LIFE

OF

ELDER JOHN SMITH.

WITH SOME

ACCOUNT OF THE RISE AND PROGRESS

OF THE

CURRENT REFORMATION.

By JOHN AUGUSTUS WILLIAMS.

"What a great failure, after all, would my long and checkered life have been but for this glorious hope of a hereafter!"—*Dying words of* JOHN SMITH.

CINCINNATI, OHIO.
THE STANDARD PUBLISHING COMPANY,
Publishers of Christian Literature.

TO

GENERAL SAMUEL L. WILLIAMS,

OF

Montgomery County, Kentucky;

AND TO

CHARLES E. WILLIAMS, M. D.,

OF THE

Daughters' College, Kentucky;

WHO, FOR FIFTY YEARS, WERE THE STEADFAST FRIENDS OF

ELDER JOHN SMITH,

IN HIS WEAKNESS AND IN HIS STRENGTH, THROUGH EVIL AND THROUGH GOOD

REPORT, AND TO WHOM

THAT FAITHFUL MAN OF GOD GAVE, IN RETURN,

THE WARMTH AND RICHNESS OF A BROTHER'S LOVE TILL DEATH,

THIS VOLUME

IS AFFECTIONATELY INSCRIBED

BY

THE AUTHOR.

PREFACE

MANY of the incidents related in the following pages were detailed to the Author by ELDER SMITH. While they are, for the most part, of a personal character, their bearing on certain great religious events, and their influence on the cause to which that remarkable man devoted his life, give them some historical interest and importance. From necessity, therefore, rather than from any design in the beginning, the writer has evolved from his subject a history, in part, of the origin and progress of the Reformation in Kentucky, which, notwithstanding its imperfections, he hopes will be acceptable to those of every name who are interested in the study or in the defense of the Faith once delivered to the saints.

He acknowledges with pleasure his indebtedness to many who, in various ways, aided him in collecting materials for the work. He begs leave to mention, in a special manner, the kindness of Elders Absalom Rice, Jacob Coons, Wm. J. Mason, Hiram M. Bledsoe, D. T. Wright, Oliver C. Steele, M. Y. Duncan, Esq., and Mrs. Emma S. Ringo, of Missouri; Elder James Challen, of Iowa; Elders John P. Thompson and Oliver P. Badger, of Indiana; Elders Henry T. Anderson and Robert Richardson, of Virginia; Elder F. W. Emmons, of Massachusetts; Elder Philip S. Fall, of Tennessee; Mrs. Maria M. Lee, Mrs. Belle D. Simrall, Mrs. Margaret Stephenson, Mrs. Caroline Wheeler, Miss Sophronia Vickery, Miss Ella Moore, Miss Mannie Powell, Miss Rebecca Henderson, A. Ward, John Bowman, Elijah Threlkeld, Archibald Redd, James G. Arnold, William Van Pelt, Andrew Steele, Landon

J. Thomas, Esq., James Harlan, Esq., Thomas Hanford, Joseph Wasson, Aaron Mitchell, Waller Small, Joseph Chinn, George Carpenter, Samuel Carrington, Dillard Hazelrigg, Elders Isaac T. Reneau, John D. Steele, Josiah Collins, Samuel W. Crutcher, William Jarrott, John A. Brooks, Aylett Raines, John Rogers, John I. Rogers, L. L. Pinkerton, George W. Elley, John S. Higgins, Curtis J. Smith and A. Adams, of Kentucky, and Isaac Errett, of Ohio.

He would likewise very gratefully acknowledge the valuable assistance of Miss Mary E. Whittington, of the Daughters' College, during the composition and revision of the work. But for the aid of her pen in transcribing the MS. for the press, its publication, owing to the engagements of the Author, would have been much longer delayed.

JOHN AUGUSTUS WILLIAMS.

DAUGHTERS' COLLEGE, April, 1870.

LIFE OF

ELDER JOHN SMITH.

CHAPTER I.

ELDER JOHN SMITH was born on the 15th of October, 1784, in Sullivan County, East Tennessee.

George Smith, or Schmidt, the father of Elder Smith, was the only son of German parents, who came to Virginia about the year 1735, and settled near the head-waters of the James River. George was early left an orphan, without kindred or friends, a lonely boy in a strange land, and among a strange people. But he soon found in Colonel Buchanan, who was an enterprising farmer of Botetourt County, a master and friend; he was taken as an apprentice into the family of that gentleman, and faithfully brought up to usefulness and virtue. In due time, he married Rebecca Bowen, an Irish maiden, strongly characterized, it seems, by the peculiar sensibilities of her people. A small farm was bought, or a piece of forest was inclosed and cultivated; and, in a few years, his labors were rewarded with comfort and thrift. His humble home was made pleasant by a cheerful wife, and healthful children blessed his riper manhood. In the midst of this prosperity, however, the war with England began. Leaving his plow to his sturdy boys, and the general care of the farm and family to his wife, he shouldered his musket, and went out to bear his part in the struggle for independence.

On the return of peace, he gave himself entirely to the work of providing for his family. Before the war, he had often thought of the growing settlements beyond the mountains; and now, anticipating the wants of his large and increasing family, he determined to remove to the wilderness of the more distant West.

Other circumstances encouraged him in this determination. He was a zealous member of the strictest sect of the Virginia Baptists; and though his brethren were numerous in the State, yet their doctrine and manners had always been offensive to the local authorities, who were devoted to the interests of the Established Church. The harshest means had been used to silence the bold advocates of Immersion and Calvinism. Before the war they had been bitterly persecuted; they had been outraged and imprisoned, sometimes on no other charge than that they were an annoyance to the country, and disturbers of the peace by their zeal as preachers. The Revolution, it is true, secured religious equality to the people; but the prejudices of other days remained, and proscription for opinion's sake was not even yet at an end. Under such circumstances the rich wilds of the West, now secure, as was supposed, from the incursions of the savage, seemed to invite thither the Predestinarians of Virginia to become the pioneers of a more democratic religion.

Early in 1784, therefore, George Smith, with his wife and eight children, sons and daughters, helped to swell the tide of immigration that was flowing westward into the valley of the Holston. On the banks of that river, after a toilsome journey along the old Indian trace that led to the southwest, he found, at last, a pleasant spot, a cabin, and repose. In that cabin, in the autumn of 1784, as already stated, JOHN SMITH was born, the ninth of thirteen children.

We ought, perhaps, to say, that he was a native of the *State of Franklin*, an unacknowledged, though duly organized, commonwealth of the olden time, whose brief annals make up a curious but interesting chapter in the history of the West.

Sullivan and the adjoining counties, at that time the most populous portion of the Western Territory of North Carolina, occupying nearly the limits of what is now East

Tennessee, had been ceded by North Carolina to the General Government, in June, 1784. Congress did not for some time accept the deed of cession. A convention of delegates from the ceded territory was in the meantime held, to consider what course the people ought to pursue in view of their political orphanage. Separated by mountains and a vast wilderness from the mother State, which had, in effect, abandoned them, uncertain of their adoption by the Federal Government, and exposed, in the meantime, to the incursions of the Cherokees, they resolved to secede from North Carolina, and to organize themselves into a separate and independent State. A Constitution was adopted by the people, and the State went formally into operation, under the style of *The Commonwealth of Franklin*, a name assumed in honor of Dr. Benjamin Franklin, of Philadelphia.*

But the State of North Carolina soon repealed her act of cession, and reasserted her authority over the revolted counties by stern legislation, and eventually by arms. A part of the colonies adhered to the mother State; the rest, under the leadership of Governor Sevier, refused to return to a condition of territorial dependence. Fierce revolutionary strife ensued. The angry partisan and the treacherous savage kept the popular mind excited continually, either with fear or with the animosities of faction. Peaceful enterprise was at an end. The social dissensions which sprung up between the new and the old State men were most disastrous. The principle of loyalty on the one side was incessantly at war with the passion of patriotism on the other. One party sent delegates to the General Assembly of Franklin; the other was duly represented at the capital of North Carolina. Rival courts sat in each county; taxes were levied and militia were enrolled by both States; in fine, before the four years of Governor Sevier's administration expired, the two conflicting governments, clashing in every department, had well-nigh reduced the aspiring young State to anarchy and ruin.

George Smith was a quiet, grave, and diffident man. He loved peace too well to quarrel with his neighbors, and was too much engaged in the work of clearing his fields to become

---

*Ramsay.

a partisan in the politics of the day. During the four years of trouble, therefore, he remained at home, and, with the help of his older boys, converted his forest, acre by acre, into field. His farm was not large, but ample enough for his force. He owned no slaves. He loved toil himself, and looked upon idleness as a vice, and upon dependence on others as the greatest misfortune; he feared, therefore, to take a slave into his family, lest his children should become helpless and haughty and learn to despise labor. Urged on one occasion to secure an interest in some slaves that were offered to him, almost as a gift, he declined to enrich himself in that way, saying that they might spoil his boys, and that he would not have a lazy son or an idle daughter for all the slaves in the Carolinas. Sometimes his older sons were away on short but dangerous campaigns against the Indians, and he was left, perhaps, at seed-time or at harvest, to do alone the work of all. But he would nerve himself for the task, and go forth alone to bear the burden of the day and the heat. His life was a daily round of simple, earnest toil, undisturbed by fretfulness or discontent. His quiet energy spent itself in cheerful, plodding industry. He was a man of few words, and of even temper—gentle in his manners and tender in his feelings. His children loved his society, and were free and natural in his presence. They were his companions in the field and at the fireside. He never scolded them, and seldom even reproved them; but his kind admonitions were always listened to with respect. In the government of the younger members of his family he spared the rod; for such was the mildness of his nature that he had not the heart to use it. His children feared to offend him; not that they dreaded his anger, but because they were pained at his distress. When their waywardness called for reproof, he gave them a kind talk, which always left them full of tears and good resolves.

He was humble-minded and earnestly pious. He held firmly, but without bigotry, every dogma of the Philadelphia Confession of Faith, as it was expounded in his day. He conscientiously sought, too, to impress his own severe faith on the minds of his children. To labor for their daily bread, and to wait, with humbleness of heart, for the Holy Ghost, were the two great commandments on which hung all his precepts and admonitions. He exhorted them to seek after God, if, haply, they might find him; yet to esteem themselves dead, and to bide the good time when, unless predestined to eternal wrath, the mysterious Spirit would give them life and open their eyes to the beauties of a Saviour. The Bible, the Confession of Faith, and a collection of hymns, were all the books that he owned or read. From these he drew the inspiration of his life, for he read them with the faith and reverence of a child. On Sunday, when the loom and the wheel were still, and the plow stood idle in the furrow, his household, in clean attire, loved to gather around him at the cabin door, while he read to them from the sacred page. Thus he dropped the precious seed, unwittingly, perhaps, into hearts uncumbered, as yet, with the thorns and thistles of life.

His kind-heartedness was felt beyond the circle of his own family. In the days of social and political distraction, when jealousies and estrangements abounded, his neighbors always came to him for counsel or sympathy. He always gave to them that asked, and from them that would borrow he never turned away. His honesty in dealing was scru-pulous, and, in some of its phases, peculiar. He could never understand the commercial value which demand gives to property. With him things had their intrinsic value only, which he thought ought to regulate their price. He used to say that a bushel of grain, when scarce, could feed no more than when the harvest was plenty; and that its honest worth was just the same. Accordingly, when corn was very scarce, and his neighbors were asking and receiving one dollar a bushel, he still refused to take more than the good old price of two and sixpence.

And yet, with all his simple-hearted goodness, George Smith was neither wasteful nor improvident. While he dispensed with an open hand to all that needed, he was careful to see to the fragments, that nothing was lost. His economy consisted rather in not wasting, than in not giving. He never suffered anything to go to ruin on his farm, or in his house, nor, if possible to prevent it, even to wear out. He mended and put in order, till things seemed to wear better from use. The eye of the visitor saw no shreds of harness, no wrecks of implements, no tattered garments;

everything was sound and ready for use. A method of his own controlled the minutest details of his business. The love of order ruled everywhere, not as a principle merely, but as a passion. Even the log heaps in the forest, the rude fencing, the furrows in the field, and every trace of his ax and knife, betrayed the strength of this principle. He had a place for everything; and, in his eye, it was a sin to lose, and almost a sacrilege to displace.

When John was old enough to run about, he was always with his father, following him through the brushy forest, or along the fresh-made furrows, gleaning after him in the hot wheat fields, or helping to strip the fodder from the ripening corn. Although he was the household pet, he bore his part in the drudgery of the cabin and the farm; for, in those days, necessity found work even for little hands to do. Care disciplined the young hearts, and toil strengthened the feeble muscles. At six or seven years of age John's term of service began; and, from that period of his life, he knew no idle days. He gathered chips and fagots in the forest, and piled them on the hearth; he hunted the shelly bark on the hills, and stored it away for the evening blaze; he pulled the purple crab-grass from the young corn, and plied his light hoe among the garden vines. Through the hot summer days it was his task to run again and again down the long grassy hill to the spring and bring back the dripping piggin for lips that were sure to chide him for the least delay. No day, except the Sabbath—no season, whether of heat or cold, found him unemployed. Economy provided work even for stormy days. A holiday afternoon was sometimes earned by the exertions of the morning; but even these hours of freedom were not hours of mischief or of indolence. The habit of always doing something useful is early acquired; and for him it was a holiday to toil in his own little garden, to weed among his vines, and to count his thrifty melons. When autumn came, he gathered nuts for the winter evening's feast, or followed his older brothers in their hunt for the partridge and the turkey on the hills, Whatever work a child might do, was left to be done by him; not that they would make him the fag of the household, or would avoid trouble themselves, but there was so much work for father and brothers to do, that it did not seem right to leave him unemployed, and to bend their shoulders to burdens that he might bear. Under these circumstances it was not possible for him to grow up in idleness or dependence on others. In fact, he did not know what idleness was, for he never saw it in those around him.

His mother, however, was not satisfied that work about the house went quietly on. Whatever her hands found to do, she did with all her might, and every one around her had to move to his task with a sprightliness equal to her own. She was a nervous, passionate woman—an impersonation of restless and untiring energy. "She ate not the bread of idleness herself, and she looked well to the ways of her household." While John saw in his father's life a constant example of patient industry, he learned from his mother to throw his whole soul into every undertaking—to move quickly, by the shortest lines, to his object—to leap at a bound over obstacles, and to carry his purpose through every difficulty, without compromise or delay. She could not, from her very nature, endure a sluggard in her house; the threatening rod, and the arousing word, kept up the glow of life among her little ones from dawn till dark. Those whom she sent, never loitered on the way; and those into whose hands she put a task, knew better than to pause till it was done.

In those simple times the mother was not a languid matron, seated in luxurious repose within her mansion, surrounded by effeminate sons and delicate daughters. The wife shared equally with her husband in the toils and dangers of the wilderness; she bore, with cheerfulness, the privations of his rude home, and brought to his aid a sound judgment, a resolute will, and skillful hands. She hatcheled the flax, and wove the linen for the summer clothing. She carded and spun the wool, and made the flannel; her buzzing wheel, or clattering loom, was heard in her cabin through all the seasons of the year. She milked and tended the cows, and cooked the food for her family. The garden, and often the patch beyond, was left on her busy hands; and, when necessary, she wielded the hoe as skillfully as the distaff or the broom. Necessity taught her many inventions. Wild osier twigs, hickory withes, the oat-straw, and even husks of corn, were useful material in her ingenious hands; hampers, and baskets, and mats, were the products of her art;

while the squash, or the gourd, the soft linden, or the sweet buckeye, furnished her hewed table with its bowls and trenchers.

But the care and education of her children was the heaviest burden on the heart of the pioneer mother. She was often their only teacher. The schoolmaster was not yet abroad in the land. By the winter's fire her little ones conned their lessons at her knees. The pastor had not yet come out into the wilderness. She alone must watch over the young lambs, and bring them, by her example and prayers, into the fold of the Good Shepherd. The great world lay far away in the distance; its books, and tracts, and papers, were unread among the scattered homes of the frontier; she must therefore recall the readings of her girlish days, and delight her children with stories of the past.

The mother of John Smith was not left to bear alone the weight of all these cares. A few years of toil, after the removal to the Territory, was sufficient to redeem her home from the poverty of the settler's hovel. Much had been done to make her family comfortable. Already the farm, and everything on it began to wear a prosperous appearance. Daughters, dutiful and industrious, were growing up to womanhood around her; and sons were ready to aid her in every domestic enterprise. At the time that John was old enough to be set to work in earnest, and when his education, as it must be termed, began, she was the mother of a well-governed family of sons and daughters, and the mistress of a house, as comfortable and as well appointed as any in all the country around. It was a double cabin, built of logs, scalped within and without, and daubed with clay. The floor was laid with puncheons, smoothly dubbed with the adze; a carpet, or a rug, was a thing unknown. A broad hearth was laid at each end of the house, and from the arches above the low chimneys were carried up with sticks and clay. A ladder led from a corner of one of the rooms below to the loft above. Shelves rested on wooden pins driven into the walls, on which were placed the nicely scoured trenchers, and a row of shining pewter plates. Occasionally the tinker came along with his molds and ladle, and gathering up the tarnished plates and spoons, melted and recast them; and the dingy ware shone in new splendor on her shelves. The wardrobe of the family hung along the walls. The precious looking-glass, the only one, perhaps, in all the house, hung over the rude stand on which the Bible and the well-worn hymn-book lay. A few spared forest trees stood before the door, and in warm days the busy mother sat there at her task, in the shade, while her daughters sang and worked around her. Piles of snowy wool lay on the grass beside them; soon came the flying cards, and then the reel and the restless broach, or the sounding wheel; and all were busy, bustling, and content.

Upon such scenes of frontier life, Rebecca Smith shed the influence of a strong but untutored mind, well stored with useful facts and Irish legends. She was remarkable for her retentive memory—her wit, and sprightly imagination. Her temper would sometimes burst forth in sudden storms, but it was never sullen or morose. Humor softened her reproaches, and enlivened even her chastisements. She upbraided in homely satire, and turned the follies of her household into ridicule. She cheered up their flagging tasks with sprightly talk, and beguiled the hours of work with pleasantry and fun. She had been brought up by a Celtic grandmother, and had learned all the wild and beautiful legends of her native land. The stories and ballads that had touched her own heart when a child, became now, in the absence of books, the literature of her cabin—her children's poetry and faith.

CHAPTER II.

WHEN John was about nine or ten years of age, the school-master came along, and, arguing wisely at each fireside, made up a school of such children as could be spared from work and indulged in the luxury of an education.

It should be remembered that teachers' wages, in those days, were not always paid in money. He ate from house to house; for the burden of keeping him was distributed among his employers. A roll of linsey, a few yards of tow linen, a woolen vest, hanks of yarn, or of thread, or some other product of the good wife's art, was often laid by as his stipulated hire. In the days of the old Franklin Commonwealth—the first State, by the way, west of the Allegheny Mountains that encouraged education by legislative action— even the Governor's salary was paid by the people in such articles as linsey, raccoon skins, beeswax, and maple sugar; and though that Commonwealth had passed away, still in the Territory of Tennessee, as the country was next called, there was but little use for money. The schoolmaster, too, was the last person in the country to refuse the bulky currency of the cabin, and to insist on gold and silver in payment for services that were regarded by many as useless to back-woodsmen.

John was permitted to lay aside his work—except on Saturdays—and was urged by his father to make good use of the present opportunity to get his schooling. On the appointed morning, with a spelling-book in his hand, and a piece of Johnny-cake in his pocket, he struck out a new path across the fields, and over the hills, to the newly raised hut of the master. It was, in fact, a hovel, built near a spring that bubbled up in the wild woods—a pen of unhewed logs, covered in with bark, or still rougher boards. A door had been made with a saw; and the crevices on all sides let in the light. The wind, too, and the rain, and the snow, came in as freely; but a huge fire-place took up one end of the house, and log-heaps, piled on by the larger boys, and set afire every morning, tempered the weather within. When John came in on wintry mornings, wet with the chilling rain, his brown face all aglow with cold, he would sit in his reeking linsey jacket before the roaring fire, and hum his task without complaining. His bench was the half of a riven sapling, raised on rude legs, with its splintered face turned up. Here sat a row of little boys with curving backs and swinging feet, and with eyes that beamed all day long with fun or apprehension. His writing-table was a long rough board, that rested, with the proper slant, on stout pins driven into the wall, where a log had been sawed out to admit the light. Along this window sat another row of boys, and sometimes of girls, bending over spattered copy-books, or idly gazing into the woods without. Usually, the genius of Dilworth, and of Pike, and sometimes of John Bunyan, supplied the frontier school with its text; and the low hum of the busy spellers, the clicking of the ciphering pencils, and the shrill voice of the solitary reader, as he stood before the master, kept up the lively discord till the sun went down. Sometimes the only reading-book was the New Testament. John passed at once from the dull columns of the spelling-book to the beautiful pages of the Evangelist. And as he learned to read the words, doubtless the influence of many a holy text fell unconsciously on his heart.

And the children of that day loved their humble school-house by the spring. An idler, or a truant, was seldom seen among them. The first to get to school in the morning was the first to say his lesson. By a dozen different paths, through weeds and brushy woods, the children every morning hurried on, careless of nuts, or birds, or flowers, each striving to be first in the race to school.

But the season for going to school was soon over; the busy seed-time came on, and the children were called to the fields. The scholars closed their books—the schoolhouse was

deserted—and the master went on his way and was seen
no more.

John Smith spent about four months at this, his first,
and for years his only, school; but in that short period he
learned to read. Beginning with the first letter of the alpha-
bet, he passed through the spelling-book, and, at the end of
the quarter, was a tolerable reader of the New Testament.
The Good Book was sealed to him no longer. His father,
anxious for his improvement, now enjoined it upon him as a
task to read the Scriptures every Sunday. Nothing was
further from his father's mind, however, than the thought
that such reading would have any religious influence upon
his child. He had no conception of any agency whatever,
in the work of conversion, save the power of that Spirit
which breathes where it lists. He would rather have withheld the Bible entirely from his boy, that the Spirit might
work freely and sovereignly on his heart, than to have grieved
it away by the presumptuous attempt to give life by means
of the Word. He was wholly innocent of any religious
aim, therefore, when he required of John a lesson every
Sunday. The Bible, however, was thus made his earliest
reading-book; and it may have been that some of its life-
giving truth was appropriated by his young mind even before
the unction of the Spirit came upon him.

The people of the neighborhood were pious, industrious,
and rigidly Calvinistic. Holston Association, the older
community of Baptists in the State, had been recently organized, and formally constituted on the Philadelphia Confession of Faith. One of the churches of the new connection had its place of meeting not far from the cabin of George
Smith; and as he was one of its most devoted members,
the preacher, who came into the neighborhood every month,
was often a guest at his house. John, it was true, was still
too young to hold, with distinctness, any article of a speculative faith; but a young mind may be warped by doctrines
before their formulas are comprehended. And surely, no
theory of religious conversion was more likely to seize upon
the imagination and heart of a child, than Calvinism as it
was understood and practically exhibited in our early western
churches.

A hell of the most appalling horrors, into which even little children might be cast—an unalterable destiny for every one, regardless of his conduct or his creed, as God might have chosen him for heaven or doomed him to hell before he was born—the dread uncertainty that rested on his fate—his utter inability to understand the Scriptures, to believe or to repent, to love God or to obey him, until endued with power from on high—the necessity of some supernatural sign or sensation, some miraculous voice or vision as an evidence of pardon and acceptance with God; the recital of these strange experiences, as they were termed, to the breathless congregation or to the solemn group around the evening fireside; the musical voice of the preacher at meetings beseeching with melancholy cant for sobbing penitents kneeling at the altar; the prayer of the almost despairing mourner, tossing on his bed at night, or, with strong crying and tears, agonizing alone in the depths of the forest: and still the exhortation, often repeated, to wrestle on till the blessing of the Spirit came, if, peradventure, it would come at all: all these, and many other phases of the early Calvinism, would strike with wonder and concern a thoughtful child, even before he could read the Philadelphia symbol. And should his own reason, or some text of Scripture, learned as a Sunday reading lesson, suggest some other view of God or man, the anointed preacher was at hand to rebuke the presumptuous thought, and thus save his young mind from every error.

John imbibed the temper of his father's creed, as freely and unconsciously as he breathed the air upon his native hills. He soon began to wonder whether the voice of the Holy Ghost would ever call to him; and he listened in the forest, when strange sounds were passing by, to hear his own name called by unseen lips. He wondered whether some glorious vision would ever bless his eyes; and he peered into the evening shades for spectral forms and beckoning lights. Woods and streams and all solitary places, were, in the dawn of his religious faith, the haunts of that mysterious Spirit that quickened the elect. He was not, of course, in the language of the times, a seeker of religion—anxious and alarmed, and waiting for the gift of pardon. His conceit was not the offspring of a guilty conscience. It

was the poetry of a dawning faith—a superstition, rather—
devoid of either penitence or prayer.

The stories of conversions that went round the neighborhood, were always full of marvelous incident and spiritual
adventure; and he listened to these narrations as he listened
to his mother's legends of the weird Banshee—with simple
wonder and a childish faith.

CHAPTER III.

THE time soon came when the farmers on the Holston began to raise a surplus, and to supply wants which, unfelt at first, became more pressing as the country grew more populous. Grain, and other produce, was now stored away for the purchaser, and every yard of cloth not needed by the family was bartered for finer fabrics, or for useful wares. Traffic stimulated industry and encouraged economy. Comforts multiplied; and a sort of wealth flowed in, but without its luxury or pride. The country was alive with enterprise, and the wilderness began to blossom like the rose. Holston Valley, at last a part of the State of Tennessee, smiled everywhere with pleasant homes and cultivated farms.

But George Smith could not, in the midst of his present prosperity, lose sight of the future welfare of his children. He had a natural wish to see them all comfortably settled around him, tilling their own land and living in their own houses. To enlarge his farm was impracticable; the price of land where he lived was too great, and the soil was not such as he wanted. He resolved, therefore, to give up his home on the Holston, and, trusting in the Providence that had hitherto helped him, plunge into the wilderness once more.

In the autumn of 1795, he sold his farm in Tennessee, and took his family into Powell's Valley. It was his purpose to leave them there, while he and John and Joseph, an older son, should cross the mountains into Kentucky, and go in search of a goodly spot, where he might build a cabin, plant a patch of corn, and prepare, as well as he could, for the family that would join him in the summer. As soon, then, as he saw them snugly sheltered in the valley, he started w..h his two boys to Kentucky. Their scanty stores, their plows and other implements of labor, were packed on horses. Two or three cows, which were to be their main dependence through the winter, were driven along before them. Following the trace which led to Crab Orchard, and thence descending into the valley of the Cumberland River, they crossed that stream, and stopped at the foot of Poplar Mountain, in a delightful valley, now a part of Clinton County. This mountain is a winding spur of the Cumberland Chain, with an elevation of from twelve to fifteen hundred feet. It extends as far as the central portion of Clinton. Within one of its singular and beautiful curves, it incloses the region known as Stockton's Valley—a fertile, densely wooded, limestone country, and, at the time of which we speak, an almost unbroken solitude.

Here, on two hundred acres of forest land, they began their labors. Two other settlers had already moved into the valley, from one of whom—Thomas Stockton—it took its name. Their farms were three and four miles distant. Besides these settlers, there was not a civilized man nearer than Burksville, twenty miles further west. With the help of these two neighbors, a cabin was soon raised. Space for a garden and corn-patch was marked off, and their busy axes were soon ringing in the smoky clearing. For a while they had no other food than milk; they had not for weeks a single ear of corn, and though game abounded, they had not the time to hunt it. At last it became necessary to procure, from some quarter, corn enough for seed. The nearest mill was on Dix Diver, in the neighborhood of Danville, more than one hundred miles distant. In that remote region corn was plentiful; but it could be carried through the wilderness only on pack horses.

The pack-saddle was an invaluable contrivance in the backwoods, where vehicles were unknown, and roads were but narrow traces winding through tangled forests. It was merely the limb of a tree which forked with the proper angles. This was cut the right length, and the prongs were chipped out so as to fit the animal's back. To this rude frame, short boards were fastened with wooden pins and the thing was complete. A good fork was not to be found every day, and the settler was sure to note any tree

that bore so rare a product. It was with a full apprecia-
tion of its value that Joseph Craig, an old pioneer preacher,
once stopped short in his exhortations to a large congregation in the woods, and while his eyes were still turned
devoutly to heaven, suddenly pointed his finger to a branch
of the tree that shaded him, and exclaimed: "Brethren,
behold up yonder a first-rate crotch for a pack-saddle."

George Smith had brought with him to Stockton's Valley two or three horses, and they were already furnished
with good pack-saddles. One evening as he sat with his
boys he said, "John, we must have some bread, and soon
we will need some corn to plant. It is more than a hundred
miles to Horine's mill, 'tis true. But you are now twelve
years old, and I know you are smart enough to make the
trip. It will keep back the work too much for me or Jo to
go. Suppose, then, that to-morrow you get ready the pack
horses, and start? Follow the trace that leads north to
Crab Orchard—people there will tell you where to find the
mill." John was ready at sunrise next morning to start
on his journey. It was wintry weather, and he was poorly
clad. His only suit, which he had brought with him from
Powell's Valley, was torn almost to tatters by the green
briars and thorns of the wilderness. His father had, it is
true, a pair of deer-skin trowsers nearly ready for him; but
hunger and seed-time could not wait. Mounting one of
the two horses, and leading the other for the pack, he started
for the northern settlement. His wallet was well stuffed
with bear's meat and wild turkey's breast, and a small buck-
skin purse held his money. Aided by a stranger, he crossed
the swollen Cumberland, his horses swimming the river at
the side of the canoe. For three or four days he threaded
the wilderness alone, haply finding each night a hospitable
cabin in which to sleep. It was nightfall when he reached
the mill, cold and hungry and tired. He would have gone
in at once to the miller's house, but a merry crowd had
already gathered there for a dance, and there was no one
for awhile to notice him. Tying up his horses, however,
he stepped to the door of the cabin and looked in. The
scene made him forget for a time his hunger and rags. A
rustic reel was beating the puncheon floor to as merry a
fiddle as ever was played. The fiddler himself was the

most conspicuous figure in the group. He was a young man of fine face and form, and was dressed in a gay coat and yellow velvet breeches. Drawn by the strains of the violin, our ragged mill-boy crept as close as he could to the genius that inspired all this mirth—and for the first time in his life, JOHN SMITH looked upon the face of JEREMIAH VARDEMAN. Next morning he retraced his toilsome way back to Stockton's Valley, having accomplished his mission to the satisfaction of his father.

Occasionally during the winter, he found time to indulge a boyish love for adventure. He explored the streams and the thickets, he climbed the mountains that lay around him, and traced the river winding through the mazes of a boundless forest. A band of Indian hunters strolled into the valley, and built their camp-fires near the cabin; a world of wonder and amusement was in store for him. They were Cherokees, on the hunt for the deer and the mountain bear—wild and cunning Nimrods, but at that time peaceful and inoffensive neighbors. He grew familiar with these fierce sportsmen, and they were pleased with him. He sat with them at their evening fires, and joined in their shorter excursions to the mountains. Having a good memory, and a thirst for every kind of knowledge, he learned their uncouth tongue, and picked up many of their traditions. Theirs was in fact the only modern language that he ever acquired, and he never afterward forgot it.

The winter at last wore away. As soon as the corn was in, and a few garden seeds were planted, they made the cabin and the dreary spot around it as pleasant as they could for the mother who was waiting with her children for a home. When all was done that their resources enabled them to do, the father set out for Powell's Valley, to bring his wife and children to Kentucky, while the two boys were left alone in the wilderness to take care of their little crop.

It was midsummer when John's ringing shout greeted his father's little caravan, as it moved into the valley. The journey over the mountains had been a safe but toilsome one. The weary pack horses—the motley herd—the guard of stalwart sons, each carrying a trusty weapon, or some implement of toil, upon his shoulder—all gathered way-worn to the cabin yard, and the trials of a frontier life began once more.

The family consisted, at this time, of thirteen children—eight sons and five daughters—several of whom were grown. Five sons and three daughters were older than John, who was now in his thirteenth year. Such a family, every member of which had been trained to labor without the help of a single slave, were well prepared to encounter the difficulties of living in the wilderness. It was not long till their united efforts, favored by a rich and easy soil, and encouraged by the rapid immigration of good citizens to the valley, placed them once more in comfortable circumstances.

John had early laid aside his childish tasks, and he now began to wield the ax, and to guide the plow. Expert enough with the rifle to bring down a buck or a bear at long shot, he nevertheless had but little fondness for a gun. More like Jacob than Esau in his taste, he left it to his brothers to procure the savory venison for the family, while he supplied the kitchen with the daily allowance of hominy and meal. In those times meal was made by beating grain with a pestle in a block of wood hollowed out like a mortar. To this contrivance a sweep was sometimes attached, when the quantity of bread required was very great. The pounded grist was shifted; the coarser part was boiled for hominy, while the finer was made into hoe-cake, or served with milk or butter in the form of mush. To beat corn at the sweep for a large family was no easy task; and among the early sounds that were heard at the cabin every morning, was the fall of John's heavy pestle pounding corn for the daily bread.

When he could be spared from labor at the cabin, or on the farm, he was sent into the mountains to dig for ginseng, for which there was, at that time, a great demand. This plant—the *Panax quinquefolium* of the botanist—was held in such estimation among the Chinese, on account of its supposed virtues as a medicine, that it was sometimes sold in their country for its weight in gold. It was about the beginning of the eighteenth century that attention was first called to its use as a panacea in the East. It was ascertained that the emperor guarded the districts where it grew, and kept several thousand natives collecting it, paying them for it an equal weight of silver, which was much less than its actual value. A decoction made from the root, or a tea distilled from the leaves, was prescribed by the Chinese physicians in nearly every case of disease. It was soon afterward discovered by the missionaries in the wooded mountains of America; and at once it became an important article of commerce. Wherever our Western settlers raised their cabins, they hunted in the neighboring hills for the ginseng; traffic was opened with the nearest villages, whose tradesmen bought it and sent it forward for shipment to the old world. As no attempt to cultivate it ever proved successful, the supply came only from the forests. It was gathered by hardy backwoodsmen alone, who, it seems, were never able to discover its virtues. A Chinese conceit alone seems to have created the demand for this plant, and a like conceit at last depreciated the American species, and lessened its importance as an article of commerce.*

With a coarse bag on his arm, and a *sang* hoe on his shoulder, John went, at the proper season, to dig for this root on the mountain slopes and in the rich, light mould of the forest. The quantity gathered during the season was sometimes very great. It was cleaned and dried, and carried to Burksville or to Monticello, where it was exchanged for such articles as the family needed, but could not produce at home.

Stockton's Valley was soon settled up by a plain and honest people from Virginia and East Tennessee. They were mostly Baptists, severe in doctrine and ardent in piety. In 1799 Isaac Denton, an humble and godly man, came out to live among them as a minister. Settling on a small farm in the neighborhood of Smith, he organized a church, of which he took the charge. His brethren soon built a meeting-house near where he lived, on the banks of Clear Fork, a small tributary of Wolf River. The spiritual interests of the Clear Fork Baptists could not have been intrusted to more faithful hands. He was kind in disposition, sound in the

---

*New American Encyclopedia.

faith, and zealous in the work of his office. Under his ministrations the church prospered; it grew in piety and in numbers; the elect were industriously gathered in, and faithfully instructed in the nature of their high vocation.

The schoolmaster soon followed in his wake; and John was again *signed* as a scholar. He had made some progress in reading since the close of his former school, though he had found but little time for study. He had read and learned by heart all the favorite hymns of the family; for he now began to love the poetry of religion as it breathed in the simply psalmody of the Church. So great, too, was the natural strength of his memory, that he was ever able to repeat any stanza that he had once read with attention.

The influence of a simple, well-written hymn on the heart of a thoughtful boy is often very powerful. He will speak to himself in some song that he has learned, till it becomes within him an ever-welling fountain of melody and truth. But John's greatest ambition, at this time, was to become an arithmetician. He was ignorant of figures; and he had already felt the need of that sort of knowledge. He was pleased, therefore, when he heard that a teacher was about to open a school in the neighborhood, but delighted when fame reported that the coming master was well versed in numbers—that he even proposed to answer any question that the best scholar of the school might ask him. His thirst for all this learning became intense, and he longed for the day to come when he would begin his studies once more.

A school-house of round, green logs was thrown up by the neighbors in a day; and on the next he stood, eager for knowledge, in the presence of the new master. He was an uncouth Irishman, who had drifted on some chance tide to the shores of the new world, and had been thrown at last, homeless and aimless, on the frontier. His unfitness for business, and his aversion to every kind of labor, forced him, by a kind of necessity, to keep school; for beggary among honest frontiersmen was too precarious a means of living.

A school in which indolence may sit unobserved, and ignorance blunder on without exposure, is, even in our own times, too often but a reputable way of escape from hard work—a mere refuge from starvation or disgrace.

This master was lazy and illiterate; too ignorant, in fact even for the unlettered people around him. He was simply a vagabond, without the skill or the industry to teach what little he knew. He was, besides, a slave to his flagon; and he would frequently sit in his school reeking with the fumes of his usquebaugh, and sleep off his stupor, while a boisterous holiday frolicked around him. John's ambition to learn died away in disgust. He was much prone to indulge a propensity for fun, which some mistook for wickedness. Even his father had watched this propensity with solicitude, and had kept him, as much as he could, in his own serious presence. But John's mirthfulness was neither wanton nor wicked; his jests were never stained with injustice or falsehood. His witticisms were harmless, and his levity was but the unconscious play of a natural humor. He saw that the neighbors had been duped by the schoolmaster; and yet they were bound to him in a written agreement. But no law, he thought, shielded the imposter from his raillery; so he determined to make him the victim of his jokes, in the hope that, without hurting a hair of his head, he might force him to quit a vocation that he only disgraced.

One day this pretender stood up before his school and bantered them to puzzle him with some question in arithmetic. John, watchful of every opportunity to annoy him, and to bring his pretensions into contempt, arose, and prudently taking his stand by the door, asked him: "Master, how many grains of corn will it take to make one square foot of mush?" The pedagogue for a moment winced at the question; but when he saw that he was only mocked by his tormentor he flew into a rage, and hastened to report him as an incorrigible offender. But father's censure was so mild, that it was construed as a license to continue the war.

A few days after this the master, again grown stupid from his cups, fell fast asleep in his chair. His persecutor, wishing to bring on the crisis, seized the wooden shovel, and lifting it full of hot embers from the hearth, poured them into the huge pocket of his linsey coat. The children trembled and stood aghast at the prank; then, seizing their books, they rushed out into the woods. The toper slept on, till the smoke of his homespun awoke him.

His pocket was consumed; like Saul of old, the skirt of his mantle was gone—his enemy had triumphed while he slept, and his scepter had departed. The school, which had lasted three weeks, was now at an end. One of the employers, getting the article of agreement into his hands the next day, threw it into the fire; the poor pedagogue bowed to his fate, and was seen in the valley no more.

The time at length came when the older sons began to look around in order to find homes for themselves. William moved into the adjoining county of Wayne, and bought and on the Little South Fork of the Cumberland; George wandered off into the country of the Green River; other sons acquired land in the valley, and lived near their father, while three of the daughters were married to respectable and industrious young farmers of the immediate neighborhood.

John felt the weight of the responsibility that now came upon him, when he saw that he was left to be the main dependence of parents that were fast growing old. Fortunately, his moral sense was tender and discriminating. Few boys ever felt greater anguish for sin, or wept more bitterly for offenses against those whom they loved. Such vices as drunkenness, profanity, and gambling, he had been taught from his infancy to hate; and though his mirthful disposition had sometimes led him astray, he had never been guilty of any of those grosser offenses; and he was now in the eighteenth year of his age.

Some of his brothers were exemplary members of the Church; but others were worldly, if not wicked, in their disposition. He was, of course, exposed at times to the influence of their evil example.

One of his married brothers who lived in the neighborhood, once brought home a pack of cards, and began to play in his own house secretly. It was not long before John was persuaded to come and join in the game. Night after night he would leave home, and steal through the dark woods to the house of his thoughtless brother to play. Finally, he would go off to the thickets on Sunday, and there play with idle companions. His father, in the meantime, suspected them; and he was distressed with that anxiety which none but a father can feel, when he fears that all is not right with his boys. But he said nothing to them; for he never provoked his children by hasty or premature censure.

One Sunday morning the good man left his house, and went out alone to pray, with the burden of his children's sins upon his heart. There was, not far off, a dense thicket overrun with wild vines, where he had often knelt in prayer, unseen by any but the All-seeing Eye. Thoughtful and humble, he now entered that leafy closet, to pour out his full heart to God. But there on the trunk of a fallen tree, in the very midst of their father's sanctuary, sat John and his brothers wickedly playing at cards.

He stood for awhile unobserved, and looked on his boys in silence and sorrow. At last one of them saw him, and whispered, "Father!" The eyes of the boys glanced upward, but instantly fell to the earth again; for the gaze of the good old man was on them, his face spoke a heart full of pain, and great tears dropped from his furrowed cheeks to the ground. He turned away from the scene that so much distressed him; and, without speaking a word, walked back through the forest.

The boys sat there for awhile in silence. At last John, whose heart was almost bursting said:

"It is wrong to distress so good a father as ours; it is a sin and a shame!"

And they all felt it; for they silently threw away their cards, and went home, resolved never to play again while they lived.

John expected a talk from his father that evening; but he was left all night long to his own bitter reflections. On the morrow, while they were together in the field, he brought up the matter himself. He owned his faults, and promised never to indulge in that pastime again. And he sacredly kept that pledge all the days of his life.

CHAPTER IV.

In the following winter a rumor reached the family that George, the brother who had settled on Green River, had fallen into the hands of the Harpes—a notorious band of outlaws from North Carolina, that had made their appearance the year before in the neighborhood of Stanford, and had marked their path through the valleys of the Cumberland and the Green River with pillage and murder. The party consisted of two men and two or three women. In their progress through the country, they had entered Stockton's Valley also, and had murdered two inoffensive citizens, neighbors of Smith. Elsewhere they had spared neither sex nor age; they seemed to be mad with a thirst for human blood, and fiendish in their hate of their fellow-men.

What the fate of George was, the family could not definitely learn; but it was judged proper that John and an older brother should set out immediately for Christian County, and if he should be alive, to give him any assistance that he might need. They started in the dead of winter, in intensely cold weather, and traversed a snowy wilderness, till they reached their brother's cabin. They found him alive and well; but he gave them a fearful account of the attempt of the outlaws to murder him, and of his providential escape from their hands.

It seems* that these strange beings, while prowling along the highway that led toward the mouth of Green River, stopped one night on the roadside near the house of a Mr. Stagall, who happened to be from home at the time. The family, duped by an artifice of the robbers, kindly received them into the house, in the belief that they were Methodist

---

*Davidson.

preachers. After they had retired to rest, the Harpes, who had got hold of an ax during the evening, murdered them all in their sleep, and, then, setting fire to the house, made their escape. The next day Stagall returned. Mad with grief and revenge, he started at once in pursuit of the murderers, with Captain John Leeper, and a few other resolute men, who readily joined the avenger. The Harpes moved rapidly on in their flight, till they reached the neighborhood of George Smith, where they halted for awhile for rest. Smith had taken his rifle and gone out to the wilds in search of some stock that had wandered. Coming suddenly upon their camp on the roadside, and seeing the women engaged in cooking, he went in carelessly among them, supposing that they were immigrants. The men suddenly seized him, and, wresting the gun from his hands, were about to murder him on the spot; but the women begged them to do the foul deed out of their sight. They dragged him into the woods, when the Big Harpe, as the larger one was called, clutched him with a tiger-like grasp, while the other got ready his rifle to shoot him. Smith, though an active and powerful young man, struggled in vain to get loose from the arms of the giant. Finding that escape was impossible, he turned to watch the movements of Little Harpe, who was ready to shoot, and waited only to get a good aim at his victim.

Almost exhausted by his efforts, George struggled in the arms of his foe now only to keep himself screened from the rifle. Again and again he saw the deadly weapon pointed, but grasping his foe closely, and dodging behind him, he managed to keep him in range of the gun. Suddenly, the women at the camp shrieked out an alarm; and, at the same moment, a band of armed horsemen dashed into view. The outlaws instantly abandoned their prisoner, and the Big Harpe, leaping on a fleet horse which he had stolen, fled with desperate speed into the wilderness, while the other escaped on foot. On came the avengers of blood. They stopped but a moment at the spot where George was sitting, panting and bewildered, on the ground. One of them, supposing him, too, to be a marauder, recklessly raised his rifle and shot him; the ball passed through his arm and leg, inflicting serious and painful wounds.

But the pursuers had not a moment to lose. One party,

under Stagall, sped on after the Little Harpe, while another, headed by Leeper, followed the trail of his accomplice. In their fierce chase, they rushed through the vines and weeds of the wild-wood like a tornado. After a fearful ride of nine or ten miles, Leeper found himself in advance of his party, and near enough to his victim to venture a shot. He fired, and brought down both rider and horse. The wounded miscreant now begged for his life, which was spared only till Stagall came up, who had abandoned as fruitless the pursuit of the other. When he reached the spot, he looked for a moment on the face of the wretch that had murdered his wife and children, and then, raising his gun, deliberately put an end to his life and his crimes.

They afterward severed his head from his body, and bending down a tall hickory sapling, they trimmed off its branches, and sharpening its extremity, stuck the ghastly thing on the point, and the tree sprung back to its place. There the revolting trophy long hung over the gloomy and desolate region known afterward in Kentucky as Harpe's Head.

When they returned to the spot where Smith had been shot, to look after that unfortunate man, they found that he had, in the meantime, crawled from the place, and, calling aloud for help, had been heard by some passer-by, and taken to his home.

When his brothers arrived, his wounds were all healed; but his thirst for adventure was satisfied, and he expressed a wish to return and spend the rest of his days among his kindred. Accordingly, he made John promise to come again in the summer, and help him to move back with his family to Stockton's Valley.

It was on this second journey to the Green River country, that, in passing through Logan County, John stopped on the roadside to witness some strange religious exercises that had been recently introduced into Kentucky, through the ministrations of James McGready, of the Presbyterian Church, and other zealous revivalists.

For some time previous to the close of the last century, religious apathy was almost universal in the West. A pious and distinguished minister of that day declares,* that not

---

*B. W. Stone.

only the power of religion had disappeared, but even its very form was fast passing away. An historian of the times testifies, * that religious worship and instruction were generally neglected, and even the forms of religion were imperfectly maintained. So deep a slumber had, in fact, fallen upon the Church that her faithful ministers had begun to despond, and the scoffer to hope that her rebuking spirit had fled forever. But the night at length wore away, the day dawned again, and the Church awoke from her slumbers in the extraordinary scenes of the Great Revival.

Zealous missionaries from the older States came out among the cabins of the West, and began to preach to a people more familiar with the whoop of the savage than with the songs of Zion. In 1799, McGready lifted his warning voice in the hills of Tennessee, and thousands flocked to the forests to hear him. So great sometimes were the numbers that gathered around this herald of the Cross, so far did they journey from their homes, and so protracted were their seasons of religious enjoyment, that the multitudes were unable sometimes to procure shelter or food. Still the awakened people continued to crowd to the pulpits. Provisions for several days' subsistence were brought along with them to meeting; blankets and straw, for the use of the families at night, were thrown into their wagons, and the vast congregations began to assume the appearance of regular encampments. Several thousands of worshipers sometimes gathered in these camps, where days and nights, and even weeks, were spent in the most fervent religious exercises.

"The scene was strange, and often grand beyond description—not unfrequently, it was awfully sublime. The ranges of tents or wagons—the fires reflected from the branches of the towering trees—the lamps and candles—hundreds of excited persons hurrying to and fro, like Gideon's army, with torches in their hands—the preaching, the praying, the singing, and the shouting, all heard at once rushing from different parts of the ground, like the sound of many waters—was enough to swallow up the powers of contemplation."

The excitement continued to spread like a conflagration through the land. In 1800 it broke out in Kentucky, and

---

* Ramsey.

extending to the northern portions of the State, reached its climax in a general camp-meeting at Cane Ridge, in Bourbon County, held in August, 1801. At that place upward of twenty thousand persons, moved by the intensest religious feeling, encamped in the groves and fields for several days and nights; the multitude dispersed at last, only because provisions failed in the country around.

These exercises were conducted mainly by ministers of the Presbyterian and the Methodist Churches, though Baptists also sometimes participated in them; but all denominations shared in the general awakening, which continued in the state for several years.

But that which most distinguished these meetings, was the prevalence of a certain nervous disorder that seized many of those who were in attendance. It suddenly struck down some to the earth, where they lay like dead men for hours; and it threw others into violent convulsions that were often fearfully protracted. This affection was involuntary and contagious, or, perhaps, epidemic. It attacked, indiscriminately, the most pious and the most profligate. Like a panic, it sometimes seized entire congregations of worshipers, until five hundred have jerked at once with strange convulsions.

It was, perhaps, naturally engendered, spreading by sympathy, among those who were not exposed to the influence of the original causes. The imagination, kept fixed for days and nights on images of the most awful spiritual import; the heart constantly stirred to its depths by a rude but powerful eloquence; the fearful denunciations of Scripture against sin, read aloud to listening thousands, and the startling applications of such texts, by earnest preachers whom the people venerated as embassadors of Heaven; and more than all, the popular persuasion that God vouchsafed to every sinner that he pardoned a miracle of grace in some outward sign or inward feeling; surely these causes all concurring and aided by the imposing grandeur of an encampment at night, were enough to produce transient, if not permanent nervous distempers.

It was regarded at the time, however, even by wise and good men, as the immediate work of God, or as the outpouring of the Holy Ghost. This notion served to increase the excitement of the people; and excesses that were often ridiculous or disgusting naturally followed. Such extremes, however, were always discountenanced by intelligent Christians, who endeavored to preserve in their congregations a decorous and solemn behavior.

Young Smith witnessed these camp scenes with feelings akin to disgust. Constituted as he was, he could not sympathize with this popular outburst of the religious instinct. Familiar with the calm, yet earnest and practical, piety of his father; more conscientious than emotional or imaginative in his nature; solemn and worshipful in his regard for things sacred: he looked on the novel and extravagant scenes around him as the result of some delusion which he could not explain, and which only offended or amused him. He did not question the soundness of the popular doctrine respecting the Holy Ghost, which these nervous phenomena were supposed to confirm; for he had been brought up in the belief of man's moral imbecility by nature, and of his arbitrary election by grace. But he could not see, in these spasms and ecstasies, any manifestation of that Spirit, whose breathings were blessedness and peace. His fine natural sense and delicate religious sentiment, more than any knowledge of the Scriptures, saved him from the enthusiasm of the times. Still religion had become the business of the people; and he now began to hear it discussed and commended wherever he went; so that he felt, at length, a more serious interest in the subject than he had ever known before.

About that time, too, he was much in the company of Isaac Denton. This good man, who, like other pastors of the day, faithfully tended his flock without tithing them, was sometimes in need of help to raise corn for his family. John, who lived close by, and was always ready to assist a neighbor, went over at seed-time and at harvest to work in his field. Denton was a kind and companionable man, always as willing to teach his young friends as they were to learn. He had a special regard, too, for John, whose probity and good sense promised much for the Church, should the Lord ever give him a new heart. As they toiled side by side along the young corn-rows, or through the ripe grain, they talked much together of the mystery of redemption.

The faithful minister labored to impress on the mind of his young friend the thought that the sinner is utterly dead, so that he could not obey God if he would; and utterly depraved, too, so that he would not obey if he could. He reminded him that he could not please God without faith, nor have faith till it pleased God to give it; that though he might acknowledge, he could never truly feel his desperate wickedness till the Holy Spirit should show him how vile and wretched a thing he was.

'You can not, my young friend," he would say, in effect, "you can not have proper views of God and his law, of Christ and his teachings, nor can you ever truly repent of your sins, or believe in a Saviour, till your whole moral nature has been changed by the power of the Holy Ghost."

"And what must I do," his thoughtful disciple would inquire, "in order to have this change of which you speak wrought within me?"

"Nothing, John; God's grace is sovereign and unconditional. If you are of his sheep, you will be called, and you will hear his voice and follow him."

"But, when, Mr. Denton, will the Lord call?"

"In his own good time, John. He has marked out your whole life, and determined your destiny according to his own wise but hidden and eternal purpose."

"How, then, may I know whether I am one of his sheep or not?"

"You will know it by your change when it comes; till then you can only wait on the Lord and hope."

"Mr. Denton, if I am left to perish, I know it will be on account of my sins; but if I should be saved, will it not be on account of my goodness?"

"The Lord sees no goodness in you, John. If you are ever brought to life, it will be solely because it was his good pleasure to choose you for himself before the foundation of the world, and that, too, without any reference to your character or works foreseen by him. True, if you should be lost, if you must perish, John, it will be on account of your sins, and to the praise of his glorious justice."

"My destiny, you say, Mr. Denton, is fixed, and I can not change it. I need not, then, give myself any concern— I have nothing to do."

"Ah! great is the mystery of godliness, John; there is something for you to do."

"What is it, Mr. Denton?"

"You must pray, John; pray in the dust and ashes to the Lord."

"Pray for what, sir?"

"That the blinding scales may fall from your eyes, and that you may see and feel what you really are in the sight of God; for you are yet in the gall of bitterness and the bonds of iniquity."

John's interest in such conversations arose, not so much from any personal concern that he felt at that time in religion, as from a fondness for argument. He had now reached an age when young men are usually prone to question the ground of their early faith, and to discuss doctrines that they had always implicitly believed. It was fortunate for him then, that, at this period of his life, he was the companion of a man who could, in some measure, confirm his faith by argument.

He had never heard of Aristotle; yet, by untaught methods of his own, he analyzed sharply, and readily invented argument or illustration to suit his purpose. He loved the debating society, and his shrewd sense and keen wit always made him a champion. On one occasion, in a debating club of the young neighbors, an awkward question came up for discussion. The affirmative was so untenable, that no one was found willing to maintain it. The speakers massed themselves on the negative, and waited for John, who promptly took the weaker side, and led off in an argument which the opposition assailed in vain. He brought over the speakers themselves to his side of the question, and carried his lame proposition with applause through the house. Not willing, however, to triumph at the expense of truth, he challenged the speakers to another contest on the spot. Changing his ground now, and arguing against himself, he reversed the decision of his hearers, and won the negative by a unanimous vote.

This activity of his discursive powers made him appear at times skeptical in disposition; but he did not doubt because he could not understand, nor deny simply because he could not prove. Still, whatever was unreasonable, was to him false, in spite of testimony. Almost without prejudice his apparent skeptical temper was but a jealous regard for truth itself.

A little incident of his childhood may serve to illustrate this trait in his mental character. A gentleman from the neighborhood of Lexington spent an evening at his father's, and entertained the family with an account of the rapid social progress of the people in that favored region. He casually remarked that a certain wealthy citizen, who had recently built a large house, had fastened on the shingles with iron nails—putting a separate nail into every shingle. The children, who sat listening, had never heard of any other nails than those which were made by the blacksmith on his anvil; nor any other mode of fastening on boards or shingles than with small wooden pins, easily made with a knife. They heard the statement of the stranger, some with indifference, others with simple wonder—but all save John, with a ready, matter-of-course faith, that never thought of calling it in question. Father, too, seemed to accept it as true, and thus to confirm it by his authority. But John mused the whole matter in silence; he reasoned for awhile, and then began to doubt, and, finally, he rejected the whole story as false. After the stranger had gone, he ventured to speak his mind.

"Father," said he, "do you believe that there is a house in the world with its shingles all fastened on with iron nails?"

"Certainly, my son," answered his father; "the gentleman told us so last evening, you know."

"But, father," replied he, "it would take all the smiths in the land a lifetime to hammer out nails enough for such a house. I don't believe they would be able to do it even then."

"But," said his father, carelessly, "the nails were not hammered on the anvil, John; they were cut."

Confidence in his father overcame his doubts for awhile, but his restless thoughts were soon busy, and he reasoned himself into doubt again. He was familiar with the cut money of the country, and with the manner of making it. He had seen his father, when he needed change, lay a silver dollar on a block, and with a cold-chisel, or an ax, divide it into halves and quarters, and even into smaller pieces. So, without discussing the matter with others any more, he still argued it with himself. He recollected how often he had seen the edge of the tools broken by the silver; and he concluded that to cut nails enough, out of iron, for the roof of a large house, would ruin all the chisels in the world; and the young skeptic would not believe.

While, from a necessity of his nature, he was thus true to his reason, no one was ever more easily led by his faith. He listened like a child to teaching or testimony concerning things that transcended his reason, or that lay beyond the horizon of his knowledge. When he could not judge, he was ready to believe; but when his mind could logically grasp a statement or a doctrine, he believed only in harmony with his reason.

The revival, of which we have spoken, at length reached the valley where he lived; and he had an opportunity of observing more closely its remarkable phases. The Baptists of Clear Fork were almost universally the victims, or the apologists, of the jerks, and other *bodily exercises*, as they were called. Young Smith attended the frequent meetings that were held in the neighborhood, and looked with a curious, but still unaffected eye, on the scenes around him. The pulpit, he saw, was not too sacred a place for the most unseemly performances. The preacher himself was sometimes seized with holy spasms, and, suddenly stopping in the midst of his harangue, would dance on the floor of the stand in wild and uncontrollable disorder. His brother William, who was a member of the Baptist Church, believing with the people that these things were from heaven, earnestly tried to persuade John also to regard them as divine, and even expressed the pious wish that, for the good of his soul, he, too, might feel these jerkings in his flesh. But John stood firm, though almost alone in his unbelief. Without pride or perverseness, he still argued, in the face of clerical and popular opinion, that it was unreasonable to suppose that God would send his Holy Spirit from the skies to afflict his people with convulsions—to buffet and mock them, and make them ridiculous.

Still, the facts were evident and inexplicable; and his reasonings were not always satisfactory even to himself. He resolved at last to examine the whole subject in the light of his inspired Reading Book, feeling assured that what was so unreasonable, he would find to be also unscriptural.

This first careful examination of his Bible, though made in the spirit of controversy, was most important in its results; for, while he found no text that either sanctioned or explained the *exercises*, he was fully convinced from his readings *that it was his duty to be a Christian.* He was under this deep and solemn conviction, when an incident occurred which led him earnestly and perseveringly to seek religion after the manner of the times.

About the close of the year 1803, his father, who had already lived out his threescore years and ten, was seized with a lingering illness, of which he died on the twentieth of March following.

The old man, on his death-bed, exhorted John to watch his gay and mirthful temper, lest it should lead him into the company of the vicious.

"When I am gone," said he, "thoughtless and profane young men, who find pleasure in a lively jest and loud laugh, will seek you as a companion, and draw you, if they can, into dissipation. This is my only fear; and yet I trust, my son, that your good sense, and your love for a father's memory, will keep you away from their revels, and lead you to seek the society of the good.

"You are now the eldest of the boys that are left at home. Your more experienced brothers are living to themselves; and they have cares enough of their own, I know. You are still young, but I must ask you to take charge of the farm, to watch over your younger brothers and sisters, and to cherish your fond, old mother, who can not long stay behind. It is my wish that you live with the family, at least till Jonathan is old enough to attend to business; that, when he and Henry are grown, the farm be divided equally between them; and that mother and the girls live with either, as they may prefer.

"And now I know, my boy, that a heavy burden will rest on your young shoulders; but do right, and the Lord, to whose care I commend you, will give you wisdom, and bless you in your undertakings."

The dear old patriarch breathed his last, surrounded by his sons and daughters, for whose welfare he had lived, and to whom he now left the richest of patrimonies—the memory of their father's pure and gentle and trustful life.

CHAPTER V.

JOHN SMITH'S study of the Scriptures had made him conscious that he was a sinner; and this consciousness, solemnized by his deep, filial sorrow, at length presented the usual symptoms of a spiritual awakening. Willing to believe that he was the subject of a Divine influence, he encouraged those feelings which, he had learned from the experience of others, must be felt in his own heart, before he could claim to be a converted man. He tried to feel, first of all, not merely that he was a sinner, but that he was the chief of sinners; and, although he believed that such a conviction must be produced by the Holy Ghost, yet he struggled to get this view of his depravity by a strict self-examination. He recalled the indiscretions of his past life, and exaggerated the follies of his boyhood; he impugned the motives of his best acts, and tried to rob himself of every virtue; still he could not feel that he was more wicked than his associates, much less that he was more depraved than those whose evil company he had always shunned.

It was the popular notion of the times that no one could know how great a sinner he was, until the Spirit of God uncovered his heart, and showed him all its dreadful pollution. "None but those who have felt it," said a preacher of that day, "can know the pungent sorrow that wrings the soul under a conviction of sin. But, in order to produce it, God puts his law into the heart; and this is done as instantaneously as the types of a press leave their characters on a sheet of paper. Thus written in the heart by the Spirit of God, it gives a knowledge of sin, and causes the convicted man to cry out, 'Unclean, unclean! I am worse than all other men!'"

In vain young Smith tried to feel this depth of depravity. He had never been guilty of any gross immorality, and, though he extenuated no offense that he had ever committed against God or man, he could not, with all his contrition and self-abasement, pronounce against himself a judgment so unjust.

But such a conviction, he had been taught, was a necessary part of all genuine religious experience; and he almost despaired of salvation, simply because he could not feel that he was too wicked to be saved.

At last, in his efforts to abase himself, he thought of the terrible Harpes, whose atrocities filled his utmost conception of human wickedness. The thought that he was worse than they, was at first false and abhorrent to his soul. But, one day, he reflected that these wretches were as ignorant as they were vicious; while he had been brought up by Christian parents, and instructed in every duty. He, therefore, had sinned against greater light, and was more guilty than murderers, who knew no law but that of the state. Reasoning that knowledge is the measure of responsibility, he finally persuaded himself that he was worse than the Harpes, and, consequently, more wicked than all other men. His fine conscience now ceased to plead in his behalf, and strangely accepted this load of fictitious guilt. He was overwhelmed with the thought of his wickedness, and so tortured with remorse that he sank down in anguish and despair.

Although such feelings were the result of his own reflections, yet his experience was none the less real and sincere. A prostration so complete, a sense of guilt so bitter and distinct, must, he thought, be the work of that Spirit who wounds to heal, and kills in order to make alive. He tried to borrow relief from his own sunny temper; but the gloom of a wrathful cloud was on him, and he lay in its shadow, stricken and dismayed.

His heart still mourned for his father; worldly cares distracted his thoughts, and severe daily toil exhausted his strength. He went about with a thoughtful melancholy that gave the family, especially his fond, old mother, much concern. Still he did not breathe the secret of his heart; he was wretched, but reserved; he shrank from sympathy, and courted solitude. He did not speak out his heart to man;

but by his bed at midnight, in the edge of the forest at noon, and in the dripping thickets at dawn, he fell on his face before God, and gave utterance to the anguish of his heart.

He tried also to get relief by an earnest and persevering endeavor to abandon his sins and to live a life of gravity and holiness. He resolved, accordingly, to quit the society of the frivolous, and to indulge no more in jests or mirthful songs. His name had recently been placed on the muster-roll of the county, and the usual parade was near at hand. He knew the temptations that awaited him, for the muster would be an occasion of merriment and dissipation. He dreaded the trial, but prepared himself for it. On the appointed day, before entering the field, he went aside to a wood, and there, kneeling down, begged heaven to strengthen him. As he came on the ground, a group of riotous companions greeted him with a noisy welcome. They had often laughed at his wit, and shouted refrains to his merry songs, and now they expected to laugh away the holiday at his jests.

"Come, John," said one of them, seizing his arm, "we are glad you have come; we want some of your best songs to-day."

"Boys," said he, with a solemn emphasis, "I have played the fool for you till I have nearly ruined my soul; I have resolved never to sing for you again while I live."

The reply was unexpected, for they knew nothing of his penitential struggles. They looked at him for a moment with surprise; and then, as if convicted by his words, quietly let go his arm, and withdrew. Firmly he thus broke friendship with the world, and gained over himself a triumph that saved him afterward from a thousand snares.

But his good works failed to give him peace. The hope that he could find relief in a reformation of conduct, perished at the thought, which now came into his mind, that the law, which had killed, could not also make alive; that, although he might in future do all that the law required, he could not thus pay off the debts of the past. Weary and heavy-laden, humble and almost hopeless, he fled like a stricken deer to a dense thicket of spice-wood that grew near the house; there, with his face in the dust, and a bitter agony in his heart, he besought his father's God to save him.

His own view of the nature of the process through which he was passing, forbade the thought of any aid or comfort from the Scriptures. The Lord, by his Spirit, had brought him to the dust, and only the Lord, by his Spirit, could lift him up. The thought that, humble and penitent as he was, he could arise and be baptized, calling on the name of the Lord, and thus have all his sins washed away, never once obtruded itself among his wildest dreams of relief. That he already believed, he did not once suspect. He supposed that faith was the gift of God, which the sinner could neither reject nor accept at will. He felt willing to obey at any sacrifice; but he had been assured that no obedience would be acceptable, unless it came from the faith which God only could give. The great desire of his heart was to be forgiven, and sealed as a child of God. This was the boon for which he wrestled morning, noon, and night; and, should it ever please God to grant it, he was persuaded that the fact would be made known to him by an audible voice—a significant vision—a well-defined feeling or mental change, that could instantly give him beauty for ashes, and the oil of joy for mourning—that would take away the spirit of heaviness, and clothe him with the garments of praise. For this great change, then, he cried from the secret places of the forest with all the earnestness of a broken and contrite spirit.

One morning, while it was yet dark, he arose from his sleepless bed, and went out to his favorite place in the spice-wood thicket to pray. The fragrant bushes were tangled with summer vines, and the dews of the night hung heavy upon them. The startled birds flitted away at his approach, and the solitude was gloomy and chill. He entered the covert, and, bowing himself in prayer, implored rest for his worn and weary soul. He knelt in hope, but arose in despair; his wretchedness and guilt seemed to cleave to him still. He started home through the dusky meadow, the stars still bright above him; but, as he went, a thought, quick and beautiful as a gleam of starlight, glanced into his soul, and dispelled his gloom. It came in the familiar words of Stennet, which suddenly occurred to him with a distinctness and power unknown before:

" Behold, the purple torrents run
  Down from his hands, his head;
The crimson tide puts out the sun,
  His groans awake the dead.

" So great, so vast a sacrifice
  May well my hope revive;
If God's own Son thus bleeds and dies,
  The sinner sure may live.

" Oh, that these cords of love divine
  Might draw me, Lord, to thee!
Thou hast my heart; it shall be thine—
  Thine it shall ever be."

Hopeless of mercy as he had so long been, he was nearly overpowered by the sudden discovery of the boundless love of Jesus. He repeated the lines of the hymn with wonder and delight. Every word thrilled him like a voice from the skies. He had long been dwelling on the terrors of the Lord as a being of infinite justice; he now fixed his gaze on the crucified One, and saw that he was a being of infinite goodness also; and the cloud of the Divine anger seemed to be spanned with the radiance of hope. He felt that this change in the direction of his thoughts could only come from above, and for a while he rejoiced.

His mind was so constituted, however, that he could not experience any sudden transition of feeling without some reflection. He stood there in the dim dawn, and thought on this new phase in his experience. He reasoned that if it was wicked to break the laws of a holy God, as he had done, it was surely tenfold more heinous to sin against a being of such goodness and love. The Divine love had just been the foundation of a blessed hope; now, it seemed, as he reflected on the subject, to be the ground of a more fearful condemnation. The goodness in which he was about to trust, could not save him; for had he not wantonly sinned against it all?

He fled back in terror to his place of prayer, and cast himself on his face in the dust. He poured out his very soul in tears more bitter, and in supplication more piteous than before. Exhausted at last by his long and painful struggles, he sank into the very extreme of prostrate wretchedness. The human heart could bear no more. His intense feeling and frenzied thought relaxed, and the repose of exhaustion succeeded the conflict. His strong mind then reacted, and he lay for some moments in a state of dreamy peace. His heart instinctively threw off its burden, and he seemed to pass in a moment from "death unto life."

The day had broken, the birds were singing in every bush, the dews sparkled in the early light, and the beauty and the freshness of the morning were around him. His heart drank in the influence of the hour, and he was happy!

He went home, though not yet fully persuaded that he was a converted man. This assurance he was to receive from those who better understood the work of the Spirit than himself. He met his brother William, who had been a member of the church for several years; he told him all that he had felt, and related particularly the experience of the morning.

"You are converted, John," said he, and joy gushed to his eyes; "you are converted at last!" and the brothers embraced, and wept together. John's doubts yielded to the testimony of his pious brother, and he spent the day in serene and cheerful meditation. But after he had slept, his mind and heart recovered their usual tone. He was able to think and feel again, and to struggle once more with despair. His doubts returned, his conscience took up its burden again, and his dream of heaven was over. He immediately sought his brother, and begged him to tell no one of his miserable hope; that it was all a delusion, a lie.

He betook himself once more to his spicy covert, and tried to pray again; but his soul was chilled with the cold-ness of despair. His appearance at length began to show plainly the effects of his mental conflicts. His mother's eye had long watched, in these outward signs, the painful travail of her boy, and she now ventured to inquire, with the deepest and tenderest concern, whether he had not experenced the happy change.

"No, mother," said he with emphasis, "I have not; and now I do beseech you, as my best earthly friend, to tell me what more I ought to do; for I would give the whole world to be a Christian."

"Ah! John," said she, and the holiest of human tears were in her eyes, "you must wait the Lord's time."

"Mother," said he, in a tone of despair, "I don't believe

that the Lord's time will *ever* come; I shall die and be lost forever!"

Isaac Denton, too, apprised of all his troubles, and anxious for his deliverance, tried to comfort him. But this good man could only tell him to go into secret, and pour out his soul to God—that he could do no more. To secret places he went; but new doubts and temptations assailed him; and he continued to sink and to rise in alternate paroxysms of feeling, till nearly two months had worn away. He believed that God had from eternity chosen certain persons for eternal life, whom he would call in due time by his Spirit and save, and that, too, without any regard to their faith or their works; all others would be left to perish, notwithstanding their struggles for life. The thought that he was, perhaps, one of the reprobate, would sometimes paralyze his heart like a touch of death. At other times he dreamed that, possibly, he was one of the elect, and could not be lost; and with this conceit, he would win a moment's respite from despair. So varied and severe were his trials, that he was at last urged by his brother to go before the church and submit the whole matter to them; they could, perhaps, resolve his doubts, and gave him the assurance which he could not obtain from his feelings.

As some experiences were to be related at Clear Fork, on the following Saturday, he determined to go and hear them, in order to see how others had been brought from darkness to light, and to learn in what respect his own experience was imperfect.

He stood in the yard without, at the side of the house, close to a crevice between the logs, through which he could see and hear all that transpired within. An ignorant and simple-hearted old man arose in the congregation to tell his experience.

"Do you begin, my brother," said the elder, "where the Lord began with you."

"One morning," said the man, "I went out into my woods to pray, and I saw the devil!"

There was a pause, and curious listeners leaned forward to hear, among whom there was none more anxious to know the Lord's way of dealing with sinners than the young penitent without, whose sad face peered through the parted logs.

"I saw the devil," repeated the man—"you may all think it was imagination; but I saw him as plainly as I now see Mr. Denton there."

"And how did he look?" asked an older brother, with more of curiosity than doubt.

"He was about the size of a yearlin'," said the man. "When I saw him I could not pray, and so I came home. But I went back next day to the same place, and he was gone! Then I was happy, for I knew that the Lord had saved me out of his hands."

Young Smith turned away from the house with sorrow and disgust. He prayed the Lord to keep his poor heart from error, and to lead him by the right way into the everlasting kingdom.

So great, finally, was the estimation in which his religious friends held his long and painful experience—so evident was it to them that a work of grace had been wrought in his heart, that they did not hesitate to acknowledge him as a brother, and to urge him to come forward and relate the facts to the congregation. On Saturday, the twenty-sixth of December, 1804, he went before the Church and gave a plain statement of his religious struggles for the past ten months. The Moderator formally submitted his case to the brethren. "All who believe," said he, "that the experience just related is a work of grace, hold up their right hand,"—and every hand in the congregation was raised in testimony of his conversion to God. The next day, he was immersed by Isaac Denton in the waters of Clear Fork; and, as soon as the congregation were seated in the house, the elder called him forward to the altar, and, praying that he might become a pillar in the temple of the Lord, solemnly laid his hands on his head, and thus received him into the fellowship of the Church.

His desire for knowledge, which had always been great, seemed to increase with his years. He mourned over his ignorance as his greatest misfortune, and wept at the thought that he was now a man without an education. Raised to labor on a rough frontier, without schools, or books, or educated society, he loved learning with a natural passion. But up to the time of his baptism, he had seen no other books than the three volumes which composed his father's library, and those in which he had studied while at school. After he joined the Church, his considerate pastor hastened to put into his hands "Toplady's Reply to Wesley"—a work of harsh and abstruse speculations on predestination and free-will. Such incidents as the fall of a leaf, the time and place of its fall, were declared to be eternally and unchangeably foreordained.

> " His decree who framed the earth,
> Fixed our first and second birth;
> Parents, native place and time,
> All appointed were by him."

Such was the sincere milk on which this babe in Christ was fed! And if he read of things which he could not understand, or, perchance, receive, his mind was quieted for the time by the assurance that "great is the mystery of godliness!"

Isaac Denton hoped that his young convert was destined for the pulpit, and that the Lord would soon call him to minister in holy things. He urged him to read, therefore, and to exercise his gifts occasionally in public prayer; in a word, he did everything he could to confirm him in the faith, and to keep his zeal alive. A desire to preach soon seized on the heart of his disciple; and he began to listen for the voice which must call him to the work. He had been taught that unless specially called as Aaron was, he could not, without daring impiety, stand before the people and expound the Scriptures. He had read of the wicked king who snatched a censer from the altar, and went with unanointed head into the presence of the Lord; and of the fearful wrath which punished his presumption with leprosy. He had read, too, of the thoughtless peasant that touched with profane hands the falling ark; and of the quick vengeance which smote him with sudden death. He trembled, therefore, at the thought of standing at the sacred desk until the Lord had duly anointed him to preach. The people generally, transferring the ideas of a primitive religious age to the Christian dispensation, regarded preaching as a priestly function, and looked on those who taught the religion of Jesus Christ as a peculiar and holy order of men. They believed, too, that the Lord not only called men to preach, but prepared them also by a divine influence for the work. An educated ministry was to them as absurd as a self-appointed one: for clerical wisdom and utterance they thought could come only from above. Learning, consequently, was despised by those whom the Spirit supplied with knowledge; and it was often the case that the less the learning, the greater was the unction.

John Smith's dream of an education was much disturbed by this desire to preach. He had been thinking of leaving home, as soon as he could with propriety do so, and of going to some more favored part of the country, where he might attend a good school, and sustain himself by his labor at the same time; but the reflection that his learning would be useless if he preached—that a knowledge of books would make him depend less on the power of the Spirit, caused him to lay aside his scheme for the present. He felt, at the time, that he could deny himself all knowledge, dear as it was to his mind, rather than destroy his influence by his learning. He waited on the Lord, therefore, for months, with patient awe; and during that time kept under, as well as he could, his desire for an education.

So constantly was his mind occupied, in the meantime, with the thought of preaching, that it frequently disturbed him in his sleep. Once, in his dreams, he stood before some imaginary congregation, and lifted up his voice so loud, that all the family were startled from their slumbers. His mother had, at last, to break the spell that was on him by going to his bedside and screaming in his ears:

"John, are you distracted, thus to preach without a call?"

But John preached on in his dreams at night, and listened for the heavenly call by day, until at last he began to despair of hearing it at all.

A more worldly project, too, soon engaged his attention. The region of country lying on the Little South Fork of the Cumberland, and formerly reserved as an Indian hunting-ground, had been recently thrown into market, and was rapidly filling up with settlers. His brother William had already entered some of this land, and John was anxious to secure a home near him. After visiting and examining the country, he purchased of a settler his headright to two hundred acres, for which he paid him the sum of fifty dollars. The land was in Wayne County, about twelve or fourteen miles southeast from Monticello, in a wild, narrow valley, called by the people "Horse Hollow," a name which had been given it from the fact that, before the extinction of the Indian title, it had been the rendezvous of a band of thieves, who used to hide their stolen horses in that secluded spot. As soon as he could make the necessary arrangements at home, he went to live with his brother, and began his preparations for opening up his farm. It had been already settled; that is, some straggling backwoodsman had acquired a title to it, notched the corner trees with his ax, raised the pen of his log cabin upon it, and called it his home; but, saving these *improvements*, it was as wild and rough a piece of wilderness as could be found.

In the midst of his preparations for farming, however, word was brought to him that a man of some learning had moved into Stockton's Valley, and was about to open a school. His desire for an education suddenly revived; the present opportunity could not be lost, and he resolved to improve it. Dropping his ax, and abandoning his wild land in the Hollow, he went back to his old home and took up his books once more.

Robert F. Ferrill, a wheel-wright by trade, had moved out from Virginia, and opened a shop in Stockton's Valley. He was a sober and industrious man. He had, for that day, a good English education, and had brought along with him a few choice books, which at once gave him great reputation among the people as a scholar. As the business of his shop would not for a while require much of his attention, he was persuaded to take up a school for the benefit of the children of the neighborhood. Every day John Smith walked nearly four miles to this school, and was always in his place at the appointed hour. For a few weeks his studies were uninterrupted. He made rapid progress; for Ferrill was a competent and faithful instructor. But there was soon a more urgent demand for wheels than for learning; and the teacher found that he could not attend to his young friends, and serve his more profitable customers at the shop. The bustling mothers clamored for their spindles, and would not wait on the schoolmaster; so he was forced to dismiss his school, and to give all his time to the making and mending of wheels.

But Ferrill was a kind-hearted man; he saw how much John loved knowledge, and how readily he acquired it; and he could not bear to turn him off in the midst of his struggle for a little learning. He invited him, therefore, to come to his house, and live with him, and to read his books, and study whatever he wished to learn. Anxious as John was to go to school, he would have declined the kind offer, had it not been made with the understanding that he could compensate his teacher by working on his farm. He would not have accepted even an education, if it had been offered as a charity. He could serve others without a fee; but a debt of any kind disquieted his conscience. He went, therefore, to work and to study with his teacher and friend. Taking quarters in the humble shop, he toiled at the bench or in the field through the day, and sat down to his lessons at night by the blaze of a light-wood fire, at last realizing the cherished wish of his heart—a few good books, and a friend competent to give him instruction.

Under the shed of this generous wheel-wright, John Smith received the most of his education. His studies were few, it is true, and confined to the rudiments of things; but what he learned, he learned well, and thus made up for the lack of variety. He pondered every word that he read, and revolved every fact and principle, until it was clearly defined in his understanding. His mind was intensely conscious of its impressions, and his conceptions of things were remarkably distinct. He grappled difficulties with an energy and patience that never despaired; and seemed to love those questions best which gave him the most trouble to solve. When Ferrill was absent, John took care of the farm, and pursued his studies alone. Night after night, by the light of his blazing pine knots, he toiled alone at some difficult problem, till the night itself was gone. If he needed assistance, while his teacher was away, he traversed the farms, for miles around, with book in hand, in search of some one to answer his questions.

When, at last, he felt that he had taxed his kind friend long enough, we went over to his mother's, and arranging the affairs of the farm so that she could get along in future without him, he left his home for the last time, and went back to live with his brother in the Hollow.

CHAPTER VI.

His neighbors, if people so widely scattered might so be called, were honest, but ignorant—a plain, hard-working and pious people, who spent the day in toil, and gathered in at night to their cabins, to sing, and to talk religion. They were, for the most part, Baptists, whose hearts still glowed with the warmth of the late revival. John's natural gifts and newly acquired attainments soon gave him prominence among them, and they often constrained him to lead at the cabin altar. His zeal was soon rekindled, and he became powerful in prayer and song. There was no church in the neighborhood, but, having brought his letter from Clear Fork, he took membership with a congregation whose place of meeting was some fourteen miles distant. There was, of course, no preacher among the people; but he went from house to house, and met his brethren in fireside exhortation and social prayer.

It was one of the popular notions of the day, that whatever might have been the experience of a young Christian he should still feel doubtful respecting his conversion, walk very humbly with his God, and, until full assurance came to him from above, only *hope* that his sins had been forgiven. Nothing caused the older members of the Church to suspect the genuineness of his conversion so much as a bold and joyful assurance. If, in view of his own experience, he could not find it in his heart to doubt, his aged brethren doubted for him. The slightest incident or phase of feeling was often deemed a sufficient ground for this self-distrust, so that the doubt was sometimes no better founded than the hope. An honest old neighbor of Smith used to relate, as a peculiar incident in his experience, and as the ground of his doubt, that, having one night obtained a hope while listening to a fervent exhortation, he found that the penitential tears which he freely shed on the occasion flowed from only one of his eyes, while the other would not weep, but was obdurate and dry. In making this discovery, he dismissed as vain the hope in which he had rejoiced, and resolutely maintained before his brethren that he had not been converted at all— but that he was a poor, weak hypocrite in the sight of God!

Assured that the Lord had once spoken peace to his soul, John Smith could not now doubt the fact. His later experience, too, tended to increase his self-confidence. Though he often tried to doubt, yet he found no reason to suspect that he was not a child of God. At length, this very confidence seemed to him like pride; and he would have exchanged it all for a little humble-minded self-distrust. He persuaded himself, in the end, that such an assurance as his could come only from the flesh; and he doubted at length simply because he could not doubt.

His interest in the religious affairs of the neighborhood continued to increase. His zeal gave warmth to the family prayers, and to the social worship. The cabins of his brethren were filled by turns, as the frequent appointment for meeting went round the neighborhood. He was often urged to exhort his brethren, and he felt a strange desire to give utterance to the feelings which these occasions always excited within him. But still he waited for a call—for some bush to burn, or other sign to appear, that would assure him of the Lord's consent. His brethren urged that, when God gives a man a talent, he gives the right to use it also; and that, if he could not preach, yet he might, without presumption, at least speak a word of exhortation to them. He was finally persuaded to lay aside his scruples, and one evening, at the social prayer meeting, he consented to say a few words to the people. His heart, on that ocasion, was full, for the song and the prayer had stirred his spirit, and the inspiration of the hour was on him. The room was crowded; the blaze from the hearth shone full upon his face, as he arose and stood with bashful emotion near the little table. He gazed on the faces around him; and a strange, bewildering torrent of feeling rushed to his heart. His mind was suddenly darkened; the thoughts which he had meditated for the occasion left him. He tried to recall them, but he could not; his lip quivered, and he was speechless. Turning from the stand, he rushed from the house into the darkness without. He fled across the yard like one affrighted, intending to quit a place where the Lord had thus rebuked him. But as he ran, his foot struck against something, and he fell, and, for a moment, he lay stunned on the ground. When he arose, the cloud seemed to be lifted from his mind; his thoughts came back to him, clear and distinct; and he felt he had the power of utterance once more. He returned to the house, where his brethren still sat. Standing in their midst again, he spoke with such fluency and fervor of soul that his exhortation seemed indeed to be with the power of the Holy Spirit.

He continued to exhort at these meetings, whenever pressed to do so; but his mind was disturbed more or less, all the while, by the want of a special call. He hoped on, however; and, as he was too unimaginative to see a ghostly vision, he watched for some simple sign, which he might, with reason, interpret as the voice of God.

It was not long before a vision came—an unspiritual one, indeed, but none the less beautiful on that account, and none the less powerful in its influence upon his life. At one of these meetings for prayer, as he thoughtfully sat and looked on the group around him, his eyes rested on the features of a young woman by the name of Anna Townsend. She had occasionally come with her parents to meeting; and had listened with some interest to the exhortations of the young stranger; but not until that moment had she ever been the object of his special regard. Now, her thoughtful and serene face, rich with the pleasing bloom of healthful and womanly beauty, strangely impressed the heart of the young man and Christian; and his destiny was shaped by the vision of that hour.

John Smith was not without susceptibility; and he was by no means wanting in a tender regard for the other sex. His respect for all virtuous women was, in fact, unbounded. But he was averse to gallantry, free from every tinge of romance, and wholly unskilled in the arts of courtship. He had a notion, too, that no young man should mingle much in the society of young women, till he had first made up his mind to marry; and that he should then proceed, in a business-like way, to seek one that was suitable, and willing to become his wife. He had conscientiously governed himself by this rule; for, although he was now in the twenty-second year of his age, he had never spoken to more than one or two young women in his life.

The impression which Anna Townsend made on his heart that evening was serious and abiding. He was now a man in years, and the owner of two hundred acres of land; he had left the parental roof forever, and he felt that he could push his own fortunes in the world. He resolved, therefore, to take a wife. After a few days' deliberation he made his first visit to the cabin of old Mr. Townsend, and on the 9th day of December, 1806, he wedded the first and only maiden that he had ever loved.

On the next morning he proposed to his wife, as his clearing was some four miles off, and he would lose too much time in going so far to his work every day, that they should move over at once to their house in "The Hollow," and live to themselves. The proposal accorded with her own wishes; for, in the mind of a young wife, the idea of domestic independence is inseparable from that of home. The preparations to move were soon made. A deep and heavy snow had fallen during the night, and the shrubs and vines were weighed down and tangled across the narrow paths, until the forest was almost impassable. An ox-sledge, drawn by sturdy yoke, was made ready. A bed, a few cooking utensils, and some provisions—the gift of the mother, and the bride's only dowry—were placed upon it. The bride herself sat bravely on the sledge, in the midst of her household stuff, while the groom, with his ax on his shoulder, stepped proudly on ahead to guide the floundering team, and to cut open a road to his cabin.

It was but an undaubed pen of logs. Through many a crevice the snow had drifted in, and it lay in piles on the earthy floor. The little square window was unshuttered and unglazed, and the entrance was closed against them by the bending shrubs. He cleared away the straggling branches, and his wife went in and took possession of her cheerless home. Gaping walls, a floor of dirt, and a stoneless hearth heaped with sooty snow, were all that met her eyes as she looked for the first time on her own fireside. But in a little while, Smith had provided abundant fuel, his flint yielded the ready spark, and a heap of logs and rich faggots soon blazed like a conflagration in the fire-place. But an empty cabin, without a puncheon or a hearth-stone, and open on all sides to December storms, was certainly no luxurious chamber for a bride, no very pleasant home for a young and hopeful wife. But she knew nothing of luxury, and, therefore, felt none of the wants which it creates. They were poor, indeed! but their poverty was unfelt; for none of their neighbors were rich, and all alike were accustomed to privation and toil.

The roaring fire soon thawed the hovel, and the dirty walls and the unsightly floor were swept again and again. Smith, having cut a few stout logs, of the proper length and thickness, brought them in upon his shoulders, and laid them down for sleepers, in a corner of the room. Across these he placed some clap-boards, found piled in the woods close by. On this rude platform the bed was laid, while a spare coverlet or two was hung against the wall to turn the cold wind which rushed in through every crevice. When the evening came on, the fire was replenished; a great log was rolled before the hearth, and the contented pair sat down together upon it in the light of the cheerful blaze, and talked over the toils of the coming day.

His task for the winter was, to clear a few acres of land, and have a field in readiness for planting in the early spring. During the day, he labored alone in the clearing—girdling the larger trees, and cutting out the undergrowth of shrubs, whose pole-like trunks he trimmed, and piled away for fencing. At night, he worked in his fire-lighted cabin, cheered and assisted by his wife. The walls were soon well chinked and daubed; a shutter was made for the window, and the awkward door was shaped and fitted till it shut out the wintry storms. His ax and wedge prepared the puncheons in the forest, which he laid down at night on the oaken sleepers, and then smoothed well with his adze. A few evenings thus spent and he stepped on as firm a floor as cabin ever had; no happier feet ever pressed a carpet in the mansions of the rich.

He next cut, from the forest, the trunk of a young dogwood tree, which forked at the proper height from the ground; and, having trimmed it, he set it up in his cabin for the outer corner-post of his bedstead. One end was let into the floor, with the augur; the other was fastened securely to the joist above. Two hickory poles, which served for rails, rested at right angles to each other in the fork of this post, and in the crevice of the log on each side of the corner. Across this frame, peeled hickory rods were laid, in close parallels, for slats; strips of clean linden bark, easily torn from the tree at almost any season of the year, were next laid down; the bed, with all its wealth of covering, was then spread, and the arrangements for repose were complete.

The labor of inclosing and cultivating a farm in the wilderness, without help, was severe; but he found time to keep alive, not only his own religious zeal, but that of his neighbors also. He had, by his fervent piety, and his force of character, come to be the religious head of a scattered brotherhood. He had persuaded them to keep up their society meetings, at which he was always present, to confirm or to comfort them by words of exhortation; and he now began to urge them to come together, and to constitute themselves regularly into a church.

His wife, who was unconverted at the time of her marriage, soon became deeply concerned on the subject of religion. He was, of course, much interested in the progress of her experience; but he reverently and hopefully left her alone with her God. The young husband, who, in any other trouble, would have succored her, even at the sacrifice of his life, abandoned her in this, the most solemn and perplexing of her trials; for no obtrusive human agency, thought he, must interfere with the work of the Spirit. She asked him one day, what was the meaning of a certain text; and he was too considerate to give her any explanation at the time, fearing that, in the simplicity of her unregenerate heart, she might improperly take comfort from it, and rely more on the Word than on the Holy Ghost. Her joyous deliverance at last relieved his own heart and fired anew his zeal for God.

His brethren scattered through the wild country in which he lived, came together at his call, and were regularly constituted into a church of seventeen members, by Isaac Denton, who, by special request, had come from Stockton's Valley to officiate on the occasion. A log meeting-house was soon built, though several miles distant from his cabin; and a preacher, Richard Barrier, was persuaded to take the young church for awhile under his ministerial charge.

It was usual among the Baptist preachers of that day, and it is yet the custom in some parts of the country, to unite four congregations under one pastorate. Although each was visited but once a month, such members as lived at a convenient distance, and were zealously enough disposed, often followed the preacher around his pastoral cycle, and thus enjoyed his ministrations every Sabbath.

It should be remembered, too, that the preachers of that day were a class of hardy pioneer farmers, who had not forgotten the church tax which they and their fathers used to pay in Virginia, to support the ministry of an established religion. They seemed to have made it a point of Christian honor, after the war was over, to preach the gospel without charge, and to support themselves independently, by hard labor, through the week. But little, if anything, was paid to them as a salary; some were even zealous enough to neglect their own families for the sake of the church, and to let their own corn-fields grow up in weeds, that they might work the more constantly in the vineyard of the Lord. The people had learned so thoroughly the lesson of muzzling the ox, that they could see their faithful pastors in want without making much effort to relieve them. In fact, they had been educated, by the preachers themselves, into the notion that it was sinful to pay men for preaching the Gospel.

Within the bounds of Stockton's Valley Association—a community dismissed from the old Green River Association, in 1804—there lived and labored for many years a gentle-hearted and godly old preacher, by the name of Barnes. He was very poor in spirit and in purse, homely in countenance and person, and exceedingly humble in his demeanor before God and man. He lived in a rude cabin among the

rocky hills, with but little worldly care beyond the maintenance of a small family, and of a faithful old horse that
had long carried him around the monthly circuit of his
four congregations.

One summer a very severe drouth came upon the land,
so that but little corn was raised, and every green thing
was withered and parched. Poor Barnes felt keenly the pinch
of famine, as bread and meat began to fail him, and as the
dry, dead leaves on the hill-side no longer furnished prov-
ender for old Gray. Still, master and beast made their
accustomed rounds, though with less and less spirit, as the
dreary year wore on. At last, at one of his monthly meetings, after the sermon of the day was over, and the church
was seated in a business session, a kind and thoughtful
man by the name of McKenzie, who had noticed the lean-
ness of the preacher's horse, arose, and proposed that if
any of the brethren could conveniently spare a little meal
or corn, they should send it to brother Barnes's family, without delay. He enforced his appeal by remarking, that brother
Barnes had been preaching for them faithfully, lo, these
many years, and yet the church had never been called on
to contribute anything for his support.

The old preacher sat near by, with his head bowed to
his lap, and his face covered with his hands, which were
brawny and brown with toil. The suggestion was at once
opposed by a brother who was zealous for the law and the
usages of the church. He argued that the Lord did not
tax his children to support the Gospel; that he had ordained
that it should be dispensed without money and without
price; that gifts, by way of compensation, to those who
preached it, were apt to puff them up with pride, and that,
though brother Barnes rode some distance to speak to the
people, many of them came quite as far to hear him.

McKenzie rejoined, that, in his opinion, the law of Christ
was explicit, clearly commanding that they who preach
the Gospel should live of the Gospel; and he urged the
proposed contribution on legal as well as charitable grounds.

But his opponent replied with emphasis, that he was
surprised to hear the Scripture in question quoted as referring to such things as meat and bread; that it was to
be understood only in a spiritual sense. "To live of the

Gospel," said he, "is to live on the sweet and heavenly feelings which the Gospel produces. On these divine things the
preacher ought to feed."

Old brother Barnes suddenly raised his head, and asked:

"But what is old Gray to do, my brother? he can't live
on them sort of feelin's."

The preacher in charge of the new church was not long
in discovering John Smith's qualifications for the ministry;
and he at once proposed to the congregation that liberty
should be given him to improve his gifts, wherever Providence should open for him a door. As a licentiate, Smith
was more than ever troubled about his call, especially in
view of the fact that he would soon be urged by his
brethren to submit to ordination. He now watched every
phase of ordinary Providence without, and every change
of feeling within, in hope, that in some incident or experience, he might find the encouragement that he sought.
For he had now persuaded himself that this encouragement
would be given, if given at all, by means of some simple
token, and in some natural way.

One day, after he had been working hard in his field, he
sat down on a log, by the edge of the forest, to rest himself. He had sat thus some time, lost in thought, when,
looking down, he saw coiled on the ground, between his
feet, a large rattlesnake. He sprang aside unharmed; for
the reptile seemed restrained, as if some spell was on it.
As he went back to his plowing, he thought of Gideon and
his fleece, and he wondered whether the Lord had not sent
this charmed snake as a sign that he, too, should help to
deliver Israel.

Having begun to interpret such incidents in this way, it
seemed to him that, for some reason, the Lord was multi-
plying his special providences around him.

Not long afterward, he bought from a drover a very
large ox, intending to fatten him for the market of Monticello. After driving him home, he found that he was a
most vicious and refractory animal. He resolved, one day,
to put a clog on him; but all his attempts to do so were
vain. He called on a neighbor for help, and they tried repeatedly to get him under control by means of the lasso.
But the ox dashed wildly around the lot in which he was

confined, and defied them. Smith kept two fierce bear-dogs, for an occasional hunt among the hills near by; he now called in these terrible allies, and dogs and men joined in the fruitless onset. The inclosure contained about four acres of ground; through this ran a small stream, across which a large beech tree had fallen. In attempting to leap this stream, the ox fell, and for a moment was caught and held fast by the prostrate branches. Smith, who had already lost his patience, determined to win the day by a *coup-de-main.* Leaping forward, he seized his victim by the nose with a powerful grasp. The indignant animal no sooner felt the touch of a human hand, than, with one mad bound, he cleared the tree, and rushed, with bellowing rage, upon him. Smith fled across the lot, but the ox kept him between his wide-spreading horns, and actually pushed him as he ran.

Though but for a moment, yet within that brief interval, Smith thought, as he was carried along between the horns of his ox, "If the Lord should be with me in this extremity, and deliver me out of this trouble, I will know assuredly that he wants me to preach, and I will no longer scruple to be ordained."

Immediately he was caught by his clothing, on a horn of the beast, and tossed in the air. On rushed the impetuous ox, and down came Smith to the ground, stunned but otherwise unhurt. The next instant he was on his feet, and before his now victorious foe could turn upon him again, he was over the fence, and safe beyond the reach of his horns.

On the subject of the call to the ministry, the Baptists of that day were by no means universally agreed. Many looked for extraordinary visions, or listened for miraculous voices, while some few believed that the Lord called only through the Church. "If a Christian has talent, and the Church says, 'preach,' he may go on safely," said an old minister, who, in his youth, however, had waited long for some supernatural call, without receiving it. "The voice of the Church," said he, "is the voice of God. The bridegroom is away, and what the bride does in his absence must certainly be valid." Thus, some were called by the Spirit and the bride; others, by the bride alone, yet all were agreed that none should preach the Gospel without the authority or consent of the Church, whatever might be his talents, his motives, or his experience. This was plainly set forth in the *Philadelphia Confession of Faith*, which declared, that the "way appointed by Christ for the calling of any person, fitted and gifted by the Holy Spirit, to the office of bishop or elder in a church, is that he be chosen thereto by the common suffrage of the church itself; and solemnly set apart by fasting and prayer, with imposition of hands of the eldership of the church."

It was, accordingly, the custom when a pastor or minister was to be ordained, to come together with fasting and prayer, and to give in their suffrages with great solemnity. The eldership examined the candidate, respecting his faith and his call to the ministry; and, if the questions asked were satisfactorily answered, they knelt down with · him, and, laying their right hand on his head, one of them offered up the ordination prayer. After this ceremony, the charge was usually delivered, and the congregation gave him the hand of fellowship. Generally, the ceremony of ordination was solemn and imposing; and the examination of the candidate, conducted in the presence of the assembled church, was edifying to all. But the examination was sometimes a mere form, if not a farce, the questions asked being simple, or even silly. "My brother," once inquired a presbyter of a young candidate, when examining him for the ministry of one of the early churches, "did you ever know a sheep to turn into a goat, or a goat to turn into a sheep?" After a long pause, the candidate could only reply that he did not recollect of having ever heard of such a thing.

The doctrine thus enforced was: "That the elect, even before conversion, were the sheep of Christ, and, as such, could never be lost; that once a sheep, always a sheep."

Not only was the notion of a supernatural call to the ministry repudiated by the bolder thinkers of the times, but even the imposition of hands in ordination was regarded by some of them as an idle and unauthorized ceremony.

It is reported[*] that John Leland, one of the most popular preachers of his day in Virginia, and one of the most eccentric and singularly pious of men, was at first ordained a minister by the choice of the church, without the imposi-

---

[*]Elder James Sims, of Kentucky.

tion of the hands of the Presbytery. He continued for some years afterward to preach and to baptize on the authority of his simple appointment, much to the disurbance of the peace of the association to which he belonged. In fact, on account of his departure from the usages of the churches in Virginia, he was not for awhile in good fellowship with any. Whether right or wrong, he openly professed to believe that the imposition of hands by the Apostles, in ancient times, was only to confer miraculous gifts; and that, consequently, such a ceremony in the Church now, was in itself worthless, because wholly unauthorized.

His brethren urged him most earnestly, for the sake of peace, to submit to ordination by the hands of the ministry; and finally, to gratify them, he consented that they might call a Presbytery for that purpose. Knowing all the ques tions which they would ask on his examination, and resolved in his own mind on the answers which he would give, he felt confident that they would not ordain him.

The Presbytery, consisting of three staunch Calvinists, was called. The day appointed for the ordination arrived, and with it came a multitude of people to witness the ceremony. The work was divided among the several Presbyters. One was to ask the usual questions concerning his faith and call; another was to offer up the ordination prayer; and another was to deliver the charge to the pastor and the church. Leland took his seat long before they appeared, and resting his arms on his knees, and burying his face in his hands, awaited their movements.

The Presbyter appointed to conduct the examination, at length began:

"Brother Leland, it becomes my duty, according to previous arrangement, to ask you a few questions upon the subject of your faith, and in reference to your call to the ministry."

"Well, brother," said Leland, slowly raising his head, "I will tell you all I know," and down went his head into his hands again.

Presbyter. "Brother Leland, do you not believe that God chose his people in Christ, before the foundation of the world?"

Leland (*looking up*). "I know not, brother, what God was doing before he began to make this world."

Presbyter. "Brother Leland, but do you not *believe* that God had a people from before the foundation of the world?"

Leland. "If he had, brother, they were not our kind of folks. Our people were made out of dust, you know, and before the foundation of the world there was no dust to make them of."

Presbyter. "You believe, brother Leland, that all men are totally depraved?"

Leland. "No, brother; if they were, they could not wax worse and worse, as some of them do. The devil is no more than totally depraved."

Presbyter. "Well, there are other questions that will embrace all these in substance. I will ask, whether you do not believe that sinners are justified by the righteousness of Christ imputed unto them?"

Leland. "Yes, brother, provided they will do right themselves; but I know of no righteousness that will justify a man that won't do right himself."

Presbyter. "Brother Leland, I will ask you one more question: Do you not believe that all the saints will persevere through grace to glory, and get home to heaven at last?"

Leland. "I can tell you more about that, my brother, when I get there myself. Some seem to make a very bad start of it here."

The Presbyter, seeing that the audience was greatly amused, proposed to his colleagues that they should retire for a few moments, and consult together. After returning, they remarked to the congregation, that brother Leland had not answered the questions as satisfactorily as they could wish, but they all knew that he had many eccentricities, for which they should make every allowance; that they had concluded accordingly to ask him a few questions touching his call to the ministry.

Presbyter. "Brother Leland, you believe that God has called you to preach the Gospel?"

Leland. "I never heard him, brother."

Presbyter. "We do not suppose, brother Leland, that

you ever heard an audible voice; but you know what we mean."

Leland. "But wouldn't it be a queer call, brother, if there were no voice, and nothing said?"

Presbyter (*evidently confused*). "Well, well, brother Leland, you believe, at least, that it is your duty to preach the Gospel to every creature?"

Leland. "Ah! no, my brother, I do not believe it to be my duty to preach to the Dutch, for instance, for I can't do it. When the Lord sent the Apostles to preach to every nation, he taught them to talk to all sorts of people; but he has never learned me to talk Dutch yet."

Presbyter. "But, brother Leland, you feel a great desire for the salvation of sinners, do you not?"

Leland. "Sometimes I think I do; and then again I don't care if the devil gets the whole of them."

Upon this the Presbyter retired again, and, having returned, reported as before, much to the surprise of Leland, who was now constrained to submit to ordination. After they had ordained him in due form, he said:

"Well, brethren, when Peter put his hands on people, and took them off, they had more sense than they had before; but you have all had your hands on my head, and, before God, I am just as big a fool now as I was before you put them on."

CHAPTER VII.

John Smith, reflecting on his recent experience, and feeling that he ought to defer as much as he could to the judgment of his brethren, consented at last to be ordained, and he was, accordingly, set apart in due form to the work of the ministry, on the third Saturday in May, 1808, by Richard Barrier and Isham Burnet, Presbyters of the Stockton's Valley Association. The Presbytery remarked, at the time, that they were so well assured of his orthodoxy, and of his ability to preach, that it was necessary to ask but a very few questions.

"We suppose, brother Smith," said they, "that you are well acquainted with the Philadelphia Confession of Faith?"

"I am well acquainted with it, brethren," replied the candidate.

"Do you adopt the Articles therein set forth?"

"I do."

Upon this, they all knelt; Isham Burnet having prayed, they all laid their hands on his head, and then declared him legally authorized to administer the Lord's Supper, Baptism, and other ordinances, and, also, to preach the Gospel. The congregation then arose and went to the stream close by, where the newly ordained minister forthwith immersed four persons who had previously given in their experience, and were waiting only till the young licentiate received authority to baptize them.

His zeal now was unrestrained. He spent every moment that he could spare in the close and earnest study of his Bible, and the doctrines of his Church, as they were set forth in the Confession of Faith. The pine-knots blazed on his hearth till a late hour every night; for he pored over the sacred text with a diligence that never tired. He saved the hour of noon, by reading while his tired yoke browsed in the shade or stood at the rick. He laid the open Bible by his side on the dinner-table, and committed to memory, over his plate, some verse on which he could ponder while at work. For he studied even in the fields, improvising sermons as he piled up his log heaps, and exhorting imaginary congregations as he plowed along.

He preached every Sunday, often riding many miles on Saturday, in order to reach the appointed place in time. He gathered the people together wherever he could—in their scattered meeting-houses, in their log cabins, in their still humbler school-houses, or in the dark, unbroken woods.

His voice was deep, rich, and heavy; his utterance deliberate and distinct. His chant was finely modulated; for he loved melody, and the taste of the times demanded that the sermon should be rendered in solemn, chant-like tones. When he stood up broad-chested, in the forest, or on some rude platform, or the trunk of some fallen tree, and spoke to the multitudes around him, his deep-toned, ponderous words rolled along the hollows, until the dwellers among the hills of the Cumberland have declared that they could sit at their cabin doors and hear him two miles off. Such a voice, then, had all the effect of eloquence itself; in the popular regard, it was a greater gift than learning, and awed like inspiration.

There were some Methodists in the neighborhood, with whom he had frequent conversations on the subject of religion. The several points of Calvinism and of Arminianism were repeatedly discussed. The texts that were supposed to bear on the question of Election, whether found in Jewish or Christian Scriptures, were examined again and again, until a zeal for doctrines, if not for party, almost consumed him.

He preached: "That all men, without exception, are dead in sin, and can of themselves do nothing to please God; that they are wholly defiled in all their faculties of soul and body; that, not only is Adam's guilt imputed to all, but his corrupt nature is conveyed to all; that consequently all are utterly indisposed, disabled, and made opposite to all good, and wholly inclined to all evil.

"That, nevertheless by God's decree, a definite number of individuals are predestinated or fore-ordained to eternal life, whom God chose and appointed personally and particularly to glory before the foundation of the world was laid, without any reference to their conduct or character.

"That these elect persons being morally and spiritually dead, and incapable of doing any thing good, are, in due time, called, and effectually and irresistibly drawn to Christ, without any agency of their own, as if co-operating with the Spirit, but are wholly passive; for which elect persons only did Christ die.

"That those who are thus elected, called, and made alive, by the Holy Spirit, are enabled, by the same divine influence, to do many things that are good and right: that they can repent and believe in Christ, and understand and obey the Scriptures; but these good works of the renewed man are not in any sense the grounds of his justification or acceptance with God.

"For God decreed from all eternity to justify the elect, although they are not personally justified until the Holy Spirit, in due time, actually applies Christ to them; that Christ's own obedience to the law, is imputed to them as their whole and sole righteousness through faith, which is the work of the Spirit, and the gift of God.

"That all who were thus justified can never fall from grace; but will certainly persevere to the end, and be saved.

"That all other persons, whether men, women or children, are reprobate—the Holy Spirit giving them neither the disposition nor the ability to do good. They can not come to Christ, nor did Christ die for them; and, therefore, they must perish in their sins.

"Finally, that elect infants, dying in infancy, will be regenerated and cleansed from Adam's sin and Adam's guilt by the Holy Spirit, and saved—while non-elect infants will be left to perish in their corruption entailed upon them, and in the guilt imputed to them."

This last doctrine he did not, it is true, love to preach; but neither did he, at that time, venture to call it in question.

In the meantime, when his friends in Stockton's Valley heard that he was preaching, they were much concerned, fearing, in their great affection for him, that his zeal or his gifts might have led him into indiscretion. They talked the matter over at the fireside, and at the social meetings, until finally it was arranged by the brethren at Clear Fork, that Philip Smith, his eldest brother, should go on a mission to Wayne, to hear him preach, and to make inquiries concerning his call.

Philip returned, with the gratifying announcement that the Lord was surely with John, and that his brethren might safely let him preach on.

And he did preach on, without hinderance or rebuke, growing daily in favor with the brethren among whom he labored. To those who had preceded him in the ministry, and whom he now often met, he was modestly deferential and attentive. He was glad to sit at their feet and learn, while they talked together of the deep things of the Spirit of God—for there were always grave points of law and doctrine that were discussed by the preachers only among themselves—a kind of esoteric theology, too profound for the people, or too much controverted to be brought before the congregation. Ambitious to learn whatever they could teach, and anxious to equip himself for successful conflict with his Arminian neighbors, who waxed bolder and stronger every day, he let pass no opportunity of attending the conferences of his older brethren—always listening with interest to their conversations, and pondering well, in his own mind, every opinion that they advanced.

One of the problems which he heard most frequently and earnestly discussed, and which baffled all the efforts of the older ministers to solve, was the reconciliation of the doctrine of the eternal justification of the elect, with the fact of their actual condemnation, as testified by the Holy Spirit at the time of their conversion. The experience of all truly converted men was, in this respect, the same. They were made to feel, not only that they deserved condemnation, but were already condemned. How, then, could this experience be reconciled with the fact that these same persons were not only justified at the time of their conviction, but had been justified from the foundation of the world? He had seen those godly old Calvinists, Isaac Denton, Richard Barrier, and Isham Burnet, grow thoughtful and solemn, when this deep question came up for discussion; and he often vexed his younger brain in fruitless efforts to explain it.

Finally, as he was working in his cornfield, one day,

he reflected that there were two distinct covenants; one of works, which concerned all men, so that, if any kept not the whole law, he died without mercy; the other of grace, which concerned the elect only, so that all whom God had chosen in Christ, would be saved unconditionally from death. He concluded that the elect stood related to both covenants, condemned by the first, and, at the same time, justified by the second; while the non-elect were related to the first only, and by it eternally condemned; that, when the Holy Spirit in conversion comes to the elect, they are made to know, first their condition as sinners, under the covenant of works, and afterward are surprised by the discovery of the fact which the same Spirit makes known to them, that they are related to the covenant of grace also, by virtue of which they had always been justified; so that the Holy Spirit, in fact, makes two successive, and not two contradictory, revelations to the sinner; and consequently, every genuine experience was in strict accordance with the received doctrine of redemption.

His solution of the difficulty was accepted by his brethren as a revelation from heaven! The very Presbyters that ordained him, when they heard the ingenious discourse that thus vindicated the Holy Spirit from all self-contradiction, and reconciled their faith and experience, believed that he was no less inspired for the work which he had done, than was Peter on Pentecost, or Paul before Agrippa. His reputation was made; his fame went abroad through all that land, and his praise was in all the churches.

During the following months, he visited the congregations within the bounds of the Association to which he belonged, and was received with every mark of respect. His well-toned voice and earnest manner, his fine common sense and unaffected piety, rendered him pre-eminently popular as a speaker; his genial humor, too, threw its sunny influence on all around him, and made him the delight of every fireside.

As his fame and influence extended, he felt more deeply his imperfections, especially his want of learning. He made no attempt to disguise his ignorance. He was honest with himself and with others. He could pretend to nothing—he could affect nothing. His ambition aimed at excellence, and not at appearance; it was not a desire simply to appear great in the eyes of men, but an aspiration to become great in the sight of God. Zeal for the Church burned on; but his singular passion for what he called an education could not be controlled.

A good school had just been opened in the village of Monticello, by Rhodes Garth, and he was soon restless with the thought that he ought not to let pass so fine an opportunity to learn. True, he lived nearly fourteen miles from the town; he was encumbered with the care of a farm, a family, and a congregation; he was twenty-five years of age, and already better educated than his neighbors; but these considerations seemed to him paltry, when urged against another attempt to get a better education. His wife, knowing his eagerness to increase his little stock of learning, did not object to his going to school, although it would take him from home, and the care of the farm would devolve on her. The lonesome days and nights, too, she thought, would drag heavily on while he was away; for there would be none to assist her—no living soul to stay with her, and keep her company in those dark and rugged woods, save the baby boy that now rolled on the cabin floor; little Eli, she felt, would help to lift off the solitude from his mother's heart.

Micah Taul, also, (a lawyer of Monticello,) urged him to go to school again, and pressed him to come and live during the time at his house. Thus encouraged, he arranged his affairs at home as well as he could, and on Monday, walked to Monticello. His purpose was to return home every Saturday, preach to his neighbors on Sunday, and walk back to school on Monday, in time for the lessons of the day. His course of study embraced the Scriptures, Arithmetic, Roman History, Orthography, and Pronunciation. This last branch of learning he deemed of special importance. He had observed that his educated brethren from the Northern Associations, whom he occasionally met as messengers, pronounced many words in a manner different from his own, and he judged that their style must be right. This led him to pay much attention to Orthoepy; for, as a public speaker, he did not wish to be guilty of a backwoods' brogue, should Providence ever call him to stand before an educated audience. His efforts to improve in this respect, gave him a precise and distinctly syllabic utterance. Careful of every element of sound, he spoke his words as if each letter had a meaning. He was particular about his accent also, and always marked the chosen syllable, whether right or wrong, with a weight of voice that never failed to give it prominence.

His first week at the academy passed by pleasantly and profitably enough. Saturday found him at home again, busy on his farm. His wife had done what she could, but he saw that, though she did not complain, yet in his eagerness for learning, he had incumbered her with cares that neither had anticipated.

On Monday, as he walked back to school, he was troubled in heart; for the love of the husband struggled with the ambition of the student; and, before he reached Monticello, he felt that he ought not to ask his wife to make such sacrifices for him any longer.

He remained at school that week, and then walked back to his cabin in the hills. The care-worn face of his wife confirmed him in his resolution, and he quit his school at once, never to become a pupil again.

CHAPTER VIII.

In the summer of 1810, at the Cumberland River Association, he again met with Jeremiah Vardeman, then one of the most influential ministers in Kentucky. Vardeman had heard of the young preacher that lived down among the hills of the Little South Fork, and when he saw him at the Association, he grasped his hand affectionately, and took him to his heart as a brother. He saw that his talents and knowledge of the Scriptures fitted him for a position of greater usefulness in the Church; and he expressed a wish to see him at work in a wider field of labor.

Smith had already become dissatisfied with the place where he lived. He felt that, if he would grow in knowledge, or in strength, he must seek a home among a more intelligent and enterprising people. With the pride of a young father, he had determined, moreover, never to bring up his children in the rough wilds of "The Hollow."

He listened, therefore, with much interest to Vardeman's description of men and things in Northern Kentucky, and he felt the full force of the argument, that he owed it to himself, to his family, and to the Church, to get away from his country, and, if needs be, from his kindred, and to go up to a land which God seemed to have blessed above all other portions of the State. "A man's gifts," said Vardeman to him, when he complained of his want of education, "a man's gifts will make room for him, and bring him into the presence of great men."

For awhile he toiled on in his fields, spending what time he could in preaching to his neighbors, and in teaching his children; for he made haste to save these from the ignorance that had darkened his own childhood. Eli, his eldest, was in his seventh year, and Elvira was two years younger; they were healthful and sprightly children, on whom he lavished an almost idolatrous affection.

At length he arranged his business for a few weeks' absence, and accepted an invitation to visit the churches in what was, even then, called the Blue Grass Region of Kentucky. On this tour, he preached with much acceptance. His own mind was lifted up, and his heart was enlarged. He was pleased with all he saw, and but for a delicate sort of pride, he would have accepted a call from some wealthy churches, and have gone to live among them as a salaried minister. But a consciousness of his inferiority in learning, as well as in social culture, his poverty, and especially the thought of living on what he regarded as the charity of his brethren, caused him to decline the proposition, and to form another plan for advancing the welfare of his family.

He returned home, resolved to seek some better country elsewhere. The war with England was going on, and embargoes paralyzed the commerce of the country. The public lands in Alabama were about to be thrown into market, and the terms would be liberal. The most splendid opportunity for speculation was presented. Choice lands would be patented at $1.25 per acre, and only ten dollars for every hundred acres would be required on entry; the remainder would be payable in four years thereafter. During the eight or nine years that he had lived on the Little South Fork, he had converted much of the forest into arable; he had built a hewed log-house for his family, put up a good barn, and collected some little stock together. By the sale of his farm and surplus stock, he could realize, he thought, about fifteen hundred dollars. With this amount he could remove his family to Huntsville, at that time a village of but few houses, erect a temporary cabin, and supply the immediate wants of his family, and still have one thousand dollars left with which to enter ten thousand acres of land. The war, he reasoned, must soon be over, the embargo would be removed, and peace re-established on a solid basis. Before the long term of payment expired, emigration would flow to the South, and the general prosperity of the country would rapidly raise the price of his land; so, that, by the sale of but a small portion of his estate, he would be able to pay up his installments to the Government, and still have enough to place him among the affluent men of the country. His scheme embraced the purchase and employment of many slaves, and the cultivation of many fields of cotton. His dreams were gilded by recollections of the wealth on which he had gazed while in the Blue Grass districts of Kentucky.

He revolved this scheme in his mind, again and again, during the summer of 1814, till, grown restless under the influence of his dream, he went to look at the country, and to confirm, by observation, the wisdom of his plan. Sub sequent events fully verified his predictions. Others were made rich; for within two years, some of that land was sold at fifty dollars per acre. But God had better things in store for him. In the very hour, almost, when he thought to put his well-laid scheme into execution, He who had called him to preach the unsearchable riches of Christ, stretched forth his hand and blighted all his earthly hopes.

He returned from Alabama, elated at the prospect that suddenly opened up before him; and he immediately made preparations to remove. He sold his farm, and some other property, for fifteen hundred dolars. Such goods and chattels as he reserved, were thrown into his farm wagon, where his four children were stowed for the journey, and where the mother also, when weary of walking, found rest on the way. A young lad, the brother of his wife, went with them, and drove such stock as they thought best to take along.

He reached his destination in the Hickory Flats, near Huntsville, on the 2d of November, 1814. He was fortunate enough to find an unoccupied cabin, which he rented till he could build on his own land. As soon as his family were made comfortable in their new home, he mounted his horse, and began a survey of the country around, with a view to select, for entry, some of the best sections of the public domain. A few Baptists had already moved into the country, some of whom were his father's old friends, from East Tennessee; but they lived some fifteen or twenty miles distant. They heard, however, that a son of George Smith had come into the State, and that he was a preacher of their own faith and order. They sent him a request, therefore, to come and see them, and to preach to them, expressing, at the same time, the tenderest regard for the memory of his father. Anxious to know those who already loved him for his father's sake, he accepted their invitation, and left home, commending with strong faith his family to God, who had so often cared for them while he was away.

It was Saturday, the 7th of January, 1815. A bright but cold sky was over him, and a charming country, beautiful even in that season of the year, lay everywhere around him. As he rode along, his mind was busy with those worldly visions which had of late so often haunted him.

"Thousands of these fertile acres are mine," thought he; for he passed through some of the very sections which he proposed to purchase. "A few years hence, a mansion will rise for me here, and gardens will smile for me yonder in those woods; farther than the eye can reach, my broad fields will whiten with the wealth of the South, and troops of dusky slaves shall gather it and lay it at my feet. The sweat of labor shall soil my face no more; Eli shall never experience the hardships of his father, nor little Elvira feel the privations of her mother. But, as all these things at last will belong to the Lord, I must be his faithful steward. I will try to do as my good old father did before me; none shall suffer from want around me; for I will make the widow's and the orphan's heart to sing for joy"—and the soul of John Smith dilated with the vision of the hour.

He reached his destination in the evening, and was received by his father's friends as a son. Little incidents of family history, the progress of events, the prospects of the country, and especially of the Church, were all talked over at the fireside till a late hour at night, and he retired to rest with a heart full of pleasant memories and still more pleasant hopes.

In the meantime, his wife at home had been called, at evening, to the bedside of a sick neighbor that lived close by. They had sent to beg that she should come and cheer the dying woman with her songs; for Mrs. Smith had a sweet voice, and sang with pathos, all the melodies of the Church. Prompt at the call, she had taken her infant in her arms, and gone at twilight on her mission of love. She had left her cabin and the three older children in the care of her brother, and of a younger sister, who also was with them. They had all gone to bed early; for they were tired of the toil, or of the sports of the day. About ten o'clock, while the mother was trying to soothe her afflicted neighbor with her songs, screams of anguish reached her ears, and the blaze of her burning house suddenly lighted up the woods. She seized her babe and rushed to the spot, for the distance was not great. The house, which was built of light poplar logs, was already wrapt in fire. Without, in the glare of the flames, stood her brother, holding one little, trembling child by the hand.

"Hiram! are they all safe? where are the others?" she cried. But he was dumb with terror; yet she saw, with the quick eye of love, the fate of her absent children.

"Eli! Elvira!" she screamed, with an agony that rent her heart, and she rushed to the blazing door. The grasp of a neighbor just saved her from leaping with her babe into the flames that were consuming her home, her husband's wealth, and the first-born children of their love. Brother and sister perished there that night together, in the very bed where, at twilight, they had fallen asleep in each other's arms, with a mother's good-night kiss upon their lips.

The fire had, by some means, first caught among the rafters of the building. Burning splinters, dropping from above, had blistered the face of Hiram Townsend, and awakened him, but too late to save the children. He hardly escaped with his life. His sister, also aroused by the dropping fire, had rushed through the flames, dragging with her the little girl, with whom she had been sleeping. Nothing, of course, had been saved. All the clothing of the family, their little furniture, and every dollar of their money, was gone.

The heart-broken mother refused to be comforted. She sat tearless and speechless by the ashes of her home, and of her children, through the long, dreary night. Two messengers and started off at midnight, to carry the word to her husband.

"Mr. Smith," said they, as they stood before the door of the house, next morning at dawn, "we are sorry to bring you bad news from home. Your house took fire last night, and everything is lost. Two of the children were burned to death!"

"O God!" cried the stricken father, and his head dropped upon his breast.

"Which of my children?" at length gasped the poor man. "Was it Eli? Was it my boy? And did Anna have to stand and see it all? O my God! my God!" and he sank down upon the steps, and buried his face in his hands.

They brought him his horse, and he hastily set out for his home, to weep his yet unfallen tears into the bosom of his wife. He passed the spot where but yesterday fancy had reared him a mansion, and laid out for him her beautiful gardens—by the place where, in his dream, the cotton had bolled, and slaves had toiled for him. Now, every prospect pained and rebuked him; for he saw in the very landscape and sky, in forest and stream, nothing but the ruin of all his hopes, and the gloom of his own distress.

The brave but wretched man endeavored to strengthen himself for the scene that awaited him. He tried to borrow support from religion, and to find, in the promises of Scripture, some solace for his wife. But the thought that, perhaps, his children had passed through the flames of their burning home only to writhe forever in the still fiercer flames of another world, sent a keen agony through his soul; he trembled with fear, and for awhile he could hardly move on in his journey.

"I can give her no consolation!" thought he. "If I tell her that our babies are glorified, the thought that possibly they were of the non-elect will only aggravate her woe." His own faith was bewildered by this thought, which haunted him like an evil specter as he rode along. He tried to persuade himself that non-elect persons do not die in infancy; but his mind would not accept the subterfuge. He dreaded, therefore, to meet his wife's look of anguish, and to hear her ask the question, "Are our children among the elect of God?" For the time being, every other grief was lost in this; and in the confusion of his mind, his faith in that harsh doctrine of his Church yielded up its strength forever.

At length, he came in view of the spot, and his eyes took in the whole scene at a glance. Standing amid the ashes of the cabin, in the very place where Eli's little bed had stood, two of his neighbors were holding by the corners a pocket-handkerchief, into which another was putting the gathered bones of his children. They saw him approaching; but they kept on at their work in silence. Other sympathizing neighbors stood around, some looking mournfully into the ashes, and some glancing through their tears at the wife and mother, who was sitting on a log near by. Some one had thrown a blanket around her; for the air was chill. One of her little children slept on her breast—the other sobbed at her side in all the bitterness of childish woe. He dismounted from his horse, and went to the place where she was sitting. He did not speak a word, but with all the gentleness of a subdued sorrow, he lifted his little sobbing girl into his arms, raised up his wretched wife, and taking her infant to his own bosom, walked slowly away with her into the forest. He tried to say something to her; but the thought of *reprobation* choked him. They reached a place out of sight, and sat down. He struggled again for some words that would comfort her; but it was in vain.

At last the thought that had held her dumb also, burst from her heart.

"Can you ever forgive me," she cried, "for leaving home as I did last night?"

He saw, from her words, that the horrible dream of an infant's hell had not yet oppressed her brain. That phantom was born of his own theology. A mother's heart had already predestined her children to glory, and all the theology of earth could not have reversed that heart's decree! The sting of her grief was the thought of her own neglect. He soothed her anguish by the assurance that she had gone that evening where duty had called her, and that for some wise and good purpose this blow had fallen upon them.

After his children's remains were buried, his neighbors came together to help him; and, in a few days, another cabin sheltered his family. But his neighbors, too, were poor, and every article of domestic comfort was scarce, so that his house was empty and bare. He drank the new milk every morning from the bowl of a cymbling, scraped out by the hands of his wife.

He recollected that a small portion of the money which he had lost was in coin. He hurried to the ruins of his cabin, to the spot where his chest had stood, in the till of which he always kept his money. He scraped among the ashes with his hands, and found a small mass of silver. This he sold in Huntsville for seventy-six dollars, which, with a balance owed him by some merchants of that place, enabled him to provide such things as were necessary to the health and comfort of his family.

But though the Lord had so severely rebuked his ambition, he soon began to lay new schemes of worldly aggrandizement. The stock which he had brought with him from Kentucky still ranged the forests; his brawny muscle, his nerves of wire, and his almost unconquerable will, remained. He could yet so arrange his affairs that, with Hiram's aid, and such help as his poor wife could give, he would be able to raise some cotton for the market. His crops would increase from year to year, and to retrieve all his lost prospects would be but a work of time.

But the pale, melancholy face of that wife never brightened again. His own sunny temper could not remove the shadow from her brow. As soon almost as she was comfortably housed in her new cabin, the good woman sickened and died, and they buried her by the ashes of her children.

They had scarcely thrown over her the mold of the forest, when he, too, the man of strong will and iron nerve, was stricken down with the Cold Plague. He lay for a long time in the utmost distress of body and mind. A month of wasting fever dragged slowly by. His wife's brother and sister had returned to Kentucky, and neighbors came by turns and watched him. Two Christian women, who lived down among his father's friends, came to see him, and when they went back, they took away his complaining children, and nursed them through days and weeks of sickness in their own pleasant homes.

Another month wore away, yet he grew no better. One kind woman, full of the temper of her Lord, came every morning, and nursed him through the day with a tenderness and skill that made the wretched man almost wish to live, for no one had ever prayed more fervently to die. Anna Miller came every morning—for she lived near by—and brought such little comforts and soothing remedies as he had begged for, or the doctor had prescribed. One thing only they denied him, though for that he begged with such plaintive agony that his nurse, and even his physician, wept when they refused it. They denied him water, cold, fresh water, though the fever parched his flesh, and fast dried up his blood! His tongue at last grew speechless; but with hollow, pleading eyes, he still begged on for water.

Another month of agony came on. Nature seemed to yield to the disease, and the doctor left him to return no more. But Anna Miller still kept watch beside him. At her instance, her father, Archibald Woods, who lived about fifteen miles off, came one day to make arrangements to move him, if possible, to his house.

"I come, Mr. Smith," said he, with much emotion, "to see if we can move you away from here. You shall be taken to my house to die. I will send for you to-morrow—now will you come?"

A fine spring of water gushed from a shaded hill-side near the house of Mr. Woods. The sick man had often thought of that spring in his wakeful hours, when the fever burned him, and had dreamed of it in his fitful slumbers. Now he seemed to hear its gushing music, and to taste its bubbling freshness. His sunken eye gleamed with pleasure, and with his bony hand he begged for water!

"You shall have it," said his friend, firmly, "if you only live to get to my house."

Archibald Woods went home, and sent his wagon for him. It came in the evening, so that he might be carried away in the coolness of the early morning. The body of the wagon was half filled with cotton yet on the seed, on which a bed was laid. They carried him at dawn in an arm-chair to the wagon, and laid him down upon the bed. The hope of water seemed to give him strength, and they moved on in their journey briskly. His impatient friend, however, had come out to meet him on the road.

"Is he still alive?" he asked of the driver.

"He was," said the man, "only a few minutes ago."

Woods looked into the wagon, and the eyes of the sick man lighted up with gratitude.

"You shall have it, Mr. Smith," said he; "you shall have as much as you want when we get home,"—and he kept by the side of the wagon till it reached his door. They lifted him out gently, and carried him into a pleasant room, and laid him down.

"Bettie!" shouted the blunt but kind old man to a servant, "run to the head of the spring and bring me a pitcher of water, quick!"

They gave him one mouthful—all that he would take—for no draught ever seemed so vile to his taste! He could not believe it was water, and he turned from it with a look of disappointment and disgust. They brought him a glass of cold still-beer. He sipped it, and then begged for more. Soon he called again for water, and his parched mouth, at last, began to feel its coolness. He drank on with a frenzied thirst, and at length dropped off to sleep.

"He is gone!" sobbed Anna Miller, as she saw the great drops gather in his face.

"It is the sleep of death!" said Archibald Woods; and the family gathered in, and stood around him.

No sound disturbed that rest. He slept on in his sweaty sleep through the evening and through the livelong night, and waked in the morning of his own accord; he was saved!

It was now July; and he had been sick since April. He soon began to recover his strength, but his nerves were much shattered, and both arms long shook with palsy. When well enough to go about and eat his usual meals at the table, they still had to feed him as a child; for he could not use a knife and fork. He now frequently heard from his little children. They, too, had recovered from their sickness, and were doing well. During his illness, he had often prayed that they might not live. Death, he had thought, would be as great a boon to them as to him, and he had often begged the Lord to take all hence and join them to those who had gone before.

But now he yearned with a childish impatience to see them. He would sometimes walk down the hot road that led toward them, till his strength gave out, and then he would sit on the road-side and weep.

"Why should I yearn for them?" thought he. "I can never take care of them, nor will they ever love me as the others did; for my worldly-mindedness has brought a life of wretchedness upon them."

Such reflections would sometimes make him so melancholy that even Anna Miller's kindness could not cheer him. In fact, the gayety of his temper was gone, and his heart was crushed by the tempest that had burst upon him.

As soon as he was able, he went to see his children, and to thank the friends that had given them each a mother and a home. After some days he returned, leaving them with their friends; for they refused to give them up, and even claimed them for their own.

He had brought with him from Kentucky some eighty-five head of hogs. They were now all gone; he never heard of one of them again. He had brought out also fifty head of good cattle. These, too, were gone, save one, which he sold, and with the money paid off the bill of his physician. A few simple articles of cabin furniture, and a wagon and team, which had been left in the care of some friend, was all the property that he now had in the world. The very clothes he wore were given to him by his neighbors. Taking a single coarse shirt for a change, and accepting from his noble old friend, Archibald Woods, a little money for his expenses, he bade adieu to his friends in Alabama, to his children, and to the graves of his lost ones, and, quitting the scene of his terrible sufferings, began his solitary journey back to Kentucky.

CHAPTER IX.

HE slowly retraced his way to Stockton's Valley, along the road by which, a few months before, he had moved with wife and children and substance, proud and expectant, to the rich wilds of Alabama. As he rode along, he reflected much on his recent experience, and began to see, in what he had suffered, the hand of the Father that scourges whom he loves. He was filled with devout wonder. The nettle began to blossom—the bitter bud was fast unfolding to a flower. He painfully pondered the subject of *election;* but the heart of the father could not accept the doctrine of Infant Damnation. "My children are happy, for they were innocent," he argued; and the faith which he had speculatively held on that point gave way. He reached the Valley in safety. Kindred and friends wept at his story, and took him at once to their homes and their hearts again.

After spending a week or two with his mother, who now lived with her son Jonathan, he went on to Wayne, to his old home on the Little South Fork of the Cumberland; for he felt the need of his brother William's pious counsel. He found awaiting him there a letter from Jeremiah Vardeman, who had heard of his afflictions, and of his return to Kentucky. That faithful friend wrote, that the brethren of Elkhorn had raised a contribution for his benefit, which they would shortly send to him by his hands; and he urged him to be present at the meeting of the Tate's Creek Association, which would soon be held at Crab Orchard. It was to be an important meeting of the churches, he said, and a great number of ministers and people would be there.

Smith set out at once for Crab Orchard. It was the last of August, the heat was great, and the roads were dusty, from a long-continued drought. Puffs of hot air stirred the soil, and the dust almost smothered traveler and beast as they sweltered along the highway. His horse was jaded and lean. Across a worn and weathered saddle he had thrown a pair of tattered saddle-bags, in which he carried his single change of homespun; this he was keeping to wear on Sunday, the great day of the Association.

He reached Crab Orchard on Saturday, with the dust of the journey thick upon him. He wore a pair of homespun cotton pantaloons, striped with copperas—loose enough, but far too short for him—and a cotton coat, once checked with blue and white, but now of undistinguishable colors; they had been given to him in Alabama. His shapeless hat was streaked with sweat and dust. His socks, too large for his shrunken ankles, hung down upon his foxy shoes. His shirt was coarse and dirty, and unbuttoned at the neck; his white cravat was in the coffin of his wife. He hitched his horse far off, to the branch of a tree, and, with his saddle-bags upon his arm, walked humbly toward the meeting-house. A great crowd loitered about the grounds, but no familiar face was there to greet him with a look of recognition. Great, indeed, was his humiliation; for the shadow of the wrathful cloud still lay dark upon his spirit. So unworthy did he feel, that he would have shrunk from recognition, even by Vardeman himself. He turned aside, and gave the way to every one, thinking it not strange that he drew upon himself their curious stare, or met their looks of pity or contempt. He reached the door of the meeting-house, and stood before it. Ministers and happy brethren were crowding the seats and thronging the aisles within. Stepping back, that a group of well-dressed people might pass in before him, he stood for a moment longer before the door, and then sat down upon the threshold. He had no heart to venture in; and he was weary and faint with his journey. They almost trod upon him as they crowded by him; for no one, it seemed, in all that vast assembly, either knew or cared to know him.

Soon a voice within, rich as music, caught his ear:

"Brother Moderator, it is impossible to transact the business of the Association in the midst of such a multitude as this. Many hundreds of people are yet without, and the house can hold no more. Let some one be appointed to preach to the people from the stand. This will engage the crowd and we can go on with the business of the morning."

It was the voice of Jacob Creath. While John Smith was listening, for the first time in his life, to the melody of that voice, his arm was grasped by an old friend, named Thomas Hansford, who had just recognized him. Only a few words could be exchanged; for the people had begun to pour out of the house, and were now hurrying to the woods.

"You must come and preach for us," said his friend; "the people will be glad to hear you."

"I can not do it, brother Hansford," said he. "If the people knew but half my story, they would not want to hear me. They would pity, and excuse me."

It was arranged by Thomas Hansford, however, that Smith should occupy the stand with two others that had just been appointed to speak. One of these was a student of divinity, who had recently come out from Philadelphia, in company with Luther Rice, who also was present on that occasion; the other was an awkward and inexperienced young preacher of the neighborhood; they now came out of the house together, and passed on to the grove. Smith arose, and walked behind them.

"Why does that dirty fellow follow us?" said one of these young ministers to the other, glancing behind him. Smith heard him, but without emotion. He had been so humbled by the chastisement of heaven, that he could not now feel the sneers of men. When he reached the stand, he found a great concourse assembled. He sat down on a log near by, and the two young ministers went up on the stand. They arose in turns, to speak; but each, after a vain attempt, had to sit down, and confess his need of grace to finish.

"If the Lord will not give it to me, brethren," said one of them, as he took his seat, "I can not get it!"

Thomas Hansford, and another, who now recognized Smith, again pressed him to go forward and say something to the people, who were disappointed, and were already beginning to disperse. At once an inspiration seemed to move him; he lifted up his head, and sat erect; he arose, and, with a firm step, walked to the stand and stood up before the people. As he looked around upon them, his eye kindled and his spirit was stirred within him. The multitude stared curiously **for** a moment at the uncouth figure before them. Some laughed outright; while others turned away from him, and left the ground.

He saw that, unless he employed some artifice to detain them, not a hearer would be left. With a noble voice, such as had so often sounded among the hills of Wayne, he called aloud:

"Stay, friends, and hear what the great Augustine said!" and they all stopped to listen.

"Augustine wished to see three things before he died," continued Smith. "Rome in her glory and purity; Paul on Mars' Hill; and Jesus in the flesh." A few now sat down, but many smiled, and started off again.

"Will you not stay," he cried, in a still louder voice, "and hear what the great Cato said?" Many returned and took their seats, and seemed willing to be amused.

"Cato," he continued, "repented of three things before his death: first, that he had ever spent an idle day; secondly, that he had ever gone on a voyage by water, when he might have made the same journey on land; and thirdly, that he had ever told the secrets of his bosom to a woman."

The people continued to come back, and began to crowd close to the stand. A few acquaintances, who had not seen him for a long time, now recognized him, and passed the word among the crowd—"It is John Smith, from the Little South Fork!" Seeing groups of persons still standing in the distance, he called again with all the strength of his heavy voice:

"Come, friends, and hear what the great Thales thanked the gods for."

"Let us go and hear the fellow," said one; "there may be more in him than we suppose." And they all, at last, sat down near by to listen.

"Thales thanked the gods for three things: first, that he was endowed with reason, and was not a brute; secondly, that he was a Greek, and not a Barbarian; and thirdly, that he was a man, and not a woman."

"And now, friends, I know you are ready to ask: 'And pray, sir, who are you? What have you to say for yourself?'"

"I am John Smith, from Stockton's Valley. In more recent years, I have lived in Wayne, among the rocks and hills of the Cumberland. Down there, saltpeter caves abound, and raccoons make their homes. On that wild frontier we never had good schools, nor many books; consequently, I stand before you to-day a man without an education. But, my brethren, even in that ill-favored region, the Lord, in good time, found me. He showed me his wondrous grace, and called me to preach the everlasting Gospel of his Son.

"Redemption! Redemption!!" he shouted, and his voice sounded through the woods like the tones of a trumpet. He had no Bible, but he quoted, in the same loud voice, his text:

"He sent Redemption to his people; he hath commanded his covenant forever; holy and reverend is his name" (Ps. iii. 9).

He spoke of Redemption, first, as *conceived;* secondly, as *applied;* and thirdly, as *completed.*

Under the first head, he explained the nature of the eternal covenant between the Father and the Son, in which the Father promised the Son a certain portion of the human race, and the Son, on his part, agreed to redeem them by his sufferings and death.

Under the second head, he discussed the question of human depravity, and the influence of the Holy Spirit upon the heart of the sinner.

Under the last head, he spoke with great fervor of the resurrection of Christ, and of the perseverance of the saints through grace to glory.

He had been speaking but a short time, when a man, who had listened with astonishment to his exordium, pressed through the audience and hurried to the house, and going up to Jacob Creath, begged him to let all business alone, and to come out immediately to the stand.

"Why," said Creath, "what's the matter?"

"Sir," said he, "the fellow with the striped coat on, that was raised among the 'coons, is up; come and hear him preach! His name is Smith."

"What! John Smith?" asked Creath; and at the mention of that name, the tears came into his eyes; for he, too, had heard the story of Smith's misfortunes. He left the house immediately, and went out to the grove, and quietly took his seat upon the platform behind the speaker. Others soon followed; for it was noised among them that some extraordinary scene was transpiring without. In fact, the morning session of the Association was broken up; preachers and people rushed out, and gathered about the platform. Many that could not find seats or places to stand, climbed the trees close by; and the very saplings swayed with people eager to see and to hear. When the speaker reached the third and last division of his subject, and began to paint the final glory of God's elect, the multitude arose and stood upon their feet; and when he closed his impassionate exhortation, every eye was weeping, and every heart and lip blessed *the man without an education.*

He turned to find a seat, for he was exhausted. Creath rushed toward him and clasped him in his arms. They had never met before; but, from that day, they never met without embracing.

"I took you to my heart, John," Creath often afterward said, "that first time I ever saw you; and I expect to do so every time I meet you, till I die."

All the preachers, even those who had reviled him, now came forward to grasp his hand; and the people continued for some time to press upon him. His sad story passed from group to group that day, and every one felt for him a tearful sympathy and tender respect. His friend, Jeremiah Vardeman, had been prevented from attending the Association; but the contribution which he had raised, amounting to $55.12 1-2, had been safely brought by the hands of another.

Smith was urged to preach that night, for everybody wished to hear again the man that had been raised among the raccoons. But he would not consent to do so, and he rather shrank from the attentions that were now pressed upon him.

On Monday, the Association adjourned, and he returned to Stockton's Valley, preaching at Somerset, in Wayne, and at other places on the road. The people everywhere heard his story, and, while they saddened to think of his misfortunes, they smiled when told how he looked that day on the stand, as he declared his origin among the raccoons and caves of the rocky frontier.

CHAPTER X.

His first care, after his return to Stockton's Valley, was to make arrangements for bringing his children to Kentucky. His brother Jonathan having offered to take them, he went down for them early in September, and brought them back in his own wagon, which he had left in the Hickory Flats.

He sold his horses and wagon for a good price, and leaving his children well cared for with his brother, he went up to Wayne again, and invested his little means in some wild land, near his old neighborhood, on the Little South Fork. He seems to have had a wish to retrace his steps as far as he could, and to correct the first sad blunder of his life.

He was now in the thirtieth year of his age, and, with the exception of a slight palsy, which sometimes shook his arms after any severe labor, he was as robust as ever. He worked as he had always done, and preached through the country with even more acceptance than before. He continued to examine the Scriptural grounds for the doctrine of personal and unconditional election, which had not ceased to trouble him since the death of his children. Isaac Hodgen, who was one of the most amiable and useful of the Baptist preachers, but who was never a high-toned Calvinist, having heard of his perplexities, asked him, one day, if he had ever read any of Fuller's works, especially his "Gospel Worthy of All Acceptation." John Smith had never heard of such a book, although it had excited much controversy, and was materially modifying the doctrines of his Church. Hodgen sent him the book, which he read with deep interest. The idea of a general atonement and special application seemed to him, at the time, plausible, and he was much comforted. But, though his Calvinism softened, he did not finally accept the views of Fuller—convinced, after reflection, that they were more inconsistent than those of Calvin himself.

Andrew Fuller, of England, believing that ultra-Calvinism was paralyzing the efforts of ministers to preach the Gospel to every creature, set himself to oppose it with all his might. The popular view, at the time, denied faith to be the duty of those to whom the Gospel came—that it was entirely the gift of God—who gave it in his own good time, by the irresistible power of the Holy Spirit, and to the elect only.

To refute this doctrine, Fuller wrote a book called "The Gospel Worthy of All Acceptation; or, The Obligations of Men Fully to Credit and Cordially to Approve Whatever God Makes Known."

"This valuable treatise operated powerfully, and set thousands upon examining their principles. A host of opponents rose up to oppose this *New Doctrine*, as it was termed; and the author had to defend himself on every side, which he did with no ordinary dexterity, taking his stand on the Word of God, with the meekness of wisdom, but with the lion heart of Luther."

About the close of the year, John Smith's friends, seeing him still depressed in mind, began to urge him, with the utmost delicacy and kindness, for his own sake, and that of his children, to marry again. In fact, his mental conflict with Calvinism, his painful struggles with himself in his loneliness, and his too busy memory, continued to cast over his spirit, at times, the deepest gloom.

There lived in the neighborhood a worthy and substantial family, whose friendly offices he had often enjoyed. The Hurts were an industrious and frugal people, distinguished for their quiet temper, and robust, common sense. Nancy Hurt combined these qualities in her own character, and had, besides, one of the kindest hearts in the world; but she was poor. Smith, whose growing popularity as a preacher, had awakened ambitious hopes in the minds of some of his friends, was urged to marry rich; and to this end he was advised to go and preach among the wealthy churches, and there seek a wife that would endow him with both love and fortune.

He set out, in December following, on a tour through the wealthier counties of the State. None but Nancy Hurt knew the real purpose of his journey; for, before he left, he had promised her to come back at Christmas—and she had plighted her word to become his wife.

The suggestion that he might become rich by a mercenary marriage, was like the voice of the tempter again; but there was no longer any worldly pride in his heart that could be aroused. Never in his life had he profaned, even in thought, the institution of marriage, by looking upon it as a means of worldly aggrandizement. Now, he listened to the suggestion, not only with distaste, but with abhorrence.

He went from home to shun officious counsel, and to escape the impertinence of idle tongues. With a prudence that well harmonized with the slimness of his purse, he made no preparations for his marriage; he did not even order a wedding suit, so that his neighbors had no suspicion of his design. They idly speculated, sometimes in the hearing of Nancy Hurt herself, on the probable issue of his matrimonial tour; and they made his sky gorgeous with their own vain dreamings. The gossips of the Little South Fork were all at fault; and, pleased with the thought, he started off on his tour to Northern Kentucky.

At Nicholasville, in Jessamine County, he was met and embraced again by Jacob Creath. An appointment had been made for him at that place, and many had come together to hear him. He preached from a part of II. Cor. i. 10: "Who delivered us from so great a death, and doth deliver." From this fragment of Holy Writ he extracted, by some ingenious process of his own, the doctrine that the Holy Ghost works directly, and with irresistible power, on the heart of the dead sinner, in order to give him life. The deliverance of which the Apostle speaks, he aimed to show, was a joyous liberation from the bands of a spiritual death, and was accomplished by the power of God alone, "who delivers us from so great a death." The doctrine of the text he proceeded to confirm by his own religious experience; his struggles at dawn, in the spice-wood thicket, and the hope that then came like a gleam of starlight into his soul, were used to illustrate the mode of that deliverance.

The people were astonished. Jacob Creath, who had purposed to follow him in a second discourse that morning,
arose, and, in his peculiar manner, said:

"Brethren, I can not attempt to preach this morning after such display of light and learning. To do so, would only
be to put out, perhaps, the light-house which the brother has
erected for the guidance of the people. But I will preach this
evening."

John Taylor, an eminent and somewhat eccentric preacher of the times, was present; and being called on to close
the meeting, earnestly prayed:

"Lord, we thank thee that while many of us are growing old, thou hast raised up this young man from the hill
country. He is now thirty-two years old. Lord, grant that
he may live yet thirty-two years longer!"

Jacob Creath addressed the people in the evening. Like
Smith, he was a man of but little culture. but of great natural powers. He was, perhaps, the most eloquent preacher
of his day, and one of the most tender-hearted and affectionate of men. His voice was toned with music; his style,
ornate; his manner, full of grace; and whether he reasoned
or exhorted, whether calm or impassioned, he always held
his audience spell-bound to the close.

He spoke on the final perseverance of the saints—a theme
that he loved—which was appropriate, too, as logically related to the subject of the morning. With a bold imagery,
he painted the Christian hero—strong, brave, and hopeful—
panoplied in heaven's golden armor, and eager for the conflict. He described his enemies as a formidable host, arrayed
against him on the right hand and on the left, lurking in
ambuscades about his path, and springing mines beneath
his feet. Troubled on every side, the true soldier of the cross
was not distressed; though perplexed, he never despaired;
though persecuted, he was not forsaken; and though cast
down, he was not destroyed. At times, defeated or discomfited, he still moved forward unsubdued, amid reverses and
alarms, to the glorious triumph that awaited him in the city
of his God. His text was: "Gad, a troop shall overcome him:
but he shall overcome at last."—Gen. xlix. 19.

From Nicholasville, they traveled together through the

adjacent counties, visiting and confirming the churches. At David's Fork, near Lexington, Smith again met Vardeman, who could not, it seems, forget either the misfortunes or the gifts of his young friend from the hill country. He kindly remonstrated with him for continuing to hide his Lord's talent, and again urged him to seek a more inviting field of labor. On Sunday, after Smith had preached to the congregation, Vardeman, whose kindness was always manifested in some substantial, if not delicate, manner, referred to his brother's history, and begged a contribution for him. Smith, though he felt that it was no disgrace to be either poor or unfortunate, burned all over with shame at the thought of appearing as a traveling mendicant of the Church. He turned his face homeward, toward the Little South Fork, and, preaching as he went, reached home on the 23rd of December. On Christmas day he married Nancy Hurt; and the New Year dawned upon him a wiser and happier man.

CHAPTER XI.

ABOUT the beginning of the present century, the Baptists of Kentucky were, for the most part, gathered into two bodies, known as the *Elkhorn* and the *South Kentucky Associations.* These two communities differed much in religious temper and doctrine. Elkhorn was rigid in her interpretation of the Creed, and her ministers, under the popular name of *Regular Baptists*, contended, almost without exception, for every jot and tittle of the Philadelphia Confession of Faith.

South Kentucky comprised those more liberal churches that attached comparatively but little importance to creeds, and held the doctrine of a General Atonement, contending sometimes, with all the zeal of Arminians, that Christ tasted death for every man—that the Gospel made ample provision for the salvation of all. They were known as *Separate Baptists.*

Two unsuccessful attempts had already been made to unite these bodies of Christians—one in 1789, and the other in 1793. But what good and great men could not accomplish by argument, was at length brought about by that strange religious excitement, which, in 1801, spread over the State, and destroyed the pride of doctrine, and the lust of priestly power, in so many hearts.

Pursuant to resolutions adopted in both bodies, two delegates from each of the churches of the Elkhorn and the old South Kentucky Association met in convention, at Howard's Creek, in Clark County, on the second Saturday in October, 1801, and consummated a union by the unanimous ratification of the following

TERMS:

We, the Committee of the Elkhorn and South Kentucky Associations, do agree to unite on the following plan:

1. That the Scriptures of the Old and New Testament are the infallible Word of God, and the only rule of faith and practice.

2. That there is only one true God, and in the Godhead, or Divine Essence, there are Father, Son, and Holy Ghost.

3. That by nature we are failen and depraved creatures.

4. That salvation, regeneration, sanctification, and justification are by the life, death, resurrection, and ascension of Jesus Christ.

5. That the saints will finally persevere through grace to glory.

6. That baptism by immersion is necessary to the receiving of the Lord's Supper.

7. That the salvation of the righteous, and the punishment of the wicked, will be eternal.

8. That it is our duty to be tender and affectionate to each other, and to study the happiness of the children of God in general, and to be engaged singly to promote the honor of God.

9. That the preaching Christ tasted death for every man, shall be no bar to communion.

10. That each may keep up their association and church government, as to them may seem best.

11. That a free correspondence be kept up between the churches thus united.

The boundaries of South Kentucky Association having been much extended during the revival by the establishment of many new churches, it was thought best that a division of territory should be made. About an equal number of churches being on each side of the Kentucky River, that stream made the line, and the old South Kentucky Association was accordingly divided into the North and the South District. North District, comprising about twenty-three churches, met for the first time in October, 1802, at Unity, in Clark County, and adopted the following

CONSTITUTION:

From a long series of experience, we, the Churches of Jesus Christ, being regularly baptized by immersion, upon the profession of our faith in Christ, are convinced of the necessity of a combination of churches, and propose to keep the rules of an Association, according to the following form of government:

1. The Association shall be composed of members sent from the different churches with letters to represent them.

2. In said letters shall be expressed their number in fellowship, those baptized, received by letter, dismissed, excluded, and deceased, since the last Association.

3. The Association thus formed shall be a council of advice, and not an authoritative body.

4. The Association shall be governed by a regular decorum

5. The Association shall have a moderator and clerk, chosen by the suffrage of the members present.

6. Any church may be received which the Association may approve of.

7. Every church in the Union shall be entitled to an equal representation.

8. Every motion made and seconded, shall come under the consideration of the Association, unless withdrawn by the member who made it.

9. The Association shall endeavor to furnish the churches with the minutes of their proceedings, provided the churches will furnish the means.

10. There shall be a book kept wherein the proceedings of every Association shall be regularly recorded by a secretary appointed for that purpose, who shall receive a compensation yearly for the same.

11. All questions shall be determined by the will of the majority in the Association, as, also, any amendment or alteration of the Constitution.

12. The Association shall have a right to withdraw from any church which they judge to act or to persist in disorder.

13. On the close of business, the minutes shall be read, passed by the Association, signed by the moderator, and attested by the clerk.

Not long after its organization, the North District Association began to exercise, in a very peculiar way, the functions of an Advisory Council. Charges were preferred against Elder David Barrow, a member of the church at Mount Sterling, by the Bracken Association to the effect that he was disturbing the peace of the churches by his opposition to domestic slavery.

Mr. Barrow had removed from Virginia to Kentucky, in 1797. He had been one of the most fearless and successful opponents of religious tyranny in his native State; for he lived in a day when the contest was going on between the friends and the foes of religious liberty. His talents were of a high order; and as a speaker he had, perhaps, no superior among the Baptists, either in Virginia or Kentucky. He was opposed in sentiment to slavery of every kind; and he did not hesitate, in Kentucky, to advocate from the pulpit the unpopular measure of gradual emancipation.

North District, having patiently heard the complaint of the Bracken churches, and David Barrow's defense, expressed the opinion that he had given cause of hurt "by meddling with emancipation;" but that his explanations and apologies were satisfactory. They aimed, however, to provide against such disturbances in future, by advising "that any minister that should propagate unsound doctrines or views, pernicious to peace and good order, might be suspended by any two preachers, until he could be formally tried by a council of five ministers, whose decision ought to be final."

Accordingly, a council of ministers reported at the next Association, which met at Grassy Lick, in Montgomery County, that they had, according to the advice given, dealt with Mr. Barrow for still preaching the doctrine of emancipation, to the hurt and injury of the feelings of the brotherhood. The Association approved the course of this council, and, after hearing the accused again in his own defense, expelled him from his seat; and, at the same time, appointed a committee to prosecute him before his brethren at Mount Sterling.

Questions concerning the moral condition of infants, began also, about this time, to excite some interest among the churches; and the doctrine of infant corruption, and infant damnation, was often discussed. Some of the more amiable, though less orthodox, ministers, ventured to speak a word in behalf of the little ones, causing much dissatisfaction by their presumptuous charity.

"What shall be done with the preachers that thus propagate infant purity?" asked the Bald Eagle Church; and North District answered:

"If they are preachers within our bounds, we refer you to *advice* already given respecting ministers that propagate unsound doctrines."

In the meantime, the Mount Sterling Church, of which David Barrow was a member, refused, on account of the proceedings against him, to send either letters or messengers to the next Association. Other thoughtful churches of the District, remembering that the Constitution declared that the Association was an advisory, and not an authoritative, body, and being alarmed at the increase of its prerogative, ventured to inquire, through their messengers: "Do the Scriptures warrant such a procedure?" To this question no answer was immediately returned. But at the next meeting, the Association revoked the act by which Mr. Barrow had been expelled; the committee appointed to prosecute him was discharged; the rule that had been devised for the trial of ministers, was repealed; and the judgment of the five ministers, who, under that rule, had already condemned Mr. Barrow, was revoked.

But the church at Mount Sterling, grieved at the course that certain brethren had pursued in this matter, refused to admit them to the Lord's Table; for which act the Association at once formally withdrew its fellowship from that church.

The result of all these proceedings was such as might have been expected. The Association began to mourn the declension of religion within its bounds. Many neglected to assemble themselves together, or came together, not for the better, but for the worse. The Church gene.ally had a declining ministry, and was a sickly, wasting society. Jeremiah Vardeman visited some of the congregations regularly, and, by his exhortations, tried to rekindle the glow of spiritual life in hearts that had already grown cold. But even his influence could not prevent dissensions from arising, for the church at Lulbegrud was, year after year, declared to be "in disorder."

In the year 1817, North District comprised twenty-one churches, with a membership of about fourteen hundred souls. Mount Sterling still remained excluded from the connection. Twenty-one influential brethren had been appointed to help Lulbegrud to an adjustment of her difficulties; and they had been so far successful as to report that church at last in order. Still, their circular presented a gloomy picture of the condition of religious society; for, though some outpourings had taken place, religion continued to languish. A night season prevailed, and the love of many waxed cold. Divisions still existed, and brethren were at variance one with another. Elder Vardeman at last withdrew his ministerial labors from them, and the churches to which he had been preaching were left destitute. They complained mournfully, indeed, that they now had no one to administer to them the ordinances of Christ! Some seemed to forsake the Church entirely, and to delight themselves more in the mysteries of Freemasonry than in the services of the sanctuary; in fact, the Association, in the continued exercise of its advisory prerogative, had, at last, to declare that it was wrong for Baptists to sit in Masonic lodges!

Such was the state of things in the North District when Jeremiah Vardeman wrote to John Smith, informing him that "he had withdrawn from the churches in Montgomery, but that the Lord had thereby opened a door of usefulness to him. The brethren there, he had no doubt, would be glad to have his services, and, he thought, they would liberally acknowledge them."

After much reflection, Smith concluded to visit Montgomery County; and he authorized his friend to say to the church at Lulbegrud, that he would be with them at their annual meeting in May. Vardeman wrote accordingly to James Mason, a prominent and devoted member at Grassy Lick:

AT HOME, May 1st, 1817.

DEAR BROTHER MASON—I have the pleasure to inform you that brother John Smith, from Wayne County, will be at Lulbegrud the third Saturday and Sunday in May, it being the time of their yearly meeting; and on the day following, will be at Grassy Lick. I think it would be to your spiritual interest to obtain his labors at Grassy Lick and the neighboring churches. I know not that he will move his residence; but it will not be amiss to try him. I am sorry that I am so circumstanced as not to be able to visit you more frequently. It has ever been a maxim with me to preach where the prospect of usefulness is the most flattering; and I am convinced that it is my duty to withdraw my stated labors from Montgomery, at the present.

We had a glorious outpouring of the Spirit in the course of last winter and this spring, in the neighborhood of Mr. Daniel Bryant's, South Elkhorn, and Mount Pleasant churches. Upward, I suppose, of three hundred persons have been baptized on the profession of their faith in Christ. . . . Their convictions for sin were in general awfully poignant; and their deliverance from guilt by the pardoning mercy of God, was no less signal. A church has recently been constituted in the neighborhood where the work began; it consists now probably of about one hundred members. I received a unanimous call to attend them; and, considering the raw and uncultivated state they were in, I felt it my duty to obey their call. . . .

The great Mr. Absalom Waller, from Virginia, has lately arrived in these parts. I heard him yesterday—much to my satisfaction. He reprobates, in the strongest terms, that antinomian fatality which some seem to mistake for the doctrine of Grace; calls upon all men everywhere to repent and believe the Gospel, as their bounden duty—that there is no impediment in the way but the want of disposition in the sinner, and that such moral inability is no excuse, etc. He is, in fine, a man after my own heart—a Fullerene. . . .

Permit me, my dear brother, to say I am yours,

J. VARDEMAN.

The brethren of Montgomery were unanimous in their desire that John Smith should become their preacher, and they now pressed him for a promise to come and live among them. They proposed to aid him in buying a farm, and assured him that, in all temporal matters, he and his family should be made comfortable.

"I am pleased with you, my brethren," Smith replied, "and I think that I could live happy among you. To be candid, I have no wish to reside any longer where I now do; but I have made it a rule never to engage in any important work, nor commit myself by any promise, till I had first counseled with my wife. I never knew a man to lose anything by taking counsel of his wife. I must go home, then, without saying more to you than this; I will talk with Nancy, and then give you my answer."

On his way home, he stopped in the city of Lexington, and preached. Samuel Ayers, a silversmith of that place, a liberal man and devoted Baptist, had said to him on a previous visit:

"This is the second time, brother Smith, that you have preached for us of late, and I have never given you any thing yet. Have you any silver in your pocket?"

"A little," said Smith; "I do sometimes have a *little*."

"Well, let me have that," said Ayers, "and I will make a set of teaspoons for your wife."

Smith gave him all he had, which was, indeed, but little. His friend, however, added the necessary quantity, and now, on this third visit, he had the spoons ready for him. Smith thankfully accepted them, and took home the beautiful gift to his wife.

Nancy Smith did not fail to show them to her neighbors. "They were of pure silver," she told them, "and had been made expressly for her by her husband's friend, who lived in Lexington." On proper occasions, when tea was served, whether of sassafras root, dittany, or Young Hyson from the store, she took delight, in honor of her guests, to bring out her silver to grace the table, which was plain, but always beautifully clean.

But the religious sentiment of her neighbors would not long suffer her to delight herself in that way. Sisters began to take offense at her departure from the usual style of living; and brethren, who took an economical view of the matter, began to fear the influence of her example. The Elders finally took the innovation in hand, and treated it as a grave offense; and, to save the peace of the church, and the influence of her husband, the good woman at last put away her spoons, and never used them on the Little South Fork again.

Mrs. Smith was unwilling to give an opinion as to the expediency of removing to Montgomery; and, feeling the need of her counsel, her husband would not act without it. So it was finally arranged for her to go with him in August, on a second visit to that county; and, from their united observations, to come to some conclusion in the matter.

She was charmed with the country and the people; for there was not, at that time, a nobler citizenship in all the land. They accordingly returned to Wayne, and, without delay, made preparations to remove. Their little farm, with its stock and crops, was sold, and, filling a wagon with their household goods, they left the Little South Fork, on the 22nd of October, 1817.

CHAPTER XII.

THE "destitute" churches of Montgomery, as Jeremiah Vardeman had described them, whose united voices had, at his instance, called John Smith to be their pastor, were, *Spencer's Creek*, *Lulbegrud*, *Old Bethel*, and *Grassy Lick*. These churches were but a few miles distant from Mount Sterling, then a thriving village of perhaps one thousand souls.

Grassy Lick was in a pleasant part of the county, five miles north-west of the town. To that church, Smith and his wife presented their letters of commendation, and in accordance with Baptist custom, they were cordially received into fellowship. He at once rented a small farm and cabin near the meeting-house, and began his preparations to raise a crop of corn. His time was taken up in working, in preaching, and in studying the Word. The influence of his ministry was soon manifest in the growth of the churches; all, save Lulbegrud, immediately began to receive accessions. The social and spiritual condition, however, even of Lulbegrud, which, it will be remembered, had been in disorder for several years, was also much improved, so that, in the course of a few months after the adjustment of her difficulties, she too rapidly grew in strength and numbers, gaining in one year more than one hundred and twenty members.

He continued to read, critically, the Philadelphia Confession of Faith, and to test its truth by his Inspired Standard. His heart had repudiated the doctrine of infant depravity and reprobation, and on other points he had softened much with Fullerism; but he was still perplexed in view of the consequences of rejecting any one article of his creed; for Calvinism, he knew, was a logically constructed body of

Divinity, and the unsoundness of any one tenet must compromise the whole system. He determined, however, if possible, to solve every knot as he had already felt every cross and sting, of its doctrine.

Each of the churches that shared his ministry, had its own peculiar religious temper and phase of belief. Lulbegrud was firmly rooted and grounded in the truth as it was set forth in the Philadelphia Confession of Faith.

Spencer had been consulted about the year 1800, by Moses Bledsoe and John Rice, on the basis of the Scriptures as the only creed of the Christian. The members of that church were generally Separate Baptists; and though they had cordially entered into the general union in 1801, they attached very little importance to the five points of Calvinism, or, in fact, to any other speculative system of belief.

Grassy Lick had, in her communion, some men of fine natural sense, of chaste religious sentiment, and of burning zeal. The names of her fathers and early messengers— Joshua Yeats, Reuben McDannold, William Jeans, Henry Gaitskill, Henry Sanford, James Sims, James Mason, David Badger, and Roger Clemens—are associated with the early history of religion in the North District. The church had enjoyed, too. the regular or the occasional ministrations of such men as Moses Bledsoe, Lewis Corbin, Ambrose Dudley, Jacob Creath. and Jeremiah Vardeman. These ministers delighted to come among the people of Montgomery, for they were always received with generous hospitality and worshipful regard. Pious mothers taught their children to love and venerate these holy men, though graceless youths, who dared not yet blaspheme the name of God, often swore with profane delight by such names as "Vardeman" and "Creath." Almost every phase of early Baptist sentiment was represented by these famous preachers; for among them were disciples, not only of John Calvin, but of Andrew Fuller and Shubal Stearns, if not of James Arminius himself. The people reflected the same diversity of opinion; yet they lived in peace as brethren, bound together by a common faith and a mutual love.

A pleasant and fruitful field of labor was open to Smith. and he went in with strong confidence, and began his work. In the first year after his removal, a committee from the four churches that were under his charge was authorized to select for him a home and farm, as central as might be to the field of his ministerial labors. It was understood that he would make the first payment, but that the churches would assume the remainder of the debt. A farm of about one hundred acres, lying two miles east of Mount Sterling, and valued at three thousand two hundred dollars, was accordingly bought. Possession would be given in November; the money which he had realized by the sale of his little farm in Wayne, with a small amount which he had already received for preaching, would enable him to make the first payment; and he never doubted for a moment that his brethren would promptly make the others.

Grassy Lick enjoyed that year, not only his usual monthly instructions from the pulpit, but the people were under his faithful watch-care all the time; and he never let an opportunity of doing them good pass unimproved.

He had a near neighbor by the name of Moses Higgins, an amiable man, whose wife and daughters were members of the church at Grassy Lick. Higgins had recently shown some interest in religion, and his wife had begun to hope that the usual manifestations of Divine grace would be vouchsafed to him. But she was distressed to find that he was only affected by the representations of certain Shakers, who, in traveling through the country, occasionally stopped at the house; for Higgins was rich, and withal a hospitable man. She went to her pastor and made him acquainted with the facts, and begged him to save her husband. In a few days afterward, Higgins himself called, and introduced the subject of the new religion.

"Can you believe," said Smith to him, "that the resurrection of the saints is an accomplished fact, and that God is now judging the world through the Shakers? Can you believe that they are the people of the resurrection, as they profess to be, and that, being such, they ought to put away their wives, and live as the angels of God?"

"These things, Mr. Smith," replied he, "they deny to me; they say that they are but the lies of the world. Two of them stayed with me the other night on their road to Daniel Dunlavy's."

Daniel Dunlavy, who lived on Spencer's Creek, was a brother of the celebrated John Dunlavy; about that time he became a proselyte to the faith of his brother.

"Then they will be at your house again very soon," said Smith; "and when they come, send me word, and I will talk over these things with them in your presence."

In a short time, he received a message from his neighbor that the Shakers were again at his house. He went over in the evening, after his work was done, and there met James Congleton and Thomas Rule. He remembered James as an amiable and intelligent man with whom he had discussed these very doctrines at Shakertown, in the winter of 1815. Suspecting that they had concealed from Higgins their more objectionable tenets, he determined to extort an acknowledgment of them in his hearing.

"Well, James," said Smith, "you still believe that you are in the Resurrection? Have you not learned better yet?"

"Nay, John," said he, promptly, and without the least effort to conceal his faith, "we are still firmly persuaded of the fact."

This point was then argued at length; other questions were discussed, and Higgins saw plainly that he had not understood their teachings. The conversation was interrupted, and he left the room for a while.

"Are you now satisfied. Moses?" said Smith, who followed him to the door.

"Yes," said Higgins, "I see that I have greatly mistaken their views and practices."

"Now," continued Smith, "I do not like to be rude anywhere, especially in a neighbor's house; but they insist, as a chief item of their profession, that they have crucified the flesh, and all that pertains to the first Adam; I would like, Moses, to put them to the test. They say, for instance, that they can not get angry under the severest provocations. I wish to convince you that they are nothing but men at last, in all things whatsoever, save in putting away their wives. I think I can make them mad."

"Try it, then, and let me see it done," said Higgins.

They were called to supper, and were soon seated together at the table. Smith was requested by the host to give thanks for what they were about to receive, which he did; but James politely asked whether he and Thomas could be permitted, without giving offense, "to do their own way." They fell on their knees, remained silent for a minute, and then arose.

"What were you about just now, Thomas?" inquired Smith, selecting Rule as the subject for his experiment; for he judged, from his physiognomy, that he was less spiritual than James.

"Giving thanks, John," said Thomas.

"How do we know that you did not pray that this food might become poison to us?"

"Nay, nay, John!"

"I don't believe, anyhow, that you ever abandoned, or even confessed, one-half of your sins when you went to Shaker-town."

"Yea, John.

"I do not believe a word of it," said Smith, with assumed earnestness.

"Why, John?" asked Thomas, with some surprise, and a little rising temper.

"For two reasons," said Smith; "first, you could not have recollected one-half of them; and secondly, if you had confessed them all, I do not know but that they would have preferred putting you in the penitentiary to receiving you into their society."

At this word Thomas sprang from the table, and stamped the floor in his anger, exclaiming:

"You are a rascal, sir!"

For a moment Smith was disconcerted; for he had excited more anger than he wished. But, remembering the purpose of his jest, he pointed his finger across the table at the raging Thomas, and tauntingly exclaimed:

"A mad Shaker, Moses! A mad angel!"

James, who had preserved his self-control, now pulled Thomas down and quieted him.

"Keep your seat," said he, calmly. "John, you must take all that back."

"When I give a man what justly belongs to him, James," said Smith, "I never take it back."

At this, they both withdrew from the table, and sat in silence near the wall. After supper, of which they refused to partake, Smith approached them in a conciliatory manner, and, rehearsing the incidents of the evening, explained frankly his design.

"My motive, James, was a good one," said he; "for it was to save my friend Higgins here from a delusion as ruinous, in my judgment, to the peace of his family as to himself. But it was necessary that I should satisfy him, who had almost become your proselyte, that you were but men, and not angels, as he had begun to imagine. I sincerely hope that the end proposed has been accomplished. And now let me beseech you, James, to awake from this same delusion yourself. You are capable of becoming a useful man in any community. Let me advise you—yes, beg you—James, to go and get your wife and children, and come away from that place."

James bowed his head in silence, and, resting his forehead in his hand, looked solemnly down upon the floor, as if impressed with the exhortation. Encouraged by his manner, Smith continued to exhort him, with many earnest and affectionate words, to save himself from his infatuation. Still his Shaker friend sat, and never raised his eyes from the floor, or said a word in reply. Moved by his own feelings, Smith drew closer to him, and continued to argue and to persuade, until the hopeful tears gathered in his eyes. Supposing at last that he had really touched the Shaker's heart, and opened his eyes to his error, he arose from his seat, and took his still silent friend affectionately by the hand.

"James, I must now go; but before I leave you, my dear friend, I want you to assure me with your own lips, not only that you forgive me for my rudeness this evening, but that I shall soon welcome you to your friends and to society again, where you can be so happy and so useful in the cause of our common Master."

"Get thee behind me, Satan!" exclaimed James, snatching his hand from the grasp of the astounded pastor, and fixing a hard look upon him; "Get thee behind me, Satan;" and he folded his arms in sullen dignity, and sat defiant as a rock.

"Thomas!" cried Smith, "didn't you hear him? He says, *Get thee behind him!*" and, seizing the morose Thomas by the arms, he thrust him behind the imperturbable James, and immediately left the room.

He took his hat, and, bidding his friend and host good-night, went home. He had been, for once, almost outwitted; but he had saved his neighbor, and the peace of his neighbor's family; for early next morning, before breakfast, the Shakers saddled their horses, and went away; nor did they ever call at Moses Higgins' again.

CHAPTER XIII.

In November, 1818, Smith moved to his farm near Mount Sterling. Before his second note became due, hard times had set in; a great financial distress, unprecedented in the history of the country, had come upon the people, and debts of all kinds went undischarged. The churches paid him nothing; so that he could do no more than parry his debt for awhile, working as he had never done before, to meet the interest on his notes. His hope was, that when the present distress was over, his brethren would come forward and fulfill their promises. In this hope, he toiled on, and preached for them with unabated zeal. He had not tried to conceal the fact that doctrinal doubts and difficulties perplexed him; for he had frankly acknowledged these things to his brethren. But he little expected that his honest avowal would be made the ground for repudiating all their promises. The creditor who held his second note at length sold it out to parties in the shape of drafts upon him. He begged them, as the churches paid him nothing, and times were very hard, to secure themselves by a mortgage on his land. But this they refused to do, preferring to take his word without security.

Finally, one who held his obligation for five hundred dollars, became bankrupt; his note passed into the hands of others, and payment was demanded. He was about to relinquish his home and everything he had, in order to extricate himself from debt, when Colonel Williams, of Mount Sterling, proposed to go with him into the Commonwealth's Bank, borrow the money, and pay off all that he owed. Smith agreed to this arrangement on condition that his friend would secure himself by a mortgage. This, however, he would not do; and Smith, at last, consented to transfer his indebtedness to the bank.

Soon after this, perhaps in the summer of 1820, he gratified a wish long felt, and went to visit his friends in Alabama. He found their hearts as full of kindness toward him as when he lay in his lonesome cabin in the Hickory Flats, stricken of God, and helpless. Many changes had taken place in the country, and among the people. The wilderness had bloomed, and mansions had arisen, but not for him. Others had realized his dreams, and grown rich by speculation; for the Lord had sent neither fire nor sickness upon them. Yet he looked on their prosperity without envy or regret. He remained in Alabama but a short time, and soon turned his face homeward, now more than ever persuaded that all his afflictions had been sent upon him in love.

He hurried forward to be at the meeting of the Stockton's Valley Association, which was to be held with the Clear Fork Church, near his old home, in Clinton (then Cumberland) County, Kentucky. He reached the meeting-house on Saturday morning, after the introductory exercises had commenced. A large concourse of people had assembled. Suddenly appearing among his old friends and neighbors, many of whom he had not seen for years and begrimed with the dust of a week's travel, he was hardly recognized. But when he entered the house, some one exclaimed, "John Smith!" and he was welcomed with disorderly greeting. The people rushed from their seats to grasp his hand, and to tell him how happy they were to see him. Tired as he was from his long journey— and he had ridden that morning twenty-five miles on horseback, crossing two rivers, and climbing over a ridge of the Cumberland Mountains—they, nevertheless, compelled him to preach that day at the meeting-house, and again, at night, at his brother Philip's.

On the next day, he was constrained to speak from a rostrum in the grove. A stand had been erected, says an eyewitness,[*] in a beautiful valley opening toward the west, through which a rill of bright clear water rippled for a short way, and then fell into Clear Fork Creek. In this stream he had been immersed by Isaac Denton, nearly sixteen years

---

[*] Elder Isaac T. Reneau.

before. Close by, still stood the old log meeting-house, in which he had told his experience. A few steps from the stand, at the base of a rocky hill, bubbled the spring from which he had so often drunk in days gone by. Not far off, were the home of his boyhood and the ever-remembered spice-wood thicket, in which he had caught the first glimpse of Jehovah's glory. Behind him, on the platform, sat his old pastor, Isaac Denton, his brother Jonathan, now a preacher, Stephen Collier, and many other ministers. Before him were his old mother, his brothers and sisters, and relatives, and all the friends of his youth, who loved him as few men have ever been loved; while hundreds of strangers gathered around the stand to see and to hear him. The day was fine; the September breeze freshened through the oaks around, and everything was inspiring. He preached from Rom. iii. 31: "Do we make void the law through faith? God forbid. Yea, we establish the law." There was every thing to arouse the speaker, and he was eloquent. The congregation sat or stood in breathless silence, for they seemed to be spell-bound, while he defined and illustrated the power of the Christian's faith. Isaac Denton, in after years, often alluded to that discourse, saying it was the best that John Smith ever delivered; but he always added, that, *even at that time, he suspected him of some sort of heresy.*

Smith returned home, and, not long afterward, publicly avowed his dissatisfaction with the doctrinal system under which he had been raised. On a certain occasion, in March, 1822, at Spencer's Creek, he was urging sinners to repent, and to believe the Gospel. "Jesus died for you," said he; "but if you believe not, you must be damned." His mind was suddenly confused with the thought that, if the elect should not believe, his preaching was false, for they would not be damned; and, if the non-elect should believe, their faith would be false, for, according to his creed, Christ did not die for them. Must the non-elect, then, thought he, be damned for not believing what is false? Or the elect be saved, though denying the truth? Too honest thus to exhort the people any longer, he closed his address.

"Brethren," said he, "something is wrong—I am in the

dark—we are all in the dark; but how to lead you to the light, or to find the way myself, before God, I know not."

He took his seat. The song hardly arose from the lips of the congregation; but a prayer for light went up in that hour from the honest heart of John Smith, that was heard in heaven by the Father of lights and Author of all truth.

The crowd dispersed, and he went directly, but silently, home, as if he would find in the sacredness of that humble spot, and in the counsel of his wife, some ray of light to dispel the darkness from his mind. Into the bosom of that wife—so often his strength in weakness and his comfort in trouble—he poured the confusion of his thoughts. They bowed down together in prayer; and, while he begged for light, he pledged himself, both to heaven and to her, that he would take God's Word as his only oracle, examine it carefully, and, calling no man master, follow its teachings, wherever they might lead him.

From the hour in which that prayer went up, and that pledge was given, we must date the commencement of that religious revolution which John Smith contributed so much to bring about in the old North District. Faithful to that pledge, and in the love of truth, he again began a most earnest and systematic investigation of the Scriptures. When the work of the day was done, and he would come in from field or forest at night, he would sit by his candle and ponder the questions that interested him, sometimes, till the day broke and called him out to labor again.

He soon saw that the doctrine of Personal Election and Reprobation, which had so much embarrassed him, grew out of the dogma that the Holy Spirit must supernaturally convert men to God. This dogma, he saw, rested on the assumption that the sinner is dead—dead in such a sense that he can not believe the Gospel, or repent of his sins until the Spirit quickens him into life; that, consequently, as all men are not brought to life, the Spirit must pass by some, and allow them to perish—not on account of their greater unworthiness, however, but simply because God in his own good pleasure did not elect them to eternal life. For these Christ could not have died, else he would have died in vain. He saw, finally, that the entire superstructure of Calvinism, as he had held and preached it, was based on the notion that moral death destroys man's free agency. Calvinism, he reasoned, depends at last on the definition of a single term. "*What, then, is death?*" he asked, as the candle burned to the socket on his little stand at midnight—and the peace of a hundred churches hung on his answer to the question!

Christians, too, are said to be dead—dead to sin. Does this death, he inquired, take from them the power to sin? May they, as free agents, still embrace error and do wrong? If, then, the Christian, who is dead to sin, can nevertheless do wrong, surely the sinner, who is dead to righteousness, may nevertheless do right.

When that conclusion was firmly grasped, he felt persuaded that the system which he had so long preached, was but a wind of doctrine without substantial basis.

Such was the state of his mind, when a friend put into his hand the prospectus of a religious paper called *The Christian Baptist*, edited by Alexander Campbell, of Buffalo Creek, Brooke County, Virginia.

CHAPTER XIV.

THOMAS CAMPBELL, the father of Alexander Campbell, had long been a minister of high standing among the leaders of the Presbyterian Church, in the North of Ireland. He emigrated to America, in 1807, and settled in Washington County, Pennsylvania, where he continued to labor as a minister among the destitute congregations of his own faith and order.

Deploring the distracted condition of the religious world, and convinced that its divisions were unscriptural, and injurious to society, he resolved to make a public effort to restore the original unity of the Church.

A meeting was called, to be held at Buffalo, August 17th, 1809,* consisting of persons of different religious denominations, most of them in an unsettled state as to a fixed Gospel ministry. After full conference, it was unanimously agreed to form a religious association, to be called the "Christian Association of Washington, Pennsylvania." A committee of twenty-one was appointed to meet and confer together, and, with the assistance of Elder Thomas Campbell, to determine upon the proper means to carry into effect the ends of the Association; the result of which conference was the drawing up of a Declaration and Address, which was agreed upon and ordered to be printed.

This Declaration and Address was not designed to be the constitution of a church; but it was simply a declaration of a purpose to institute a society of voluntary advocates of church reformation. The sole purpose of this organization was to promote simple, evangelical Christianity; and for this end they resolved to countenance and support only those

* Memoirs of Thomas Campbell.

ministers who practiced that simple, original form of Christianity, expressly exhibited in the sacred page; who would inculcate nothing of human authority, of private opinion, or of inventions of men, as having any place in the constitution, faith, or worship of the Christian Church; who would, in a word, teach nothing as a matter of Christian faith or duty, for which there could not be produced a "Thus saith the Lord," either in express terms, or by approved precedent.

Alexander Campbell, after spending some months at the University of Glasgow, followed his father to America, and reached Washington in October, 1809, just in time to read the proof-sheets of the Declaration and Address. He heartily joined in the effort to unite the churches on this basis of a simple, evangelical Christianity.

A congregation was soon formed and constituted on the principles set forth in the Declaration. A house of worship was erected, and ministerial duties were regularly performed conjointly by father and son, who had been duly ordained pastors of the church.

The doctrine of weekly communion in the Lord's Supper being acknowledged and practiced in this congregation, its incongruity with infant church membership became, to Alexander's mind, more and more apparent. He began to press upon his father's attention also, the incongruity of thus demanding an express precept or precedent for every ordinance, and yet practicing infant baptism, for which neither the one nor the other could be produced. For some time, however, his respect for his father's judgment held him in abeyance.

Finally, the subject was formally introduced and discussed, the whole question was examined thoroughly and impartially, and Alexander became fully convinced, not only that the practice of infant sprinkling could not be sustained by Scripture evidence, but that immersion in water, upon a profession of faith in Christ, alone constituted Christian baptism. He immediately made known to his father the conclusions at which he had arrived, and his determination to be immersed. Thomas Campbell, influenced, doubtless, by the example of his favorite son, now examined the subject with more care, and finally yielded the point. On the 12th of June, 1812, with several other members of the Brush Run congregation, they were both immersed by Elder Mathias Luse, of the Baptist community.

This occurrence, of course, caused a division in the congregation. Those who were attached to infant baptism, or opposed to immersion, withdrew from the church; the remainder, as a congregation of immersed believers, were received into the Red Stone Baptist Association. It was carefully stipulated at the time, however, that "no terms of union or communion, other than the Holy Scriptures, should be required."

*"From the moment that Thomas Campbell concluded to follow the example of his son, in relation to baptism, he conceded to him, in effect, the guidance of the whole religious movement."

Alexander, as a messenger of the church at Brush Run, made use of his many opportunities to present to his Baptist brethren his view of the ancient Gospel, and to urge its acceptance upon them. While his doctrine was indorsed by some, he excited considerable stir in the Association in 1816, on Romans viii. 3, known as his "Sermon on the Law," that created the greatest sensation, and aroused against him the most violent opposition. His design in that discourse was to show that Christians are not under the law of Moses, but to Christ. In doing this, however, he maintained, contrary to the received doctrine, that there was no necessity for preaching the Law, in order to prepare one for receiving the Gospel.

Notwithstanding the opposition which he had thus provoked, he was chosen to debate the subject of baptism with Mr. Walker, in 1821; of which debate two editions were soon published. Still, opposition to him was manifest every year, with increasing bitterness, in the Red Stone Association, until, finally, he determined to withdraw from them. The church at Brush Run agreed to dismiss about thirty of her members, including Mr. Campbell, to Wellsburg, where they constituted a new church. They were, some time afterward, admitted into the Mahoning Association, of Ohio—a body of Christians distinguished for their liberality of feeling and knowledge of the Scriptures.

Believing that his discussion with Mr. Walker on the

---

*Memoirs of Alexander Campbell, vol. 1, p. 401.

subject of baptism had been beneficial to the cause of truth, he was induced to debate the same question with Mr. McCalla, of the Presbyterian Church, whom he accordingly met at Washington, Kentucky, in the autumn of 1823. In that debate Mr. Campbell contended that baptism, or immersion, is a divine institution, designed to put the legitimate subject of it into actual possession of the remission of his sins; that to every believing subject it did formally and in fact convey to him the forgiveness of sins. He subsequently remarked, in reference to this matter, that it was with much hesitation that he presented this view of the subject at that time, because of its perfect novelty. He was then assured of its truth; but it was subsequent to that period that he developed more fully the import of the declaration, that baptism is for the remission of sins.*

The debate at Washington was listened to with much interest; for the publication of the "Sermon on the Law," and of the "Debate with Walker," had already given to Mr. Campbell great reputation among the Baptists as a man of learning and power. In fact, Jeremiah Vardeman, whose word at that time was authority, declared, that if all the Baptist preachers in Kentucky were put into one, they would not make an Alexander Campbell!

In the meantime, Mr. Campbell had commenced the publication of a monthly paper, with the design to "restore a pure speech to the people of God—to restore the ancient order of things in the Christian kingdom—to emancipate the conscience from the dominion of human authority in matters of religion, and to lay an imperishable foundation for the union of all Christians, and for their co-operation in spreading the Gospel throughout the world."

In the prospectus, which he issued in the spring of 1823, he says: "The *Christian Baptist* shall espouse the cause of no religious sect, excepting that ancient sect called Christians first at Antioch. Its sole object shall be the eviction of truth, and the exposure of error in doctrine and practice. The editor, acknowledging no standard of religious faith or works, other than the Old and New Testaments, and the latter as the only standard of the religion of Jesus Christ,

---

* Christian Baptist, vol. 5, p 121.

will, intentionally at least, oppose nothing which it contains, and recommend nothing which it does not enjoin."

John Smith received a copy of the prospectus soon after the debate with McCalla, and he read it with profound interest. He ordered the paper to be sent to him, and induced a few others to subscribe for it. He hoped, from the reputation of Mr. Campbell as a man of learning and piety, that his discussion of Scriptural themes would greatly assist him in arriving at a solution of his own doctrinal difficulties.

He had now fully persuaded himself that the system of religion embodied in the Philadelphia Confession of Faith was unscriptural. He had examined all the modified phases of Calvinism, and found that he could accept none of them as being in full harmony with the Word of God. The Arian, Socinian, the Universalian theories had all been likewise considered and rejected. Yet, he felt assured that the truth must be found somewhere among the systems of the day. In this belief, he had resolved to select from each such tenets as he could approve, and unite them into a system of his own, which should be consistent with itself, and accordant with the Word of God. On this vain task he was wasting his fine powers, when the first few numbers of the *Christian Baptist* reached him. He hastily glanced through its small, solid pages to learn what, at that time, he was most curious to know—whether the editor was a Calvinist, a Fullerite, or an Arminian. He did not dream that it was possible for a man, especially a learned man, to be a Christian, and yet belong to no religious party; for he had, as yet, no conception of an undenominational Christianity. But, instead of meeting with elaborate essays on the perplexing dogmas of the day, he read with variable feelings of pleasure, surprise, and painful suspicion, such passages as the following:

To convert the heathen to the popular Christianity of these times would be an object of no great consequence, as the popular Christians themselves, for the most part, require to be converted to the Christianity of the New Testament.

*   *   *   *   *   *   *

The societies called churches, constituted and set in order by the ministers of the New Testament, were of such as received and acknowledged Jesus as Lord Messiah, the Savior of the world, and had put themselves under his guidance. The only bond of union among them, was faith in him, and submission to his will. No subscription to abstract propositions, framed by synods; no decrees of councils, sanctioned by kings; no rules of practice, commanded by ecclesiastical courts, were imposed on them as terms of admission into, or of continuance in, this holy brotherhood. In the apostles' doctrine, and in the apostles' commandments, they steadfastly continued. Their fraternity was a fraternity of love, peace, gratitude, cheerfulness, joy, charity, and universal benevolence. Their religion did not manifest itself in public fasts nor carnivals. They had no festivals, no great and solemn meetings. Their meeting on the first day of the week was at all times alike solemn, joyful, and interesting.

Their religion was not of that elastic and porous kind, which at one time is compressed into some cold formalities, and at another expanded into prodigious zeal and warmth. No; their piety did not at one time rise to paroxysms, and their zeal to effervescence, and, by and by, languish into rigid ceremony and lifeless form. It was the pure, clear, and swelling current of love to God, of love to man, expressed in all the variety of doing good.

The order of their assemblies was uniformly the same. It did not vary with moons and seasons. It did not change, as dress, nor fluctuate, as the manners of the times. Their devotion did not diversify itself into the endless forms of modern times. They had no monthly concerts for prayer; no solemn convocations; no great fasts, nor preparation, nor thanksgiving days. Their churches were not fractured into missionary societies, Bible societies, education societies; nor did they dream of organizing such in the world. The head of a believing household was not, in those days, a president or manager of a board of Foreign Missions; his wife, the president of some female education society; his eldest son, the recording secretary of some domestic Bible society; his eldest daughter, the corresponding secretary of some mite society; his servant-maid, the vice-president of a rag society; and his little daughter, a tutoress of a Sunday-school. They knew nothing of the hobbies of modern times *In their Church capacity alone they moved.* They neither transformed themselves into any other kind of association, nor did they fracture and sever themselves into divers societies. They viewed the Church of Jesus Christ as the scheme of heaven to ameliorate the world; as members of it, they considered themselves bound to do all they could for the glory of God and the good of men. They dare not transfer to a missionary society, or Bible society, or education society, a cent or a prayer, lest, in doing so, they should rob the Church of its glory, and exalt the inventions of men above the wisdom of God. *In their Church capacity alone they moved.* The Church they considered the pillar and ground of the truth; they considered, if they did all they could in this capacity, they had nothing left for any other object of a religious nature. In this capacity, wide as its sphere extended, they exhibited the truth in word and deed. Their good works, which accompanied salvation, were the labors of love, in ministering to the necessities of saints, to the poor of the brotherhood. They did good to all men, but especially to the household of faith. They practiced that pure and undefiled religion which, in overt acts, consisted in taking care of orphans and widows in their affliction, and keeping one's self unspotted by (the vices of) the world.

*   *   *   *   *   *   *

We happened upon the truth, when we published as our opinion, about seven years ago, that *"the present popular exhibition of the Christian religion is a compound of Judaism, heathen philosophy, and Christianity.*

*   *   *   *   *   *   *

From the whole of the premises it is evident, that the professing world is far gone, yea, very far, indeed, from original ground; for such was the import of the Gospel testimony, as we have seen, that all who professed to believe it, whether they were intelligent persons or not, understood, *at least, so much* by it, that it gave assurance of pardon, and acceptance with God, to every one that received it, that is, to every baptized believer; consequently, every one that was baptized, making the same profession, he both thought himself, and was esteemed by his professing brethren, a justified and accepted person. Hence we do not find a single instance on the sacred record of a doubting or disconsolate Christian.

*   *   *   *   *   *   *

The dominion of the clergy, though much impaired, still exists to an alarming extent; and their eagerness to have an unrivaled control over the public sentiment in all religious affairs, remains unabated. Behold the arrogance of their claims, the peerless haughtiness of their pretensions! They have said, and many of them still say, they have an exclusive right, an *official* right, to affix the proper interpretation to the Scriptures; to expound them in public assemblies; in so much, that it would be presumption in a layman to attempt to exercise any of those functions which they have assumed. They must "christen" the new-born infant; they must catechise and confirm the tender stripling; they must celebrate the rite of matrimony; they must dispense all ordinances in religion; they must attend the corpse to its grave, preach a funeral sermon, and consecrate the very ground in which it is laid. From this dominion over the consciences and feelings of mankind, it was not difficult to slide the hand into the purse of the superstitious. The most artful, and, indeed, the most effectual way to get hold of the purse, is to get a hold on the conscience. The deeper the impression is made on the one, the deeper the draft on the other. Thus it came to pass that the clergy obtained worldly establishments, enriched themselves, and became an order as powerful in the State as in the Church.

*   *   *   *   *   *   *

When I hear a modern preacher, either with or without a diploma in his pocket, saying that he is an embassador of Christ, sent of God to preach the Gospel, moved by the Holy Ghost to take upon him the work of the ministry, I ask him to work a miracle, or afford some divine attestation of his being such a character. If he can not do this, I mark him down as a knave, or an enthusiast; consequently, an imposter, either intentionally or unintentionally.

*   *   *   *   *   *   *

When there is a voluntary association of any number of disciples of Christ, met in any one place to attend to the duties and privileges of a Church, should they call any one of their *own* number, who possesses the qualifications belonging to the bishop or overseer, laid down by the Holy Spirit in the written word, and should they appoint him to office, as the Holy Spirit has taught them in the same written word, then it may be said to such a person, "Take heed to yourself, and to the flock over which the Holy Spirit has made you overseer." But this bishop of whom we have now spoken, is neither priest, embassador, minister of religion, clergyman, nor a reverend divine; but simply one that has the oversight of one voluntary society, who, when he leaves that society, has no office in any other, in consequence of his being an officer in that. His discharge of the work of a bishop is limited by, and confined to, the particular congregation which appointed him to office. If he should travel abroad and visit another congregation, even of the same views of that of which he was or is bishop, he is then no bishop; he is then in the capacity of an unofficial disciple. To suppose the contrary, is to constitute different orders of men, or to divide the Church into the common classes of clergy and laity; than which, nothing is more essentially opposite to the genius and spirit of Christianity.

*   *   *   *   *   *   *

If it is true (as we shall see from Scripture it is) that the body of Christ is united in its several members by the belief of this matter of fact, viz.: that Jesus is the Son of God, and that it is increased by the confession and belief of it, then a number of very important corollaries are deducible from these two revealed propositions: First, the peace and union of a Church of Christ are not the result of any sort of ecclesiastical government. Secondly, the increase of Christ's body is not predicated on anything so exceedingly exceptionable as modern confessions of faith, but on the confession of the first truth. Thirdly, the worshiping establishments now in operation throughout Christendom, increased and cemented by their respective voluminous confessions of faith, and their ecclesiastical constitutions, are not Churches of Jesus Christ, but the legitimate daughters of that mother of harlots, the Church of Rome.

*   *   *   *   *   *   *

We have no system of our own, nor of others, to substitute in lieu of the reigning systems. We only aim at substituting the New Testament in lieu of every creed in existence; whether Mohammedan, Pagan, Jewish, or Presbyterian. We wish to call Christians to consider that Jesus Christ has made them kings and priests to God. We neither advocate Calvinism,

Arminianism, Arianism, Socinianism, Trinitarianism, Unitarianism, Deism, or Sectarianism, but *New Testamentism.* We wish, cordially wish, to take the New Testament out of the abuses of the clergy, and put it into the hands of the people. And to do this is no easy task, as the clergy have formed the opinions of nine-tenths of Christendom, before they could form an opinion of their own. They have, in order to raise the people's admiration of them, for their own advantage, taught them in creeds, in sermons, in catechisms, in tracts, in pamphlets, in primers, in folios, that they alone can expound the New Testament; that without them, people are either *almost*, or *altogether*, destitute of the means of grace. They must lead in the devotion of the people, they must consecrate their prayers, their praises; and, latterly, they must even open a cattle-show, or an exhibition of manufacturers, with prayers and religious pageantry.

*   *   *   *   *   *   *

The popular belief of a regeneration previous to faith, or a knowledge of the Gospel, is replete with mischief. Similar to this is a notion that obtains among many, of a "law work," or some terrible process of terror and despair, through which a person must pass, as through the pious Bunyan's slough of despond, before he can believe the Gospel. It is all equivalent to this, that a man must become a desponding, trembling infidel before he can become a believer. Now the Gospel makes no provision for despondency, inasmuch as it assures all who believe it, upon the veracity of God, that they are forgiven and accepted in the Beloved.

*   *   *   *   *   *   *

Enthusiasm flourishes, blooms under the popular systems. This man was regenerated when asleep, by a vision of the night. That man heard a voice in the woods, saying, "Thy sins be forgiven thee." A third saw his Saviour descending to the tops of the trees at noonday. A thousand form a band, and sit up all night, to take heaven by surprise. Ten thousand are awaiting in anxiety for a *power*, for a power from on high, to descend upon their souls; they frequent meetings for the purpose of obtaining this power.

*   *   *   *   *   *   *

Like the Phœnix in the fable, they and the preacher have gathered a bundle of dry sticks, and they set about clapping their wings with one accord, that they may fan them into a flame—which sometimes actually happens, if our faith could be so strong as to believe it.

From all this scene of raging enthusiasm, be admonished, my friends, to open your Bibles, and to hearken to the voice of God, which is the voice of reason. God now speaks to us only by his word. By his Son, in the New Testament, he has fully revealed himself and his will. This is the only revelation of his spirit which we are to regard. The popular preachers and the popular systems alike render the Word of God of none effect.

*　　　*　　　*　　　*　　　*　　　*　　　*

John Smith read these papers with avidity—with a suspicious, critical eye, that overlooked nothing—and with an admiration for its style that was positively extravagant.

But in vain, the pen of Alexander Campbell charmed, or his piety and genius inspired confidence; Smith, true to himself, accepted no doctrine, and renounced no error, till compelled to do so by the Word of God.

CHAPTER XV.

The contents of the eighth number of the *Christian Baptist* gave great offense to many of its readers. The article on "Experimental Religion" was regarded as a positive proof that, however great might be the learning and talents of the editor, he was utterly destitute of heart-felt religion.

Smith himself, who had failed to find out to what theological school Alexander Campbell belonged, was almost persuaded, on reading the article in question, to concur in the general opinion, that he was a very erudite, but wholly unregenerate, man.

Some, whom he had induced to subscribe for the paper, came to him and ordered it to be discontinued. Among them was his brother Jonathan, who had recently moved from Stockton's Valley, and was now living but a few miles distant from him.

"You are wrong, Jonathan," said he to his brother, "you ought still to read that work. I do not myself indorse all that Mr. Campbell has written. But I am willing to pay him one dollar a year, were he Satan himself, and his writings destitute of truth, just for his manner of saying things. You are a young preacher, and may well afford to read it, just to learn how to say great things in few words. Study its manner, my brother, and, if you choose, let the matter go."

*Shortly after the publication of the article on "Experimental Religion," in the spring of 1824, Mr. Campbell visited Kentucky. Hearing that he would be at Flemingsburg, about twenty miles distant, and that it was his intention to come on to Mount Sterling from that place, Smith proposed to some of his brethren, that as an act of courtesy to a dis-

---

* See article in *Millen. Harbinger*, vol. 7, No. 5, contributed by Albert Allen.

tinguished stranger, they should go and meet him at that point. But so great was the prejudice which his recent essays had stirred up against him, that they were not willing to ride to Flemingsburg, and show him the way to their village! Smith, therefore, went alone. He reached Flemingsburg on the day Mr. Campbell had appointed to preach there. On entering the town, he was met by Elder William Vaughn, a Baptist clergyman, with whom he was well acquainted.

"Brother John," said he to Smith, "have you seen brother Campbell yet?"

"No, sir," he replied, "I have not; have *you* seen him?"

"Why, I have been with him for eight days and nights, through Mason and Bracken Counties, and have heard him every day!"

"Do, then, tell me what his views are on doctrinal points. Is he a Calvinist or an Arminian, an Arian or a Trinitarian?"

"I do not know," said Elder Vaughn; "he has nothing to do with any of these things."

"Well, I can tell, when I hear him, just what he is."

"How?"

"If he is a man of sense," said Smith, "and takes a position, even though he should not run it out into any *ism*, I can do it for him, and tell exactly where he would land. But tell me, brother Vaughn, does he know anything at all about heartfelt religion?"

"Bless you, brother John, he is one of the most pious, godly men that I was ever in company with in all my life."

"But do you think he knows anything about a *Christian experience?*" still inquired Smith.

"Lord bless you, he knows every thing," said Vaughn. "Come, I want to introduce you to him."

They went into the house, where Mr. Campbell was. He was taking off his sherryvallies, in which he had been riding that morning; for the roads were muddy. As he arose to receive the stranger, "*his nose*," as John Smith used to say, "*seemed to stand a little to the north.*"

"Brother Campbell," said Elder Vaughn, "I wish to introduce brother John Smith."

"Ah!" said he, "and is this brother John Smith? I know brother Smith very well, though I have never seen him before."

An introduction was not all that John Smith desired. He wished to sit down where he was, to look upon him without interruption; to scan and to penetrate, if he could, the man who had been so much talked of, and who in his writings had already put so many new thoughts into his mind. But the hour appointed for the address had come; and they all started to the meeting-house together.

The house was small, but preparations had been made for seating the congregation in the yard, where a small platform had been erected against the wall for the speaker. Still there was not room enough for the people, and many had to stand. Smith took his seat on the floor of the platform, near the feet of the speaker, so that he could catch every word that might fall from his lips. He was determined now to find out the theory of religion he held to, if, indeed, he held to any; for he was still full of doubt and suspicion.

Mr. Campbell arose and read the allegory of Hagar and Sarah, in the fourth chapter of Galatians. After giving a general outline of the whole Epistle, and showing how it ought to be read, in order to arrive at the Apostle's meaning, he took up the allegory itself. In a simple, plain, and artless manner, leaning with one hand on the head of his cane, he went through his discourse. There was nothing about the man to call off the mind of the listeners from what he was saying. He seemed, as Smith afterward remarked, to move in a higher sphere or latitude than that in which the *isms* of the day abounded. When the congregation was dismissed, Smith immediately remarked to Elder Vaughn:

"Is it not hard, brother Billy, to ride twenty miles, as I have done, just to hear a man preach thirty minutes?"

"You are mistaken, brother John; look at your watch. It has surely been longer than that?"

He looked at his watch, and to his surprise, saw that the discourse had been just two hours and a half long. Holding up his watch, he remarked:

"I have never been more deceived. Two hours of my life are gone, I know not how, though wide awake, too, all the time!"

"Did *you* find out, brother John," now asked Vaughn, "whether he was a Calvinist or an Arminian?"

"No," replied Smith, "I know nothing about the man; but, be he saint or devil, he has thrown more light on that Epistle, and on the whole Scriptures, than I have received in all the sermons that I have ever heard before."

It was arranged that Mr. Campbell should go a few miles that evening toward Mount Sterling, and spend the night at a Mr. Cannon's, who lived on the road. As they rode along, Smith drew to his side and remarked:

"Brother Campbell, I do not wish to meet any man at the judgment, having entertained an unfavorable opinion of him without good grounds. I will now say to you what I have never said to any man before—I am, religiously speaking, suspicious of you; and, as I have an unfavorable opinion of you, I am willing to give you my reason for it."

"Well, brother John," said Mr. Campbell, "if all my Baptist brethren would treat me as candidly as you have done, I would think more of them; it would afford me a better opportunity, too, to explain to them my views. I expected," continued he, smiling, "that when I saw you, I would know all you thought of me; for I heard recently, that at the Bracken Association, held in Carlisle, last September, when a number of preachers that had gone to a certain house to dinner, were abusing me terribly for the attack I had made upon the clergy, you said that the clergy needed a castigation so much that you were willing to be whipped almost to death yourself to get the others killed."

"Yes," said John Smith, "and I said it sincerely, too. But, brother Campbell, I now wish to say to you that I think it strange you should have written that piece on Experimental Religion, which I read in the eighth number of the *Christian Baptist.* You can not be so ignorant as the piece would seem to prove. There must be something kept back or hidden behind it all; for you understand as well as any one what the *populars* mean by *Experimental religion.*"

"My father," said Mr. Campbell, in reply, "gave me a scolding for publishing that piece so soon; for, as he thought, the people were not ready for it. But I have a series of essays on hand, on the work of the Holy Spirit, which will explain the whole matter; this was thrown out only to call the attention of the clergy."

After further conversation, they reached Mr. Cannon's. Other preachers had accompanied them, and the social hours of the evening were protracted by conversation on various Scriptural topics. The subjects generally were proposed by Smith at the suggestion of his Baptist friends, who seemed to be unwilling to ask Mr. Campbell their own questions.

At last, the host handed the Bible to Mr. Campbell, and requested him to conduct the devotions of the evening. He, however, appealed to those around him to relieve him of this office; but they refused. In a serious and solemn manner, he then remarked:

"I have reason to think hard of my Baptist brethren in Kentucky; for I have spent nine or ten days among them, have spoken, for the most time, twice each day, and have conversed the greater part of the night, until much worn down; and yet I have never been able to get any one of them to open a meeting for me, even by singing and prayer!"

Turning around to Smith, he said, "Brother John, will you take the book and proceed?"

"If brother Campbell is a Christian," said Smith, taking the book, "he can make as much allowance for my imperfections as any one present; but if he be a poor, unconverted sinner, I do not care what he says or thinks about me."

With this he read and offered up the prayer of the evening. On the next morning, he and his companion went on their way together, toward Mount Sterling. He had a good opportunity of conversing on many of the doctrinal points that at that time especially interested him, which greatly conduced to his correct understanding of Mr. Campbell's religious views.

As they rode along together, he remarked in his own frank and peculiar manner:

"Brother Campbell, I have seen some of these preachers who were educated for the ministry in the eastern colleges; and I was much surprised to find in you an entire want of gesture and manner. You leaned upon your cane easily, though somewhat awkwardly, and *talked* as men commonly talk."

"I long ago studied all those arts of elocution of which

you speak, brother John," said Campbell; "but I have conscientiously refrained from any attempt to use them."

Smith looked at him with curious surprise.

"The apostles," continued Mr. Campbell, "were sent forth as witnesses to a certain great fact. Suppose that one of them should, in making his statement before the people, have plied his arms in gesticulations, stamped his foot in vehemence, and declared his testimony in the ears of the people, in a loud, stentorian voice?"

"I would not have believed one word he said," interrupted Smith.

"But how weightily fell the words of these first preachers," said Mr. Campbell, "when, with composure of manner, natural emphasis, and solemn deliberation, they spoke forth the words of truth and soberness!"

After crossing the Licking River, and while slowly riding up the hill beyond. Smith, who wished to understand Mr. Campbell's view definitely on the subject of Christian Experience, inquired:

"Brother Campbell, I suppose you had something that the populars call an *experience*, did you not?"

"Oh! yes, I had an experience," replied Campbell.

"Well, I want you to sell it to me," earnestly said Smith; and he drew closer to the side of his fellow traveler.

"My father," proceeded Mr. Campbell, "intended to make a clergyman of me, and always kept me near him. From the time that I could read the Scriptures, I was convinced that Jesus was the Son of God, and was fully persuaded that I was a sinner, and must obtain pardon through the merits of Christ, or be lost forever. This caused me great distress of mind; for I was much exercised under the workings of a guilty conscience. Finally, however, I was able to put my reliance on him, the only Saviour of sinners; and from that time I have had peace of mind. It had not yet entered into my head to investigate the subject of baptism, or the doctrines of the creeds. Afterward, when I came to the United States, I was led to think on the subject of baptism by a question asked me one day by an old Christian woman; and I became convinced, after thorough investigation, that immersion is the only mode of baptism. Persuaded that any bap-

tism in infancy was not Christian baptism, and feeling that
every command of the Saviour should be obeyed, I was accordingly immersed."

Smith was satisfied with the *experience*, thus summarily
stated, and he felt that he could now give Mr. Campbell his
hand in fellowship.

"And now," said Campbell, "I would like to hear yours."
After Smith had given succinctly his own religious experience,
Mr. Campbell said to him:

"I have never doubted or denied the reality of these various workings of the mind as modified by the different tem-
peraments of those who are exercised by them. But I do
object to the use that is made of them by the clergy. We
should not make them tests of one another's Christianity; nor
is there anything in the Book that requires a man to tell all
the workings of his conscience, as a prerequisite to baptism."

At Mount Sterling, Mr. Campbell delivered three discourses,
and then proceeded to North Middletown, in Bourbon County;
at which point John Smith parted from him, with a better
understanding of the character and views of his distinguished
brother and friend.

CHAPTER XVI.

JOHN SMITH continued to ponder the bold words of the *Christian Baptist*, quite sure that he had always been wrong, but still doubting whether Mr. Campbell was right. At last, he ceased to speculate, and he began to read the Scriptures as a child would read them. His mind now cast off its fetters forever, and he was free!

Familiar with every text and argument by which the popular systems were defended, he was well prepared to discuss them before the people; and he resolved to begin the controversy. As he would have to remove prejudice as well as refute error, he studied to present the truth in the least offensive form, and in the most impressive manner. The churches everywhere stood in need of reform; and, reflecting on his own history, he felt that he had been called by Divine Providence to the work of urging that reform. He knew that in renouncing his former opinions, he would cast off old friends; and that in proclaiming the new faith, he would arouse the animosity, if not hate, of the clergy. It was a solemn hour, when, closing his Bible, very late one evening, he turned to his wife, and, with a heart dilated with the greatness of the work before him, began with her to count up, one by one, the sacrifices which he would have to make. No man ever had a warmer or more constant heart for his friends; and now alone by the fireside that evening they sat, and called over by name the friends that would soon discard them. No man ever held more sacred his Christian reputation; and now they mournfully talked together of the calumnies that would soon be heaped upon him. He was still in debt, and, like his father, he was so constituted, that even an unpaid bill rested on his conscience like guilt. His brethren still neglected to meet the calls of the bank upon him. "Will they not now," thought he, "turn from me, and, forgetting all their pledges, leave me bankrupt, friendless, and without a home?" They talked together of those still deare: friends far away on the Cumberland, and they wept to think that even mother and sister and brother must be forsaken. But houses, and lands, and friends, and fair name, and life itself, if need be, they resolved to sacrifice for the Truth— rejoicing, even in the midst of their tears, that they should be counted worthy to suffer all these things for his Name's sake. He had no hope, he said to his wife, that the Ancient Gospel would prevail in his day; but he prayed that he might live long enough to see a few young men of another generation raised up to push forward the good work to its consummation.

In 1825, he began to preach the great facts of the evangelical history, and to call on all men to believe them on the testimony of the inspired writers. He began to declare the commandments of Jesus as the only Head of the Church, and to urge all men to obey them.

"However much the sects may differ about other matters," said he, "one thing is certain: whoever does not believe the Gospel must be damned. The Arminian denies the doctrines of Calvin, and yet he is well assured that the Calvinist may be saved; Calvinism, then, is not the Gospel of Christ. He denies, also, without danger of hell-fire, the speculations of the Universalist; Universalism, then, is not the Gospel. The strict Calvinist disowns the Fullerite, and will not fellowship the Arminian; and yet even he will admit that these may be saved. Neither Fullerism nor Arminianism, therefore, can be the Gospel. It is not, therefore, the distinctive feature in any of these systems of theology; it may be a common element in the *faith* of all, but it can not be found in the *ism* of any."

He began to teach, also, that the Bible is the only revelation of God to man; that the New Testament contains all that is necessary to be believed or obeyed in order to the enjoyment of pardon and eternal life; and that inspired penmen wrote to produce faith; for faith comes by hearing the Word of God, and is simply confidence in Christ, and in all that God has said, promised, or threatened in the Scriptures. The

Sacred Writings, he contended, are sufficiently plain on all matters of duty, when interpreted in harmony with the laws of language and of thought; and it is the inalienable right and imperative duty of every man to read and to interpret them for himself, calling no man on earth master. The Christian Confession is formally contained in the proposition that *Jesus is the Messiah, the Son of God*, the cordial acceptance of which is the faith that, in full dependence on him, works by love and purifies the heart. The penitent believer is introduced into the Church, or Family of God, by a birth of water. This birth, as distinguished from his quickening, is an immersion into the name of the Father, and of the Son, and of the Holy Spirit. Submission to the ordinance of baptism is, moreover, the initial act of obedience to Jesus Christ, in the due performance of which the believing penitent is authorized to regard himself as accepted with God the Father, through faith in his Son. He maintained that the Scriptures do not warrant the dogma that the Spirit, by a special, abstract influence, produces faith. He taught, however, that it was an outward witness to the world; because through the words of the apostles, it convinces the world of sin, of righteousness, and of judgment. If these views were held at that time by any order of Protestants, he contended that they were held speculatively only; but that by all classes they were practically denied.

In his earlier study of the Word, John Smith had often been much embarrassed by the recurrence of obsolete terms and antiquated forms of speech. He had memorized the greater part of the Christian Scriptures, and had studiously pondered them in his mind; but still the vail lay on many a verse and page as he read. Quaint terms and puzzling phraseology, that defied every rule of interpretation, and discrepancies which he could not reconcile, had often tried his patience and baffled his skill. He felt sure that the apostles wrote to be understood, and that it required no special aid of the Spirit to interpret what they had written; and he used to wonder at such phrases as, "We do you to wit," though persuaded at the time that the fault was in his own mind. He had not yet called in question the learning or the faithfulness of the king's translators; nor had he reflected that a living language is continually changing, and that, consequently, any translation must, in time, become antiquated and obscure.

About that time a series of articles appeared in the *Christian Baptist* on the "History of the English Bible," evidently designed to prepare the reader for a new translation of the Scriptures. The objections to the common version, which had often been made by intelligent students of the Scriptures, were prudently but forcibly presented; certain imperfections were pointed out, and, finally, proposals were issued for publishing a *New Translation*, which the editor indorsed as the best in the English language.

This version, reprinted substantially from London editions, and often improperly called "Alexander Campbell's Translation," was made by George Campbell, author of the "Philosophy of Rhetoric," James McKnight, author of a "Harmony of the Four Gospels," and Philip Doddridge, the celebrated author of the "Rise and Progress." The first two were Doctors of Divinity of the Church of Scotland; the last, a Congregationalist.

In his prospectus of the work, the American compiler and publisher remarks: "One improvement of considerable importance ought to be made in this work, and to which we shall attend. Sundry terms are not translated into English, but adopted from long usage. Those terms are occasionally translated into English by Campbell and McKnight, but not always. We shall uniformly give them the meaning which they have affixed to them, wherever they occur, and thus make this a pure English New Testament, not mingled with Greek words, either adopted or anglicised. *But in doing this, we shall not depart in any instance from the meaning which they have declared those words to convey.*"

In April, 1826, the first edition of the New Translation was issued from the press, and Smith sat down to its perusal, not only without prejudice, but with eagerness and delight. Many an obscure passage was at once made clear; unintelligible words and phrases disappeared; discrepancies were reconciled; and the sacred page seemed to grow transparent as he read. Texts on which he had once relied as the foundation of his religious system, lost, in the phraseology of the new version, much of their doctrinal importance. Still, he accepted no rendering until he had tried it by his own canon of criticism, that whatever word or phrase is inconsistent with the context, or with common sense, will be found, on due examination, to be also unscriptural.

When he had, by this rule, approved any rendering, he would adopt it, and quote it thenceforth as the Word of God. He had, for example, when immersing, always used the formula, "I baptize you *in* the name of the Father, and of the Son, and of the Holy Ghost." But when he read in the new version of *immersion into* the Name, he approved it; for he reasoned that inasmuch as all authority in heaven and on earth had been given to the Son, it could not be proper to baptize disciples *in the name*, that is, by the authority, of the Father too, and of the Holy Ghost. And, as baptism introduced the candidate *into* a new state, or *into* a new relation, he did not hesitate, though ignorant of Greek, to adopt that language also.

He told his brethren, on one occasion, that as *baptize* was a foreign word, he would always in future translate it for them. "In fact," said he, "as not many of you have the gift of tongues, or of interpretation, I am resolved to speak to you in Greek no more."

He once heard an evangelist declare from the pulpit that the word *baptize* should be erased from the Book, because it was neither English, nor Greek, nor Latin. It meant *to sprinkle*, if one chose to affix such a meaning to it; or, it might mean *to pour*, or *to immerse*. In popular use, it meant anything or nothing. On the next day, he heard the same evangelist, when immersing a candidate, use the word *baptize*. As soon as he had the opportunity, he took the inconsistent preacher to task:

"Brother, I do not rank myself among learned men, but superior age gives me some privileges among those who are younger than myself. Yesterday, you taught us that the word *baptize* is neither Greek, Latin, Dutch, nor English; that it is, in fact, a word without any meaning at all."

"And do you not think so too?" said the evangelist.

"I was inclined to take your word for it," replied he, "as you perhaps understand some of these languages; but why did you, in administering the ordinance of immersion to-day, solemnly use the very word which, yesterday, you said belongs to no language on earth, and has no fixed meaning among men?"

Had these little innovations appeared only in his conversation, they might have given but little offense to his brethren. But the more solemn and public the occasion, the more fit was the opportunity, in his judgment, to exemplify a pure speech. About the first public use that he made of the new version was to revise, by its aid, the formulary words of baptism.

Smith never infringed on any custom from mere caprice, of from a spirit of innovation. He was constitutionally steadfast and conservative. Nevertheless, he could break up any habit of thought or speech, and adopt with enthusiasm the most progressive ideas, when truth or consistency required it. To erase from the memory and the heart, for truth's sake, phrase after phrase of Holy Writ, learned and loved in childhood, and to train the ear and the tongue to unfamiliar texts instead, evinces a devotion to truth at once beautiful and strong.

He did not, however, approve of every change from the common version. He dared to criticise, and sometimes to reject; but this he always did in the same spirit in which he approved. One evening, as he sat by his table reading the new version of *Acts of Apostles*, he came to the question of the Philippian jailer, rendered by Doddridge thus: *"Sirs, what must I do that I may be safe?"* Turning to his wife, and reciting the passage aloud, he said:

"Nancy, this rendering is wrong, and I will not accept it. They have not been faithful to the Greek."

"What in the world do you know about Greek, Mr. Smith?" asked his wife, smiling at his humorous pretensions.

"I may be a barbarian, wife, but I know something of the mind of the Spirit. Neither prophet nor apostle, when moved by the Holy Ghost, ever spoke or wrote one word of nonsense. The jailer was in no danger; for the prisoners were all present, and he knew it. Besides, Paul's advice to him, had he followed it, would have done him no good; for faith in the Lord Jesus Christ would certainly have brought down on his head the vengeance of both Pagan and Jew. Brother Campbell is a great man, Nancy, and I think he is a good one, too; but for that very reason we must beware of him. Such a man can the more easily mislead others, should he be wrong himself. They have certainly put a wrong question into the mouth of the jailer, and a hundred Campbells could not make me think otherwise."*

Great was the offense, however, which the New Translation gave to many of his clerical brethren. One of them, having purchased a copy and compared it diligently with the old version, piously condemned it, and burned it to ashes!

His own study of the new text, and his occasional public use of it, his growing indifference to doctrines, his persistent efforts to rise superior to denominationalism, and especially his departures from some of the customs of the Church, not only provoked criticism, but incited against him, at last, a formidable and organized opposition. His brethren in the ministry throughout the District were offended by his heresies; while the staunch old lay brethren, whose religious ideas were set with age, were deeply grieved by his innovations. He had some friends among the young, it is true; but their influence in the Church was not yet felt. His good sense and moral courage had gained for him, too, the respect and admiration of many unbelievers; but that sort of popularity served only to increase the dissatisfaction of his brethren. He was accused of misleading the young, and of consorting with publicans and sinners.

With no colleague to aid him, he saw the storm gathering wrathfully about him, but he stood ready for the bolt which he knew must soon descend upon him.

The old rendering of this passage was afterward restored.

CHAPTER XVII.

THE church at Mount Sterling had been received into the Association again; and John Smith, entreated to come and break to them the Word of Life, had, in 1823, withdrawn his services from Lulbegrud, and accepted the call.

It should be here mentioned that Elder David Barrow died about that time, much lamented, notwithstanding he had grieved so many of his brethren by his zeal as one of the founders of the Association of Baptists, known as *The Friends of Humanity.* But those who opposed, and even those who persecuted him, acknowledged, at last, that he was one of the best of men.

It ought to be added, also, that John Smith had continued to invite this bold man, as long as he lived, into his pulpit at Grassy Lick; for he had resolved never to cast a stone at him, nor to hold the clothes of those who did. During Elder Barrow's last illness, he had visited him as a brother; and. though differing from him in some of his opinions, had conversed freely and affectionately with him on the subject of emancipation.

"I have no more doubt," said David Barrow, in the last words that he ever spoke to his friend, "that God will one day deliver the African from slavery, than that he once rescued Israel, with an outstretched arm, from the bondage of Egypt. Poor Kentucky! Poor Kentucky!"

But the excitement which had grown out of this early movement to abolish slavery in Kentucky subsided soon after the death of David Barrow. All estrangements were in time reconciled; and every trace of the impression which had been made on the public mind, seems, in a few years to have disappeared.

It was among the strenuous Calvinists of Lulbegrud, then, who had not enjoyed the ministrations of John Smith since 1823, that the dissatisfaction, already spoken of, first found a decided and formal expression.

It was the custom of each congregation in the District to send, by the hands of duly appointed messengers, an *Annual Letter* to the Association, and to report therein, according to the requirements of the Constitution, the number of members that were in fellowship, the number that had been baptized, dismissed, and excluded, and that had died during the year. Queries and complaints against churches, and even individuals, were often appended; and, sometimes, these inquisitive or censorious postscripts were made the burden of the correspondence.

On the third Saturday in July, 1827, the church at Lulbegrud met, according to custom, to prepare her letter. The Association was to assemble on the following Saturday at Cane Spring, in Madison County—a church which, though south of the Kentucky River, had, at her own request, been received into the North District Association as early as 1803.

Smith, in the meantime, learned that charges would be brought against him; but what they were, he could not definitely ascertain. He knew only that his brethren, generally, censured him, and condemned his doctrine; yet such was his confidence in the power of the truth, that he did not doubt that some of the more pious and thoughtful would stand by him in the proclamation and defense of the ancient Gospel.

But as the day for the meeting of the Association drew nigh, he saw that professed friends began to fall away from him. Many that had often listened to his plea for reform stood off, and awaited the action of his enemies. He was left, in fact, almost alone; yet, while he deeply felt his isolation, he clung the more closely to the cause he loved, and now girded himself for the conflict.

Some time before the meeting of the Association, one of his children was taken sick. He lay for weeks in his little bed, racked with torturing pains, and slowly wasted away. For sixteen days and nights the father kept an almost sleepless watch at the bedside. On the 26th of July, the agonies of the little sufferer ceased, and they laid him to rest among the vines of the garden. As they walked back from the grave, the faithful preacher reminded his wife that the Association would meet on the next day, at Cane Spring. "Many things will be said against me," he gently urged, "and no one will be there to defend me, or to speak a word for the cause we love. I must then go. But, wife, I can not leave you here alone in your bereavement; so I beg you to go along with me."

Call it not weakness, if, in that dark hour, John Smith, forsaken by friends, and afflicted of God, turned to his stricken wife for comfort and support.

They had now five children, the oldest of whom was but ten years of age. To leave them at home with strangers would be wrong; the mother's heart would not consent. Joshua Hurt, therefore, an unmarried brother, for whom the little boy that died was named, urged her to go, and promised to stay with the children himself, and to take good care of them, till she returned. She was finally persuaded, and the horses were hastily made ready for the journey, for an appointment to preach that very night, at Howard's Creek, twenty miles distant, had been sent on some time before.

They started immediately, and reached the neighborhood of Howard's Creek just at dark. The preacher that had been requested to make the appointment for him had refused to do it, but had warned the people against this apostate from the faith. But they had learned, from other sources, that John Smith would preach in the neighborhood that night; and they came to hear him.

His wife was much distressed by these increasing evidences of ill-feeling toward him; and she anxiously inquired, as they rode along together next day, what he would do if they should say anything against him in the Association.

"Wife," said he, "they will hear of our bereavement, and feel too much for our distress to do anything unkind."

He reached the meeting-house in good time, on Saturday, and took his seat among his brethren as a messenger from the church at Grassy Lick.

Elder David Chenault, of Cane Spring, presided as Moderator, an office which he had filled successively for many years. He was comparatively unlearned in books, having read but little beyond his Calvinian text; but the sternness of his character, his sober piety, and his impenetrable orthodoxy, had given him influence among the more rigid of the Baptists

When the name of Lulbegrud was called, her letter was presented and read, and Smith then learned the nature of the charges against him. After setting forth the general condition of the church, the letter grievously complained that one of their preachers had departed from Baptist usage in several particulars, in substance, to-wit:

1.   That, while it is the custom of Baptists to use as the Word of God King James's translation, he had, on two or three occasions in public, and often privately in his family, read from Alexander Campbell's translation.

2. That, while it is the custom in the ceremony of baptism to take the candidate into the water, and solemnly pronounce the words, "I baptize you, my brother, in the name of the Father and of the Son and of the *Holy Ghost,*" he, on the contrary, is in the habit of saying, "*By the authority of Jesus Christ,* I *immerse* you *into* the name of the Father and of the Son and of the *Holy Spirit.*"

"And there is no *Ghost* in it at all," indignantly exclaimed some one present.

3. That, in administering the Lord's Supper, while it is the custom of the Baptists for an ordained preacher to stand at the table and give thanks, and break the loaf into bits, or morsels, small enough to be readily taken into the mouth, and then for the deacons to pass these around in a plate, or some like convenience, yet he leaves the bread in large pieces, teaching that each communicant should break it for himself.

As some ground for this last charge, it must be admitted that Smith had, on several occasions, declared, that, as Christ's body had been broken for all, each should break the loaf for himself; that anciently the disciples came together to break bread for themselves, and not to see it done by the holier fingers of some preacher or priest.

In due time the queries and complaints of the several churches were taken up. As other congregations, besides Lulbegrud, complained of the reading of the New Translation, they proceeded, first of all, to the consideration of that offense, as understood to be charged against John Smith.

The indictment sent up by Lulbegrud closed with words like these: "We do not of ourselves know that any brother has been guilty of all these departures from Baptist usage; but we have been assured by reliable authority." Having heard the accusations again read, Smith arose, and, fixing on the solemn face of the Moderator a look of kind but defiant humor, he remarked:

"My brethren from Lulbegrud need not feel the least concern for evidence to sustain their charges; I plead guilty to them all."

According to the usual order of business, the consideration of such matters should have been postponed till Monday. But an impatient spirit of controversy seized the Association: and much wrangling, about established usages and ancient landmarks, occurred on Saturday. By a rule of decorum no member was allowed to speak more than twice on the same subject without the consent of the Association; nor more than once on any proposition, until all had spoken that might wish to speak.

Smith was now assailed on the right hand and on the left; for there were more than fifty messengers present, and every speaker among them rose up against him. He wasted some irony, and flung away upon them a pearl or two of truth in repartee and rejoinder, during the earlier part of the discussion, intending to reply at length after the opposition had expended all its strength. But by this improvidence of speech he had placed himself at the mercy of his enemies; for, when he came to make his defense in form, he was abruptly called to order—he had already spoken twice, and could not speak again without the consent of the house. He now begged for the privilege of replying fully to the things that had been said against him; but, in all that assembly of messengers, he had not one friend to support so reasonable a request. He sat down, with more of sorrow than of anger in his heart. He had turned from the grave of his child to come and brave the presence of those who were stirred up against him; he had come to defend his reputation, and to conciliate, if he could, the opposition that he had provoked. But instead of receiving sympathy, or even justice, at their hands, he was made to feel that he was but an outlaw among his brethren. Yet he continued to mingle, without offense, in their little social circles, and to maintain, under all the provocations of the hour, a serene mind and a prudent tongue.

Just before the adjournment, on Saturday, the Moderator announced to the messengers and strangers present, that the people of the neighborhood were all prepared to enter- tain them; and that they must feel free to go wherever they wished, for they would find a Christian welcome every- where. Elder Chenault's residence was only about half a mile from Cane Spring—in fact, the meeting-house was on his farm—and Smith, supposing that his more influential opponents would lodge with him, resolved to go and spend the night with them. He thought that it would be better for the cause to go with his enemies than to stay and enjoy the company of his friends. He had learned, also, that cer- tain brethren from Cumberland and Wayne, who had come as corresponding messengers, would be at the elder's house that night, and he wished to talk with them about his present religious views, before they returned home. He said to his wife, therefore, who still sat in the meeting-house with her friends while the crowd were slowly dispersing in the yard:

"Nancy, several brethren are here from our old home, and they are all going to brother David's to-night, and I intend to go there too."

"They do not want you to go, Mr. Smith," said his wife.

"I know it, Nancy," replied he, "and that is one reason why I want to go."

"But," she replied, "I have not been invited, and, of course, they will not expect *me*."

Here was an unexpected dilemma. He could not ask his wife to do what her sense of propriety forbade; and yet, duty to himself and the cause required him to be, for the night at least, a guest of the Moderator.

But John Smith never cared for dilemmas. "Will you go," said he, "if brother Chenault invites you?"

"Certainly I will," said his wife.

He went immediately to the door, and, looking over the crowd that still filled the yard, discovered the Moderator just passing out through the gate. Standing on the steps, he called, with a voice which all the people heard:

"Brother Chenault, I am going to your house, to-night;

but my wife here says that she is unwilling to go unless you invite her."

"'Come along, sister; come along!" said he; "we have nothing against *you*."

"There, Nancy!" said he, turning to his wife, "brother Davy says you must come along. Now, let us go."

And to David Chenault's they went, and, of course, they were most kindly received.

He met his opponents, as he expected; and there, too, he found messengers from the Cumberland River Association, whose esteem he wished, if possible, to retain.

The afternoon was warm, and chairs were brought out and placed under the shade-trees in the yard. When all were seated, he began:

"Brother Collier, and you other brethren from the Cumberland River Association, from what you heard to-day you must think that I have gone wild in religious matters. Here around me sit the very brethren who have accused me; and now I beg them, as they love truth and justice, to name the errors that I have committed. Here, at least, I may have the liberty of speaking in my own defense."

To these words there was no reply, and he continued:

"Concerning my reading of the New Translation, perhaps enough was said to-day. But I have been accused also of changing the formulary words of baptism. Brethren, as all authority was given to the Son, and as the apostles went forth by that authority to preach the Gospel and to immerse, is it repugnant to good sense, or to the Word of God, to say, now, that we baptize by the authority of Jesus Christ? Will you, who condemn me, tell me, too, if you can, the difference between baptizing and immersing? And, finally, is not a *ghost* the spirit of a dead man? Is it not a term unfit to be applied to the Holy Spirit? Do you say that a man must be born of water and of the ghost? Or, that God is a ghost, and that we must worship him as such?"

He discussed these points fully, but he could elicit nothing in reply.

He then spoke of his manner of distributing the loaf, and showed that it was consonant with Scripture and reason for the disciples themselves to break the loaf, which is but an emblem of the body that was broken for them. John

Taylor, who was present, and had sat an attentive listener all the time, now remarked, with emphasis:

"Brethren, I believe that on this point brother Smith is right, and I shall introduce his mode of breaking bread among my own churches."

Stephen Collier also approved; but the rest were silent. Smith then turned to his opposers, and earnestly entreated them to point out a single departure that he had made from Baptist usage, except where Baptist usage had departed from the Word of God. Still they made him no reply.

"Then, brethren of the Cumberland Association," said he, with earnest dignity of manner, "you may go home, and tell those who know me there, and whom I still love as I did, exactly where I stand."

On Monday, the complaints of Lulbegrud were formally taken up. One after another of his opponents arose, and, waxing warm with zeal, boldly asserted that the New Translation was not the Word of God. The Moderator sat upon his chair, gathering warmth and strength for the final blow. When each less distinguished brother had spoken, he called some one to preside, and descending to the floor, closed the argument against the translation by saying that he had never seen the book, and never wished to see it. "But Elder Waller," said he, "did right when he burnt it to ashes." That elder, it seems, after comparing the translation with the common version, had burnt it in January.

Smith at last gained the floor. The love of truth and of his brethren, mingling in a heart chastened by recent affliction, and humbled by a sense of loneliness, made him eloquent. Having replied to the charges, and rebuked the unkind spirit that had assailed him, he turned in conclusion to a certain elder that had declared the King's version to be the only Word of God, and asked whether he really meant to say it.

"Yes," said the elder, bravely, "I said so, and I still say it."

"How long, my brother," said Smith, "has it been since the king made his translation?"

"I don't know," said the elder, defiantly ignorant.

"Was it not about two hundred and twenty years ago?"

asked Smith of the clerk, who, perhaps, had read more than his brethren.

"I believe it has been about that time," he replied.

"Then is it not a pity," continued Smith. "that the apostles left the world and the Church without any Word of God for fifteen hundred years? for, as these intelligent citizens around me know, they wrote in Greek, without the least knowledge of the language into which King James, fifteen hundred years afterward, had their writings translated! But, if nothing is the Word of God but the King's version, do you not, brethren, pity the Dutch, who have not that version, and who could not read one word of it, if they had it?"

His remarks produced a fine impression on the minds of the people that crowded the house. In fact, the manifestations of sympathy for him were unrestrained, and some disorder ensued. Excited by the fact, which could not be disguised, that the verdict of the people was in his favor, the anger of his opponents waxed hot. Some scowled upon him; and one, unable to bear it any longer, suddenly sprang to his feet. He gnashed his teeth, and stamping the floor, exclaimed:

"Brother Moderator, I can not stand it! I would rather die than be run over in this way by a Campbellite!" and he shook his orthodox fist in the Campbellite's face.

Smith, who had, during the whole of this extraordinary scene, preserved a kind and tranquil temper, turned this last indiscretion to the benefit of the cause.

"Brother Moderator," said he, dispassionately, "I came here to defend myself against charges of wrong-doing, that, I feared, might affect my usefulness, if they were not refuted. I have stood for two days before you, alone, and, accused by all my brethren, trying, in the very presence of an overwhelming opposition, to vindicate an humble name from the charge of infidelity to the truth I love. But, friends," said he, turning to the audience, "if this is the fruit of that Spirit whose influence in conversion I am charged with denying, then do I plead guilty to that charge. For, whether such a spirit as this is from God or not, I leave you all to judge."

Fifteen or twenty of the more influential brethren now withdrew to consult together, requesting the Association to remain in session till they returned. They concluded that

John Smith was too good and great a man to be spared from the Church, and too wise to fall away into any dangerous heresies; and that time should be allowed him for reflection. They agreed, therefore, to recommend that the whole matter be laid over for one year, feeling assured that by that time the heresy of *Campbellism* would be forgotten, and Smith would return to the faith of his fathers.

The Association, without debate, adopted the suggestion; they added, however, a protest against any translation of the Scriptures except that which was in common use, and they advised the sister churches to do likewise.

They then adjourned, to meet again at Lulbegrud, on the fourth Saturday in July, 1828.

CHAPTER XVIII.

JOHN SMITH returned home, and began to reflect on his recent experience. His reply to his brethren, at Cane Spring, had won for him friends among those who were without; but he looked over the District in vain to find one minister to whom he could go for counsel or support. His financial embarrassments continued to weigh heavily upon his heart. His bank debt, still unpaid, destroyed his peace of mind; and, though indulgence had been given, it served only to protract his disquietude. There was no prospect of help from the churches, nor, indeed, from any other source; so that he was left to bear all his burdens alone. After consultation with his wife, he resolved, first of all, to release himself from debt. But, to do this, he must stay at home, and, dispensing with hired help, cultivate his farm with his own hands. He had once thought of giving up all that he had, and of returning, penniless, to the frontier whence he came; but the reflection that such a course, now, would seem to be an abandonment of the truth which he had professed, or an ignoble flight from persecution on its account, forced him to dismiss the thought. He took up his ax, and went out to work. Day after day, he toiled alone in the woods, with maul and wedge and handspike, from early dawn till the stars came out at night. He thus worked on until the close of the year 1827, when God, who had called and prepared him to preach the Gospel of His Son, now, by one of those mysterious, but not uncommon, impulses which move like inspiration, took him away from his log-heaps, and brought him to stand before the people once more.

One day, in the month of January, as he was bending to his labors in those lonesome, sleety woods, he thought of the cause that he loved, and remembered that there was no one in all the land to advocate it but himself. He thought, too, of the prediction made at Cane Spring—that in one year he would see his errors, and the heresy which he had preached would be forgotten. The storm, it was true, had subsided; but would not his silence now be construed as an acknowledgment that he had erred? He threw down his ax at the thought, and went to his house; he dropped off his coarse apron at the feet of his wife; and, filled with enthusiasm, he exclaimed:

"Nancy, I shall work no more! Get whom you please to carry on the farm, but do not call on me! In all the land, there is not one soul to open his mouth in defense of the best cause under the sun! I am determined, from this time forth, to preach the Gospel, and leave the consequences to God."

His wife had cordially entered with him into all his little schemes of economy and finance, and, with frugal and industrious hands, had been toiling and saving to help him pay off his debt. Now, she as readily caught his new spirit, and as cheerfully accepted the responsibilities of her new position—agreeing to carry on the farm, to provide for the family, and to relieve him of every temporal care, while he should give himself wholly to the preaching of the Word.

So thoroughly in earnest was he, that he did not wait for opportunity or occasion to begin his work. A mile or two off was the schoolhouse of a young man named Absalom Rice, whom he had already baptized. He walked over, and requested the master to announce, through the children, that he would preach that evening at the house of a neighbor by the name of Mosley, and that he wished all to come and hear him. Returning to his house, he sat down, and, with his wife's assistance, arranged the order of his appointments for the week. Possibly, he might be rejected from the houses of the people; for it was generally understood, that, though the further consideration of the charges against him had been postponed for a year, yet he was virtually under the censure of the Association. It required no little courage, on the part of his brethren, to open their houses to him, that he might inculcate the very heresies for which he had already been condemned. Fortunately, many of his neighbors were members of the church at Spencer—a congregation composed at first, as we have said, of Separate Baptists, and constituted on the Scriptures alone. They, consequently, had but little regard for distinctive, speculative dogmas. Before that congregation, it will be remembered, he had first publicly avowed his dissatisfaction with Calvinism; and there, too, he had first baptized penitent believers on the simple profession of their faith in Jesus.

Among the first fruits of the Ancient Gospel at Spencer, were Jacob Coons and Absalom Rice—two young men, who presented themselves for immersion, the former in 1825, the latter, not long afterward. They had been diligent students of the Scriptures, and had learned to discriminate between the facts of the Gospel and the speculations of men. Smith had sympathized with them through all the stages of their spiritual development, and had anxiously watched till the Christ was formed within them.

When young Coons came forward, Smith, who had extended the invitation, told him *to go on in his own way,* and say to the church whatever he pleased. The candidate remarked that he had been, for some time, concerned on the subject of religion, but had seen no strange sights and had heard no strange sounds; that he believed with all his heart that Jesus was the Christ, and wished to obey him.

Smith arose and said: "Brethren, with the Bible in my hand, if I were to die for it, I do not know what other question to ask him!" Coons was examined no further, but was admitted to baptism on that simple confession. This incident, occurring as early as October, 1825, and taking place with the approbation of a church that had no constitution or creed but the inspired Word, may be recorded as the first exemplification of the Ancient Order within the bounds of the District, if not of the State.

Jacob Coons had, some time before his immersion, married the daughter of a Presbyterian clergyman, who lived in the neighborhood. She had been baptized in her infancy; but at the time of her marriage, she was a thoughtless, worldly-minded woman. Jacob's immersion displeased her family, who had hoped to see him one day in full religious accord with his wife. Fearing now that the influence of his example and teaching might lead her from the faith of her church, they let pass no opportunity of confirming her in her early religious belief. They loaned her books and pamphlets, and urged her to read them with her husband, for whose salvation also they seemed to feel a deep concern. They recommended especially to her perusal a tract by Finley on the doctrine of *Infant Church Membership.* The impression which that pamphlet made on her mind, disturbed Jacob; for, after reading it, she declared with emphasis, that it was God's truth. In his perplexity, he laid the matter before Smith, and begged his advice.

"Does your wife profess to be a Christian?" Smith inquired.

"She acknowledges that she is a vain and giddy creature," said he; "and she even confessed to me the other day that she was a great sinner."

"Inquire of her, then, whether she is in the Church or not. If she says that she is, ask her if it is right for such a sinner to be in the Church of God; if she says that she is not, then ask her when they turned her out."

Jacob did as he was instructed; his wife denied that she was a member of the Church, but was confounded when asked when and why they had excluded her.

In her perplexity, she went to see her father, and Jacob, anxious for truth's sake and his wife's, went along with her, to hear the explanation.

"Father," said Jane, "am I a member of the Church?"

"Yes, my daughter, I initiated you when you were an infant."

"But, father, you know that I have always been a worldly-minded girl; do you think that it is right for me to say that I am in the Church?"

"Daughter," replied he, "you remember that, in the Church, there are both tares and wheat; so the Savior teaches in the parable. You are but a tare, Jane! you are but a tare, I fear!"

This was satisfactory to her; but Jacob, still perplexed, reported, the next day, the whole matter to his friend and pastor. After receiving from him the proper counsel, he returned home.

"Jane," said he, carefully following the advice of Smith, "didn't your father say that *he* had put you into the Church when you were a child?"

"Yes, but he said that I was only a tare," replied his wife.

"Your father surely could not have put you there, Jane; for the Book says, he that sows the tares is *the devil!*"

Jane read, and forthwith went again to her father to have this startling difficulty solved.

"Father," said she, "did you not tell me that you had initiated me into the Church yourself?"

"Yes, my daughter; but what is it that bothers you now?"

"Why, father, look! *He that sows the tares is the devil!*"

The old man looked at the passage, and groaning aloud, began to walk the floor; but he made his daughter no reply.

From that time, Jane listened to her husband's expositions of Scripture, and, under his teachings, soon presented herself for immersion.

Absalom Rice, early taught by pious parents of the Baptist Church to love the Scriptures, had long sought religion according to the manner of the times; but not experiencing the usual operations of the Spirit, he had stood aloof from the Church, though assured by his teachers that it was unnecessary for some persons to wait for special manifestations. Still, his theory of religion demanded a miraculous evidence of the Divine favor, and he had prayed continually for it. But his well-balanced temperament unfitted him for such experiences; so that, after fervent praying, and long waiting, he had renounced his theory, and, taking up his New Testament, resolved to do what it enjoined. Just at that time, John Smith, from the pulpit at Spencer, began to preach a simple, evangelical Christianity, and Absalom Rice, and his wife, another close student of the Word, confessed their faith in Jesus as the Messiah of God, and were immersed for the remission of their sins.*

---

*In 1831, Absalom Rice removed to Callaway County, in the State of Missouri. There was at that time, in the county, but one church organized on the Scriptures alone; it was a small congregation, about twenty miles distant from his residence. In a short time, other friends moved out from Kentucky and settled in his neighborhood; and, in 1833, a church was organized, of which he took the oversight; the cause prospered greatly under his ministrations. He still lives—1870—and, though more than three-score and ten, still preaches the same gospel that he heard at old Spencer in 1825, from the lips of John Smith.

A few other such spirits had early been brought in under the influence of John Smith's teaching; and now, in the beginning of the year 1828, they were ready to open their houses to him and welcome him to his appointments. He exhorted his brethren, that came to hear him, to throw away their creeds as bonds of union, and to adopt the Bible alone as the standard of their faith and practice. He called on sinners to believe and obey the Gospel, declaring that Christ died for all, and that whoever would believe on the simple testimony of God's witnesses, and obey him in immersion, would enjoy the pardon of his sins. He urged all, saint and sinner alike, to read and to reflect for themselves, and not to be led off into idle speculations by a partisan clergy. The country around soon blazed with excitement. Many listened with good and honest hearts, and searched the Scriptures to see whether these things were so. The field of his labors gradually widened, until all the churches of the county felt the influence of his zeal. As soon as the season permitted, he met the people in the woods; and, from the rude stand, or the trunk of a fallen tree, he proclaimed the Gospel in its simplicity and power. At Spencer, he soon baptized other believers upon a profession of their faith in Jesus; and converts to his doctrine, by hundreds, gathered around him. They caught his own spirit; and in the ardor of their enthusiasm, and, according to the measure of their knowledge and ability, went everywhere preaching the same Gospel. It was not unusual for his new religious friends—men and women—to quit their ordinary business, and to go from house to house, or from grove to grove, and, appealing to the Scriptures as their only authority—a copy of which they always carried in pocket or satchel—to plead for the *Ancient Gospel* and the *Ancient Order of Things.*

When the leaven began thus to work among the churches, some of his friends came to him, and tried to dissuade him from preaching with so much boldness and warmth. "Your more influential Baptist brethren," said they, "will abandon you; you will get nothing for your preaching; your debt will press you to earth; and your farm and home must eventually be given up."

"Conscience," said he, "is an article that I have never

yet brought into market; but, should I offer it for sale, Montgomery County, with all its lands and houses, would not be enough to buy it, much less that farm of one hundred acres."

His old Calvinistic brethren, who feared to meet him in debate, tried to impede the progress of the new heresy by censuring or ridiculing the young, who, generally, were the first to accept his teachings. When they met a young Reformer by himself, they would assail him with reproof and argument, perplex him with obscure texts of Holy Writ, and overpower him with ponderous words about Predestination and Free Will. No art, either, was left untried to entice them back into the old paths again. But when discomfited by these attacks, the young disciples would go to their pastors, sometimes by night, and, supplying themselves with weapons from his arsenal, turn upon their opponents with fresh courage, and put them to flight. A young man who lived about two miles from Smith's house, having embraced the new faith, found himself, one evening, while debating with the family, sadly in want of an argument to sustain his position: leaving the fireside abruptly, he ran to the house of his pastor, and, getting from him the proof that he needed, returned, and, almost in the same hour, silenced the logic of his Calvinistic father. Whenever Smith paused for awhile in his labors and came home to seek a day's rest in the bosom of his family, his young brethren flocked around him, and he often wore away the nights of his sojourn in giving them counsel and instruction.

Taught by observation, and his own experience, how prone young minds are to lean with almost religious trust on the preacher, he tried to save them from such a bondage to human authority by leading them to the Scriptures as the only Oracle of God. He would tell them that he had unconsciously preached error for many years to people that never knew it, simply because he and they were alike ignorant of the Scriptures; but that, now, since they had discarded all human creeds, and professed to stand together on the Bible alone, it behooved them to read it by day and to meditate on it by night; and to be ready, at all times, to cite a *"Thus saith the Lord"* for everything that they held as faith, or imposed on others as duty. Such exhortations, no less than the opposition of brethren, filled the churches with students of the Scriptures. They soon became distinguished for their knowledge and love of the Truth, and for the readiness with which they quoted and applied the Word.

He preached at least two discourses every day, besides filling his regular appointments at Spencer, Mount Sterling, and Grassy Lick; for those meeting-houses were still open to him. He soon began to meet vast crowds of hearers, who listened to him with the most intense interest. Many came a great distance to hear him contrast the Gospel with the old systems of religion, as expounded by the clergy of the times. At all these meetings he was without assistance. None of his ministerial brethren ventured, as yet, to stand up with him before the people. Exhaustive as his arguments were, they aroused, but did not satisfy, inquiry. When he closed a meeting, the young, who wished to learn, and the old, who would refute, still gathered around him and pressed their earnest questions on him. They crowded to his side as he rode along the highways. Little congregations followed him from house to house, and sat with him at hospitable firesides, where he himself was but a guest, and hung on his words till the night was far spent.

He often baptized, at night, those who had made a profession of their faith during the day; for he could seldom tarry till the morning, and he did not think it right to postpone obedience to the Lord's command. Many a night, in that memorable year, the torches and lanterns of the multitudes flared on the ghostly sycamores that grew along the streams, while soul-stirring songs, from hundreds of voices, rolled over the waters, and died away in the dark and distant forests.

His intemperate zeal threatened, at last, to bring on disease. But he disregarded sickness, and moved forward in his work with an enthusiasm that never languished. He was once seized with a painful disorder while on his way to his regular meeting at Grassy Lick. A great crowd was expecting him, for it was to be an important occasion. He had many friends in that church, but he had not yet baptized any converts in the neighborhood. Now he was about to make an earnest appeal to the young men about Grassy Lick, some of whom, he knew, already believed. When he came upon the ground, he was pale and tremulous from exhaustion, and he had to confess that he was unable to preach. He lay down to rest in the yard near the house, while the congregation, broken into little, social groups, dispersed through the grove. As he lay there, faint and suffering, he overheard a conversation between Reuben McDannold, a firm Calvinist, and General Samuel L. Williams, who, though not a member of the church, was one of his most devoted personal friends, and in full sympathy with his religious views.

"Why is it, General," said McDannold, "that, while brother Smith has immersed so many at Mount Sterling, and Spencer, and other places, he has not baptized a single man at Grassy Lick?"

"I will tell you," replied the General; "your brethren long ago taught us that we can do nothing of ourselves, but that we must all wait the Lord's time."

"But that can not be the reason, at least, for your own impenitence, General," replied the Calvinist; "for you say that you do not believe our Gospel, and yet you refuse to be saved even by your own!"

"True," replied he, "I do not believe one word of your doctrine; but your preachers have so hammered it into the people, that, though we now reject it as absurd, we still strangely act under its influence."

This conversation aroused the sick man, and he now went into the house, nerved by the thought that, perhaps, many of the people of Grassy Lick were, like his friend, still under the influence of errors that they had already renounced. The multitude crowded in after him; inspiring songs arose, and the speaker, who seemed to be moved by some supernatural energy, ascended the pulpit. He began his argument; but the excitement soon overcame him, and he begged his audience to indulge him in a moment's rest. Eight times thus, during the delivery of that discourse, distressing paroxysms forced him down; but he as often rallied his prostrate energies, and went on with his argument. During this singular strife between the spirit and the flesh, his brethren frequently remonstrated, and begged him to desist, but without effect. A physician of the neighborhood, also, in vain warned him of the probable consequences of his indiscretion. He still spoke on, though in pain and weakness, till, with a most persuasive exhortation, he closed his address. Many were that day convinced of error, or of sin; and a generous revival soon warmed up even the good old Calvinists of Grassy Lick.

CHAPTER XIX.

ALTHOUGH the Union of 1801, on the *Terms* already given to the reader, had been cordially ratified by the Separate Baptists of Kentucky, and by all the forty-six churches of the Elkhorn Association, save one, yet the weakness of the bond that held them together soon became apparent.

Not long after the act of union, several churches were dropped from the Associations to which they belonged, on account of their Unitarian sentiments. Many persons were excluded for unsound opinions concerning the future punishment of the wicked. The Emancipationists, generally, withdrew from the Union, and, being numerous, constituted themselves into an independent body, under the leadership of David Barrow and others. But the most serious defection was the withdrawal of several prominent ministers and influential churches from the Elkhorn Association, and the formation of a new and, for some time, antagonistic body, under the name of the *Licking Association of Particular Baptists*. This separation grew out of certain matters of discipline, which, in the beginning, concerned but a single congregation—the same, by-the-by, that had opposed the union in 1801. But other churches, the press, and, finally, the entire Association, were involved in the controversy. The withdrawing ministers, holding to the dogma of "Particular Atonement," styled themselves *Particular Baptists*, generously providing that their new name should not be allowed to interrupt their correspondence with such churches as might choose to remain in the Union. They held strictly to every item of doctrine as set forth in the creed of the Regular Baptists, and condemned, in strong language, those who departed therefrom.

"The day in which we live," said they, in 1818, "is dark and gloomy; many are engaged in corrupting the Scriptures, by propagating doctrines to seduce the people from the truths of the Gospel. The pretender—who tells you that Christ died for the sins of all the world, and who says that he has Christ and salvation to offer you on the condition of your obedience, faith, and repentance, set him down as a blind guide."

"Some of the churches," continued they, referring to the more liberal Baptists, "are in the habit of receiving members without special examination; some of those received, perhaps, holding to the doctrine of particular unconditional election, while others hold to that of conditional election. This brings on schisms and divisions in the body.

"See the corruption and errors of doctrine and discipline that have already crept into society, and the further innovations that they are still making! And yet, degenerate sons of the Church are constituting churches vaguely on the Bible, as if the words and doctrines of that precious book had no definite meaning attached to them! This is calculated to open the flood-gates of error, and to increase numbers at the expense of the truth. Avoid such; have no fellowship with them; 'receive them not into your houses, neither bid them God-speed.' Those who have honest and right views of the Word of God, are not afraid to publish them to the world, to contend earnestly for them, and to unite in a covenant to support them."

In 1825, North District Association, looking upon these divisions in sorrow, addressed the following words to the churches—words which were sent forth, with the name of John Smith, as Moderator, subscribed:

"Schisms and divisions," said they, "have done much to impede our progress in Kentucky. Short as the period is, since the first churches were constituted in our State, it has been marked by several divisions, each productive of widely-extended distress. We now have six kinds of Baptists, all of which—the *Universalists* and the *Friends of Humanity* excepted—are numerous; they are supplied with preachers, and they bid fair to extend and increase in numbers.

"What is to be the end of these things? They are a

source of sorrow and anguish to some, at least, among us. Must they be perpetual? Are these wounds incurable? Who can tell but that we—the United Baptists—are to be the happy instruments to heal these splits and schisms? Let us make the first advances, and He who said, 'Blessed are the peacemakers,' will crown our efforts with success."

As an illustration of the spirit of schism, which at that time was so rife in the land, we may cite the case of a church which stood connected with a certain Association of United Baptists. It had been constituted, in early times, on the Bible as the only creed of Christians. After many years of prosperity, it received into its membership a preacher who had some zeal for orthodoxy; and, in deference to him, the church added to its inspired Constitution a few articles explanatory of the received doctrine of grace. The preacher, on account of the infirmities of age, did not long discharge the duties of his office. Another was invited to take membership, with a view to the better edification of the brethren. But he insisted, as a condition of becoming their pastor, that they should make still further additions to their creed; and that, as a declaration of their orthodoxy, they should take the name of *Particular Baptists*. This they agreed to do; and he was duly installed as their pastor. But this proceeding gave offense to the milder brethren, and several of them went off and joined other congregations.

Consistency now required the unstable church to withdraw from the Association, and to join the community of Particular Baptists. But, when the moment for decision came, her members had not the heart to break off from a sisterhood of churches with which they had been so long associated. They, therefore, struck from their creed the dogma of *particularism*, renounced their new name, and reassumed that of the United Baptists—determined, at all hazards, to live and to die in the fellowship of the old Association. But now the more orthodox pastor, and all that believed with him, took offense. Calling for letters, they set themselves afloat; leaving the remnant of the once prosperous church to take care of themselves.

Another illustration of the same spirit may be seen in the attempt of John Smith, in 1825, to induce the church at *Bald Eagle*, in Bath County, to throw away her creed, and to substitute the inspired Book as her rule of practice and her standard of faith. That church had been much disturbed by the efforts of certain extreme Calvinists, to entice her from the general Union, and to associate her with the Licking community. The effort was resisted by Jonathan Smith and other moderate Baptists; and much excitement was produced. A meeting was called to reconcile the two parties, and John Smith was invited by his brother to be present. He went, intending, however, to take no part in a strife in which both sides were evidently wrong.

Elder Thomas came to the conference as the representative of the Particular Baptists, bringing his creed with him, which, of course, was strongly Calvinistic; and Jonathan Smith appeared with his milder articles of faith. Discussion failed to bring the parties together, and every attempt at compromise seemed but to widen the breach between them.

At length John Smith arose, and, approaching the table, which was in full view of the audience, he placed the two creeds before him, one on each end of the table, and then put the Bible between them.

"Since, brethren," said he, "neither will accept the creed of the other, let both come together on this Bible, as the only Word of God, and the only bond of union."

"It will never do!" said Elder Thomas, hastily, and with much excitement. "It will not do at all! Such a course would let in Arians, Arminians, and every other kind of errorists! It will never do!"

"I can not agree with my brother," replied Smith. "In my judgment, the Word of God excludes all sectarians. But, if the Bible, as he says, would admit them, how dares he form a creed to reject them."

But his proposition met with no favor, and the two parties remained divided.

One of the measures of reform, therefore, which Smith advocated most earnestly, in 1828, was the union of all Christians on the basis of *faith in Jesus as the Messiah, and obedience to him as the only Head of the Church.* The belief of one great fact on the testimony of the inspired writers, and submission to one outward ordinance expressive of that belief, he contended was all that heaven required of any man in order to his admission into the Church.* While to sinners he preached that great fact, and enjoined upon them obedience to that one institution, to the several discordant sects of Baptists he declared that their one faith and one baptism already made them brethren, and, as the subjects of one Lord and children of one Father, they should unite as one body, without regard to differences of opinion.

Believing that authoritative creeds were divisive in their tendency, and, therefore, contrary to the will of God, he boldly, but prudently, assailed the confessions and covenants of the denominations, and insisted, as the first step toward a Scriptural union, that these walls of separation should be torn down. These once removed, he believed that the people of Christ would come together on the common ground of faith in him, and obedience to his commandments. It was not the opinions, which had found expression in the creeds, so much as the creeds themselves as bonds of union, that he opposed; for, in his view, any human creed, whatever might be its doctrines, was schismatical, if its adoption was made a test of character or a condition of fellowship.

But the proposed ground of union was soon found to be practically incompatible, not only with ecclesiastical creeds and covenants, as such, but with some of the opinions, also, which generally prevailed among the churches. A penitent believer, for example, according to the *ancient order*, was not to be so much as asked whether he was a Calvinist or an Arminian, a Trinitarian or a Unitarian; and yet his baptism on the simple profession of his faith in Jesus, without examination of his experience, was at variance with the popular theories of conversion.

Whether, therefore, he preached the primitive Gospel to sinners, or presented it as a ground of union among Christians, he found that he must make war upon both creeds and opinions. Especially when he began to call upon the churches to abandon every ordinance of human origin, and to walk according to the example of the primitive churches, he found that he set himself in opposition to every sect in the land, presenting in the aggregate of his teachings, what his opponents called a *new religion*, altogether different

* Christian Baptist, vol. 1.

from the prevailing forms of denominationalism. Thus he began, by inveighing against creeds and party names; but his plea soon grew to be radical and revolutionary in its demands, until, at last, in harmony with the doctrine of Mr. Campbell, he assumed that the churches in general had apostatized from the original faith and order; and that, to reform them, not only must creeds and sects of every name be destroyed, but the Apostolic Gospel and Order of things must be restored.

As a proclamation, the Ancient Gospel, as it was termed, was simply the joyful tidings that the remission of sins, and the gift of the Holy Spirit, were assured to every penitent believer on submission to the ordinance of Christian baptism.

As a theory, or systematic arrangement of ideas, in which form it was sometimes presented in the teachings of that day,[*] it consisted of six points, to-wit: Faith, Repentance. Baptism, Remission of Sins, the Gift of the Holy Spirit, and the Resurrection. These items were sometimes grouped into triads. The first, being conditions or duties required of man: the second, being promises or gifts bestowed by God. Should the sinner believe, repent, and be baptized, God promises to remit his sins, to give him the Holy Spirit, and, if faithful unto death, to raise him again to eternal life. Respecting the sinner and his sin, six things further were usually considered, to-wit: the love, the practice, the state, the guilt, the power, and the punishment of sin. Faith was represented as destroying the love of sin; repentance, the practice of sin; and baptism, the state of sin; while pardon removed its guilt; the Holy Spirit, its power; and the resurrection, its punishment.

While the Ancient Gospel was thus supposed to embrace everything in the doctrine of Christ necessary to make disciples, the Ancient Order included everything necessary to preserve and perfect them as disciples. It had special reference to the organization and government of the Church; to its worship, its ordinances, its discipline, and its customs; in all of which respects, it professed a strict adherence to the precepts of the Apostles and the example of the primitive churches.

------

[*] "Evangelist," vol. 1, p. 14, by Walter Scott.

Those who, in 1828, came into the churches under the preaching of John Smith, cordially accepted his doctrine on these points. They sat around him, whether in house or grove, with Book in hand, like earnest children in the schools, jealous of their traditions and customs, yet willing to be taught the truth. They advanced more rapidly, however, in knowledge, than in practice; for opinions are more easily changed than customs. Some, for instance, who had renounced the doctrine that the Holy Spirit, by an abstract influence, changes the heart of the sinner, still called for the recital of the usual experience as a prerequisite to baptism.

The work of theoretical instruction, then, was comparatively easy; but it required much address to persuade his converts to reform in conduct as they advanced in knowledge.

Friends rapidly multiplied around him. The churches were almost daily strengthened by accessions from the ranks of the young: and fathers and mothers, too, soon began to lose their interest in the old dogmas, and to turn with delight to the contemplation of the Gospel as the power of God to save every man that believes it.

James Mason, one of the elders of the church at Grassy Lick, in a letter, dated April 19, 1828, remarks:

"John Smith is certainly a host within himself. The sectarian leaders here have found it out, and are barking at him; but the people are following him in crowds, and he is teaching them the Ancient Gospel with astonishing success. You would be amazed to see with what adroitness he handles the weapons burnished and refitted for him in the *Christian Baptist.* The old, profane swearer and the long-professed deist,—many that, to all appearances, were given over to hardness of heart and reprobacy of mind, have bowed to King Jesus. At our last meeting, thirty-six were immersed and added to our church. On last Lord's Day, at Mount Sterling, thirty-seven were immersed, among whom were some of our most respectable citizens—men of the highest position in civil society.

"But I can not deny myself the pleasure of telling you how my soul was filled with joy at seeing a beloved brother, according to the flesh, make the confession. Unconscious of it himself till he heard Brother Smith proclaiming the Ancient

Gospel, he had been a believer in the Lord Jesus Christ for more than twenty-six years; but, because he could not tell what we have always been in the habit of calling a *Christian experience*, he has been kept out of the fold of God ever since, till a few days ago, when he found that to believe in the Lord Jesus Christ, and to obey his commands, was all that the Gospel required; he then went down into the water and told Brother Smith he wished him to say *immerse*, instead of *baptize*. Like the eunuch of old, he is now going on his way rejoicing, as happy a man as can be found."

Revivals, such as those alluded to in this letter, were now of frequent occurrence. In fact, for several months in succession, he immersed about thirty persons every week. These results did not fail to alarm the orthodox even among the distant churches of the Elkhorn, the Licking, the Bracken, and the Boone's Creek Associations. In order to defend the doctrine of grace, as set forth in the creed, some of the ablest ministers of those Associations visited Montgomery, and upheld their distinctive tenets by every argument that they could produce.

One of the most learned of these divines, gathering a large concourse of people together at Grassy Lick, addressed them at much length, and, by means of a pleasing and powerful argument, left them so deeply impressed with the reasonableness of the Calvinian theory that the friends of the Ancient Gospel were no little disconcerted.

He argued that obedience to any physical law presupposes physical life. The plant, for instance, that unfolds its leaves in the light of spring, obeys a vegetable law by the power of a vegetable life, previously imparted. A dead tree puts forth no leaf, or blossom—it can obey no law. In the animal world, also, there are certain physiological laws which each living creature obeys—not by the energy of a vegetable, but of an animal life. Obedience, therefore, does not confer life: the animal must first be made alive, before it can begin to obey. It is so in the spiritual world; there must be spiritual life, before there can be obedience to spiritual law. For argument's sake, indeed, it might be admitted that life is afterward enjoyed only so long as the quickened man continues to obey; but the first act of obedience, whether it be to repent or to believe, is impossible until life is given by the Spirit of God.

"How absurd, then," he concluded, "is the doctrine of some, that the gift of life is conditioned on an act of obedience! Rather is obedience conditioned, in the very nature of things, on the previous gift of life. Without life imparted by the Holy Spirit, then, it would be impossible, not only to obey, but even to understand the law.

"Yea, though I were to read and ponder the Word for a hundred years," said he, "I would not, at the end of that time, unless quickened by the Holy Ghost, have any more knowledge of its meaning, or ability to obey it, than my horse hitched to yonder tree."

At the next regular meeting at Grassy Lick, Smith learned the points of this argument from his brethren, and gave them a brief, but characteristic reply:

"If there is any reason in the argument of my distinguished brother," said he, "then it follows, inevitably, that the devil will never get any of our race, *except the elect.* For if no man can *obey* a natural law without natural life, neither can he *disobey* without natural life. For the same reason, he can never disobey a spiritual law without spiritual life; for, universally, obedience or disobedience to any law presupposes the life to which that law appertains. Now, as sin is the transgression of spiritual law, no one can commit sin till God gives him enough spiritual life to disobey. And as death is the wages of sin, it follows that none can ever die and fall to the devil's share save those only who have been first made alive by the Holy Ghost."

Another minister, who was a leading member of the Licking Association, visited the church at Mount Sterling, already leavened with the new heresy, and sought to restore there the doctrine of the creed touching the nature and extent of the atonement. He faithfully set forth Jesus Christ as the actual surety of his people, and taught, with emphasis, that he had literally paid off the debt, which, as sinners, they owed to God.

Such teaching was at variance with the simplicity of the Gospel as preached by Smith, and, in his judgment, it tended to lead the people into unprofitable controversy. He reminded his brethren, therefore, that such speculations were idle; that they formed no part of the Gospel, and served only to dismember the body of Christ. But while he warned them against confounding any religious system with religion itself, the spirit of inquiry and discussion, then so prevalent in the land, required that they should be armed with brief, cogent arguments against all the more common forms of speculative error.

"If the doctrine be true," said he, "that Christ, as a surety, has actually paid off the sinner's debt, then it follows that God can never forgive any but *the non-elect*. For, if Jesus, as a surety for the elect, has really paid their debt, then God can no longer have any claims upon them. Can a creditor forgive a debtor after his debt has been canceled by his surety? If Jesus, in a like sense, has paid off the debt of my brother, it follows that God has now nothing against him, and, of course, can never forgive him!"

It is said that the brother, thus answered, honestly accepted the conclusion to which his doctrine was reduced, and that he afterward preached it, congratulating the elect in that they needed no forgiveness, and giving over the non-elect to everlasting despair.

It was sometimes the case that, while he was preaching with much success, some jealous brother would call away the attention of the people from him by gathering the orthodox together in the neighborhood and stirring them up to a counter revival. His mode of replying to such opposition was peculiar. He never suffered it to irritate him; but always met the interference with perfect good humor. Armed at every point against the logic or the malice of his enemies, and penetrating their designs at a glance, he moved about among them with an artless, good-natured sort of familiarity, that made them always dread his approach.

One day, during a revival, after he had baptized about forty persons in the waters of Grassy Lick, he announced that one of the opposing brethren was about to begin a meeting not far off, and would preach that very night; and that he wished them all to go and hear what he had to say. He went himself, and took his seat in the crowd, and looked about him with a face that beamed with kindness on them all. After the preacher had closed his argument, he called for remarks from any brother that might feel disposed to address the congregation.

Smith arose, and, with great fervor, began to exhort every sinner present to believe and obey the Gospel. He called for a song, and the congregation responded with enthusiasm; for many of his own converts were there, and their voices swelled the chorus. As they sang, he went through the congregation, cordially shaking the hands of the people, till the whole assembly, in the warmth of the moment, seemed to glow with brotherly love.

The preacher alone looked with displeasure on the unexpected scene. He stood apart; and when the song grew loud and tremulous, he folded his arms stiffly on his breast, and stifled his sympathy. The obtrusive exhorter at last approached him, too, and held out his hand to him, warm with the grasp of the brethren. But the offended preacher only locked his arms the more closely together, and fixed a stoic look upon the wall before him. With a quiet, sudden force, Smith wrenched his arms apart, and, grasping his rigid hand, shook it in the presence of the people with a strength of fellowship that could not be resisted. The occasion became his own, and the meeting, with all its results, passed into his own hands.

CHAPTER XX.

ONE would misconceive the object of John Smith's preaching to suppose that he wished to build up a new sect, by means of a schism in the North District Association. He still preached and proselyted as a member of the Baptist Church; and those who, under his teaching, had renounced the Calvinian theory of conversion, still lived in formal, if not cordial, fellowship with those who stood resolutely by the old church covenants. True, the two parties were incessantly discussing the new issues; but neither, in the beginning, dreamed of a separation. One was laboring to reform; the other, to reclaim. Smith hoped that all his brethren would one day accept the Ancient Gospel, and adopt the Ancient Order of Things; many of them, on the other hand, looked on his abandonment of the old paths as an error from which he would soon turn, with all whom he had led astray.

The prevalent belief that conversion was the direct and exclusive work of the Holy Ghost, was the most formidable obstacle to his success as a Reformer. The great question, at last, between him and his Calvinistic brethren was, whether faith is produced by testimony or imparted by inspiration; whether, as antecedent to baptism, it should be confessed as a voluntary act of the mind, or experienced as an irresistible influence from above. That the Holy Ghost supernaturally prepares the heart of the sinner to receive the truth, was almost universally held as a first principle of the doctrine of Christ. It was, also, the last dogma of the old system that the Reformers consented to renounce; and, even then, they still loved to hear their younger brethren in Christ tell what wonderful things the Lord had done for their souls.

Old brethren, from habit, still required to be satisfied that the young had experienced the work of grace in their hearts; and even the young themselves, though believing the Gospel on the testimony of the apostles, felt that more should be required of them as a prerequisite to baptism than the mere confession of that belief.

He was, for awhile, much embarrassed by this state of things; and he anxiously wished for the day to arrive when all the congregations, like that at Spencer, would admit to baptism a penitent believer on the simple confession of his heartfelt faith in Jesus. Until that time should come, he boldly preached the Gospel in the words of Peter, and raised no strife with his brethren about the examination of candidates for baptism—satisfied that those whom he instructed in the way of the Lord, would relate no experience at variance with the doctrine that faith comes by hearing the Word of God.

At length an incident occurred at one of his meetings, in the spring of 1828, that relieved him of all further embarrassment in this matter. He was preaching in the woods, on the banks of Slate Creek, in Montgomery County, to a great multitude of people, that had come together from every quarter to hear him. At the close of his discourse, he invited any that believed with the heart that Jesus is the Christ, to come forward and confess that faith before men. Two or three at once presented themselves, and, as usual, gave a brief history of the change through which they had passed. There was present on that occasion, Colonel John T. Mason, who had come out from Virginia, some time before this, and purchased an interest in the iron works on Red River. He was an intelligent gentleman, a lawyer by profession, the father of Governor Mason of Michigan, and justly esteemed one of the first men in Kentucky. He had often heard John Smith contrast the "Ancient Gospel" with the systems of the day, and he well understood the nature of the reform that was now urged.

When the invitation was extended a second time to believers, Colonel Mason arose in the congregation, and, with much dignity of manner, said:

"Mr. Smith, it is my wish to be a Christian, and I now

present myself for that purpose. I do not wish, sir, to blunder at the start. I could tell you much concerning the workings of my mind in reaching my present conclusion, but I do not believe that such a statement is divinely required as a condition of baptism. I believe, with all my heart, that Jesus is the Christ, the Son of God; and upon this simple declaration I wish to be immersed."

The preacher, grasping him warmly by the hand, replied:

"I thank you for this, Colonel Mason. I have long been convinced that there is nothing in the Book that requires a sinner to tell all the workings of his guilty conscience, before he can lawfully be baptized."

He now exhorted the people to wait no longer for miraculous visions or changes; but, if they believed in Jesus the Messiah, to arise and be baptized for the remission of their sins, calling on the name of the Lord.

A dozen persons or more arose, and, following the example of Colonel Mason, were forthwith immersed in the waters of Slate Creek. From that day Smith never received an experience again.

A heresy that thus seemed to deny the direct influence of the Spirit on the heart of the sinner, was, to many, no better than infidelity itself. Under the name of *Campbellism* it was stigmatized as a cold, proud, and unspiritual system of religion that flattered the unregenerate with the promise of the Holy Spirit and of heaven, on the condition of an historical faith, a worldly repentance, and a baptism in water!

Great was the excitement in many congregations when they saw that Smith persisted in immersing men and women without the consent of any church, and without even assuring himself, by the usual examination, that they had been born of the Holy Spirit. But he had now laid aside all reserve; and he not only defended his course as scriptural, but henceforth waged unrelenting war against the popular doctrine of spiritual regeneration. Disciples thus baptized without the usual evidence of conversion, not being received into some of the congregations, he encouraged them to meet together in their own houses for devotional exercises, and the study of the Word. At Sharpsburg, and at Owingsville, in Bath County, he organized them regularly into churches, constituting them on the Scriptures alone as the only creed and code of the disciples of Christ.

On the banks of the Slate, where he had liberated himself and so many of his brethren from the thraldom of an unauthorized custom, he organized a church of one hundred members, and called it *Liberty.* The church at Owingsville numbered fifty members; that at Sharpsburg, thirty-six.

In opposing the doctrine of regeneration by the direct influence of the Holy Spirit, and advocating that of life through the belief of the truth, he offended not only the Calvinist, but the Arminian also; and it was not long till he found himself assailed on all sides by Methodists and Presbyterians as well as Baptists.

Not far from the town of Mount Sterling, on the banks of the Stepstone, in a dense grove of oaks and maples, the Methodists of Montgomery usually held their great campmeetings. The wildest enthusiasm prevailed on these occasions. Religious frenzy seized both saint and sinner, and the multitudes, persuaded that these seasons of refreshing came only from the presence of the Lord, vehemently sang and shouted together. It was the spring of 1828. The Methodists had pitched their tents and spread their straw on the Stepstone for a great revival, and, with prayer and song, they began to invoke the baptism of the Holy Ghost and of fire. Soon some strange influence seized the people: convicted sinners fell upon the ground and cried for mercy, while penitents wept in crowds about the altars. The old saw visions, and the young dreamed dreams. Strange voices fell upon their ears; unseen wings rustled around them; and glorious sights, ever and anon, flitted before their eyes.

Amid these scenes of rapturous disorder, one man leaped from the straw where he had long been agonizing, and, running to a maple near by, up which a wild grape-vine climbed, gazed into its branches with burning eyes, and shouted:

"I have at last found him whom my soul has long been seeking! I see him in the tree-top! Come, friends, and help me get my Savior down!" and he pulled at the hanging vines till he fell exhausted to the ground.

Another, who had for days and months wrestled with

principalities and powers, in the vain hope of a spiritual deliverance, meeting, late one evening, the arch enemy of his soul, as he supposed, in a bodily form, fell upon a harmless wight of the neighborhood with desperate courage, and, striking him to the earth with a sudden blow, pounded the imaginary devil to his heart's content.

Smith's spirit was stirred within him by these things—for he had witnessed some of the scenes on Stepstone—and he determined to lift up his voice against them. As soon as the camp-meeting was over, he announced that he would meet the people on the same spot, and inquire whether such scenes were in harmony with the Word of God; and he invited Mr. Jameson, then the pillar of Methodism in that region, to be present. He chose a week day, as he said, because it was more suitable for the discussion of such a subject than the Lord's day. In the presence of a large assembly of citizens, who wondered at his boldness, he affirmed that the law of the King required everything connected with his worship and the proclamation of his Gospel, to be done decently and in order. The recent exercises of the camp were neither decent nor orderly, and for that reason, they could not be the work of the Good Spirit. If, however, people chose to engage in such extravagances as mere amusements or animal exercises, he had nothing to say against them; if any had a taste for such exhibitions, let them indulge it.

"But," continued he, and he raised his voice and stretched out his arm toward heaven, "they shall not, God being my helper, do such things any longer under the name of religion!"

Jameson replied that the Scriptures, in many places, called on the people of God *to shout;* that if any one, therefore, wanted authority for shouting at a Methodist meeting, he could find it on many a page of Holy Writ.

"But, in the name of all the prophets and apostles," rejoined Smith, "where do we read in the blessed Book that a sinner ever *treed his Savior?*"

A few days afterward, it was announced that another camp-meeting would be held in Bath County, and that Mr. Jameson would be there, to show that such meetings were not only right, but necessary; it was further stated, that if any objected to them, they could come here and make their objections known, or forever afterward hold their peace.

On the former occasion, Smith had opposed these excesses in the presence of his friends: now he was challenged to come into the midst of his enemies, whose wrath he had already stirred up, and speak whatever he had to say. None, but those who knew him well, believed that he would thus venture into the stronghold of his enemy. The day for the sermon of Mr. Jameson came on, and Smith was sick—so sick, in fact, that his friends used all their influence to keep him at home. But he mounted his horse as he was, and repaired to the camp. The preachers and people for many miles around had come together; and when he went in among them, their scorn for the man who had blasphemously ascribed the work of the Holy Spirit to the play and passion of animal blood, was openly manifested. When Mr. Jameson closed his argument, Smith, tottering with weakness, walked to the stand, and, looking composedly around upon a thousand angry faces, again protested, in the name of reason and Scripture, against the excesses that had profaned the Methodist altar.

"Do you think that you can stand alone, sir, against the whole world?" shouted Jameson to him, on that occasion, with much excitement.

"I can, at least, do one of three things," replied Smith, "I can maintain my ground, be whipped, or die!"

"Can't some of you, my brethren, knock off his horns for me?" said a venerable elder to the ministers that sat around. "See how terribly he pushes and gores!"

Smith now notified Jameson that he would, on a certain day, in the court-house, at Mount Sterling, discuss the question, *"Is Methodism the Christianity of the New Testament?"* and he requested him to be present. Accordingly, after much preliminary correspondence, they met at Mount Sterling in public debate.

He thus gained what he had long desired—an opportunity of publicly exposing what he regarded as a fanaticism of the day, and of defending the Ancient Gospel from the misrepresentations of its enemies.

Soon after this he began to immerse many Methodists,

so that he provoked that denomination to even greater jealousy, if possible, than before. His preaching was setting the son against the father, and the daughter against the mother; for he sometimes immersed the children of parents that looked on him as an enemy to religion, and regarded his doctrine with unaffected abhorrence.

"What shall be done with him?" asked Mr. Jameson one day of a Presbyterian elder and physician. "He is distracting society, sowing dissensions in families, and overturning churches; yet the law will do nothing with him."

"You need not give yourself the least uneasiness about John Smith, sir," replied the doctor. "I know something of the human constitution; and no man on earth can continue to do the amount of work that he is doing without breaking himself down. He will not live six months."

Having baptized several members of a certain family in his own neighborhood, he shortly afterward met the father, who had always been his personal friend.

"Good morning, my brother," said Smith to him kindly.

But the old man fixed a scornful look upon him and said: "Don't call me brother, sir! I would rather claim kin with the devil himself!"

"Go, then," said Smith, "and honor thy father!"

While immersing in the neighborhood of Spencer, a young lady presented herself for baptism, much to the astonishment of the congregation, for she had been a zealous Methodist, and was the flower and pride of a Methodist family. Great was the indignation of her friends when they heard that John Smith had corrupted her faith also, and had immersed her for the remission of her sins.

"When you led that dear young girl into the water, sir," said an old Methodist sister, almost bursting with indignation, "you led her that much farther toward hell!"

"Sister," said Smith, in the blandest tone, "when you read your Bible more, and your Discipline less, you will learn that people do not go to that place by water, for there is barely enough on the road to sprinkle a baby!"

A few days after this, several other Methodists were immersed by him. In fact, converts from that sect were received at almost every meeting that he held. The same old lady, seeing so many of her brethren and sisters deserting her, was again moved with wrath, and charged him with a wolf's fondness for Methodist lambs.

"I do love them, sister," said he, "but I can not bear them till they are *well washed.*"

"He surely has a devil," said the offended woman; and she turned away to mourn over the distress that had come upon her Zion.

His teachings were everywhere grossly misrepresented, so that it became necessary for him to spend much of his time in rescuing his doctrine from caricature. The clergy around had great influence with the people, and it was consequently hard to correct their misrepresentations of what he believed and taught. He usually laid off his discourses, which were two or three hours long, in three divisions, according to the objects that he had in view: in the first, he corrected misrepresentations; in the second, he exposed popular errors; and in the third, he presented the simple Gospel to the people.

His wife often remonstrated with him on the frequency and severity of his animadversions on the doctrines of the creeds.

"Nancy," said he to her, one day, holding up before her a glass of water, "can I fill this tumbler with wine, till I have first emptied it of water? Neither can I get the truth into the minds and hearts of the people till I have first disabused them of error."

But opposition served only to brace him up, and he almost courted it; persecution rather pleased him, for it made him strong, and increased the number of his friends. Sometimes he was even threatened with personal violence; and on one occasion, three men conspired together, and bound themselves under a curse, to chastise him. But such things excited in him neither anger nor fear. He had once felt the yoke that now oppressed the people, and, though they might love their bondage, he resolved, if possible, to deliver them from it. He preserved his equanimity, and even cherished kind feelings for his enemies. He smiled with unaffected good humor when they frowned, and blessed them when they cursed. "Kindness," he often said, "is the best sort of revenge, and wins more victories than wrath."

His labors, however, grew daily more and more exhausting. He constantly borrowed time from sleep, never resting during the day, and seldom retiring till after midnight. His hair rapidly turned gray; and his robust form at last began to show the effects of his incessant conflicts and toil.

CHAPTER XXI.

ABOUT that time, a scheme was laid by some of his Pedo-baptist opponents, which threatened to weaken, if not to destroy, his influence with a certain class of his brethren. With the Baptists generally, he held the sentiment that the immersed could not, without injury to the cause of truth, invite the unimmersed to commune with them at the Lord's table. Dr. James Fishback, of Lexington, a man of some learning and decided talents, was invited by certain Methodists to come to Mount Sterling and expose the inconsistency of the doctrine and practice of the Reformers.

In 1824, that able minister had zealously defended the Baptist custom of restricted communion in the Circular Letter of the Elkhorn Association. His argument was in dorsed at the time as a complete vindication of his brethren from the imputation of sectarian bigotry. He seems, however, to have imbibed afterward the sentiments of Robert Hall, of England; for he came, in time, to regard Christian character, and not baptism by immersion, as the scriptural prerequisite to communion.

In 1827, he was the pastor of the *First Baptist Church* in Lexington, Ky., or rather of a church previously known by that name, but which, in that year, began to call itself the *Church of Christ on Mill Street*. This repudiation of the name *Baptist* gave great offense to the Elkhorn Association. Influenced by such men as Jeremiah Vardeman and Jacob Creath, they unanimously rejected the letter of the newly-styled church, and accepted one from the minority, who zealously clung to the old name, and refused to be called simply a "Church of Christ." Moreover, they solemnly warned Dr. Fishback of the awful danger of causing divisions in society by introducing a system of things that would essentially change the name and character of the Baptist denomination; and they adjured him and his brethren in love to return to the Church from which they had rent themselves.

"Dr. Fishback has torn down the Baptist flag," exclaimed Jacob Creath, during the discussion of the resolution to reject the letter of the *Church of Christ on Mill Street*.

"I know that I am a *Baptist*," said a Calvinist, on the same occasion, "but I do not know that I am a *Christian*."

"Where now are these *Mill Street Christians?*" said Jeremiah Vardeman, after the resolution rejecting them had passed. "Let them seek an asylum," said he, "wherever they can find it!"

Dr. Fishback, having thus induced his brethren on *Mill Street* to relinquish their denominational name, easily persuaded them also to accept the teachings of Robert Hall, and to commune with their Pedobaptist neighbors whenever invited to do so. He and his brethren, having been disowned by the Baptists, maintained, for awhile, the peculiar position of an independent and dissociated church, contending, in opposition to the sentiment of many of that day, that a heartfelt faith in Jesus Christ, and a sincere and honest obedience to him, is the only true ground of ecclesiastical union and Christian fellowship.

It was under these circumstances that he was called, by the Methodists of Mount Sterling, to come and speak to the people on the subject of free or unrestricted communion. When he reached that place he learned that John Smith was absent, preaching and baptizing in another part of the District. He was requested, however, to postpone his address for a day or two, in order that Smith might be present. But the Methodists would not consent to any delay, and he proceeded to discuss the question in Smith's absence; and, by his powerful argument, greatly excited the people, and unsettled the minds of even some of the Reformers.

He argued, from Rom. xiv., that it was wrong to make the mode of one's baptism a condition of communion with him, since Christians are commanded to receive one another without regard to differences of opinion.

He argued that the strict communionists are inconsistent in rejecting from their Table believers with whom, nevertheless, they are willing to commune in other acts of worship; "for if we may not break bread with the unimmersed," said he, "neither may we pray or sing with them."

He contended, moreover, that an exclusive Table engenders a sectarian spirit, than which nothing is more opposed to the spirit of Christ.

Especially was it inconsistent in Reformers, such as John Smith, to refuse to sit at the Table of the Lord with Pedobaptists, and yet to commune with the United, or the Particular, Baptists, who, as Smith declared, had apostatized from the religion of the New Testament.

But his main argument was that sprinkling or pouring is baptism to those who honestly esteem it as baptism: for God, he believed, would accept the *honest intention* to obey, and pardon the *unpresumptuous mistake* in the manner of obedience.

When Smith reached home, he was surprised to learn that Dr. Fishback had already delivered his address, and that the religious community was in a state of great excitement. He was distressed to learn, also, that the minds of his young converts, and of some of his older brethren, were much confused by his argument. He felt that an advantage had been gained in his absence by his enemies, and that he must, at any sacrifice, recover the ground which he had lost.

Fortunately, his friend Absalom Rice had noted down every material point in the Doctor's discourse, and from these notes he understood the argument of his opponent. He also learned that Dr. Fishback had, perhaps, already gone into the hills of Red River; for he had appointments to preach there.

Smith rested at home that night; but, early next morning, his horse was at the gate, and he was equipped for a journey.

"When will you be at home?" asked his wife, as usual; for on leaving home, he always set an hour for his return, and, though it might be days, or even weeks, ahead, he seldom disappointed her. He would sometimes ride all night long, in order to keep his word; at other times, he would rein in his horse, lest he should anticipate the hour.

"When shall we look for you again?" she now inquired.

"Nancy," replied he, with unusual earnestness, "never will I put my foot within this door again to the day of my death till I have found Dr. Fishback; for find him I will, if he is on this side of the ocean!"

He went on to town early that morning, before the hour of meeting; for it was known that he had returned home, and an appointment to preach that day had been made for him by his friends. He went in early, that he might learn more definitely the extent of the damage which had been done to the cause. He expected, of course, that the Doctor was on Red River; but to his surprise he found him in town.

"Dr. Fishback," said he, "I was told that you had gone to Red River; but I am truly glad to meet you here."

"I did intend to go," replied he, "but you have worked such wonders in these parts, that, hearing you would preach in town to-day, I concluded to stay and learn how it is that you effect such great things."

"Brother Fishback," said he, courteously, "will you not preach to-day yourself?"

"No," he replied, "I will not; I stayed to hear you."

As they walked on together to the meeting-house, which stood on a hill in the western part of the town, Smith, in a frank but kind manner, inquired:

"Brother Fishback, did any of my brethren ask you to postpone your discourse till my return?"

"Yes," replied the Doctor, "but my Methodist friends judged it best that I should do as I did."

"You have treated me most unkindly in this matter, brother Fishback. But Absalom Rice has furnished me with notes of your discourse; and, now, I say to you in all candor, that if you can argue no better than you seem, from these notes, to have done, I never will believe but that I can handle you like a baby! Where, Doctor, will you spend the evening?"

"With my brother-in-law, James Mason," he replied.

"Then I am going to brother Mason's, too," said Smith, "and I will there try the strength of your argument."

"Try it this morning—try it here," said the Doctor, bravely, as they entered the meeting-house together.

"No, sir!" said Smith; "I have too much generalship for that. I will meet you to-night."

In his discourse that morning he made no allusion whatever to the visit of Dr. Fishback, or to the subject of controversy. After the immersion of several persons, that afternoon, he stood in his dripping garments on the banks of the Hinkston, in the presence of a throng of people, and announced simply that he would spend the evening, and, if necessary, the night, too, with Dr. Fishback, at the house of Colonel Mason.

When he got there, he found many of his brethren already assembled. A number of Methodists, also, had come to witness his defeat. He introduced the discussion by remarking:

"I have come here, brethren, to meet Dr. Fishback, and to test, by the Word of God, his position on the subject of free communion."

Calling for a Bible, he turned to Rom. xiv., and, while the company stood or sat around him with the open Book in their hands, he argued from the context:

"That, with reference to things indifferent, such as the eating of meats or of herbs, there was liberty of opinion and of action; for, concerning such things, the King never specifically legislates. But positive ordinances are not to be included among things indifferent, seeing they are expressly commanded. It is presumption, therefore, to teach that baptism, which is an ordinance of Christianity, is a thing indifferent, and may, therefore, be neglected or modified at pleasure."

He argued that the true ground of Christian Union, as advocated by the Reforming Brethren, justified communion with all immersed believers—communion with them in every act of worship, and in every deed of love; for the ground of that union is faith in Jesus and immersion into his name. But such fellowship does not necessarily extend to all the opinions, sentiments, and practices of the immersed, and is not to be construed as indorsing them either as faultless Christians or as a perfect church. But communion with Pedobaptists, he contended, must compromise the bond of union itself by acknowledging as Christians those who, though they profess to believe in Christ as their Savior, refuse to obey him as their Lord.

After reading several paragraphs from the Doctor's defense of close communion, as indorsed by the Elkhorn Association in 1824, and thus placing the Doctor against himself, he brought the discussion to a close by suddenly asking his opponent, whether pouring was an ordinance of the New Testament?

"It is not," replied he.

"By what logic, then," continued Smith, "do you make it Christian baptism?"

"Neither pouring nor sprinkling is baptism to *me*," replied the Doctor; "but those who honestly believe that it is baptism, to *them* it is baptism. Let every one be fully persuaded in his own mind."

"If I judge a thing to be *wrong*, brother Fishback," replied Smith, "to me it is wrong; but, if I judge a thing to be *right*, I am not, therefore, always guiltless if I do it. For me to think that a thing is right, does not necessarily make it right to me. I do not charge you with the consequences of your doctrine, but your logic leads to this: That not even faith in the existence of God is with you always a condition of fellowship. One may deny that Jesus is the Christ; another, a future state; and another, the being and attributes of the Godhead. Yet, if each is fully persuaded in his own mind that he is right, then—get out of it if you can—you must admit him to your communion."

The discussion closed for the night; but Smith gave notice that on a certain day, he would speak in Mount Sterling in exposition of the fourteenth chapter of Romans; and that, as he would handle the arguments and the name of Dr. Fishback freely, he hoped that gentleman would be present.

The day arrived and he redeemed his promise. The large meeting-house could not contain the people, and they built a stand for him in a grove near by. Dr. Fishback was not present; but the discourse was regarded by all the Baptists as a most triumphant defense of restricted communion. His own brethren were confirmed, and the churches around, on this subject at least, had rest for a season.

Soon after this, he went out on Slate Creek, and began to preach the Ancient Gospel among the Methodists and

Baptists of that region. An itinerant of the Methodist Church was already on the ground, and the attention of the people was soon divided between the two preachers. Smith had but few brethren in the neighborhood, and the views of the Pedobaptists generally prevailed. The two congregations met in groves not far apart, and each emulated the enthusiasm of the other. Soon a number of anxious penitents found religion at the Methodist altar; and soon Smith began to immerse believers on the profession of their faith in Christ.

One day, a mother brought her infant into the Methodist congregation, that it might receive baptism at the hands of her preacher. Water was applied according to the custom of his Church, no regard being paid to the cries and struggles of the child, that with all its strength resisted the ordinance.

On the next day, Smith, in the presence of all the people, who crowded the banks of the beautiful stream hard by, led forth ten persons, one by one, into the water, and immersed them for the remission of sins. Seeing the Methodist preacher in the crowd, he walked up from the stream, and pressed through the place where he stood. The song went on; for the people supposed that another candidate was about to be buried in baptism. Seizing the preacher by the arm, he pulled him gently but firmly along toward the water. Resistance would have been in vain; for the *Dipper*, as the people now began to call him, was a man of powerful muscle.

"What are you going to do, Mr. Smith," said the man, uncertain what the strange procedure meant.

"What am I going to do!" said Smith, affecting surprise at the question; "I am going to baptize you, sir!"

"But I do not wish to be baptized," said the man, trying to smile at what he deemed to be rather an untimely jest, if, indeed, it was a jest at all.

"Do you not believe?" said Smith.

"Certainly I do," said the preacher.

"Then come along, sir," said the Dipper, pulling him still nearer to the water; "believers must be baptized!"

"But," said the man, now uneasy at the thought that possibly it might not be a joke at all, "I'm not willing to go. It certainly would do me no good to be baptized against my will."

Smith now raised his voice so that the multitude could hear, for the song had ceased, and every ear was open to catch his words. "Did you not," said he, "but yesterday, baptize a helpless babe against its will, though it shrunk from your touch, and kicked against your baptism? Did you get its consent first, sir? Come along with me, for you must be baptized!" and with one movement of his powerful arm, he pulled the unwilling subject to the water's edge. The preacher loudly and earnestly protested, and the Dipper released his hold. Looking him steadily in the face, he said:

"You think, sir, that it is all right to baptize others by violence, when you have the physical power to do it; but when you yourself are made the unwilling subject, you say it is wrong, and will do no good! You may go for the present; but, brethren and friends," said he, lifting up his voice to the people, who now perceived the purpose of the jest, "let me know if he ever again baptizes others without their full consent; for you yourselves have heard him declare that such a baptism can not possibly do any good!" But little mirthfulness was excited by this scene, for it deeply impressed the people; in fact, a thousand arguments could have done no more.

CHAPTER XXII.

WE have said that Mrs. Smith entered heartily into the resolution of her husband, to give up the farm to her, and devote himself to the proclamation of the Gospel. Her zeal, henceforth, was no less than his; her sacrifices, perhaps, were as many and as great. The care of a farm, not yet paid for, nor set in order, and of five or six little children, whom she must feed and clothe with her own hands, heavily taxed her energies. During the entire year, her husband could give no attention to secular or domestic affairs. In truth, he was so absorbed in studying and teaching the Word, that he felt no interest in any worldly thing. Even when stopping to rest for a night at home, he would sleep and read by turns, awaking and lighting his candle at midnight, to examine some word or text not yet understood, and which, perhaps, had confused him in his dreams.

She had exacted from him a promise to look in upon his home, if possible, every week. But so great, now, was the interest of the people in religious matters, that it was impracticable for him always to keep his promise. He would tarry in some distant place, preaching and baptizing, till the week was nearly gone, and then, dismissing the people at a late hour, ride hurriedly home through darkness, sometimes through mud and cold and tempest, in order to keep that promise to his wife. At other times, when going from one part of the District to another, he would pass along by his own house, but too much hurried to stop and rest, would linger awhile at the gate, and gathering strength from her words of cheer, press on to his distant appointment.

Once he stopped as he was thus passing, and, without dismounting, called her to the gate:

"Nancy," said he, giving into her hands the saddle-bags in which he carried his clothing, "I have been immersing all the week. Will you take these clothes and bring me some clean ones right away? for I must hurry on."

"Mr. Smith," said she, pleasantly, but with a touch of sadness in her voice, "is it not time that you were having your washing done somewhere else? We have attended to it for you a long time."

"No, Nancy," said he; "I am much pleased with your way of doing things, and I don't wish to make any change."

After a kind good-bye to her, and a few playful words to the little ones, whose brown hands and browner feet clung to the rails of the fence close by, he passed on to meet the congregation that would wait for him that day in some young convert's house, or, perhaps, in some hospitable grove.

Once, after many days' absence, he returned home to spend there a few hours of needful quietude. It was the seed-time of the year. His wife, with the help of an indolent hired man, had done what she could to put in the necessary crop, and she now wished to have the benefit of her husband's advice. But when she proposed to him to go out into the fields, and see how everything went on, he tried in vain to dismiss the Gospel from his mind, and to let in the world again. He walked the floor, and with a strange enthusiasm in his manner that startled her, sang aloud:

> "O tell me no more of this world's vain store,
> The time for such trifles with me is now o'er!"

He could not, even for that one hour, descend from the height to which months of earnest religious toil and study had raised him.

Sometimes it was impossible for her to hire a man at the proper time to work on the farm. Once, when it was necessary to weed the corn, and help could not be had, without incurring, as she thought, too much expense, she took her infant in her arms and went out to the fields alone. Laying the child down under the elder bushes that grew along the fence, she toiled down the hot corn-rows, nerved to her drudgery by the same spirit that was giving her husband voice and power in the congregations.

At another time, her grain grew ripe, and long waited

in vain for the reapers. The field lay there near the house, and every day she saw it burning in the summer's sun. She was troubled, and at length began to despond; for he was far away, and her poor babes could give her neither sympathy nor help. One night, she awoke from a troubled sleep, for she had dreamed of her unharvested grain, and of little children in distress. She arose from her bed, and, kneeling down in prayer, begged for strength to labor and endure. The full moon shone serene without, and all the fields were silvered with its light. As she walked the floor in her wakefulness, her wistful eye glanced out through her window, and, to her amazement, she saw that her field was already reaped, and every sheaf stood bound and gathered to its shock! Her bewildered heart rose in gratitude and wonder to him that answers prayer. God,

" Who oft, with unexpected joy, the fervent prayer of faith surprises –"

had put it into the hearts of some young converts of the neighborhood, when their own tasks for the day were done, to come by night, and, noiselessly banding themselves together, reap her grain for her, in the strength and beauty of their love!

No harvest shouts or noisy revels had broken the stillness of the hour; but there were happy songs in those reapers' hearts which were heard that night in heaven!

For all his labor and sacrifices, John Smith received but little compensation. From the day of his bold renunciation of Calvinism, at Spencer, in 1822, to the year of grace 1828. he had received nothing for his preaching from any source whatever, save that, in 1825, a kind-hearted merchant of Mount Sterling gave him the amount of his account for merchandise that year, which was about $18.00. Though not a professor of religion, he did the same in 1826, and also in 1827. In 1828, that merchant, charmed with the simple Christianity which Smith taught so well, and illustrated so consistently in his life, embraced it himself. Neglecting his counting room, he went through the borders of the land, with his father in the Gospel, and, like Timothy of old, preached the Word with boldness, being urgent in season and out of season.

The new doctrine recognized no such order of men in

the Church as *preachers*, in the popular sense of that term. It was maintained as the privilege and duty of every member of a congregation to proclaim the Gospel to the full extent of his ability. It will be remembered that, in his essays on *The Clergy*, Mr. Campbell denied the popular doctrine of a divine call to the ministry, declaring that, when a modern preacher claims to be sent of God to preach, he should work a miracle in attestation of his call. If he could not do the sign, he must be set down either as a knave or an enthusiast.

"I do not mean to say," said he, in 1824, "that every man and woman that believes the Gospel is to commence traveling about, as the popular preachers do, or to leave their homes and neighborhoods, or employments, to act as public preachers. But the young women are to declare to their coevals and acquaintances—the elder women, to theirs—the young men and elder men, to theirs—the glad tidings, and to show them the evidence on which their faith rests. This, followed up by a virtuous and godly life, is the most powerful means left on earth to illuminate and reform the world. In the meantime, the bishop of the church, in their weekly meetings, teaches the religion in its sublime and glorious doctrine and bearings, and thus the members are still educating and building up in the most holy faith. When the bishop rests from his labors, the church of which he has the oversight, by his labors, and by the opportunity afforded all the members of exercising their faculties of communication, and inquiry in the public assembly, finds within itself others educated and qualified to be appointed to do the same good work. The Church of the living God is thus independent of theological schools and colleges for its existence, enlargement, comfort, and perfection; for it is itself put in possession of all the means of education and accomplishments, if these means be wisely used."

"My very soul is stirred within me," said he, "when I think of what a world of mischief the popular clergy have done. They have shut up everybody's mouth but their own, and theirs they won't open unless they are paid for it."

"No man believes any fact but he can tell the reason why, and produce the evidence on which he believes it. This is all the New Testament means, and all I mean by *preaching*.

A bishop must be *'apt to teach;'* but nothing is said about being *'apt to preach,'* for *teaching* and *preaching* are two things essentially different. To have said that a bishop must be *'apt to preach'* in that age would have been absurd when women as well as men could preach. Paul mentions women of note who were his fellow-laborers; and all know how Priscilla explained to the eloquent Apollos the way of God more accurately. Euodia and Syntiche are mentioned as women who labored with the apostle Paul in the publication of the Gospel. Yet, in the Church, they were not allowed to teach, nor even to speak in the way of asking questions."

The influence of this teaching was early felt throughout the North District; for John Smith accepted it, and he impressed it, in his own peculiar manner, on his young brethren and sisters. Philips and Aquilas arose in every congregation, and Electas and Priscillas labored at every fireside. Young converts went everywhere preaching the Gospel, while the more aged contended for the restoration of the Ancient Order in the churches.

Among those disciples who, by their devotion to the cause, and their knowledge of the Scriptures, rendered him the earliest and most efficient aid, were Jacob Coons, Absalom Rice, and the merchant, Buckner H. Payne; while, among the women most distinguished in that year for their co-operative zeal in the social circle, must be mentioned Dulcinea Ryan and Eliza Payne.

As yet, there were but few, if any, among all his brethren in the ministry that were in full sympathy with him, or his work.

Jeremiah Vardeman, pre-eminently a revivalist, and never a strict Calvinist, did, indeed, in the years 1826 and 1827, preach BAPTISM FOR THE REMISSION OF SINS, and advocate, with great ability and success, the doctrine that the New Testament is the only standard of a Christian's faith and practice. In 1827, he introduced into the Elkhorn Association a resolution declaring the individual churches to be the highest ecclesiastical authority known in the Word of God, and affirming that they should never bring their difficulties into an Association for adjustment. His wish was, as he said, to convert the Elkhorn Association into a simple worshiping assembly. But soon afterward, he began, it seems, to reconsider the doctrine of baptismal regeneration. At the Association, in 1828, he preached the introductory discourse, from Eph. ii. 8—"By grace are ye saved through faith; and that not of yourselves: it is the gift of God;" on which occasion, he was understood as opposing the leading principles of the Reformation. Certainly, in 1829, while he still condemned the strong features of Calvinism, and was by no means an advocate of creeds, he professed to be chagrined and mortified at the conduct of the Reformers; and he turned back to the OLD DISPENSATION, as he styled the faith and order of the Baptists. It was in reference to the course of this justly distinguished man that Jacob Creath once said:

"He set out in the Reformation before me; but, after I had enlisted under its banner, and started out to battle for it, I met my old comrade and brother, now disgusted and discouraged, coming home again, with his knapsack on his back."

Jacob Creath, when he last parted from John Smith, which was in 1827, was a preacher of Calvinism; and when they met again, which was some time in 1828, he was still in full fellowship with the Baptists, and only in partial sympathy with the Reformation, zealously opposing, however, all authoritative creeds, councils, and Church covenants. It was after this that he embraced the principles of the Reformation; and he eloquently defended them to the day of his death.

Jacob Creath, Jr., a man of more learning than his uncle, was distinguished for the boldness and severity of his character. He wielded the most ponderous arguments, defended his positions with obstinate courage, and assailed error and errorists with singular energy, though sometimes with a harsh, yet ever honest, spirit. But he was not in Kentucky during the eventful year of 1828, until near its close.

William Morton, of the Boone's Creek Association, was one of the first among the Baptist preachers of Kentucky to advocate a return to the Apostolic basis of Christian union. He was one of the most amiable and honorable of men, a Christian gentleman, and a model minister of the Word. His mild and just temper early led him to doubt the doctrine of imputed sin, and of man's utter helplessness by nature; for which amiable heresies, complaints were made by some of the churches, and he was subjected to a kind of trial, or examination, as early as 1825. He readily accepted the doctrine of Alexander Campbell, but was of too gentle a nature to become a bitter partisan. He was firm, without dogmatism; aggressive, indeed, as a reformer, but without rudeness. His pure teachings fell from his lips like the dews, and sanctified the hearts of a people that loved him. He was not a man for storms. He shrunk from all ill-tempered controversy, and drooped with the grace of meekness under sectarian abuse. He clung to the truth, however, with a love that never compromised or betrayed it; and vindicated it as well by the beauty of his life as by the strife of argument.

George W. Elley, while living within the bounds of the Long Run Association, received, in the spring of 1827, from a Baptist church, authority to speak in public. But he had been a constant reader of the *Christian Baptist* from the beginning; and now, in his first attempts at speaking, he betrayed the influence of his readings. His brethren became suspicious, and charged him with unsoundness; and, finally, they began to doubt whether the Lord had ever called him to preach! But he preached on, nevertheless. At length, he began to urge his brethren to meet together to celebrate the Lord's death according to the ancient custom—on every Lord's day. But this they refused to do, saying that such was not the custom of the Baptists. His efforts to reform only called forth rebukes from the preacher in charge, who declared that while there was no authority for altering the customs of the Church, there was a plain injunction, to mark such as caused divisions among them. He also said to the people that Alexander Campbell, in spite of his greatness, would fall, and that all those who now stood by him would fall with him.

Young Elley arose and answered him. A great noise was immediately raised; for, in his presumption, he had even dared to contradict a preacher!

At the next meeting of the congregation, the ominous question was raised:

"Is the church pleased with her young gift?" and the church voted that her young gift was not profitable! But the licentiate replied that, though they might put to silence their own officers and agents as they might see proper, yet, as for himself, he felt that he was authorized, by the Word of God, to preach to any congregation willing to hear him.

On their refusing to give him a letter of dismission, which he now asked for, and even to make the facts in the case a matter of record, the young reformer arose and said:

'Brethren, I was born free; and, as the Church of Christ is not a prison, I withdraw myself from you!"

He accordingly went out from them, though not intending, at the time, to leave the Baptist connection. He continued to speak to the people of the neighborhood, and became, in time, one of the boldest and most successful preachers of the Ancient Gospel in Kentucky.

Other pious and thoughtful ministers of the Bracken, the Franklin, and the Tate's Creek Association, also, about this time, began to re-examine the popular theories of religion: but they did not yet commit themselves fully to the cause of Reform. John Smith for awhile, therefore, stood almost alone among those who had been his co-laborers for so many years. But others were won by the truth. Friends continued to gather to his side, for he proselyted them by hundreds from the world and from the sects, and he thanked God and took courage at the thought that in a few weeks more they would all meet him at the Association, and fill, with their songs, the groves of Lulbegrud.

CHAPTER XXIII.

BOONE'S CREEK ASSOCIATION was formed in 1823, by churches dismissed for that purpose from Elkhorn, Tate's Creek and North District. It comprised, in the year 1827. thirteen churches, with an aggregate membership of nine hundred and eighty-five persons. These, for the most part, lived in the counties of Bourbon and Clark, and were in constant religious intercourse with those brethren of the North District who lived along the adjacent borders of Montgomery. Smith, passing the bounds of his own Association, soon began to preach among the people of Boone's Creek also. They gladly received his word, and hundreds were immersed by him in the streams of Indian Creek and Stoner. At Lower Bethel, or North Middletown, Friendship, and Mount Zion, his labors, during the spring and summer of 1828, were specially blessed; he introduced many converts into those influential churches, not a few of whom became, in the new acceptation of the term, *preachers* of the Ancient Gospel.

The churches of Mason and Fleming Counties, composing the Bracken Association of United Baptists, had already felt the influence of the doctrine of Alexander Campbell, and a few good men, such as Jesse Holton and Walter Warder, had begun to commend some features of the Ancient Gospel with much boldness. When John Smith appeared among them in 1828, resolutely attacking Calvinism, and proclaiming that every penitent believer might find in baptism the assurance of pardon, the people crowded to hear him; the great issues were sharply defined, and the controversy, growing more and more earnest, became, at last, in some of the churches, passionate and bitter.

In his hurried tours through the country, during the early

part of the summer, he touched on the borders of the Elkhorn and the Licking Association. He went among the churches of Tate's Creek, also, and gathered strength from the sympathy and companionship of such men as Josiah Collins and Oliver C. Steele.

But the Calvinists of Lulbegrud and Cane Spring were unaffected by the revival which he had excited. They looked upon it as an unholy passion, which bad zeal had stirred up, and with which the Good Spirit had nothing to do. They had hoped that the errors into which he had fallen would pass away with the year, and that he would then stand up before his brethren and honestly renounce them all. But the year was almost gone; the meeting of the Association was near at hand, and *Campbellism* not only lived, but was wide-spread and rank throughout the land. They had neglected to crush the germ, and had nursed it in the very bosom of the Church; but now, they would rise up in the strength of the united churches, and destroy it forever!

Many of them, indeed, thought of the fate of John Smith with sorrow, for they could not but respect and love him. But they had borne with him long, hoping to save him, and yet he persistently refused to be saved! His doctrine was corrupting the people, too, and destroying the peace of the churches; and, since he would not return, he must be cut off, with all whom he had led astray. This they now resolved to do, gracing their resolution with pity for his infatuation, and turning their censure upon the great apostle of the new Gospel, who, through the pages of the *Christian Baptist*, had sent such a strong delusion upon him.

Lulbegrud was still aggrieved because the Association had temporized with Smith's heresy in 1827, and had not duly hearkened to her complaints. But now, it was agreed that the blunder committed at Cane Spring should be corrected, and that Lulbegrud herself should be satisfied.

According to Baptist custom, an Introductory Address was delivered before the Association, at each annual session, by some minister appointed to that honor the year before. That there might be no disappointment or confusion, another was always selected to take his place should he be absent: to him the honor of the Introductory for the ensuing year was always awarded. In 1826, John Smith had received such a provisory appointment, and he would have preached at Cane Spring in 1827 had not the principal, Thomas Boone, been present. It was his duty, therefore, according to Baptist usage, to deliver the opening address to the Association in 1828. But the Calvinists of Lulbegrud and Cane Spring took counsel together how to silence Smith should he propose to preach in the face of the offended churches. But they could do nothing; for they dared not disregard an old, established custom themselves, and afterward seek to cut him off from their fellowship for a similar offense; for he had been arraigned, and was now soon to be judged, for alleged departures from Baptist usages. Satisfied that the charges already brought would be held to be good ground for his excision, and knowing that accusations of heresy in doctrine could be sustained, if necessary, they concluded, rather than to incur the charge of inconsistency themselves, to let him introduce the exercises of the Association, if, indeed, under the circumstances, he could feel any inclination to do so.

The time for the churches to prepare their usual letters, and to select their messengers, came on. The church at Spencer's Creek reported one hundred and seventy-six baptisms during the year; Grassy Lick reported one hundred and two baptisms; Mount Sterling, one hundred and fourteen; in fine, a general report would have shown that, during the year, and mainly during the six months from January to July, nearly nine hundred members had been received into the churches of the Association, the greater part of whom had been immersed by Smith; five new churches also had been constituted on the Bible alone; so that North District now comprised about twenty-four churches, with an aggregate membership of more than two thousand souls.

It was impossible, however, to determine beforehand the exact religious temper of the Association. Many were still inquiring; some wavered, or waited; some watched the signs of the times, intending to trim to the popular gale; others were indifferent, or double-minded, and not a few loyally resolved to abide the action of the Association.

The newly-constituted churches had been taught that authoritative ecclesiastical creeds and courts were wrong, and they consequently hesitated to ask for admission even into an advisory council of Baptists; but, when they reflected that he who had constituted them might need their aid to stand against his enemies, they appointed as many messengers to Lulbegrud as custom allowed. At the church meetings in other parts of the District during the months of June and July, the contest between the two parties for representation was earnest, and often angry. "Shall John Smith be put down?" was virtually the question raised in nearly all the churches; and it was answered in the character of the messengers appointed.

The fourth Saturday in July came. Ministers and messengers and excited brethren crowded the meeting-house at Lulbegrud, or gathered in the groves without. Spencer, Mount Sterling, Grassy Lick, and other churches favorable to the restoration, not only sent their full complement of messengers, but followed on in masses to the spot. Lulbegrud, with all her adverse influence, was present in a body, demanding that her complaints should now be heard. Thither came also crowds of zealous Calvinists from Cane Spring, Goshen, and Howard's Creek. Messengers from corresponding Associations in due time arrived; but Smith saw with mortification, that those foreign brethren, whose counsel and support he had hoped to have, were not among them! It was the first great organized struggle in the State for Primitive Order. and he was almost alone. Boone's Creek, it is true, had sent William Morton, and Elkhorn had accredited Vardeman and Creath, but they did not come; neither did Jesse Holton nor Walter Warder, from Bracken. On the other hand, John Taylor came, representing the Calvinism of the Franklin Association, and Ryland T. Dillard, the Hyper-Calvinism of Licking. Others were with them, not gifted with speech, it is true, but firmly set against innovation, and darkly frowning at heresy. The messengers of the newly planted churches were there, but doubting whether they would be received; they had no creed or covenant to exhibit, and were reputed to be rank with heresy. But the Opposition saw that to reject them because their only creed or constitution was the Scriptures, would dissolve the union of 1801, and give just cause of offense to many separate churches that, like Spencer, had, from the beginning, known no other creed but the Word of God. They concluded, therefore, to receive the new churches into fellowship, though they felt at the time that it was a dangerous policy to do so.

When the hour came, Smith arose to deliver the introductory discourse. The house, though large, could not contain the people and he went into the grove and preached from the stand. As he looked upon the thousand faces before him, he read the certain triumph of his cause; for he saw that the people were with him, though the rulers might still be against him. There, on the logs before him and behind him, sat those who had accused him of innovation, heresy, or apostasy, and who had refused, a year ago, to hear him speak in his own defense. There beside him sat some of the ablest defenders of the Faith that he was trying to destroy, reverenced, too, by many of the people, as the chosen ambassadors of Christ. Sitting in the congregation were foes from other sects, curious to see the end of the bold enthusiast that had dared to lift up his single arm against all the churches in the land. And there, too, with faces bright with the confidence of victory, sat hundreds whom he had baptized with his own hands, and many hundreds more whom he had turned from sectarianism to the freedom of the Gospel. There were the young reapers that had gone by night and saved the harvest for his wife and children; and the women that had labored with him through good and evil report; and many gifted young brethren from the shops, the farms, and the counting rooms, some of whom were already beginning to preach the Ancient Gospel.

Solemnly conscious of his responsibility, he arose with dignity, and, in a voice that hushed every whisper, read:

"You see your calling, brethren, that not many wise men, according to the flesh, not many mighty, not many noble call you. But God has chosen the foolish things of the world, that he may bring to shame the wise; and the weak things of the world has God chosen, that he may put to shame the strong; and the ignoble things of the world, and the things that are despised, has God chosen, and the things that are not, that he might bring to naught things that are: that no flesh should glory in his presence.

* * * * * * * *

"And I, brethren, when I came to you, came not with excellence of speech or of wisdom, disclosing to you the testimony of God. For I determined not to know anything among you but Jesus Christ and him crucified. And I was with you in weakness and in fear, and in much trembling; and my speech and my preaching were not in persuasive words of man's wisdom, but in demonstration of the Spirit and of power, that your faith might not be in wisdom of men, but in the power of God.

*　　　*　　　*　　　*　　　*　　　*　　　*　　　*

"The natural man receives not the things of the Spirit of God; for they are foolishness to him; neither can he know them, for they are spiritually discerned. But the spiritual man discerns all things, yet he is himself discerned by no one. For who has known the mind of the Lord, that he might instruct him? But we have the mind of Christ."—*I. Corinthians.*

He had long since ceased to teach that God calls men in some extraordinary way, to preach the Gospel of his Son. The fact that Christ once chose unlettered fishermen, and qualified them, to instruct the simple and confound the wise, had been expanded by the clergy into a rule for themselves: they, too, claimed to have been called as Peter was; they sometimes emulated his supposed ignorance and rustic behavior, and even boasted of their lack of learning. Nor had they any the less influence with the people on that account. Their very ignorance enhanced their authority, so that not unfrequently an entire community has unconsciously worn the yoke of some anointed dolt.

Smith had often discussed before the people what Alexander Campbell called the *arrogant pretensions of the clergy;* but he had never before had the opportunity of challenging those pretensions in the presence of the clergy themselves. He believed that the people could not be saved from their errors so long as they were in bondage to their preachers; and, since they had been brought into that bondage through the priestly device of a divine call to the ministry, they could not be made free again till that device had been exposed. Prudence, perhaps, required that he should say nothing to offend the ministers that sat around him, since they were about to call in question his own right to preach among them. But the temptation to say to them what he had already said to the people about them, was too great for him to resist, and he could not afford to let the opportunity pass.

He argued that the modern clergy was a self-constituted order, or an abrogated Jewish estate revived in the Church of Christ; whereas, by the proclamation of the King, his people were all priests, ministers of holy things, and preachers of the Gospel of his kingdom. He declared that in the quotations from Paul, which he had read in their hearing, there was to be found no more authority for specially called preachers than for weak and foolish ones; that, if such a call is a doctrine of the text, then ignorance, imbecility, and meanness must be encouraged as the scriptural conditions of the call; and it would be true—as they were slanderously reported as saying—that the bigger the fool the louder the call!

Following the Apostle's doctrine to the close, he discussed, in conclusion, the office of the Holy Spirit, and assailed, with earnestness and much effect, the popular theory of spiritual regeneration.

Letters from the churches were then read, and the names of their messengers were enrolled. Till this time, the numerical strength of the Reformers in the Association was unknown, even to themselves. The people without were generally with Smith; but the interesting question was:

"Will he carry a majority of those within?"

Some kept tally of the messengers as they took their seats, and silently the friends and the foes of Reform were reckoned up. But the hope of the Reformers, at last, was in the representatives of the new churches, whose letters were next presented, and for whose admission they were resolved to contend to the last. But when they saw that no opposition was made, they could hardly restrain their joy. After their admission, the Association at once addressed itself, quietly and earnestly, to business. A majority were now Reformers; but they determined to conciliate, if they could, all jealousies, and to confound all party distinctions. David Chenault was re-elected Moderator; he and John Smith were placed together on committee; John Taylor and Ryland T. Dillard, with Josiah Collins, were selected to preach on Sunday; and, then, after the usual courtesies to corresponding

Associations, they adjourned, without discord, to meet again on Monday.

"It has been arranged, Brother Smith," said a friend to him that day, after the many greetings, that had brought the tears into his eyes, were over, "it has been arranged for you to go home with me to-night. Many brethren and friends will be there, who wish to see you, and you must go."

"No, my brother," replied Smith, "I thank you. You are all friendly there; the Opposition, I learn, will be with Brother French to-night, and I must go to his house," and he turned off to search for the Clerk of the Association. He found him inviting many guests, for he lived not a great way off, and was a most hospitable man.

"Brother French," said he, "you ought to ask me to go along with these brethren, for I will undertake to make them all behave themselves."

"Do come, Brother Smith," said French, smiling hospitably. "Come along with them, and make yourself perfectly at home."

He went; and by his pleasant, conciliatory humor, smoothed some brows that had been ruffled all day long. But David Chenault, who was present, was grave, though less from anger than from real distress of mind. That good man feared that heresy had at last triumphed in the Association; and, if so, the blame would be laid at his door, for he had tampered with it at Cane Spring in 1827. He replied to none of Smith's arguments, nor could he find it in his heart to smile at his witticisms. The scenes of the day were before his mind, and he was solemn, reticent, and severe.

The company, in due time, retired for the night, and Smith, with several other guests, was conducted to a large room, where four or five beds had been made ready. In the freedom of the hour and the place, his wit was unrestrained. The general humor was freshened, too, by draughts of delicious cider, which the host brought in, and pressed upon them. But David Chenault was inexorably grave—proof alike against the inspiration of the hour and the raillery of his heretical brother. With all the unruffled dignity of office still upon him, he went to bed and left the genial company to themselves.

In all his life, John Smith never had an unkind feeling

for his Calvinistic brother. In fact, he loved him, but it was with a good-natured sort of love, that nothing could solemnize nor chill. He had failed to thaw him into fellowship that evening by any of his pleasant words, and he could not see him now turn away thus, and lie down alone in a disconsolate bed.

"Brethren," said he to the others, as they were lying down, "these July nights, I know, are hot, and you do not need that any warm-hearted Christian should crowd with you; yet I must turn in with some of you, anyhow. Brother Davy," said he, going to the bedside of the Moderator, "make just a little room for me, for I must sleep with you to-night."

It was vain to protest against the intrusion; so John Smith and the Moderator of the North District Association lay down that night together, and slept till morning in amity and peace!

On Monday, the session of the Association was again harmonious; the Opposition, though surprised at the state of things, acquiesced, for the time, in silence, while the majority, satisfied with their triumph, behaved with prudence and magnanimity. The question of *Free Communion* was the only subject of importance discussed; they decided not to correspond with any Association that would retain in its connection a church that communed with Pedobaptists or with *Arians*.

No mention was made of any complaints from the church at Lulbegrud, nor indeed from any other source; for no one there dared to say aught against the character or the doctrine of Smith. And so the Association adjourned, in apparent harmony, to meet again at Unity, in Clark County, on the fourth Saturday in July, 1829.

CHAPTER XXIV.

JOHN SMITH kept no journal; but, for awhile in 1828, he noted down the results of his labors each week: and now, after he had sat one evening at home, reviewing the work of the past few months, he announced the result to his wife.

"Nancy," said he, "I have *baptized* seven hundred sinners, and *capsized* fifteen hundred Baptists; so we have made two great mistakes."

He had said to her, at the beginning of the year, that the Reformation would not prevail in his lifetime; yet six months only had passed by, and it was already established in the hearts of the people. He had counted up the sacrifices, too, that he would have to make, and had talked of the persecutions that he would have to endure; but now he felt that the struggle was over, and that he would henceforth be called to labor only in pleasant fields. He ascribed all this success to the Truth itself; for, in the very hour of his triumph, he seemed to be unconscious of his power. He thanked God, and his wife, for what he had accomplished, and, with strong hope and unabated zeal, he resolved to work on in the good cause as before.

About this time he received a letter from Walter Warder, of Mason County, urging him to be present at the meeting of the Bracken Association, which would soon convene at Wilson's Run, in Fleming County. He learned at the same time that there would probably be some sharp contention in that Association, growing out of the attempt of certain religious leaders to impose some grievous ecclesiastical yoke upon the people.

It appears that, in 1827, Bracken had requested a correspondence with Licking, and had said, in her letter to that body, that it was unnecessary to set forth the articles of her

faith, as the brethren all knew that she was the eldest daughter
of Elkhorn. But Licking rejected her messengers, and demanded a more definite statement of her present faith—
appointing a committee, however, to bear a letter to Bracken,
when convened at Wilson's Run, which letter set forth the
terms on which she would correspond. It was soon noised
abroad that Licking had resolved to require of Bracken a
pledge to support the Philadelphia Confession of Faith. Such
a pledge would doubtless have been given readily in 1827;
but, in the meantime, Smith had passed the borders of North
District, and preached among the churches of Mason and
Fleming; and such men as Walter Warder and Jesse Holton,
already moved by the plea of Alexander Campbell for reform,
and encouraged by the boldness and success of Smith, were
favoring the heresy of the *Ancient Gospel.*

Much discussion had arisen, therefore, during the year,
as to the course which Bracken ought to pursue; and, as the
time for the meeting of the Association drew near, the two
parties arrayed themselves against each other, advocating or
opposing the proposed correspondence with much bitterness
of feeling; so that all looked forward to the approaching
meeting with much anxiety.

It was under these circumstances that Warder wrote to
Smith, giving him to understand that an effort would be made
to commit Bracken to a correspondence with Licking, on the
terms already indicated, and begging that he would not fail
to be present.

He went as a messenger of North District. The letter of
Licking was read on Saturday. It declared, in response to
the request of Bracken for a correspondence, that Licking,
under proper circumstances, would not object; and that she
would ask of the daughter, as a condition, nothing more than
what had already been required of the mother *—to maintain

---

*In 1825, Elkhorn had expressed a wish to cultivate a *Christian union,
fellowship,* and *correspondence* with Licking. The latter, after adjusting some
minor differences, consented to a correspondence with Elkhorn, upon the
inviolate maintenance of the doctrine of grace as revealed in the Bible, and
set forth in the Philadelphia Confession of Faith—with the distinct understanding that each Association would protest against any departure therefrom. Elkhorn accepted these conditions, stating that she had always maintained the doctrines of grace as revealed in the Bible, and set forth in her
Constitution, and hoped that Licking would unite with her in maintaining
the same, and in promptly correcting every departure therefrom.

inviolate the doctrine of grace as taught in the Bible, and as set forth in the Philadelphia Confession of Faith.

Much discussion followed the reading of this letter, during which John Smith sat silent, but watchful, waiting for a favorable moment to strike a blow at what he called the *Papal Calf of Licking*. Finally, after the debate had become somewhat inflammatory, James G. Arnold, a messenger from the North Bend Association, moved that the terms proposed by Licking be rejected, and that all further correspondence with that body be dropped. Smith arose to support the proposition. Taking from his saddle-bags a small, worn copy of the Philadelphia Confession of Faith, he began by saying:

"Brethren, Licking requires of Bracken an utter impossibility. No one can maintain inviolate the doctrine of grace as revealed in the Scriptures, and, at the same time, defend that which is taught in the Philadelphia Confession of Faith; for the doctrine of the Creed is not the doctrine of the Bible. No two books in the world differ more than these; and on no point do they differ more widely than on the doctrine of salvation by grace."

He proceeded to contrast the teaching of the New Testament with that of the Confession; and, when he closed his argument, nearly all seemed to be satisfied that the terms proposed by Licking were contradictory, for the proposition to reject was carried almost unanimously.

Smith was now chosen by the Association to address the people on Sunday; and he did not fail to improve the opportunity to enlarge upon the freedom of the Gospel, and to urge the people to throw off every ecclesiastical yoke. They were all charmed by his manner; many were convinced by his reasonings, and he at once became the master spirit of the Association. In the words of a prominent actor in the scenes of that day, "*It was John Smith that gave impulse and tone to the Reformation in Bracken, as he had already done in North District, Boone's Creek, and other Associations.*"

On Monday, Bracken resolved to recommend no creed or confession of faith to the churches, save the New Testament.

When the Association adjourned, Smith took a short tour through Mason and Bracken Counties before he returned home. He went from Wilson's Run to Mayslick, followed by many from the Association, who it seems, could not be satisfied with hearing him. From Mayslick he passed on to Washington, and thence to Ohio Locust, a meeting-house near Germantown—the people following him from place to place.

At Ohio Locust, the first discourse of the day was delivered by Buckner H. Payne, the merchant, who was already preaching the *New Gospel* with much success. The people wondered that one so young could preach with so much power, for they looked on him as a novice, and all knew, besides, that he had never been specially called to the ministry. During his discourse, he occasionally spoke of the Holy *Ghost;* but his father in the Gospel, who sat behind him, promptly corrected him before the people. "Say the Holy *Spirit*, my brother!" Smith exclaimed more than once, as the young speaker blundered against the New Translation.

When Payne had concluded, a man came to Smith, as he was about to rise, and, in a whisper, directed his attention to a stranger, of good appearance, standing in a remote part of the congregation.

"That man," said he, "is John P. Thompson: he has come all the way from the White River country, in Indiana, to destroy *Campbellism*, and to lead back the people to the old paths again."

"Are you acquainted with him?" inquired Smith.

"Yes," said the brother; "he used to preach here some years ago."

"Then, when I am done, I want you to introduce me," said Smith, "for I must know the man that has come all the way from Indiana to oppose what he believes to be an error."

Smith arose, and, in his artless manner, introduced the subject of his address.

"While my brother was speaking," said he, "I was thinking, as I have no doubt you all were, of that passage of Scripture which saith: 'The natural man receiveth not the things of the Spirit of God; for they are foolishness to him: neither can he know them; for they are spiritually discerned.' Now, I am going to speak to you from that very passage, just three-quarters of an hour."

He labored to show that, by a fair exposition of the context, the declaration of the Apostle could not be made to support Calvinism. While he spoke, the stranger stood in an attitude of fixed attention; but, when the discourse was concluded, and the speaker came down to seek him, he could not be found. They searched for him through the scattered congregation, but in vain. Next day, they heard that he had gone back to Indiana, with a suspicion, if not conviction, that Calvinism had no foundation in the Word of God!

"I went to Kentucky," says Elder Thompson, speaking of this incident, "to learn by what means so many of my old neighbors and friends had been turned from the old paths. I heard Elder Abernethy, a leading Reformer in Bracken, defend the new heresy, but I saw no reason to distrust the soundness of my own faith. I was about to return home, when I learned that John Smith, already renowned throughout the land, would preach, next day, at Ohio Locust. I determined to hear him, assured that, if I was wrong, he could make it so appear. I listened with attention to the introductory remarks of Buckner H. Payne, but, when he sat down, my armor was still sound. I rebuffed his arguments with the text, which came frequently into my mind, 'The natural man receiveth not the things of the Spirit of God.' When John Smith arose and cited that very text, I said to myself: Now, my brother, if you can do anything for me, so be it. He began, and, with the skill of a master-workman in forty-five minutes stripped me bare of my armor, under which I had long fought the battles of moderate Calvinism! I saw that, if his view of the Scripture was correct, I might say, as Napoleon said at Waterloo—'All is gone!' I shall ever believe that God caused John Smith to meet me that day at Ohio Locust."

When Elder Thompson reached his home in Rush County, Indiana, he entered upon his investigations of the Scriptures with fear and trembling. He resolved to open his understanding to every ray of light, and to follow the truth of God at any sacrifice of property, friends, or reputation.

Soon a meeting was held at a house in his neighborhood, and a large congregation came together. Elder Thompson arose to declare once more to his neighbors "the unsearchable riches of Christ." He did not intend, at the time, to bring any strange things to their ears, but his mind was full of great ideas recently acquired, and his heart was swelling with love to God and man. When he was about half through with his discourse, his spirit overleaped all barriers, and, as if suddenly inspired, he proclaimed to his astonished hearers the fullness, the freeness, and the simplicity of the Gospel of Christ! That morning's service was the beginning of a great reformation in Eastern Indiana.*

The Boone's Creek Association was now soon to meet at Friendship, in Clark County, and John Smith hurried home from Bracken, to attend it. Like North District and Bracken, Boone's Creek was passing through a great religious revolution. In her circular letter of 1827, evidently written by William Morton, the Association had held the following language:

"We hear from some of the churches that they are endeavoring to return to the Ancient Order of Things: they have renounced all human devices in matters of religion, and they recognize the Scriptures alone as an entire and sufficient rule of faith and practice. We believe that Christ has made his churches free from all ecclesiastical power on earth, and that he alone is King in Zion, and his Word the only law of his kingdom."

In the spring and summer of 1828, there had been an increase of about eight hundred and seventy members by immersion, many of whom had been brought in through the preaching of John Smith. The propriety of creeds and constitutions had, of course, been much discussed during the year among the people; and even the lawfulness of Associations as advisory councils had been called in question. Lower Bethel, or North Middletown, and other churches, now sent up a request, through their messengers, that the Association should so amend her Constitution as to make it more compatible with the Word of God.†

The Association, comprising a large delegation from the thirteen churches, met on the third Saturday in September. William Morton delivered the Introductory Address, and, on Sunday, John Smith preached to the vast concourse of people. Jeremiah Vardeman followed with general arguments from

---

* Pioneer Preachers of Indiana.

† Messengers of Lower Bethel were James Sims, Thomas M. Parrish, Nimrod L. Lindsay, Charles E. Williams, and James M. Cogswell; of Friendship—William Morton, Z. Ridgeway, Josiah Ashley, Griffin Kelley, and Smith Jeffries; of Mt. Zion—William H. Blady, Robert V. Bush, Elliot Holladay, Walter Holladay, and Henry T. Chevis.

the Scriptures, and Jacob Creath closed by one of his eloquent exhortations. On Monday, after an exciting debate, the following resolution was adopted, in answer to the petition of the churches for a more Scriptural Constitution:

"This Association, having taken into consideration the request of some of the churches for an amendment of her Constitution, after mature deliberation, is decidedly of opinion that the Word of God does not authorize or prescribe any form of constitution for an Association in our present organized state; but we do believe that the Word of God authorizes the assembling of saints together for his worship;

"We, therefore, recommend to the churches the abolition of the present Constitution, and, in lieu thereof, the adoption of the following resolution:

"*Resolved*, That we, the churches of Jesus Christ, believing the Scriptures of the Old and the New Testament to be the Word of God, and the only rule of faith and obedience given by the Great Head of the Church for its government, do agree to meet annually, on the third Saturday, Lord's Day, and Monday, in September, for the *worship of God;* and, on such occasions, voluntarily communicate the state of religion among us by letters and messengers."

The question was thus thrown back upon the churches for their consideration, during the ensuing year of 1829; and, in the meantime, the objectionable Constitution which we give below, was ordered to be printed for the benefit of the people.

We, Baptist churches of Jesus Christ, believing it to be for the glory of God and the prosperity of the Kingdom of the dear Redeemer to form ourselves into an Association, adopt the following as the fundamental principles of our

CONSTITUTION.

We take the Holy Bible, the Old and New Testaments, as the only rule of faith and practice in religion, and are united in the belief of the following doctrines as contained in the Scriptures:

1. That there is one God and one Mediator between God and men, the man Christ Jesus, and that in the Godhead are Father, Son, and Holy Ghost.

2. That mankind, without exception, are, in their natural

state, sinners, totally destitute of holiness, and are entirely helpless in themselves.

3. That faith in Jesus Christ is the alone instrument of justification, according to the Scriptures, and is the gift of God, and is ordinarily wrought in the heart by the Spirit, by and with the Word, heard or read.

4. That salvation is wholly of the free and sovereign grace of God through the atonement, righteousness, and mediation of Jesus Christ, by the sanctifying influence of the Holy Spirit and the belief of the Truth; and that the saints will persevere through grace to glory.

5. That there will be a resurrection of the dead, both of the just and the unjust, and a general judgment; that the righteous will be received into everlasting happiness, and that the wicked will be driven into everlasting punishment.

6. We hold that the visible church of Christ is composed of such as profess saving faith, and that those only who exhibit credible evidence of faith in Christ, should be baptized, agreeably to his command, by being immersed in water in the name of the Father and of the Son and of the Holy Ghost, and that it is the duty and privilege of such to celebrate the Lord's Supper.

7. That notwithstanding children, who are not capable of professing faith in Christ, are not fit subjects for baptism and the Lord's Supper according to the Gospel, yet we hold it to be our duty to bring them up in the nurture and admonition of the Lord.

8. We believe in the divine appointments of the Christian Sabbath, scripturally called the Lord's Day; and that it is the duty of Christians to sanctify it to the service of God, according to the example of primitive saints. We believe that the moral law of God is a rule of obedience for all men through faith, and that the Gospel should be preached to all men, and all that hear are commanded to believe it.

9. This Association regards the independence of the churches inviolable, and disclaims any right to exercise power in the government of them; and declares her only aim and intention to be, to assist, advise, and encourage the propagation of truth and the cultivation of practical piety.

10. No query shall be brought before the Association from any church, unless the church has previously investigated

the subject-matter of it, with the aid of helps obtained from other churches, without having been able to determine it; and, should any difficulty arise in a church, or between churches, the same steps shall be taken to settle it as in the above case, as a prerequisite to an appeal to the Association; and, should an appeal be taken, the Association shall give advice.

11. Each church shall send to the Association, by her messengers, a written statement of her number received on profession of faith and baptism, and by letter, or restored, or dismissed by letter, deceased, or excommunicated.

12. The Association may employ part of her time in a free and familiar conversation about the state of religion in the churches composing her body.

13. Any church applying to join the Association shall present a copy of her Covenant, which shall be subject to examination, and, if received, shall be filed among the archives of the Association by the Clerk.

14. The number of messengers from any church shall not exceed five.

15. This Constitution shall be subject to amendment by a majority of two-thirds of the members present. Any proposition for amendment shall be made and seconded at a previous meeting.

16. This Association adopts the terms of the General Union, as ratified at Howard's Creek, Clark County, in 1801, as a bond of connection between her and the United Baptists.

Such was the Constitution which North Middletown and other churches requested the Association to make more scriptural, and which the Association, in reply, advised the churches to abolish entirely. Several of these churches had themselves already renounced "humanly devised forms, or confessions of faith, and adopted the Word of God as their only constitution and directory—conceiving it to be the great charter of all their privileges and rights."* They, of course, approved the recommendation of the Association, and resolved. if possible, to carry a majority with them at the next meeting, to be held with the Hind's Creek church, in September, 1829.

---

*Minutes of 1828.

Within a few miles of Lower Bethel, or North Middle-town, there was at that time an influential body of Particular Baptists, belonging to the Licking community, known as the *Stony Point* church. They had long enjoyed the pastoral care of Lewis Corbin, and, occasionally, the able ministrations of Ambrose Dudley, and other prominent Baptists of the old Regular Order. It was a stronghold of Hyper Calvinism, whose adverse influence had often been felt by Smith, when preaching among the churches of the Boone's Creek Associa-tion. So he resolved to try the power of the Ancient Gospel on the firm-hearted Calvinists of that region. A few had already softened under his preaching at North Middletown, and they now invited him to come and preach the same Gospel to their neighbors also. He went; and Gurdon Gates, the pastor of the church at Paris, went with him, with many others from that congregation. The young and zealous Reformers of North Middletown met him there. As they rode along toward the place, Gates expressed his fear that the house would be closed against them; but Smith felt no concern about it, for, though the day was chilly, he was sure the groves would receive the people. But they found the house open, and already filled with people. Groups of men stood in the yard, waiting for the man whose word, it seemed, could move churches from their foundations, and who now had the boldness to come and preach a strange Gospel among the orthodox at Stony Point. He went in and took his seat at a table near the pulpit. The strong and cheerful voices of his young brethren greeted his entrance with the fine old song, from manuscripts:

> " How firm a foundation you, saints of the Lord,
> Have laid for your faith in his excellent Word."

While they were singing, an old man came in, and approaching Smith, said something to him that he could not understand, for the whole multitude had caught up the strain, and were singing with enthusiasm. Smith rapped on the floor with his cane, and the song ceased.

"This gentleman," said he, "wishes to say something that I can not well hear."

The man now informed them that the trustees of the meeting-house had directed him to come and say, that John

Smith could not preach in that house, but that Elder Gates might do so if he chose.

Smith arose, and repeating the order of the trustees, said:

"I came here, friends, by special request, and I am perfectly willing to preach wherever the people may choose to assemble."

Several at once proposed their own houses; some said one thing and some another, for there was much confusion. He met the crisis, however, in his own peculiar way. When order was restored, he took up his hat, and while every eye was on him, walked toward the door.

"Though we are not apostles, nor even successors of the apostles," said he, turning to the messenger, and speaking through him to the trustees, "yet we come to you bringing the apostles' doctrine, and since you will not receive us into your house, nor hear the Word that we bring, we shake off the dust from under our feet as a testimony against you," and the dust of his shoes was left on their inhospitable threshold. Two Christian women, who loved the Word that he preached, now arose and followed him, and, imitating his example, their lighter footfalls were distinctly heard as they, too, shook off the dust from their feet at the door. The whole congregation followed, and gathered around him in a grove near by. There he stood in their midst, at the root of an old maple, and while heaps of forest brush blazed near by, he preached the Gospel that he loved, to a multitude that were willing to endure cold and fatigue and ridicule to hear him.

In the assembly, that day, there stood a man much respected for his strong, natural sense, and his firm and honest heart. He listened with intense interest; for he, too, was prayerfully investigating the Scriptures, and suspiciously examining the foundations of his Calvinism. That discourse gave to his mind new light, and helped him to a more perfect understanding of the plan of salvation. Hiram M. Bledsoe, soon afterward, modestly, but firmly, embraced the principles of the Reformation, becoming, at length, one of the most solid of the pillars of the Church.

That night John Smith preached at a farm-house a few miles off, and many, that had gone to Stony Point, followed him thither also. And thus they continued with him some

days, as he went preaching from house to house among the
people.

He returned home, and, for the remainder of the year
1828, confined his labors within the bounds of North District—preaching regularly at Spencer, Mount Sterling, and
Grassy Lick—and giving what time he could to the new
churches that he had planted.

On one occasion during that year, as he was preaching
to the young disciples at Sharpsburg, the Methodists and
the Presbyterians held meetings also, and divided the attention of the people. At the close of his discourse one evening,
a young man of very plain appearance, but of fine sense,
came forward and demanded baptism forthwith. Lights
were procured, for the night was dark. The entire congregation turned out with one accord to escort him to the
water. The crowd shaped itself into something like a procession, and, with uplifted torches, and waving lanterns, they
moved on through the streets, singing with fervor,

> "In all my Lord's appointed ways,
> My journey I'll pursue."

It chanced that their way to the water led by the Presbyterian and Methodist meeting-houses, at both of which places
there was preaching that night. As the procession passed
by, the congregations poured out of the doors from both
houses, and, leaving their ministers behind them, moved on
with the throng to the water. Even the solemnity of a baptism at night, could not hush the irreverent titter of the
people, as they thought of the two preachers standing there
in the pulpits, indignant and alone.

The wife of the young man who was immersed that night
was a devout Methodist. On the first opportunity, afterward,
he went with her and attached himself to the Methodist
Church. Her religious friends boasted no little over this
unexpected capture of one of John the Dipper's disciples; they
indulged in much raillery at the Reformers, who could not, in
their chagrin, see any reason for the strange behavior of their
convert, nor any occasion for merriment in their opponents.

On the next visit of the circuit-rider, the young man was
appointed class-leader; for he was very pious, and well read
in the Scriptures. But he arose and expressed some scruples

at accepting an office for which he could find no authority in the Word of God, and which, withal, he felt utterly unqualified to fill; and he drew out a New Testament from his pocket, and asked for the text that authorized such an appointment. The preacher replied that the appointment was strictly in accordance with the Discipline of the Church. But the young man persistently refused to accept it. Not long afterward, another was made class-leader in his place; but again he arose, with his New Testament in his hand, and said that no man could lead him in religion; for it was written, "One is your leader, even Christ." And thus it was with every measure that they proposed for which there was no authority in the Book; he stood up and respectfully, but firmly, opposed them.

At last, they determined to get rid of him, and accordingly arraigned him, on some frivolous charge, before the church. They sat on his trial with doors closed, for they knew that the people sympathized with him. Many of his friends gathered around the house, anxiously awaiting the result, and curious to catch some word or incident of the trial as it progressed. The preacher spoke low and cautiously, that he might not be heard by those without; but the accused, conscious of the fact that friends were near by, repeated the preacher's questions, and made answer to them in a voice that was distinctly heard in the yard. At last the minister called for the class-rolls, and solemnly erased his name. But now, his wife arose, and, strengthened by her love for her husband, said:

"If you thus treat your members for conscientiously adhering to the Word of God, take off my name, too, from your book." And they both went out, and soon afterward united with the Disciples.

About this time, a young man—Curtis J. Smith—who lived in Madison County, and who had recently joined the Presbyterian Church, and received the usual call to the ministry, came to Montgomery County ostensibly to visit some relatives, but really to converse with John Smith. He was soon to enter the Presbyterian College at Danville, to fit himself for the ministry; but, in the meantime, from his preparatory reading, he had become no little perplexed on the subject of baptism. Smith soon learned that he had reached the neighborhood, and, meeting him one day, cordially invited him to his house. He accepted the invitation and went.

"You feel, no doubt, that you have been divinely and specially called, my young brother, to preach the Gospel?" inquired Smith.

"I do," said he.

"Why, then, do you not begin?"

"My brethren," answered he, "say that I must go to college four or five years first, and qualify myself for the work."

"Do your brethren, then, think," said Smith, "that the Lord has mistaken your qualifications? How can they dare to keep you back five years from doing what the Lord calls you to do now?"

This set the young stranger to thinking, for he did not see how to reconcile the Lord's will and man's decree.

Not long after this, he found the desired opportunity to talk with Smith on the subject of baptism. He was young and modest, but anxious to know the truth. Summoning up the necessary courage one day, he opened the Bible, and, reading what Ananias said to Paul, he inquired:

"When it says, 'Arise, and be baptized, and wash away thy sins,' what does it mean, Mr. Smith?"

"It means just what it says, my young brother."

The answer, thus simple and suggestive, was, however, unsatisfactory, and the prejudices of the young man were aroused. He was discouraged, and he determined never to affiliate with a people that, as he supposed, taught that water could wash away sins. But before he returned home, his thoughtful friend put a copy of the New Translation into his hands, for he appreciated his difficulties, and knew how to remove them. That book satisfied his mind fully on the subject of baptism. He soon afterward renounced the faith which he had professed, and became, not only a convert to the Ancient Gospel, but one of its most eloquent and popular proclaimers.

The year 1828 now drew to its close. Smith, after reviewing his work, and prayerfully considering the interests of the cause and the condition of his family, concluded, with his wife's consent, to preach another year as he had already done.

He had lately received some small donations in money, which enabled him to pay some of the interest on his debt. He hired a negro man, also, for sixty-five dollars, with whose help his wife, ever ready to do what she could, undertook to carry on the farm for another year.

CHAPTER XXV.

SILAS M. NOEL was, at that time, perhaps the most learned preacher among the United Baptists of Kentucky. He had been educated for the bar, but, being religiously disposed, had early laid aside the law, and taken up the Gospel. He was for awhile pastor of the church at Frankfort, but, his zeal increasing, he gave up his charge to another, and, traveling through the country as an evangelist, preached far and near, with much success. The church at Frankfort not prospering, he was recalled, and soon became the leader of the Franklin Association.

In 1826, in the Circular Letter of the Association, he defended, with much tact, the propriety or necessity of creeds, and his very able essay was held by his friends to be conclusive on the subject. There was not in the State a more powerful opponent of the Reformation than Silas M. Noel—though he was charged at one time with being an admirer of Alexander Campbell.

Shortly after Smith had begun to preach the *Ancient Gospel*, he was urged to go and proclaim it to the orthodox community of Frankfort.

"I was called on," says he, "to go up to the capital of the State and storm the sectarian fort of Dr. Noel. No one was there to help me at that time, so far as I knew, but Philip S. Fall. I authorized him, therefore, to make the appointment, but they closed every church in town against me! In his extremity, Brother Fall went to Judge Owsley, for court was in session, and he was upon the bench. I had baptized some relatives of the Judge, and he had, perhaps, already heard something of me. Brother Fall appealed to him, for it was winter, and the people could not gather in the grove. 'What!' said the Judge, 'is it John Smith, of Montgomery? What is the matter with the people, that they shut their houses against such a man? Tell him I will adjourn the court, and he can preach in the court-room.' I suppose Philip had heard that little anecdote about my sermon at Crab Orchard, 1815, and, perhaps thinking that some of the representatives from the lower counties might remember me, he wrote a notice, and stuck it up everywhere about the town, to the effect that *Raccoon John Smith* would preach, that evening, in the court-room. Everybody read it, wondered at it, and came to hear me. The room was crowded to overflowing—lobby, aisles, and windows were filled. Every member of the Legislature was there but four; and even Silas himself couldn't stay away. Of course, my ugly name was fixed on me from that time; for members of the Legislature carried it to every county, and, when I afterward appeared in any part of the State, I always found that some knew me as 'Raccoon John Smith, of Montgomery.' " *

Smith arose that evening in the presence of one of the most imposing audiences that he had ever addressed. He had never stood up to plead the *Ancient Gospel* on a more important occasion. He was to speak before the representatives of the people; he was to assail a popular doctrine in the presence of its ablest advocate; he was to present to the people a strange Gospel, unfit, the clergy had said, to be preached from any orthodox pulpit in the city; and, besides, the representatives present would soon return to their respective districts, and carry with them the impressions of the hour; yet he arose without embarrassment, and, opening the Scriptures at a certain place, read:

"And when *John* came to *Frankfort*, his spirit was stirred

---

* Elder P. S. Fall, in a note to the author, disclaims altogether the prefixing of the word "Raccoon" to the name of John Smith. True, in the advertisements that were posted about the town, and that were written by him, the word occupied its place before the name of Smith; but he had never heard him spoken of, or distinguished from any other John Smith, except in that way. He thinks that, if any one originated that epithet, it was Jacob Creath, Sen., who, at an Elkhorn Association, made an appointment for him, and, on being asked who John Smith was, replied, "He is a singe-cat from somewhere among the raccoons."

Elder Fall is of the opinion that this visit of John Smith to Frankfort was at a later period.

within him when he saw the city wholly given to *secta
rianism.*"

Pausing a moment, and adjusting his spectacles, he re
marked:

"I believe, friends, that I have not read it exactly as it is
in the Book! The city spoken of, it seems, was wholly given
to *idolatry.* But, really, the difference between sectarianism
and idolatry is so slight that the error is hardly worth correcting; for I do aver, my friends, that sectarianism has
done the cause of Christianity more harm than all the idolatry
in the world!"

He then proceeded to contrast the Church of Christ, constituted and governed according to the law of the King, with
a sect founded on a human creed, and governed by human
traditions and commandments. He was heard with profound
attention by all present, many of whom had always accepted
the doctrine of their preachers without the least examination.

Not a great while after this, he went to Frankfort again;
for he was hopeful that, in spite of the opposition of Dr.
Noel, the standard of the Apostolic Gospel might be planted
at the capital of the State. He hoped, too, that he would
meet with a more favorable reception from the people than
before. When he reached the city, he inquired at once for
the house of his opponent; and, on his way thither, he met
the Doctor in the street.

"Brother Silas," said he, "I am on my way to your house.
You may not want me to come, but I am going anyhow, and
I expect to be well treated."

"I will, indeed, be glad to see you there, Brother Smith,"
replied Noel, for he was a courteous and kind-hearted gentleman. He immediately turned back, and conducted his guest
to the house; nor could Smith have wished for a warmer
greeting or a more hospitable fireside.

He had been sitting but a little while, when he saw
through the window that his horse, which had been hitched
at the gate, was loose, and wandering about the street. He
went out, and soon caught and hitched him again, for he had
only slipped the bridle.

"Brother Smith," said Noel, "your horse ought not to be
blamed for slipping his bridle, for his master has already
done the same thing himself."

"Silas," retorted Smith, "don't you know that up yonder, in Montgomery, the very brutes are so well taught that they refuse to wear human yokes? But down here, in Frankfort, I am told, you have your subjects so cowed that they will wear anything you choose to put on them."

There was quite a stir in town that afternoon, when it was known that John Smith had come again, and that he was going to preach in Dr. Noel's church; for the Doctor did not, on this occasion, refuse the use of the meeting-house. But his brethren, and especially some of the sisters, murmured, and did all they could to keep away the people. However, they went themselves, though under a kind of protest against the liberality of their pastor. Noel himself, too, not only went, but even sat in the pulpit with him.

Before rising to speak, Smith turned to him, and said:

"I expect you to reply to everything that you may not like, Brother Noel; for I wish to be set right, if I am wrong."

"No," said Noel; "that would lead to controversy."

"Well," replied Smith, "that is just what I want it to lead to, for I think that controversy at this time will do good."

At the close of his discourse, he told the audience that he had begged his brother to correct him if he should say anything that was wrong; for he would esteem that man as his best friend who would save him from error. It was due the people, also, he said, that every error in religion should be exposed. But Dr. Noel declined any controversy, and the congregation was dismissed.

"We are a *horned* set here, Brother Smith," said the Doctor, next morning, alluding to the opposition that had been made to Smith's preaching, especially by some of the sisters—"we are a horned set."

"That does not surprise me," he replied. "We know from the Book, Silas, that the *Beast* has horns."

"But, then, we are the sheep," said Noel. "You know that they, too, are sometimes horned."

"But the sisters, Silas: you say they are particularly hostile: do they, too, wear horns?"

"Well," said the Doctor, recovering himself, "I have seen even *horned ewes*."

Noel accompanied his guest as far as South Benson, and there took leave of him. After visiting Lawrenceburg, and other places in Anderson and Woodford Counties, Smith returned home, much encouraged by the results of his short tours beyond the bounds of his old field of labor.

He now formed the rather bold resolution to go and preach the *Ancient* Gospel from the pulpit of David Chenault! He believed that he had accomplished much good even at Frankfort, and at Stony Point: why, then, might he not make some impression on the Calvinists at Cane Spring also? This church, as well as that at Lulbegrud, had been unaffected by the revival of 1828: they had strengthened their stakes, indeed, but they had not lengthened their cords. Cane Spring had even fallen off in numbers, though she had lost none of her orthodoxy and zeal.

Smith sent word that he would be at Cane Spring on a certain Lord's Day in February; and, on Saturday, he reached the house of Josiah Collins, a prominent member of the Flat Wood's Church, in Madison County, and one of the earliest reformers in the Tate's Creek Association.

"I am going," Smith said to his friend, on arriving at his door, "to preach to-morrow at Cane Spring, and I am now on my way to spend the night with Elder David Chenault, and I want you to go along with me."

Collins was astonished, and at once refused to go; but Smith urged him, and he finally consented. It was a blustering, wintry day, and they reached the house at dark, in a storm of snow, weary and cold. Smith called aloud, at the yard fence, and the Elder himself came to the stiles.

"Brother David," said he, "I know you always have good fires, and warm beds, and plenty of everything to eat, besides; Brother Collins and I have come to stay all night with you."

"I suppose you can do so, brethren," said he, somewhat confused, for he was evidently not expecting such guests; "I have no particular objection."

"It would make no particular difference if you had, brother David," said Smith, pleasantly, as he dismounted and hitched his horse, "for we have come on purpose to stay with you; so get down, Brother Collins, and come in and warm yourself."

A large fire soon blazed in the best room, and the travelers were made comfortable. After the usual compliments, however, Elder Chenault remarked:

"Brother Smith, I do not feel willing to talk with you on the subject of religion here, in my house."

"Why, Brother David?" said Smith, taken by surprise.

"Because," replied he, "my wife and children will hear you, and your words may unsettle their faith."

"But, if your wife and children are of the elect, what I would say could do them no harm; and, if they are of the non-elect, you can never do them any good."

"But," said the old gentleman, "you might disturb their minds."

"Well," said Smith, "if you will agree not to attack any doctrine that I preach, I will let you and Brother Collins do all the talking."

In a few minutes, Collins and Chenault were discussing the influence of the Spirit in enlightening the mind of the sinner before his conversion. Smith sat by, ready to speak should the conditions of his silence be violated. In his zeal, the Elder at length made some allusion to the dangerous teachings of his silent guest. Smith instantly rejoined, and his words put an end to the discussion.

"Brethren," said he, "you may rest assured that the Spirit can not enlighten a sinner's mind, except through words, for we must think in words; nor can we even imagine any thing without first naming every idea as we form it."

"Brother Smith," said the Elder, annoyed with this piece of philosophy, "you are not to speak!"

"Then mind the conditions better, Brother Davy," said Smith, and he relapsed into silence again.

But the hour for prayer now came. A devout neighbor had dropped in during the evening, and to him the host handed the Bible, requesting him to read, and to offer the prayer.

"No," said he, "I do not think it is right for me to lead in worship when preaching brethren are present: we will follow them."

"Brother Chenault, I fear, objects even to our praying in his house," said Smith.

"Yes, Brother Woods, I do," said the Elder, "and you must worship with us. The time has been when I could have let these brethren pray in my house; but I can not do it now— they deny the Holy Spirit."

Woods led in devotion, and the company afterward retired to rest. Very early next morning, Elder Chenault came into their room.

"Good morning," said he, "you philosophers that can not think without words! I have come to let you know that I have thought of a thing that has no name—a thing, too, that I never saw or heard of in my life."

Smith saw at once that the mind of his host had been busy all night with the thought which he had dropped that evening at the fireside.

"Do, then, let us have it, Brother David," said he.

"Well, sir, I have thought of an animal that is one-fourth horse, one-fourth hog, one-fourth ox, and one-fourth bear. I have no name for it. I never saw or heard of it before. Did you? Have you a name for it?" and he laughed at Smith's philosophy.

"Have you ever seen a bear, Brother David, or an ox?"

"Certainly," replied he; "but have you ever seen *my* animal?"

"Not the whole of it at once," rejoined Smith; "but I have seen and named every quarter of it. But think now of a quarter of anything that you have never seen, and have no word for, and I will surrender."

The Elder, though a man of fine natural sense, found nothing to say in reply.

After breakfast, Smith invited him to go with him over to Cane Spring and hear him preach.

"I will not go," said he; "and, besides, you will not preach there yourself to-day. The principal members of the church, having heard that you were coming, met yesterday, and locked up the meeting-house; they nailed up every window, too, and carried away all the fuel."

Smith was really perplexed; the day was cold, and the ground was covered with snow, and there was neither house nor barn convenient that he could occupy; but he was soon resolved.

"I will go over anyhow," said he. "But it is too cold a day for people to stand out in the snow to hear preaching; the women can not endure it: nor, indeed, can the men. I will go over and see whether we can get in. If not"—and he arose and took his stand at a middle door, between the two rooms, and measured the space around him with his eyes—"if not, I will just come back and stand here, Brother Chenault, and talk to as many as can get into these rooms. I know *you* will not turn your neighbors out, in such weather as this. Yes, Brother David," continued he, seeing the Elder's looks protesting, "I will do that very thing."

"Lord!" sighed the Elder.

"Yes, Brother Chenault," said Smith, "I can not see them standing out-doors this bitter day. I will go and bring them right here by this great, roaring fire."

When he reached the meeting-house, which was but half a mile distant, he found a congregation of men and women already assembled. The fuel had all been removed; but groups of people were gathered around piles of brushwood, which had been fired in the woods near by, and they were waiting, with much patience, for the preacher that never failed to meet his appointments.

The doors of the house were locked, the windows were securely fastened, and every means of entering, save one, was out of the question. Some, who claimed to have an interest in the house, came to him and proposed to force an entrance; but he would not permit it to be done. Calling a little boy to him, he said:

"Run over to Mr. Chenault's, my son, and ask him to be kind enough to send us a key that will unlock the meeting-house. Tell him that the people can not stand in the snow, even to hear me preach, and that, if we can not get a key, *I must take them to some other place.*"

A key was sent. The doors were quickly opened, and the house was soon made warm, and John Smith went in and sowed the seeds of an abundant harvest that day from the pulpit of Elder Chenault!

The opponents of the Reformation were not long cast down by their quiet, but signal, defeat at Lulbegrud in 1828. They had been surprised and discomfited; but they did not yet despair. Though *Campbellism* seemed to be growing apace in the land, they were resolved that it should not long thrive among the churches of the North District. They thought that they would be able to withstand the influence of Alexander Campbell and his paper, if John Smith were only out of the way; and so they determined, if possible, to rid the Association of him. A scheme was accordingly laid to reach him through the church at Grassy Lick, of which he was still a member; they would persuade that church to send a more orthodox messenger in his place, even though it should require his exclusion from that congregation!

Smith was absent so much of the time during the spring of 1829, preaching in other parts of the State, that he had no suspicion of any plot against him. It had once been the custom of the church at Grassy Lick to have the Covenant—which was a creed of fifteen Articles—read at every stated, or monthly, meeting; but that custom had, of late, been dropped, and the Covenant was now seldom read, and only by special request. But at the stated meeting in May, a member of the church, by the name of Hokerson, called for its reading; and after hearing it read, he declared that, as a Christian, he could not live under it any longer. Much debate ensued. Smith, who sat as Moderator, persuaded that the time had come for delivering his brethren at Grassy Lick from the bondage of a human creed, arose, and, taking the document in his hand, said:

"Brethren, when I came among you, in 1817, I joined this church in good faith, believing and defending every item of her creed as I then understood it. But I am now fully convinced that some of the articles of that creed are at variance with the Scriptures, and, therefore, I can not conscientiously teach or defend them any longer."

Taking up the several items of the Covenant, one by one, he endeavored to show wherein they contradicted the Scriptures.

"But, brethren," continued he, "I desire to live with you in peace. I propose, therefore, to lay down my gift, that you may call whomsoever you please to serve as your preacher in my stead. All I ask is, that I shall be left at liberty to preach wherever the people may wish to hear me. This much, my brethren, I feel bound, as an honest man, to say to you."

James Mason replied: "Brother Smith, no one here has complained of you, and you ought not thus to complain of yourself." The church, accordingly, declined to consider his resignation.

David Badger, wishing to remove every cause of offense,

proposed that the church should express her present sentiment respecting the Covenant; and the vote having been formally taken, it was abolished by the voice of nearly two-thirds of the members. Before adjournment, the clerk was directed to prepare the usual letter to the Association, which would meet in July, and to submit it for approval or rejection at the meeting of the church in June.

But the Calvinists of Grassy Lick were much offended at what had been done, and, doubtless, instigated by others, they determined to withdraw, as a body, from Smith and all his anti-creed brethren. They accordingly drew up a Covenant, and went around privately among the disaffected, and obtained their signatures. The document set forth, in explicit terms, that the *direct work of the Holy Spirit in conversion* is a vital point in religion, and that those who believed it, and those only, were to be considered members of the church at Grassy Lick! Having thus clandestinely covenanted themselves into a church, and virtually excluded all others from their fellowship, they, too, prepared a church letter, and appointed messengers to bear it to the Association.

The meeting of the church in June came on. The regular clerk, as directed in May, had drawn up a letter, which he now offered to read. But the critical moment had come, and Reuben McDannold, a leading Calvinist, arose to speak:

"Brother Moderator," said he, "it is unnecessary for your clerk to read what he has written. We, who stand together upon the old Covenant, and we only, can be regarded as the legitimate church at Grassy Lick. We have had our meeting, written our letter, and duly appointed our messengers!"

He then proceeded to read the letter which he had written, and to announce the names of those who had been appointed to bear it; Smith's name, of course, was not among them. Though taken by surprise, he penetrated their scheme at a glance. He had but a moment for reflection; but in that moment he deliberated, decided, and was ready for action.

"Brethren," said he, "this procedure, as you must be well apprised, is all new to me. I still declare my wish to live with you in peace; but I now say again that I must resign my place as your preacher, and go wherever the people may call me, or where the Lord may direct."

But Reuben McDannold now replied: "Your resignation as a preacher here, Brother Smith, will not remedy the evil; for, should you leave, a worse might be called in your place; and, to be candid, we would rather have you here than any other preacher of your sort."

Seeing that they would not accept his resignation, he proposed that they should give him a letter in fellowship, so that he could join some church that would receive him with his present views, and he would ask no more. This they agreed to do, and the clerk was ordered to write the letter. His wife, also, without any conference with her husband, now called for her letter, which of course was granted. David Badger, also, and his wife, asked to be dismissed. Others were about to follow their example, when McDannold, who was growing impatient, and who had an eye to business at all times, said: "Brethren, this is too tedious, it consumes our time. Have you anything against those members, who, in May last, voted against our Covenant, except, indeed, that they would not stand by it? If not, let the clerk be authorized to give letters to all that wish to leave us on that account."

The motion prevailed, and forty-three members made application for letters that day. On Sunday—the next day— the multitude crowded to the meeting-house at an early hour, for it was noised abroad that the church had *split*, and that there would be a struggle for the occupancy of the house. But those who knew John Smith were confident that he would control the storm, and maintain peace, if not fellowship, among his brethren. Seventy-four others now applied for letters, making, in all, about one hundred and twenty.* It was now apparent that a large majority of the church were resolved to go with their pastor. They might justly have claimed the right to occupy the house one half of the time. But Smith, anxious to preserve good feeling, and still loving those whom he was about to leave, said:

"Though we might, with propriety, call ourselves the Grassy Lick church—and we deny that we are, in any sense, a faction—yet we wish to go from you in peace. We leave you, therefore, the house, the books, and the Covenant;

---

*The letters showed that nothing whatever had been alleged against their moral or Christian character.

and all that we ask of you is, that we may meet here and consult together, whether, under all the circumstances, we should join other congregations, or form a new church to ourselves."

The request was granted, and, on the next Wednesday, the *Disciples* met, and resolved to come together at an early day as a *Church of Jesus Christ*, on the Bible as their only covenant and creed. Smith informed them, however, that he could not, for certain reasons, go with them into their new organization; but he promised to preach for them as long as they wished him to do so. They then adjourned, to meet another day.

Thus the disciples went forth from old Grassy Lick, under the leadership of John Smith. No cross word was spoken, and no unkind act was done to give offense; but they departed in tears, and with Christian good-will toward all whom they left behind.

CHAPTER XXVI.

THE church at Mount Sterling had, in 1828, voted out her Covenant, yet she continued to correspond with the Association. Like Sharpsburg, Owingsville, and Spencer, though satisfied that Associations were unauthorized by the Scriptures, she chose to remain in connection with them for awhile, in the hope of soon seeing them converted into general assemblies for the worship of God. They were constrained, too, by their love for Smith, to stand around him, a wall of defense, as long as there was a hand or a voice in the Association to be lifted up against him.

It will be remembered that the usual time for the meeting of the North District Association was the fourth Saturday in July, and that Smith had withdrawn from the church at Grassy Lick at its stated meeting in June. He now hastened to present his letter to the church at Mount Sterling, which came together for business on the second Saturday in July, and he was cordially received into their fellowship. They had already appointed their messengers to the Association, however; but when Smith told them that, for certain reasons, he wished to have a voice in the meeting at Unity, they recalled those whom they had appointed, and sent him, with three others, in their place.

Just before the Association convened, he went to meet the remnant of the church at Grassy Lick for the last time. It was the day of their regular meeting, and, notwithstanding the defection that had reduced their number, many came together. At the proper time, he arose and said to them:

Brethren, about twelve years ago, I moved from Wayne and settled among you, as your preacher, in good faith; and in the same spirit, you agreed to assist me in paying for a home. In 1818, you appointed a committee, who, in connection with brethren from other churches, joined me in selecting a farm. We found a place containing about one hundred acres, and bought it. You, brethren, helped me to make the first payment. Hard times came on, and the circulation of money almost ceased. Soon afterward, I began to change my views respecting some of the doctrines set forth in our Confession; and, as I departed from your faith, you thought proper to render me no more assistance. My creditors sold out the debt upon me to my neighbors, and I went into the Commonwealth's Bank, borrowed the money, and paid off the debt. What I yet owe for that farm, stands against me yonder, in the bank at Mount Sterling.

I now ask you to appoint a committee of brethren to make a settlement with me. I propose that if you will refund to me what I advanced out of my own pocket, and assume my present indebtedness to the bank, which I have already reduced, I will deed back to you the land, and you may settle any preacher on it that you please.

When he had made this proposition, Reuben McDannold said:

"Brethren, I have been making a calculation, and I believe that we are in his debt! for all that we paid for him on the land, in 1818, does not amount to as much as fifty dollars a year for his preaching; and we have never paid him anything else for his services! I, therefore, oppose the proposition, and suggest that we, the church at Grassy Lick, assure him that he owes us nothing at all." This assurance having been unanimously given, Smith departed from them again in peace, but to return no more.

In the meantime, the Disciples that had withdrawn from Grassy Lick, met together again, and resolved to build a meeting-house as soon as practicable. The site selected was a richly wooded hill that overlooked the Somerset, two miles east of Grassy Lick, and six miles north of Mount Sterling. There, in a maple grove, they met for awhile, united by a common faith, and constituted on the Word of God, the creed of each disciple. Until the house was completed, they continued to worship in the grove, where they had erected a rude stand, and rolled the logs together for seats. They met at first monthly, on the third Sunday; for Smith had promised to be with them, on that day, as long as he could. They had no elders for sometime; but David Badger and Franklin Taylor were chosen deacons; afterward, when they began to meet weekly, Philip Hathaway, Newton Lane, David Cassady, and Samuel Carrington were ordained elders. The church continued to grow in influence and in numbers, and faithfully tried to conform, in all respects, to the Ancient and Apostolic order of things.

The following words, from the lips of Elder Smith, have special interest in this connection:

I have sometimes been asked why I left the Baptist Church, and I have, on several occasions, answered, in substance, as follows:

I. I did not believe the doctrines of the Philadelphia Confession of Faith to be in accordance with the Word of God; and, of course, I could not conscientiously teach them.

II. I could not find such a thing as a *Baptist Church* named in the Bible.

III. I found that the kind of experience which they required was unknown to any of the saints of the New Testament. I recalled my own experience, and compared it with the conversions given in the Bible; and I was astonished to find that sinners, when convinced of sin and desiring salvation, instead of agonizing for months, as I had done, did not wait a single day to find it; except, perhaps, Saul of Tarsus, who waited and prayed three days before he was told what to do. In bringing every thing to test, however, I found these points in my experience:

1. I believed sincerely in the Lord Jesus; this I knew the Word of God required, and I felt conscious of its qualifications.

2. I was conscious that I had repented of all my sins; this, also, I knew the Word of God demanded.

3. I knew that I had been immersed; and this, I saw, the Lord required of every believing penitent.

I saw clearly that instead of being required to tell all the workings of my mind, they should have required these three things and nothing more, in order to my admission into the Church. True, when I was immersed, I submitted to it simply as a command of God, without knowing the blessings connected with it.

IV. I found, also, this glaring inconsistency among the Baptists: while they taught that a man must be a Christian in the Bible sense of that term, before they could admit him to baptism, yet, until he was baptized, they allowed him no more privileges among them than a pagan or a publican.

V. I was well persuaded that God never authorized any man or set of men to make Articles of Faith or Rules of Practice for the subjects of his kingdom.

VI. I was convinced, moreover, that it was not the custom of the ancient and apostolic churches to eat the Lord's Supper, monthly, or quarterly, but that the disciples met together for that purpose every first day of the week.

Now, convinced as I was that the Baptists taught many erroneous, and some dangerous, doctrines—that they had given their church a name unauthorized by the Scriptures— that their practice of admitting members to baptism by *experience* was also unauthorized—that they assumed the authority to make laws and rules for the government of Christ's Church—and that they neglected to celebrate the Lord's death more than two, or four, or twelve times a year; seeing all these things, I could not conscientiously remain a Baptist, *especially when they were not willing for me to preach and practice among them what I believed to be the truth.*

The North District Association convened at Unity meeting-house, in Clark County, on the fourth Saturday in July, 1829. The introductory sermon was delivered by Elder Thomas White, who earnestly enforced the exhortation of the Apostle, *"Let brotherly love continue."* There was a full representation from nearly all the twenty-four churches of the District. Lulbegrud still complained, declaring that in consequence of changes which were taking place in the Association respecting the administration of the Lord's Supper and other matters, she could not commune! Goshen complained of new forms of words adopted and used in the administration of baptism, etc., and she now begged the Association to give ear to her complaint! The letter of Cane Spring also breathed a sad and complaining spirit.

The letter from Grassy Lick, brought by the hands of

Reuben McDannold and others, was in due time presented, and every ear listened as the names of her accredited messengers were announced.

"He is left out!" said an old Calvinist, and he brightened all over with delight. "He is left out at last!" and an undignified chuckling enlivened the benches around him. The countenance even of David Chenault relented, and a sort of sober joy shone in his gray eye.

Smith sat by, patient and demure, betraying none of the humor that was secretly welling up within him. The letter from the church at Mount Sterling was in due time read. It closed with something like these words: "We send this letter by the hand of our brethren, Buckner H. Payne, Kenaz Farrow, William Orear, and our beloved Bishop, John Smith!" At the mention of that name, the countenance of Goshen, and of Cane Spring, and of Lulbegrud, and of Calvinistic Grassy Lick, instantly fell; the chuckling benches grew solemn, and that ghost of a joy which had appeared in the Moderator's face vanished away!

The Reformers at Unity manifested the same conciliatory and fraternal spirit that had animated them at Lulbegrud in 1828. David Chenault was re-elected Moderator, James French, Clerk, and Buckner H. Payne, his Assistant. John Smith and David Chenault were placed together on committee; while John Taylor and Jacob Creath, Jr., Ryland T. Dillard, and William Morton were elected to address the people from pulpit and stand on Sunday!

When the proper committee met to decide what matters should be presented on Monday, Smith insisted that the complaints of Goshen and Lulbegrud should receive attention. He rejoiced that an opportunity had now come, when all those things for which he and his brethren had been so much censured, would be thoroughly discussed. But the Calvinistic members of the committee strenuously opposed the introduction of these matters. His own presence, and that of so many of his brethren, evidently disconcerted them, and they knew not what to do. His argument at last prevailed, and they agreed to bring forward the complaints of Lulbegrud and Goshen. But on Monday they reconsidered their action, and refused to pay any attention to the complaints of the churches. David Chenault, on the other hand, arose, and declared:

"Brethren we can do nothing; for those who are complained against are more numerous than those who complain. There is only one course that is left to us, and that is, *to withdraw ourselves from them.*"

Thus fell the unfortunate words that drove away the spirit of compromise, and invited that of jealousy and party strife! Those words, deliberately uttered, were caught up by the churches, and afterward repeated as a watchword by such as were resolved to stand by the old landmarks against all innovation or reform.

After adopting a Circular Letter which breathed the spirit of brotherly love, they adjourned to meet at Spencer, in Montgomery County, on the fourth Saturday in July, 1830.

Smith returned home, encouraged at the triumph of the Apostolic Gospel, but sad with the thought that a minority of his brethren were resolved to divide the Association.

The Elkhorn Association convened that year at Lexington, and he was present as a representative, or corresponding messenger, from North District. Elkhorn seemed to move sluggishly in the work of Reform. The influence of such members as Vardeman and Waller, supported by Dillard, Noel, and Dudley, checked the spirit of revolution, and steadily held that community to its ancient Constitution. Nothing of special interest occurred during the session of 1829, save, perhaps, the adoption of a new rule of representation. It was agreed that, henceforth, "all the churches composing the Association should be entitled to at least two votes; if, however, any church was composed of one hundred members, three votes; and then one vote more for every additional hundred members;" and they recommended that the churches should, in future, send messengers according to that ratio. This new rule of apportionment deserves mention here on account of its bearing on subsequent events.

It should be mentioned, also, that at this same meeting Jacob Creath, Sen., introduced a resolution, proposing, that inasmuch as all the corresponding Associations, except Licking, acknowledged the *Terms of Union*, while few ever saw the Philadelphia Confession of Faith, from the present time

the *Terms of Union* should be made the basis of correspondence with the churches and associations. But this proposition
was rejected.

A circular letter, which had been prepared by Jacob
Creath, Jr., was also rejected, probably on account of certain
references which it contained to the two great *isms* of the
day, to the orthodox doctrine of Grace, and to the traditions
of men as opposed to the Gospel of Christ. It was, however,
recommitted to its author, in connection with Jeremiah
Vardeman and John T. Johnson, at that time a messenger
from the church at the Great Crossings, who, in a short time,
reported a letter that was read and unanimously adopted.

The Tate's Creek Association met on the fourth Saturday
in August, at Red Lick meeting-house, in Madison County.
John Smith had often preached within the bounds of that
community, especially to the people of Flat Woods, White
Oak Pond, and Silver Creek. The leaven had early begun to
work in those churches; for they had among them such men
as Josiah Collins, Thomas S. Bronston, and Oliver C. Steele.
But a majority of the Association bitterly opposed the Reformation, not so much, perhaps, from any intelligent conviction
respecting it, for they seem, for the most part, to have mis-
understood its principles, as from a common prejudice that
rejects, without examination, every doctrine that tends to
abolish old religious customs.

The teachings of Josiah Collins and others, that faith is
a simple, heart-felt trust in Jesus as the Messiah, that it is
produced by inspired testimony, and that it works by love,
and purifies the heart, was construed into a denial of all
spiritual agency and Christian experience. It was, moreover,
declared that the holding of such views by any church was a
violation of the Constitution of 1793, and that it furnished
good grounds for its exclusion from the Association. The
friends of Reform consequently felt some concern, when the
meeting came on, lest they should be rejected. They desired
to continue their correspondence with the Association, for
the sake of the influence which they supposed such
a connection would give them; for they felt that, should
they be cast out in the hour of their weakness from fellowship with their brethren, they might not be able to gain the

ears of the people, and stand up alone against the opposition of the clergy.

In this exigency they turned their eyes to John Smith; and, when he appeared among them on the day before the meeting, they felt that with such a man to plead their cause there was no danger of defeat. On Saturday, therefore, he demonstrated before the Association, from the Constitution itself, that those who were called *Campbellites* had not violated that Ancient Confession in any item whatever. The representatives of the heretical churches were finally admitted to seats, the more readily, perhaps, because they seemed to be but a helpless and harmless minority. But when the question came up on Saturday, who should preach on Lord's Day, it was obvious to the Calvinists, from the balloting, that some powerful influence was working against them among the people; for John Smith, in spite of clerical opposition, was elected to speak. After conference with his friends, he resolved to seize the opportunity and to tell the people plainly what the Reformation was; and to give his reasons for every departure that he had made from Baptist doctrine or custom.

When he was about to rise on Sunday afternoon, after three others had already spoken, one of the Calvinistic preachers, who sat near him on the stand, thinking, perhaps, that he could draw off a portion of the people, prepared to leave. He announced, at the same time, that, under the circumstances, he felt it to be his duty to withdraw. But Smith, maintaining his self-control, begged him, in the hearing of the people, to remain and hear him.

"I will tell you," said he, "all about *Campbellism*. Stay, brethren, and hear me," for he saw that others were about to leave the stand.

They sat down; and the people now crowded up from all parts of the grounds where they had been dispersed. He proceeded to name every item of Baptist faith and practice that he had given up, and to explain his reasons for doing so. He spoke at length, for the interest of his hearers seemed not to flag for one moment. He was frank and explicit in his statements, but kind and conciliatory in his manner. The people were more than pleased; they were delighted and convinced. Even the preachers could find nothing to gainsay or condemn. [He closed his address, and, while his eye still beamed with the inspiration of the hour, and his heart throbbed with the fervor of his melting exhortation, the very preachers that had scrupled to sit by and hear him, now came up to him in tears, and affectionately grasped his hand. Some happy heart in the congregation burst into singing, and hundreds caught up the strain. People, overpowered by their feelings, rushed to the stand, and, crowding upon it, seized and shook his hand with unrepressed raptures.] In the midst of this strange scene, Smith raised his voice and exclaimed, in the hearing of the multitude:

"Now, brethren, if you will only live like Christians, a great victory for the Gospel will be gained."

"Brother Smith!" shouted Bronston, at the very top of his voice, "'tis gained already! That 're is to say, the victory is gained now!"

And so, indeed, it was, as subsequent events abundantly proved.

CHAPTER XXVII.

At the Bracken Association, which met in September, at Poplar Run, in Fleming County, Smith and two other preachers, friendly to the Reformation, were chosen by ballot to speak on Sunday. Just after the last discourse on that day, Elder William Vaughn announced to the congregation that he would, on the next day, at the stand, reply to all that had been said. At the appointed hour, while the Association was sitting in the house near by, he met a large assembly in the grove, and, for two hours, controverted the positions of Smith, assailing with some force, the doctrine that forgiveness is graciously obtained only through faith and obedience; in other words, that the Gospel must be obeyed, as well as believed, as a condition of pardon. He contended that justification is wholly of grace, and not of works—alleging that those who preached baptism for the remission of sins virtually denied the blessedness of that righteousness which is without works, and gave up that salvation which is by grace through faith.

It devolved on Smith to reply; for both Abernethy and Gates, who had preached on Sunday, refused to answer. When he arose, Vaughn took up his hat to leave.

"Where are you going, Brother Vaughn?" said Smith, in a loud voice, that fixed the attention of the congregation upon him. "Surely, you are not going away."

"Yes," said Vaughn, "I am on my way to the house."

"But, Brother Vaughn, I am going to reply to you; you will certainly stay and hear me."

"No," persisted Vaughn, "I must go."

"Brother Billy," expostulated Smith, "are you willing to confess, by such a course, that you have taken positions which you can not maintain?"

"Not at all," said he; "but I can not remain."

"I will give you twelve pistareens," urged Smith, "if you will only take a seat and listen to me."

But he would not accede to the proposition and seemed rather to be annoyed by the importunity of Smith, and by his apparent effort to construe his departure into a flight.

"If you will come back," persisted Smith, "I will promise not to expose more than thirteen of your blunders; for I am satisfied that the people have, without difficulty, discovered the others for themselves."

But Vaughn went on to the house, where business, doubtless, called him. Just then a note was handed up to Smith from the crowd, requesting him to make inquiry of the people for a certain dun colt that belonged to some old sister present, and which had wandered off the day before. He no sooner proclaimed the matter to the congregation, than a farmer of the neighborhood arose, and said that the colt was at his house, not far off, safe and sound.

"Do you believe it, my sister?" asked Smith, speaking aloud to her from the stand. "Do you believe what this gentleman says about your colt?"

"Certainly I do," replied the lady.

"But do you think that your faith will ever bring that colt back to you? Must you not now go or send for it, before you can be benefited by your faith?"

"Yes, I must!" she said.

"Now friends, here you see an illustration of the nature of faith, and how it is that, without works, it is dead!"

"There now!" said an honest fellow in the crowd, loud enough to be heard by all around him, for a new idea had flashed into his mind, "if all that Billy Vaughn has said in two hours hasn't been kicked to pieces by a little dun colt!"

But the good Elder, unconscious of the injury done to his cause, by such means, had already reached the meeting-house, and was sitting unconcerned among the pillars of his church.

When the Association adjourned, Smith set out for Mayslick, for he had an appointment to preach there the next day. Elder Vaughn, who really had the kindest regard for him, and who, of course, had refused to listen to him on Monday from no ill-will, went with him, to hear him preach, and, if necessary, to reply to him again. He sat in the pulpit with him with his pencil and paper in hand.

"Write down carefully, now, Brother Vaughn, what I may say," said Smith, aloud, "for I shall speak very candidly to-day."

Having concluded, he turned and said: "You seem to have used your pencil but very little; what was the matter?"

"I heard but very little to condemn," said Vaughn.

"And yet," replied Smith, "I never preached what you call *Campbellism* more plainly in my life." For he had opposed the popular notion that the Spirit is given to the sinner before faith, in order to produce faith; affirming that God had nowhere promised the Spirit to any man in disobedience, or unbelief.

The next day, Smith was to preach at Bracken, and he went home with Jesse Holton, who lived in the neighborhood. Elder Vaughn rode along with them the greater part of the way; for he, too, lived not far from Bracken, and he wished to have still further conversation with his reforming brother.

It should be borne in mind, that the excitement among the churches of Mason and Fleming was at that time very great; for it was understood that the policy of the North District Calvinists would be adopted, and that such churches as were tainted with heresy would, after proper admonition, be rejected. Such a policy was, in fact, announced afterward substantially in the following words to the churches:

"Seek first to reclaim these reformers from their errors. If your efforts should fail, invite them to leave you, and to practice their reformation to themselves. If they will not go at your request, separate them from you in the best way that you can."

All expected that the work of excision would soon begin, and each party was already laboring to get a majority in every church.

Early on Wednesday morning, Elder Vaughn came over to Jesse Holton's, and called for Smith.

"I have come," said he, "to talk with you some more,

and to go with you to meeting to-day, for I wish to hear you again."

"I am glad of this, Brother Billy," said Smith, "and I hope you will hear me honestly."

"I have been studying much about your new doctrine," said Vaughn, "and reflecting especially on our own main position—that the Spirit must enter into the dead sinner, and quicken him, before he can believe or obey."

"Well, Brother Vaughn, have you found any promise yet in the Gospel that the Spirit will be given to any man in disobedience? I labored this point at some length, you know, on yesterday."

"Brother John," replied Vaughn, in the most unreserved manner, "I confess that no promise of the Spirit is given to the sinner while living in disobedience. In fact, I can see that such a promise would have been wrong; for it would have encouraged the sinner to abide in his disobedience."

"You are certainly apprised, Brother Vaughn," said Smith, pleased with the idea of making so distinguished a convert, "that this is giving up all that we ask? But I wish others to hear this." So, when he had called in the family of Jesse Holton, he continued:

"Now, Brother Vaughn, I want you to say here, before these friends, what you have just said to me, that there is no promise in the Book that God will ever give his Spirit to a sinner while in disobedience."

Smith did not see how Vaughn could admit so much without renouncing his whole system of religion; but the Elder had his own way of escaping from the dilemma.

"Yes," said Vaughn, boldly, "I say that God has nowhere made such a promise."

"And did you not say, too, Brother Vaughn, that such a promise, if made, would have encouraged sinners to disobey?"

"Yes," replied Vaughn, "I said all that; but, mark, I did not say that God does not, nevertheless, give his Spirit to them! He has not promised it to them, I know; *but he gives it notwithstanding.* I did not promise to come here to-day, but yet I came anyhow."

Smith looked at him with surprise; and then, in a tone of humorous remonstrance, replied:

"Billy, just look at the attitude in which you have placed yourself! You say that God never promised to send his Spirit to sinners, because such a promise, if revealed, would have had a bad effect upon them. Still, you teach that God will give his Spirit to them nevertheless! When did God, who, you say, never published such a promise, make you his confidant in this matter, and let you into his secret counsel? And why do you blab it all out to sinners, as you do, every time you preach, when, as you say, God don't want the people to know it? Billy," said Smith, affecting great indignation, "you ought to be killed outright for such a breach of confidence!"

Smith preached at Bracken, according to appointment; and on the next day he went to Minerva, and thence to Washington, and then, preaching through Fleming and Bath, he returned home in time to be at the Boone's Creek Association.

That Association, it will be remembered, was, in 1828, in favor of abolishing her Constitution, but had laid the matter over for another year, in order to have the deliberate voice of the churches. Accordingly, in 1829, at Hind's Creek, in Madison County, letters were read from thirteen churches, seven of which voted to retain the Constitution, and six voted to abolish it. These letters, though they expressed the most conflicting sentiments on the subject of creeds, breathed no unchristian spirit. The Circular Letter of that year declared that the whole correspondence evinced that temper of mind which the Head of the Church delights to behold in all his disciples.

The minority raised no disturbance on account of their defeat. They resolved to be bound by no uninspired creed themselves; and they were disposed to allow others also to do as they pleased. They were not inclined to be schismatic, for they desired to live in peace with their dissenting brethren. So long, then, as no attempt should be made to bring them, as Christians, or as churches, under subjection to a human Constitution, they would not seek a separation; but they declared that they would not be bound by any confession of faith or rule of discipline other than the Word of God.

When the sessions of the Associations for the year 1829 were over, John Smith turned his attention again to the churches of the North District; for the state of affairs in that community interested him most deeply. It will not be forgotten that David Chenault had declared, at Unity, that there was but one course left for the faithful to pursue, and that was, to withdraw to themselves. Accordingly, not long afterward, in the fall of 1829, the clerk, James French, announced that a meeting extraordinary would be held at Lulbegrud, in April, for the purpose of taking the affairs of the District into consideration; but only such churches as stood on *Baptist ground* were invited to be present! It was by no means the purpose of the offended Calvinists to abandon the Association; but, like their brethren at Grassy Lick, they resolved to withdraw from the majority, and to take with them the books and papers, the Constitution, and their name. In a word, their plan was to assume all Associational authority, and, under the name of a withdrawal, to drop the majority from their communion!

There was one man among the many opponents of Smith that seemed to comprehend the real issue between the Reformers and their brethren. James French saw that it was more than a question about ecclesiastical creeds and covenants and names; for he knew that many Baptist churches had been constituted on the Scriptures alone, and had not, on that account, been rejected by their brethren. He saw that the success of the Reformation involved the utter extinction of every sectarian or denominational Church in the land; that the design of Mr. Campbell was to re-establish what he called *Apostolic Christianity*, from which, it was alleged, all denominations had apostatized. French felt, as every other good man, that the Baptist churches stood in need of reformation; but he hoped that, when reformed, they would be Baptist churches still, pruned of their faults. He saw that Mr. Campbell's doctrine, if carried out, would not only reform, but revolutionize, and ultimately destroy, the Church of his fathers; and, therefore, he persistently withstood John Smith, not as a reformer, but as a revolutionist.

He was a man of great shrewdness; he had a strong,

but well-governed, temper; was thoughtful and reticent, but uniformly polite in his bearing. He had well studied men and things, and was not without some knowledge of the literature and the theology of his day. He was, for a long time, a Magistrate, or County Judge, and had gained some influence among the people. Usually, he carried a point by strategy; for he seldom stormed an obstacle, or openly quarreled with an enemy. He would quietly plan, while others would almost unconsciously carry out his designs. Sometimes, his purposes seemed to ripen of themselves into execution. He was, indeed, the wisdom of the opposition; in a word, it was James French, and not John Calvin or David Chenault, that so obstinately withstood John Smith in the North District Association.

"We have often been thrown in collision, Brother French," said Smith, when visiting him in his last illness, long after these exciting scenes were over, "but I have no unpleasand recollections of anything you ever said to injure or to wound. You talked but little; but I used to think that you devised many things. I do not say this, now, to criminate you in the least; on the contrary, I want you to feel assured that I have not an unfriendly feeling toward you in the world."

In the meantime, Smith, and other leading Reformers, were anxious that the disciples should bring forth fruits worthy of reformation. Having pleaded so long for the restoration of the *Ancient Order*, they felt that they should exemplify it more consistently in their practice. Accordingly, it was agreed that religious meetings should be held in different parts of the country, and that the brethren should be urged to come together for social worship and exhortation, *"without regard to human rules, institutions, or commands."* One of those "three-days' meetings," as they were called, was held at Mount Zion, in Clark County, in the month of October, 1829.

"I expected greater enjoyment," writes one who was present, to the *Christian Examiner*, "than we commonly experience at Associations, and I can assure you that it exceeded my most sanguine expectations.

"The peace, love, and harmony which prevailed, both in the public assembly and in the private circle, were truly edifying. If I ever saw the fruit of the Spirit *manifested* in a large and lengthy meeting, it was at Mount Zion.

.   .   .   .

"The remarks of Brother Smith, on that occasion, upon *the Desire of a Union among Christians*, were worthy of serious and faithful consideration. He observed that the different denominations of professed Christians were praying for what God could never grant, to-wit: a union upon each of their respective systems of opinions. The Presbyterian prays for a union with *his* people; but to know how far he is willing to go to effect this union, ask him if he will lay aside the confession of opinions formed by the Westminster Assembly. He immediately answers, 'No; we can not keep out heretics without that!' The Baptist prays that all true believers may be united in faith, peace, and love. But ask him if he is willing to put away the Philadelphia book, or the Terms of General Union, and take the *Word of God* for his rule of faith and practice. 'Oh, no!' he answers, 'there can be no *union* without these Terms.' The same is true of the Methodist, with his Discipline; of the Episcopalian, with his Thirty-nine Articles. The Presbyterian expects that, in the millennium, all will be Presbyterians, and so with the others; but God can never answer them in this way, nor will he unite us on any plan but his own.

"I congratulate the brethren living near Mount Zion for. their great advancement in the divine knowledge; yet I think there are some things which are necessary to their further advancement. They are in want of a *purer speech,* which would be greatly assisted, if, on every Lord's Day, they would meet together in suitable and convenient places, and carefully read and examine the Scriptures. They would increase in knowledge, love, and peace.

"The disciples of Jesus have been so long priest-ridden that they do not know their own privileges or abilities. They have lost or given up that system which should have made them kings and priests to God our Father; and they do not God and learn his ways *without a humanly constituted priest or clergyman at their head.* It seems as difficult to convince the great majority of the professed disciples of this day that they can meet and worship without a clergyman in the *sacred desk,* as it would have been, about half a century ago, to convince a European that a nation could exist without a king on its throne. But the United States has fairly demonstrated the absurdity of this hypothesis; and I have strong reasons to believe that, before half a century to come, it will be fully proved that a congregation of believers in Jesus can walk together in the Lord with only a president (as the early Christians were wont to call their Bishop or Elder) chosen from among the brethren."

About that time, also, the first well-authenticated report of Elder Vardeman's defection reached John Smith, and he felt so much concerned, that he went to David's Fork, to one of Vardeman's regular meetings, in order to have an interview with him. After the usual discourse, Smith arose, and, referring to the reported change in his brother's views, remarked to the congregation:

"As I desire above all things to know what is right, and to do it, I hope that Brother Vardeman will tell me, and this audience, what passage in the Word of God has convinced him that he was wrong. This I beg him now to do, not only for my sake, but for his own good, and that of the people."

"You know, my brethren," said Vardeman, in reply, "how much I have always loved Brother Smith, for I have long known him to be a good man and one that wants to stand in the truth of God. But to do what he now desires, would only lead us into controversy, and I do not wish to dispute about doctrinal matters with such a man as he."

Smith replied: "What Brother Vardeman has said only makes it the more imperative on him to give me the reason which led him to abandon us. He says *I love the truth;* he must know, then, that whatever passage of Scripture condemns me, I will, as an honest lover of the truth, accept with all my heart. He says *he loves me;* how then can he bear to see me in the wrong, and not enlighten me? Besides, he has the promise that he that turns a brother from the error of his way, will save a soul from death, and hide a multitude of sins."

But Elder Vardeman said: "I feel satisfied, Brother Smith, that a controversy here would do no good; and I will, therefore, proceed to dismiss the assembly."

"If now you do refuse," continued Smith, "to cite the

proof that we are wrong, whom you so lately declared to be right, the people will justly conclude that you have abandoned us without any scriptural reason at all."

But Elder Vardeman declined the discussion, and the congregation was dismissed. The people became suspicious; and perhaps more was immediately effected by this bold but fruitless challenge than would have been accomplished by the most protracted controversy.

CHAPTER XXVIII.

JACOB CREATH, JR., after an absence of two years from Kentucky, was, on his return, in December, 1828, invited by a portion of the Baptist church at Clear Creek in Woodford County, to visit them once a month, with the understanding that his preaching would not interfere with the regular worship of the church, under her chosen pastor, George Blackburn, an amiable man, and a firm and prudent moderator.

Clear Creek, the oldest daughter of South Elkhorn, was for many years one of the most influential and orthodox Baptist churches in Kentucky. But personal contentions had arisen, and roots of bitterness had sprung up, until some of her best members had withdrawn in order to escape the continuous turmoil. To increase her distress the question was at length raised: " Are not authoritative human creeds, as tests of fellowship, contrary to the will of God, and a source of discord among his people?" The frequent discussion of that question, by such men as Jacob Creath, Sen. and William Morton, in 1828, had given offense to many who were resolved, at all hazards, to stand by their Constitution. The close of the year consequently found the church not only torn by personal jealousies, but divided on the great question which was then agitating so many other churches in the land.

Jacob Creath, Jr., at this juncture, accepted the call of the anti-creed party; and while George Blackburn pleased the majority of the church by his defense of the Confession, and his patient exposition of its doctrines, Jacob Creath delighted others, on the first Sunday in every month, with arguments against all ecclesiastical creeds and covenants. A few impulsive spirits helped to keep up the strife between the parties, until, at last, the question was raised: Whether it was good order for a few members to employ a man to preach stately in the meeting-house without first consulting the church? The design of this question was obvious; and the anti-creed brethren, desiring to live in peace with all men, agreed to assemble in the woods. There they worshiped during the summer months, though, when winter came on, they returned to the house.

It was while they were holding their assemblies in the grove that they deeply wounded the feelings of the church, and furnished the grounds, or the pretext, for which she afterward withdrew her fellowship from them. Clear Creek had not, on account of the dissensions referred to, celebrated the Lord's Supper for nearly two years. The anti-creed brethren, at peace among themselves, felt a strong desire to observe the ordinance. Accordingly, at one of their monthly meetings, with many from Versailles, and other places, who sympathized with them, they spread the table in the grove, and sat down together to the sacred feast. But their brethren were deeply grieved at their course; some of them declared that it was an outlandish thing for a mere faction to go into the woods and commemorate the Saviour's death! At last, the church took the matter formally in hand, and, as the offense was repeated again and again, they solemnly decided that such conduct was disorderly, and their censure was put to record. Jacob Creath, Sen., and even John Taylor, tried to have the decree reversed, but in vain. The condemned party, unwilling to abandon the table of the Lord, determined, as a last resort, to constitute themselves into a Church of Christ, on the Word of the Lord alone.

The younger Creath was with John Smith, preaching to the churches of Bath and Montgomery, when this resolution was taken; but he met with them on the appointed day, and helped to constitute them into a church.

He had been preaching at Clear Creek but a little while when the church at the Great Crossings, in Scott County, which had formerly enjoyed his teaching, having heard that he had brought back with him some strange doctrines, kindly requested him to visit them, and give his views publicly on the subject of *experimental religion*. He promptly appeared before them, and maintained that the Word, or Gospel, without any Divine influence superadded, was worthy of belief; that it had power to save all that would believe it; and that, in order to produce faith, nothing more was necessary than an honest attention to the testimony of the inspired witnesses.

The elder Creath, who was present, was not at that time fully prepared to accept this teaching. He was inclined to believe that the Hoy Spirit went with the Word and gave it efficacy to the elect, without which they could not believe it to be true.* But not long afterwards, he met with John Smith, and, during a protracted interview, the question of spiritual influence was fully and freely discussed; the position of the nephew was reviewed, and the expediency of his course in declaring his views before the people at that time, was considered. Smith defended the policy of the younger Creath, and gave the doctrine which he had promulgated at the Crossings, his unqualified indorsement. This was a critical period in the history of the Reformation within the bounds of the Elkhorn Association. Jacob Creath, Sen., though not fully satisfied, yielded a general assent to its principles; and other preachers, emboldened or convinced, soon began to teach without reserve what John Smith had so fully indorsed.

Not long after this, Smith himself visited the Crossings, and delivered a discourse on the main points of Calvinism, which was long remembered for its clearness and power. The impression which it made on the minds of his Calvinistic hearers, in spite of prejudice, was deep and lasting. Elder Thomas Henderson, aroused to investigation by it, at once began a correspondence with him on the subject of foreknowledge and election.

The following letter, which Smith addressed to him, contains so much that is characteristic of the temper and the style of its author, that we give it entire, for the satisfaction of the reader:

MONTGOMERY COUNTY, KY., Nov. 16, 1829.

Dear Brother Henderson:—Having got through a multiplicity of engagements, I now embrace the first opportunity of attending to your friendly communication of the 20th ult.

---

* Autobiography of Jacob Creath, Jr., in *Christian Pioneer.*

I know not when I received a communication which produced the same kind of sensations in my mind.

I doubt not your sincerity. I think I can fully enter into your feelings and difficulties from my own experience. In the year 1822, I had the same thoughts, the same feelings, the same difficulties about the same texts of Scriptures, and deed many others, which you suggest in your letter. My parents were Calvinistic Baptists, and, when I first made a profession of religion, all the Baptists in the neighborhood where I lived were of that sentiment. Under that kind of teaching, I embraced the doctrine of *Election* and *Reprobation* in the strongest terms in which it was expressed in their creeds, or covenants, and even the doctrine of *Eternal Justification*. When I began to speak in public, I preached it; having received those opinions as true, I strove with all my power to maintain them. Not long after I found difficulties in the system which I could not reconcile with the justice, the impartiality, and the love of God, and the universal exhortations with which the Bible abounds. A friend and brother, who lived fifty or sixty miles from me, ascertained my difficulties, and sent me Fuller's *"Gospel Worthy of all Acceptation"*— a book which I had never before seen. Some sentiments, therein exhibited, seemed to make the universal exhortations of the Bible more consistent with what I had been taught to call the "Doctrine of Grace," but I finally concluded that if the blessings offered were entirely out of the reach of those to whom they were offered, unless God afforded some immediate or physical aids, the offer was a perfect mockery to all those from whom such aid was withheld. About the years 1821-22, I expressed my difficulties to several of my friends, and determined to search the Scriptures over again, and whatever I found to be the truth, I would receive and teach at all hazards; and if I found any error in my former opinions, I would give it up. The result of my inquiries you heard in part at the *Crossings*.

Now, Brother Henderson, I have made the above statements, that you may see that your difficulties are not yours only, and that I can, from my own experience, enter into your feelings.

Your difficulty about the foreknowledge of God, I think,

must arise from blending foreknowledge and fore-ordination as if they were the same. Now, the word *foreknowledge* is found in only two places in the Bible that I recollect, viz., Acts i. 23, and I. Peter i. 2. In the first of these places, the Apostle was speaking of the death and resurrection of Christ for the benefit of the world, and he brings to view that which God by the mouth of the prophets had said long before it came to pass; that it had now taken place according to those predictions, and in this way introduced the words *foreknowledge*, etc. In the latter, the Apostle is explaining the means by which God had elected those to whom he wrote, to eternal life, viz.: "through sanctification of the Spirit," etc., for the Spirit was promised to them that believed. The fore-ordination of God, as set forth in the Scriptures, is joyful to think of. In I. Peter i. 20, we learn that Christ was fore-ordained for the salvation of sinners. In a word, all things that we read of God's fore-ordaining are for the good of mankind. Now it is certain this God foreknew all the evil as well as the good; and, if foreknowledge is equivalent to fore-ordination, it follows, that all the sins and abominations that have ever cursed, or ever will curse, the world with wretchedness and ruin, were fore-ordained of God; and if God foreordained nothing contrary to his will, then it follows that the liar, the thief, and the murderer do the will of God as perfectly as the most virtuous and pious. It is a fact, which should never be overlooked, that the Bible nowhere teaches that the foreknowledge of God ever was or ever will be the immediate cause of any body's being justified or condemned. Neither is the foreknowledge of God spoken of as the cause why any body will be admitted to heaven or cast into hell at the last day. But I rejoice in contemplating the wisdom, the knowledge, and the counsel of God in devising, executing, and adapting his way of salvation to the condition of such sinners as we are. Now, Brother Henderson, that the doctrine of *Election and Reprobation* is a Bible doctrine, I have never doubted; but I do deny said doctrine as set forth in our Calvinistic creeds, and by our Calvinistic preachers from the pulpit. But the limits of a letter will not admit of entering fully into the merits of this subject. I shall, therefore, just glance a little at the texts to which you referred in your letter, firmly believing that no fair construction can place them at variance with my views on the subject of faith, as I explained at the *Crossings*.

That the text in John xv. 16, has special reference to the Apostles, I have no doubt, and the fifteenth and twenty-seventh verses of the same chapter, with many others, prove it. There you will see that things are said of them which can not, with propriety, apply to any other persons from that time to this; in a word, that certain men were personally, and, according to the sovereign pleasure of God, elected to certain offices for the benefit of the world, is a joyful truth. So it was with these men, the Apostles; they were his special witnesses. So far from others being reprobated to eternal death, when they were chosen to be Apostles, they were, by virtue of that choice, to be for salvation to the ends of the world (Acts xiii. 47). So I understood in the passage in Ephesians. If the *us* and *we* spoken of from the first to the twelfth verse, includes all who are elected to eternal life, who are those alluded to in the thirteenth verse? The *us* and *we first* trusted in Christ. The *ye*, Gentile believers, also trusted in him, "after they heard the word of truth." As to the passages referred to in Romans—that it was a *national* election is evident from the following facts and Scriptures, unless it be where the Apostle has reference to character:

1. It does not appear from the Bible that it ever was the design of God, in making a revelation of himself, and of his love to mankind, to reveal the awful fact to a mother, that, before her child was born, or had done good or evil, it was reprobated to eternal wrath. What must have been the feelings of a mother who loved God, and what the effects of such a revelation, would be hard to tell. Perhaps Christian mothers form the best or most correct idea.

2. Esau never did serve Jacob in his own person. But God did defend the tribes of Jacob, and he did lay waste the heritage of Esau; *i. e.*, Esau's tribe for the dragons of the wilderness. The following are a few of the many passages to prove, without doubt, the above-stated proposition: Gen. xxvi. 22, 23; Mal. i. 2-6; Jer. xviii. 1-11. These Scriptures, and many others, are quoted by Paul in Rom. ix.; and go to

show plainly that the eternal salvation of Jacob and the reprobation of Esau as individuals, was not the object in view. The characters spoken of in Rom. viii. 29, 30, were all justified, etc., at the time that Paul wrote this letter; for it is spoken in the past tense, and, therefore, can have no allusion to you or me any further than we sustain a similar character. That Ezekiel's vision of the dry bones had no direct allusion to the conversion of a sinner under the Gospel, is evident from the connection in which it stands. When we attend to the thirty-sixth and thirty-seventh chapters of Ezekiel's prophecy, and hear Israel as a nation spoken of— the land which the Lord gave their fathers—the cause of their dispersion—their being divided into two kingdoms— their complaints, "our bones are dried," etc.—the Lord showing how they should be united—how they should be cleansed— promising to restore them to the land of Israel—that they should be no more two kingdoms—that there should be one king over them; even David—and that these bones were the whole house of Israel;—I say, when we see all these things in the context, which so plainly show the meaning of the prophet, is it not evident that the direct allusion was to the deliverance of Israel from captivity, and restoration of them to their own land, and not the state of sinners, or their conversion to Christianity under the light of the Gospel? Might we not as well say that the sprinkling and cleansing, spoken of in the same connection, has a direct allusion to baptism under the Gospel? A word to the wise is sufficient.

I had nearly forgotten the saying in John xiv. 16, 17. Here let it be noted that the unbelievers are all considered worldlings. Believers are not of the world, and whether you would consider that miraculous gifts were intended or not, it is plain that the unbelievers or worldlings could not receive them. *Now if unbelievers can not receive the Spirit, how can they be regenerated by the Spirit before they believe?* Read John viii. 38, 39; and there you will see the matter made plain. Then you may understand why it was that faith or repentance was the first thing urged upon the world by all the preachers of the Gospel, from John *the Dipper* to the end of the apostolic age. You will also see why it was that none of them ever preached the Spirit to unbelievers, but preached Jesus, that they might receive the Spirit by faith in him. There is no promise, no account of any body's receiving Jesus by faith in the Spirit; but there is a promise of receiving the Spirit by faith in Jesus Christ. A few remarks more, and I will close this letter.

When God intended to send a message to men, of which the world had never heard before, he did, of his own sovereign pleasure, elect men without consulting them, without asking their consent, and sometimes before they were born. This was the case with Jeremiah (see Jer. i. 5), John the Dipper, and others. Indeed, while God was making a revelation of himself and his will to the world, I have no doubt but all those instruments employed in making such a revelation of new things, were thus elected and called, even from the calling of Abraham in the land of Haran, to the calling of Saul between Jerusalem and Damascus. In fact, no man had any right to fill, neither *could* any man fill, such an office, or perform such a work, unless he was thus elected and called. But this is quite different from talking about things *after* they have been revealed; for *then* they become *common* property, and we may obey or disobey, and receive or renounce accordingly. And is it not strange that any person should ever think that some are elected and called to obey the Gospel and enjoy everlasting life, and others rejected in the *same* way that those men were elected and called to fill their respective offices, and others rejected from said offices?

Now, Brother Henderson, without the least thought of vain speculation, I have suggested some thoughts on topics of great importance. I hope you will examine them impartially, and let me hear from you again as soon as convenient. And, believe me, your sincere friend and brother in Christ,

JOHN SMITH.

Elder THOS. HENDERSON.

CHAPTER XXIX.

It was not long till John Smith, after due notice given, appeared among the divided brethren of Clear Creek. When he reached the neighborhood, John Taylor came to him and informed him that the regularly-constituted church had determined to occupy the meeting-house next day themselves. "And now," said he, "what, under the circumstances, do you propose to do?"

"Brother Taylor," said he, "I propose to let you all alone. Do you meet in the house, and I will go to the woods."

But Taylor called again early the next morning, and said to him that they had decided to let him preach in the house, agreeably to his appointment, but that Elder ———— must speak first, Smith might follow, and he himself would deliver the closing address; each speaker, however, would be limited to one hour.

"I care nothing for the other discourses," said Smith; "and it is a matter of indifference to me who speaks first or last, but I will not consent to be limited in time."

Taylor finally agreed to give him what time he might wish, and then went away. Jacob Creath, Sen., who was present, was much concerned that Smith had thus put himself in the power of his enemies.

"Brother John," said he, "your discourse will be torn to pieces by Elder Taylor; and he has so arranged it that you can not reply to him, or defend yourself."

The conflicting appointments had brought many together, and they were all curious to see how Smith would meet the opposition that had been so unexpectedly concentrated against him. When the hour came, Elder ———— arose and read his text: "Is it well with thee? is it well with thy husband? is it well with thy child?"—2 Kings iv. 26.

The dead child was made to represent the sinner, dead in trespasses and sins; the prophet was Christ; and the staff was the preacher. The prophet first sent his staff to give life to the child; but it could do no good: so Christ first sends the preacher to the sinner, who tries in vain to save him. Finally, Christ goes himself, as did the prophet of old, and he puts his eyes to the sinner's eyes, and his mouth to the sinner's mouth, and his hands upon the sinner's hands; and he stretches himself down upon the sinner, *till the dead one sneezes, and opens his eyes.*

"Brother John," said Creath, softly, for they sat together in the pulpit behind the speaker, "do you think that you can carry the flag safe through all that?"

But Smith was unabashed. When his time came, he arose and read the third chapter of Paul's letter to the Philippians. He made no allusion to the allegory of the staff and the prophet, nor any criticism on the doctrine which the speaker had extracted from the story of the Shunamite's son; but he noticed, in complimentary terms, the exhortation with which he had closed his performance, for he had, in concluding, said many good things. Smith's eye, while speaking, was on him who was to follow. When he sat down, Taylor arose, and alluding to the chapter which had been read, remarked, in conclusion:

"My brother has preached to us to-day from twenty-one texts of Scripture, and yet I can not object to anything that he has said! I don't believe, after all, brethren, that John Smith is so bad a man as we have heard. All that he has said to-day I can heartily indorse, and I now give him my hand;" and with these words he walked down from the pulpit. But an old Calvinistic elder, who was present, cried out at this, for his zeal for good order and orthodoxy had almost consumed him: "Brother Taylor, if you give your hand in that way to a *Campbellite*, we never want you to come into Clear Creek meeting-house again!" But the hand was given, and Taylor went in and out at Clear Creek as before; nor were the doors ever closed even against John Smith from that day.

Not long after this, Smith informed by a notice in the public papers that the friends of the Reformation, under the name of *Baptist Reformers*, "would hold a three-days' meeting at Clear Creek, similar to that which had been held at Mount Zion," returned to the neighborhood, and, with the Creaths and others, labored to remove still further the prejudices of that community against the "Ancient Gospel," and to confirm those who, through much evil report, were struggling to be free from the bondage of human authority. While at Clear Creek, he sent over a written notice to Elder George Waller, who was then at Hillsborough, a church about six miles distant, saying that he would preach at that place on the following Wednesday; and he requested the Elder to make announcement from his pulpit on Sunday.

Waller received the note, but neglected to read it to the people. Nevertheless, when Smith arrived at the spot, he saw a large congregation assembled in the yard; for the house had been shut and locked against them. A winter rain had recently fallen, and women, anxious to hear the strong man preach, were standing patiently on the cold, wet ground. Smith, no little embarrassed, turned aside to a spring not far off, and having revolved the matter in his mind, determined that, as the house had been closed against him, he would preach to the people in the woods, if they would stay and hear him. But in the meantime, a young man of the neighborhood, a stranger to Smith, but a friend to Elder Waller, came upon the ground, and seeing the ladies standing without, immediately rode up to a window, and, having opened it from the back of his horse, climbed in, and, unlocking the door, admitted the people.

Smith saw them crowding in, and he expressed, to certain brethren who were with him, his mortification and regret that the door had been forced open; and he declared that even now he would preach in the woods. But learning how the house had been opened—that it had not been done violently, nor by any of his own brethren—he at last consented, though reluctantly, to go in and speak to the congregation.

It may serve to illustrate the spirit of the times to relate that after he had returned home, he was published throughout the land, in a leading religious journal, as a *clerical housebreaker!*

"On Wednesday morning, after Christmas," says some writer in the *Baptist Chronicle*, a paper published at that time in Georgetown, Ky., "John Smith, to whom the meeting-house had already been publicly refused, came on to Hillsborough, nevertheless, with Jacob Creath and others, and found, of course, every door and window closed against them. But they were not to be thus foiled. A wicked young man, in their presence, and under their auspices, and, as we understand, encouraged by John Smith, who proffered to indemnify him if he should be sued, proceeded to break open one of the windows, enter the house, and open the doors. We state these facts with little comment; but we believe that a similar outrage can not be found in the history of the Reformation. Let an intelligent community say whether such men are to be countenanced and encouraged."

On his way home from Hillsborough, Smith stopped at the house of Jeremiah Vardeman to pass the night, for he was still anxious to learn the real views of his friend, who was now certainly preaching again those things which he had once labored to destroy. Smith again asked for some reason for the course he had taken; but his host tried persistently, though pleasantly, to waive all discussion, saying that he would not be drawn into controversy with a brother whom he so much loved.

"Should Brother Campbell's views prevail, however," said Vardeman, in the course of the evening, "one result will inevitably follow: the ministry will be put down."

"But we profess to be governed by the Scriptures," replied Smith, "and we should be willing, if we are wrong, to be put down by the Scriptures. Where, then, is the proof that we are in error?"

"Brother Smith," said Vardeman, evasively, "you know how stingy the Baptists already are toward their preachers. But you will now get nothing at all for your preaching; you must all starve."

"Still you give me no proof that I am in error. Men have been martyred for the truth in times past; and, for one, Brother Vardeman, I would rather starve for its sake, now, than to fatten on error, though I should get to be like the man's buck that cut two inches on the shin-bone. But you do much mistake Brother Campbell's views; *his object is to establish a Gospel ministry, in opposition to the hireling priesthood of the day.*"

They had much friendly conversation together, and in many things they were still agreed, particularly in condemning authoritative human creeds, and the severer points of Calvinism. Not long after this visit, it was reported that Smith had abandoned the principles of the Reformation, and that, at the house of Elder Vardeman, he had confessed that he had been in error. His brethren informed him that such a report was current, and begged him to correct it. About the same time, he received a letter from the editors of the *Christian Examiner*, a paper then published in Lexington, who assured him that the report was doing much damage to the cause. Averse, as he always was, to taking any notice of the evil things that were said about him, he determined to correct this mistake, not, however, on his own account, but for the sake of the cause which he loved more than he loved himself. He accordingly addressed the following letter to one of the editors of the *Examiner:*

MOUNT STERLING, KY., April 1, 1830.

*Brother Norwood:—*I have several times been informed that there is a report in circulation in Lexington and its vicinity—but how it got there, or how it originated, I know not—that when I spent a night with Brother Jeremiah Vardeman, on my way home from my last visit to Frankfort, in a conversation between Brother Vardeman and myself, *I gave up every point that we discussed, and agreed to every thing which Brother Vardeman contended for.* This is substantially the report as I heard it. At first I paid little or no attention to it, believing that no *honest* man present at that conversation would make such a statement, and that the report would consequently die of itself; but hearing it so often repeated, I think proper to send you the following statement; and, if you think circumstances require it, you are at liberty to give it a place in your paper; if not, you can do what you please with it, without fear of embarrassing my feelings:

On the evening of the seventh of January last, I called, in company with three other brethren, upon Brother Vardeman, and stayed all night. Much friendly conversation passed between us. Many things were named, in which we both agreed. But I do assert that I did not give up *any* sentiment that I ever contended for, either *then* or *at any other time*, since I have renounced *human systems and the traditions of men* for pure Christianity. You will know that the principal grounds on which our Baptist brethren differ from us, especially those of the liberal sentiments of Brother Vardeman, are our views of the work of the Holy Spirit in the salvation of men, the call to the ministry, hum n creeds, and the necessity of reformation. These four topics, I well recollect, were all spoken of by him and myself that night, and I am sure that Brother Vardeman will never say to me that I yielded one iota of my views on those points, but that its origin is with those who adopt the Quixotic notion of many of our would-be champions of the present day, who boast of victory where none was gained, *behind the backs of those they fear to face in argument.*

I do not recollect whether we said anything about the *Law* or not—that is, whether people in this age of the world are under Moses or under Christ. If it was mentioned, I am equally sure that he will say that I yielded nothing of my views on that topic. I heard neither reason nor Scripture proof sufficient to convince me of error, or even to make me doubt that I was right; and, therefore, could not have changed or even given up my views, either in whole or in part. I am happy to say, that in our conversation about creeds, Brother Vardeman did not attempt to defend them, but rather joined in condemning them. We both agreed in condemning the strong features of Calvinism, etc.

In relation to my views of the Gospel, which I have labored to defend for several years past, if you hear any man say that I have denied or given up any of them, tell him to set his time, and write me the word, and I will come to Lexington at any time, to hear him *attempt to prove it;* for assertion without proof is not current. At the same time, be it remembered that I am open to conviction; and that, should I, at any time, be convinced by the word of truth, of any error that I may be in, I will give it up, and confess it as publicly as I ever promulgated it.

Respectfully, your brother, in the kingdom and patience of Christ, JOHN SMITH.

It will be remembered that Alexander Campbell, in withdrawing from the Redstone Association, with which he had first stood connected, joined the Mahoning Association of Ohio. Through his influence, mainly, the last vestige of what was called *sectarianism* soon disappeared from Mahoning, so that in August, 1829, she was rejected by the Beaver Association of Pennsylvania, and perhaps by other communities of Baptists, on the ground that she had departed from the faith and order of the Gospel church. A copy of the Beaver resolutions was soon forwarded to Frankfort, Kentucky, and the church at that place, in charge of Silas M. Noel, immediately sent up a request to the Franklin Association, which was about to convene at the Forks-of-Elkhorn meeting-house, in Woodford County, that the charges of Beaver against the Reformers should be indorsed and published by the Association. Franklin, after due consideration, not only complied with the request, but advised all the churches in her connection to discountenance the several errors and corruptions for which Mahoning had already suffered excision.

Those *Errors* and *Corruptions* were set forth in the following terms:

1. They, the Reformers, maintain that there is no promise of salvation without baptism;
2. That baptism should be administered to all who say they believe that Jesus Christ is the Son of God, without examination on any other point;
3. That there is no direct operation of the Holy Spirit on the mind prior to baptism;
4. That baptism procures the remission of sins and the gift of the Holy Spirit;
5. That the Scriptures are the only evidence of interest in Christ;
6. That obedience places it in God's power to elect to salvation;
7. That no creed is necessary for the church but the Scriptures as they stand; and
8. That all baptized persons have the right to administer the ordinance of Baptism.

Not long after the publication of these charges, by the Franklin Association, it was rumored that an attempt would be made to spread them upon the Record Book of South Benson, the oldest and largest church in that connection.

John Smith, in his travels through the country in the winter and spring of 1829, had visited that congregation, as we have related, in company with Doctor Noel, then widely differing from him in religious sentiments. On that occasion, he did not hesitate to declare that the Church of Christ ought to have no other constitution than the Word of God, and that opinions could not be the proper foundation of a Christian Church, nor the bond of a Christian brotherhood. The Creaths also had visited South Benson frequently during the same year, and preached the same doctrine; so that many of her members were now ready to surrender their creed, and lay aside their denominational name.

When, therefore, these anti-creed brethren of South Benson heard that the Beaver Resolutions were to be brought up for adoption at the meeting of the church in November, they took alarm, and sent for Jacob Creath, Sen., and Josephus Hewett, a young man of much promise, who had recently been ordained to the ministry; they were both still members of the Baptist church at Versailles. The bill of heresies was, at the time proposed, brought up for consideration. The day was inclement, so that only about seventy-five, out of a church of three hundred members, were present.

Discussion, it appears, was confined mainly to the seventh item, involving the sufficiency of the Scriptures as the creed of the church, and it was carried on with much animation, chiefly by George Waller and Jacob Creath. The day was consumed in debate, and, when the vote was taken, at dark, it was found that forty were of the opinion that the Scriptures as they stand were sufficient, while thirty-three still maintained that a human creed also was necessary, for the constitution and government of the church. At the next monthly meeting, which was in December, the church reconsidered the question, and Doctor Noel, the champion of the creed party, by his personal influence and address, succeeded in reversing the former decision, although John Brown, an unordained member, eloquently maintained that the Scriptures alone should be the creed of Christians. The creed party, having thus triumphed, caused this item of error and corruption to be entered on record along with the others.

Such a record was painfully offensive to the anti-creed party, and they resolved that at the next meeting of the church, which would be in January, they, in turn, would have the whole question discussed again; and they invited Jacob Creath, Sen., and his nephew, to be present. The meeting came on, and Silas M. Noel and George Waller were there to sustain the recent action of the church. Their brethren urged every argument, and used every art of persuasion to induce the church to give them a new hearing, but in vain; they declined to reconsider the action that was now giving the minority so much offense.

The aggrieved party still begged that the December action, which charged them with error and corruption, should be repealed, expressing a willingness, in that event, for the sake of peace, to live quietly under the old Constitution. Even Doctor Noel himself, and, in fact, all the preachers present, at last relented, and urged the majority to expunge the offensive resolution; but they persistently refused to do it. Every effort at reconciliation by the milder spirits of both parties having failed, the minority came together, and, with the assistance of Jacob Creath and his nephew, constituted themselves, on the Scriptures alone, into a *Church of Jesus Christ.* For that alleged schismatic conduct, they were unanimously excluded from the Baptist church at South Benson, at its regular meeting, in February, 1830.

CHAPTER XXX.

SMITH had received but little compensation during the
year 1829, even from those for whom he had specially labored; but his wife, with the help of the hired man, had
raised a good crop, and, by this means, had still further reduced the amount of his indebtedness. But he now felt
that, in justice to her, he ought to take charge of the farm
for the ensuing year, and try to do something for the
greater comfort of his family. But the good woman suggested that, with the same servant to help her, she might
still cultivate the farm profitably; and she assured him of
her perfect willingness to undertake it. He thought of the
probable result of the deliberations of the Convention which,
it will be remembered, James French had called to meet
at Lulbegrud, in April, and he felt that a crisis in the religious
affairs of the Association was at hand. His whole heart was
in the Gospel, and he doubted whether he could consistently
or profitably give his mind to any thing else. He concluded,
finally, that if he could hire the same man again, he would
continue to devote his time to preaching; and that, as soon
as affairs in the District would allow, he would again visit
more distant parts of the country. But his poverty embarrassed him. He could not pay off the note which he had
already given for hire in the preceding year, and he was
unwilling, under the circumstances, to burden himself with
additional debt.

"Brother Hansborough," said he, "I owe you sixty-five
dollars; I have property, but no money; and now I beg
that you will come and select what you wish, and pay yourself."

"Brother Smith," said he. "go on and preach, as you

have been doing. Never mind that note. Take my man another year, and give yourself entirely to the cause."

Those few kind words, spoken at an anxious and critical moment, fixed him in his purpose; and, giving up every thing at home again to his wife, he deliberately planned the campaign for 1830, and aroused himself for the coming conflict of the churches.

In the meantime, the churches and parts of churches that were resolved to stand on old Baptist ground, had been again duly summoned, by James French, to assemble in extraordinary council at Lulbegrud, and the day appointed for the meeting now drew near. The anxiety of the people became intense. "How many of the twenty-five churches of the District will send messengers?" "What will they do when they come together?" "What, according to Baptist usage, will they be able to do, should a minority only of the churches be represented?" "If they meet as an advisory body, what advice will they give?" "And to whom will they give it?" Such questions were asked again and again, and the people speculated till the hour for the meeting came on.

Excluded from any part in their deliberations by the very terms of the invitation, Smith resolved, nevertheless, to be a spectator of their proceedings. He had studied the nature of the present crisis thoroughly, and though, as he believed, a rupture in society must come, yet religious principle, as well as sound policy, required that he should maintain fellowship with his Calvinistic brethren as long as possible. He was willing to live in communion with them, and to accord to them the same liberty of opinion and action that he claimed for himself. His language to them was: "We are willing, brethren, on our part, to confess that some among us have been, at times, guilty of improper words and actions; but do not condemn the cause we advocate for the improprieties of a few individuals. Although we can not consent to be bound by customs which the Word of God does not enjoin, yet we desire to live with those who differ from us, provided they will allow us the privilege which we accord to them, of thinking and acting for ourselves." He was resolved to leave the responsibility of dividing the churches to his opponents, by refraining from the slightest act that would hasten the schism, and by doing all that he could to maintain unity and peace among them. He had but little hope, it is true, that the great brotherhood of Baptists could be held together much longer; but to the sectarians among them he would leave the work of schism; and to this policy he constantly exhorted his brethren.

With such feelings, he took his seat in the old log meeting-house, at Lulbegrud, a mere spectator in that most singular assembly of his brethren. Only seven churches sent either messengers or letters, to-wit: Lulbegrud, Salem, Howard's Upper Creek, Goshen, Unity, Mount Tabor, and New Providence; in all of which churches, as Smith well knew, there were many friends of the Ancient Gospel.

Thomas Boone was chosen Moderator; for David Chenault, for some reason, was not there. A committee was appointed to examine the Records, Correspondence, Decisions, and Reports of the North District Association, from the day of its constitution, in 1802, to its last session, at Unity, in 1829; and to report such results as they might deem to be of interest to the Council. In due time, the Committee made the required examination, and reported in substance, as follows:

1. That the Constitution of North District Association makes it the duty of the Association to have a watch-care over the churches, and gives it the right to withdraw from such as act disorderly.

2. That the Association exercised this watch-care over both churches and preachers, until their session at Cane Spring, in 1827.

3. They find that, at that Association, Lulbegrud complained of a new mode of breaking the bread, when administering and receiving the Lord's Supper; but the Association neglected to notice the conduct of such churches.

4. They find that Cane Spring complained to the Association when in session at Unity, in 1829, and no attention was paid to her complaint.

5. They find, also, that in the same year of 1829, Goshen complains to the Association of new forms of words adopted and used in the administration of baptism, etc.; and yet, though the church requested it, no attention was paid to her request.

6. In 1829, Lulbegrud again complains that, in consequence of changes taking place among the churches respecting the administering and receiving of the Lord's Supper and other matters, she could not commune; and yet, no attention was paid to her complaint.

The Council then formally declared that North District Association consisted of such churches only as continued to practice the ordinances of Baptism and the Lord's Supper, according to established usage, and adhered to the old way of administering the Constitution of the Association and the Terms of Union; and they instructed the clerk to take charge of all the records and papers, and to keep them until legally called for by the Association.

Having thus accomplished all for which they had come together, they appointed a second convention, to be held in June, which should consist of messengers to be sent by those churches or parts of churches, and those only, which were satisfied with the Ancient Usages.

But before they adjourned, much discussion arose as to the place where the next convention should be held. North District Association was by adjournment to convene at Spencer; but it would be an awkward thing for the seceding churches also to meet there; and it would be a violation of a well-established usage to meet as the North District Association anywhere else. Besides, to resolve to go elsewhere would be a final separation; and the embarrassing question would not fail to arise: Whether the minority that refused to go to Spencer according to a resolution unanimously passed in 1829, was the North District Association, or merely a disorderly and schismatic faction?

The Council was divided; some were for meeting at Spencer, others at Goshen. In their embarrassment, an old Calvinist, by the name of Treadway, turned to Smith, who was sitting by him, and inquired of him in a whisper: "What do you think of our going to Spencer?"

During the whole of this extraordinary conference, Smith had sat among them, silent and observant. He had made no attempt to speak, though he had longed for an opportunity to do so. But he knew that they would not suffer him to open his mouth, and he had borne the restriction as patiently as he could. He now replied to the question asked him, but in a voice too low to be distinctly understood. Treadway, however, arose, and urged the Council to meet by all means at Goshen; for the Reforming brethren, as he had just been informed, did not wish to see them at Spencer. "Am I not right, Brother Smith?" said he; and he turned, expecting to see the head of that Reformer nod assent.

"No!" said Smith, in a loud voice, "you are wrong in that, Brother Treadway, as you are in everything else!"

"Well, what *did* you say?"

Smith felt that the time for speaking had come at last. He arose with the purpose, not only of correcting his brother, but of improving the opportunity to enlighten the Council on other points. But he was no sooner on his feet, than they cried out from one end of the house to the other: "Don't let him speak, Brother Moderator!" "Put him down! Put him down!" He turned and looked on them for some time, with a face that calmly brightened, as their frowns grew dark. When their noisy protestations were over, he said:

"Will you not let me tell the brother what I said?"

"Put him down!" was everywhere repeated, and their cries became louder each moment; for he stood there and patiently smiled at their clamors. The Moderator, for awhile, utterly failed in his attempts to enforce the decorum; but a happy expedient at last occurred to him, and he made one more effort to quiet the tumult. Calling the boisterous messengers to order with a loud voice, he said:

"I decide that Brother Smith ought to be allowed to explain himself; but he must do so in a whisper to Brother Treadway, who will then report it to the Council."

"Whisper it again, Brother Smith," said Treadway, softly.

Smith, still standing, looked down into the upturned face of Treadway, and, speaking in a voice that was heard distinctly by all that were in the house, and by some that were standing without, fully fifty yards off, *he whispered:*

"I said, Brother Treadway, that if you will all come to Spencer AS BRETHREN, we shall be glad to see you; but, if you expect to come there to padlock people's mouths, as you do here, you had better go anywhere else in all the world than to Spencer's Creek! Now, tell the Moderator what I said!"

"You have already told it yourself, sir," said an indignant Calvinist, who foresaw that the words of Smith would be reported throughout the entire District, and that, consequently, no apology could now, in the eyes of the people, justify their factious assembly at Goshen. But, resolved on a separation from their heretical brethren, at any cost, they now boldly adjourned, to meet at Goshen, in Clark County, on the fourth Saturday in June, one month before the day that had been regularly appointed for the annual meeting of the Association at Spencer. They subsequently invited all such churches or parts of churches belonging to North District, as were content with the former usages of the churches, and were pleased so to do, to send letters and messengers to the meeting.

In reference to the singular decision of the Lulbegrud Council, that North District had violated her Constitution in not hearkening to the complaints of certain churches, it will be kept in mind that the very individuals who, in 1827, at Cane Spring, had voted to postpone, for one year, the consideration of those complaints, now composed that Council! In 1828, no complaints were made by any church. In 1829, at Unity, Smith did all that he could to induce the Opposition to listen to the complaints which were then made; for he wished the grounds of the dissatisfaction to be discussed before the people. But the Calvinists themselves, who now censured the Association for neglect of duty on that occasion, were the very individuals who prevented it, and had turned a deaf ear to the churches.

"You not only withdraw from us," said Smith, to one of their elders, "but you exclude us from your fellowship for faults of your own!"

"No, no, Brother Smith," replied the Elder, "we do not assume any such authority; you know that we are only an advisory council."

"But when you advise a church or preacher, and they do not choose to follow your advice, what do you do with them?"

"Well," said the Elder, "we have to withdraw from them, of course."

"But are you, in this matter, as honest as the Catholics, who come right out boldly and decree their refractory members to death? I would as soon be decreed, as advised, to death."

Referring to these and other events already related, James Mason wrote a letter to the editor of the *Millennial Harbinger*, in May, 1830, from which we make the following extracts:

The happiness I once enjoyed in the society has been destroyed by the schism that has taken place in the church at Grassy Lick, on account of an old written creed, as old as the church itself, called the "Church Covenant," which held forth, in eleven or twelve articles, the old system of John Calvin, and which a majority of the church, with Brother John Smith at their head, were determined no longer to put up with. After voting it out, they asked for letters, and constituted in less than two miles, where they meet to themselves, and have as little to do with those they left as Jews and Samaritans.

I plead with these *Campbellite* brethren, as they are called, to be patient, and let the old Covenant alone. I disbelieved it as much as any of them; but rather than cause a division of the church, I was willing to let it die a more lingering death; for I had no doubt but that Brother Smith's preaching the Ancient Gospel, as he was constantly doing, would kill it without any other aid. I thought it would be better to take the fort by siege than to risk the lives of our men; but I could not prevail, and things are as above stated. I am yet in the old camp, viewed with a jealous eye by both parties, and not very popular with either; and although my views as respects the Gospel of Christ are pretty much in accordance with these reformers of yours, I am afraid to venture myself on board their boat, lest they run foul of a sawyer.

I spent an evening with Brother Smith lately. I told him *it was in vain to profess and preach Reformation, unless the world could see it in practice; for, if those who profess to have got out of Babylon do not manifest more of that love and humility, and more of the spirit of meekness and forbearance which dwelt in the divine Savior, than do those they left behind, they will make but little progress in doing good.* This temper and spirit, I am afraid, are much needed among them. The war seems at present to be waxing very hot; and I think that, during this summer, the great battle will be fought, which will drive every one to his proper standard. The North District Association has already had a swarm out of her hive. An old man who has long been clerk to that body, and has had possession of her papers and records, has lately taken it into his head to call a Council of such churches as he thought would favor his designs; seven only attended by their letters and messengers. These have, according to his designs, advised him to keep possession of the records of North District. They have appointed an Association to meet on the fourth Saturday in next month, [at Goshen,] and have invited all the churches, or parts of churches that favor their designs, to meet with them; they will consider themselves the North District Association. I was instrumental in stopping the church at Grassy Lick from sending delegates to their first [council at Lulbegrud], but I am of opinion that I shall not succeed in stopping them again, as a majority of those whom your Reformers left behind [at Grassy Lick] are of the old Calvinistic stamp; so that no doubt remains that when the North District Association meets [at Spencer], at the time appointed, their records and papers, with eight or ten churches, will be missing.

The fourth Saturday in June, which was the day for the Calvinists to assemble at Goshen, came on. Messengers, representing a minority of ten churches or parts of churches, gathered themselves together. There were David Chenault, James French, John Treadway, Reuben McDannold, and others, severe with orthodoxy, and grave with the responsibility which they had assumed. Elder Chenault ascended the chair, and James French took up his clerkly pen. Two questions were immediately raised, by the Council, and they were as promptly answered:

1. Has North District, by abandoning the supervisorship of the churches and preachers, departed from her Constitution? [and the Council answered]: They have so departed!

2. Has a church that takes upon herself the right to introduce and practice usages unknown among the churches of Elkhorn and South Kentucky Associations at the time of their Union, departed from the Constitution and gone out of the Union? [and the Council answered]: They have gone out of the Union!

"Our reasons," said they, "for deciding that North District Association has departed from her Constitution, are contained in the proceedings of the meeting at Lulbegrud, in April last. In point of *Doctrine*, their departures from what was believed in the churches of either Elkhorn or South Kentucky Association, at the time of their Union, are so entire, that to attempt an illustration throughout, would be too long and tedious a writing. They even deny *the special operation of the Spirit in quickening the dead sinner!* And by way of ridicule, they ask, 'Where did the Spirit hit you? Was it in the shoulder, or under the fifth rib?'

"As to departures from church usage, they are so general that, if any one thing in church customs, as practiced in the churches of Elkhorn and South Kentucky Associations at the time of their Union, remains unchanged, we know not what it is. Constituting churches, ordaining preachers, eating the Lord's Supper, words of baptism, the action of putting under water in baptism—all are varied. Can it be thought strange that these innovations, all beating on the churches at once, should produce distress, confusions and schisms?"

We would not be understood as saying that all these things have been adopted and gone into by all the churches, except the ten above named; nor that these things are advocated by all the preachers; but they are more or less adopted in several of the churches, and advocated by several preachers. To our own mortification, we acknowledge that we have connived at these departures, changes, and alterations, until we are reduced to the necessity of trying to maintain old North District ground unincumbered by any of those new and discordant things. We do, therefore, agree as follows:

That North District Association be held at Howard's Upper Creek meeting-house, in Clark County, the fourth Saturday in July, 1831; that the proceedings of the Council at

Lulbegrud, and the proceedings of this meeting, be published together; that a copy thereof be furnished to those who meet at Spencer's Creek in July next; that a copy be sent to each Association with whom North District is in correspondence, and to each church registered on the minutes of the North District Association at its annual session in July last. Each church that shall send letters and representatives to the Association when convened at Howard's Upper Creek next year—except the ten churches represented in this meeting—will please to state in their letters:

"1. What translation of the Bible they consider the Scriptures of truth;

"2. What words of baptism are used by the administrator of such church;

"3. What manner of breaking bread in eating the Lord's Supper is practiced;

"4. What is the mode of putting the person baptized under the water."

After the adoption of the foregoing Report and Recommendations, which we have here condensed, the Goshen Council, notwithstanding they had already excluded the majority of the churches of the Association for departing from the customs of the Baptists, proceeded to appoint James French, John Treadway, David Chenault, Reuben McDannold, and others a committee "to report at the next Association, one year from that time, what has been the uniform custom of the Baptists in attending to the ordinances of baptism, the Lord's Supper, etc."

The Council then instructed their committee that had been appointed to carry copies of their proceedings to Corresponding Associations, "that if they should find any Association split, they should present copies to such parts only as stood on the old church usages, and the terms of Union."

Finally, before they adjourned, they declared themselves withdrawn from all churches that had departed as before alleged; but that their fellowship was not to be considered as broken with those minorities, or individual members, who were content with the former usages of the churches.

The example now set by the Calvinists of the North District was soon followed by other Associations. Not long after the meeting of the Council at Lulbegrud, in April, notices were sent around to the several churches of the Franklin Association, signed by Silas M. Noel, and others, announcing, that in consequence of the late disturbances at the South Benson church, and other proceedings tending to distract the churches, a called meeting of the Franklin Association would be held at Frankfort, on the second Friday in July, when and where the churches were requested to send their usual number of messengers.

"Although we are not certainly acquainted with all the objects of your meeting," said, in effect, the church at Hopewell, in reply to this call, "yet we send you our messengers to sit in council with you, and to represent us in your assembly. We have been told that one object of the meeting is to decide on the propriety or impropriety of continuing a correspondence with Elkhorn Association in case she refuses to discountenance certain Teachers and Elders of that body, against whom charges have been exhibited in a certain pamphlet, and made against them in other ways.

"We would respectfully suggest, that as steps have been taken to decide on these charges, it seems improper to declare a discontinuance of your correspondence, while that investigation is still pending. . . . We do sincerely believe that the strife now pervading the churches, is in defense of words to no profit; and that, if the Church of Jesus Christ is ever to be perfectly joined together in one mind and in one judgment, it must be when our faith shall stand not in the wisdom of men, but in the power of God, and when our teachers unanimously say, 'I am determined to know nothing among you but Jesus, and him crucified.'

"The advice given at your last session, to reject as erroneous and corrupt, such persons as consider the Bible a sufficient rule of faith and practice, has been the cause of much division and discussion in South Benson church; and we do sincerely hope that no such advice will be given again, and that no more strife will be sown by your decisions."

The usual time for the meeting of the Franklin Association was in September. Grieved, however, at the course which the anti-creed men had pursued at South Benson, and especially at the conduct of Jacob Creath, in constituting them into a church, they assembled thus early in an

extraordinary session, evidently to move the Elkhorn Association, to whose jurisdiction the Creaths belonged, to take
action in reference to their alleged disorders. Silas M. Noel,
John Taylor, and others, were accordingly appointed messengers to bear a letter to Elkhorn. In that communication,
Franklin declares her determination to drop her correspondence with Elkhorn, if such schismatic teachers as Josephus
Hewitt and the Creaths should be retained in her fellowship.

Silas M. Noel, John Taylor, and others, were also appointed a committee to prepare a Circular Letter to the churches
of the Franklin Association; and, on the next day, they reported a document, evidently written by Dr. Noel, from which
the following extracts are taken:

DEAR BRETHREN:—You will learn from our Minutes the
[action] of our Association. Before Alexander Campbell
visited Kentucky, you were in harmony and peace; you heard
but the one Gospel, and knew only the one Lord, one faith,
and one baptism. Your church Constitutions were regarded,
and their principles expounded and enforced by those who occupied your pulpits. Thus you were respected by other denominations as a religious community. Often were you favored with refreshing seasons from on high, and many of your
neighbors and your families were brought to a knowledge
of the truth. How delightful were your morning and evening
interviews, cheered by the songs and prayers and exhortations of brethren, and by the presence of Him who has promised that where two or three are gathered together in His
name, to be in the midst! Have not those happy days gone
by? In place of preaching, you now may hear your church
covenants ridiculed; your faith, as registered upon your
church books, is denounced, and you yourselves are traduced,
while the more heedless and unstable abjure the faith, and
join with the wicked in scenes of strife, schism, and tumult.
The fell spirit of discord stalks, in open day, through families, neighborhoods and churches. If you would protect yourselves as churches, make no compromise with error—mark
them who cause divisions, and divest yourself of the last
vestige of *Campbellism.*

As an Association, we shall esteem it our duty to drop
correspondence with any and every association or church

where this heresy is tolerated. Those who say they are not *Campbellites*, and yet countenance and circulate his little pamphlets, are insincere—they are to be avoided. When they say they are persecuted because "they will not swallow the Philadelphia Confession of Faith," you are not to believe it, for no church has called one of them in question on that point, so far as we know. It is not so much their objection to this book as *our* objections to *their* Confession of Faith that makes the difference.

When they tell you that the Holy Spirit begins the work of salvation, that he carries it on, and that he perfects it, they may only mean that all this is done by the words of the Holy Spirit; that is, by the Testament read or heard, and not by the quickening energies of God's Spirit directly. All super- natural, immediate influences are discarded by them as mere physical operations. All that we have esteemed religion— the work of God's grace in the soul directly—is rejected. Mr. Campbell calls it a whim—a metaphysical whim! And, that you may know the full extent of our objections, we herewith send you several articles, gathered from the *Christian Baptist* and the *Millennial Harbinger*, with references to the pamphlet and the page, where you can read and judge whether they are or are not the tenets of the Reformation.

Thirty-nine paragraphs, sentences, and parts of sentences, extracted from the pages of the *Christian Baptist* and *Millen- nial Harbinger*, follow these remarks, concerning which ex- tracts the editor himself afterward remarked:

In forming, for me, thirty-nine Articles of Faith, the writer —Dr. Noel, as I am informed—has ascribed to me words, sen- tences and articles which I never uttered or wrote; and many others are, by a perverse ingenuity of quoting, made to speak a language antipodes to any thing I ever taught.*

When this circular letter was read before the Franklin Association, and a motion was made to adopt it, much dis- cussion ensued. Jacob Creath, Jr., who, with other Reform- ers, had come to witness the proceedings, tried in vain to

---

* Millennial Harbinger, vol. 1, p. 373.

speak a few words in defense of himself and his brethren; he was forced down by the noisy interruptions of the messengers. Jacob Creath, Sr., also endeavored to gain the floor, declaring, in their hearing, that he could refute every thing that had been charged against them; but he was loudly called to order from every part of the house. He stood there before them with composure till the disorder subsided; and then, laying his hand on his white head, he said:

"Brethren, I am now sixty years old; I have been forty years in the service of my God and my country, and this is the first time in my life that I have known men to be arraigned before any tribunal on any charge and the constitutional privilege of answering for themselves denied them!" But loud and repeated clamors for order forced him to silence.

John Smith also, who was a deeply interested, but unrecognized spectator on this occasion, next arose to speak, but even his voice was drowned in their cries, and he was compelled to take his seat.

During these strange proceedings, some allusion was made in the discussion to the fact that the Reformers and the Baptists of the North District Association had separated, and the question was raised, whether the letter ordered the year before to be written and sent to that Association when convened at Spencer, should not now be recalled. The question excited much interest, during the discussion of which, John Smith again arose, and asked for the privilege of giving the history of that unfortunate division: "For if Franklin," said he, "wishes to act wisely and justly, she will listen to the facts in the case." But he was answered only by impatient cries of "order!"

"I do not wish, brethren," continued he, "to argue any question of doctrine or policy; but to give you a simple statement of facts for your own advantage."

"Don't let him do it, Brother Moderator! Don't let him do it!" and the cries for order grew more earnest and noisy.

"Brethren," at last said John Taylor, "I have known Brother Smith a long time, and I know him to be a truthful and candid man. I move that we allow him the privilege of speaking." But the motion was quickly voted down.

"Then," persisted Taylor, "do let us allow him the privilege of talking just five minutes, if no longer."

This proposition was debated for nearly one-half hour, but was finally carried. Smith instantly arose, and out came the watches in every part of the house.

"Brethren," said he, "if North District has violated her Constitution as charged, by neglecting the supervisorship of her churches or preachers, then those who met in June at Goshen, and not we, are guilty of that violation.

"When letters came up to the Association last year, at Unity, complaining of new customs introduced, we, whom you are about to condemn, urged those very brethren who have now withdrawn from us, to attend to those complaints, and they would not do it! They now charge us with that neglect, which was all their own! They have withdrawn from the majority; and, taking with them our books and papers, have styled themselves the *North District Association*, and affected to exclude us for faults which they, and they only, have committed!"

But the mind of Franklin was already made up, and the letter heretofore ordered to be written to North District was recalled.

The circular letter, that had been drawn up by Dr. Noel and approved by the Franklin Association, was ordered to be printed, and circulated among the churches, and they then adjourned *sine die*.

On his way home, Smith stopped at the house of Thomas Bullock, Esq., the able moderator of the Elkhorn Association, and one of the most honorable and upright of men. There he again met with John Taylor, who had with him a partisan pamphlet which he had recently published, called "A History of Clear Creek Church, and Campbellism Exposed." This production was very severe against the Creaths, William Morton, and Josephus Hewitt, on account of the part which they had taken in changing the faith and customs of the orthodox churches. Smith himself had not escaped the critical pen of Taylor; but he was more surprised to find in the book so many things that he thought must certainly have been written in ignorance of the facts. He called the attention of the author, in his usual candid way, especially to what was written against William Morton, affirming that the pamphlet did that good man great injustice, as he could abundantly prove. He then made to Taylor such a statement of facts as he supposed would fully vindicate Morton, feeling no concern at all about any thing that had been written against himself.

CHAPTER XXXI.

On the fourth Saturday in July, the North District Association met at Spencer's Creek, pursuant to the resolution adopted at Unity, in 1829. Elder Thomas Boone being absent, the Introductory Sermon was delivered by John Newton Payne. Thomas White was chosen Moderator, and Buckner H. Payne, Clerk. Of the twenty-six churches of the District, all but eight sent messengers and letters as usual. Neither Lulbegrud nor Grassy Lick was represented. Cane Spring sent her four delegates; but David Chenault was not among them!

In spite of all the vigilance of that steadfast Baptist, the heresies which he so much dreaded had taken root and sprung up at Cane Spring. The church that he had planted, and watered with so much care, and for whose increase he had spent so many prayers, had at last been wasted by John Smith. It deeply grieved his heart to witness all these things; and surely it was enough to bring down his gray hairs with sorrow to the grave! He had faithfully represented a small minority of his congregation in the Convention at Goshen, but all his influence had not been enough to save his beloved church from apostasy; so, turning away from those who had forsaken the old ways, he resolved to remain and die with the few who were true and faithful to the covenant of their fathers.

It had not been the purpose of the church at Somerset to seek a connection with any Association. But after the secession of the Calvinists at Goshen, the Reformers determined, as soon as practicable, to convert the meetings of the Association into annual assemblies for Christian worship and communion; and, in order to bring about such a

revolution without debate or delay, they judged it expedient to come together once more as an Association, at Spencer. Accordingly, Somerset, though refusing to be called a Baptist church, or to wear any other denominational name, concluded to send her messengers, David Badger, James Allen, Jonathan Masterson, and Henry Darnall, who were all cordially admitted to seats.

Never, perhaps, in the history of North District had so large a concourse of people assembled as that which now crowded the groves of Spencer. There were Jacob Coons and Absalom Rice, the first fruits of the Ancient Gospel in the State, and Thomas Mosley, whose house was the first one thrown open to John Smith, when, in 1828, he stood up alone against the whole North District Association and boldly preached the heresy for which they had condemned him. And there, too, were such men as David Bruton, Joseph Bondurant, Thomas White, William Orear, Buckner H. Payne, Moses Ryan, Asa Maxey, and John Newton Payne. From other Associations came Jacob Creath, Sr., and Jacob Creath, Jr., Josephus Hewitt, Oliver C. Steele, and Josiah Collins. Present also was David S. Burnet, the youngest of those who then preached the Ancient Gospel, and Aylett Raines, who had ceased to speculate that he might believe, and Thomas Campbell, of Bethany, venerated as the Father of the Reformation.

One of the first acts of this Association was to receive the messengers who had been sent by the Council that met at Goshen. They bore a printed copy of their proceedings, which was filled with allegations of heresy and disorder against undescribed churches and unnamed preachers. Nevertheless, it was allowed to be read, and the messengers were courteously invited to sit with the Association.

There were many things stated in the Goshen manifesto which, in the judgment of the Association, were erroneous, or needed explanation. John Smith, therefore, with the Clerk, proceed to draw up a paper in the form of a circular letter, in which the actions and the arguments of the Goshen convention were reviewed, and on Monday, the Association read and approved that paper, and ordered it to be printed with the minutes. The circular says, in substance:

Justice to ourselves and to the world requires that we take some notice of the charges published by a few discontented members of some of the churches, who were convened first at Lulbegrud, and subsequently at Goshen.

In the first place, we deny that North District has ever departed from her former way of administering her Constitution, or has abandoned any supervisorship that she has ever claimed over either churches or preachers, in any instance where a charge was brought according to the law of Christ or the custom of the Baptists.

In the next place, we affirm that no church of North District has ever been convicted, or even accused, of introducing or practicing usages or customs unknown among the churches of South Kentucky and Elkhorn Associations at the time of their union. This her records clearly prove.

But were the customs and usages of either Elkhorn or South Kentucky ever adopted as a rule for the churches? The customs and opinions of those Associations were different; one was constituted upon the old London Confession of Faith; the other, upon the Bible. One preached particular atonement; the other, a general atonement; one, an effectual calling; the other, a calling common to all men. One was fond of written creeds and decorums; the other was content with the Bible alone. One was fond of washing the saints' feet; the other did not think it incumbent upon them to do it.

But, on the other hand, Elkhorn and South Kentucky agreed at the time of the union to take the Word of God as their only rule of faith and practice, and to tolerate each other in differences of opinion and custom, as Christians ought to have done, and as they ought still to do.

But what is most astonishing, those individuals who met at Goshen, after withdrawing from us, as they say, *on account of our departures from the customs of the Baptists*, proceeded to appoint a committee to find out what Baptist customs are!

In addition to all this, never have they attempted to call either individuals or churches to account to reclaim them, or even to make them sensible of any fault, if fault they had! They even denied some of us the right to be heard on the insinuations contained in the publication, and refused us the privilege of explanation! If this be Baptist custom, or Christian charity, we have it to learn from them, and not from the Elkhorn or the South Kentucky Associations, nor yet from Jesus Christ or his Apostles.

They allege that North District has departed from her Constitution, and they deny that those who now meet at Spencer are the North District Association at all; but they declare that they themselves are the Association, and they have agreed to meet as such at Howard's Upper Creek, on the fourth Saturday in July, 1831. Now, if it be the fact that those only who met at Goshen are the North District Association, it follows that they only are the transgressors of whom they complain; and, according to their own decision, they have gone out of the union! Thus, like frantic Saul, they have fallen upon their own sword.

But we are still more surprised at the blinding influence of sectarian prejudice which made those brethren say *"that, in point of doctrine,* the departures from what was exhibited and believed in the churches of either Elkhorn or South Kentucky Association at the time of their union, are so entire that to attempt an illustration throughout would be too long and tedious a writing."* Now, did not both Elkhorn and South Kentucky believe in only one living and true God, who created and upholds all things? that Jesus Christ is the Son of God and the only Saviour of sinners? that all men are sinners and guilty before God? that Christ died for our sins according to the Scriptures? was buried and rose from the dead according to the Scriptures? that he ascended into heaven? that he is the only Mediator between God and man? that sinners must believe in the name of the Son of God, repent of their sins, and obey the Gospel, or they can not be saved? Did they not believe that there is one Body, and one Spirit, one hope, one Lord, one faith, one baptism, one God and Father of all? Did they not believe that there will be a resurrection of the dead, both of the just and the unjust, and that all will be judged according to their works? and that the wicked will go away to everlasting punishment, and the righteous into life eternal? But we have neither denied nor departed, in the smallest degree, from any of these Gospel facts or truths; we have, on the other hand, always insisted upon them. Now, as there is a perfect agreement, in these and other matters, between what was believed by the churches of Elkhorn and South Kentucky, and what is believed by us and all the churches of the North District, can any one suppose that our departures in doctrine are as entire as they are represented to be?

You, brethren of Goshen, have made but one specification in reference to the matter of doctrine; and that is not correctly stated. It is true that, under peculiar circumstances, *one individual*, not a church, as you say, when speaking of faith as coming by hearing, and of the promise that the Spirit will be given to those who believe, in opposition to the doctrine of receiving the Spirit without the use of the senses, or the aid of the Word, did ask if the Spirit enters not through the senses, *where does it enter?* But the individual who used the expression does not justify himself in it. Why do you thus select an improper expression, uttered by an individual two or three years ago, and publish it to the world now, in false colors, as a sentiment of the churches?

You say, also, "that departures *in practice or church usages* are so general, that, if any one thing as practiced in the churches of the Elkhorn and South Kentucky Associations at the time of their Union remains unchanged, you do not know what it is!" Now, brethren, we again ask you: Was it not their custom to receive and dismiss members by letters? to receive by profession of faith in the Lord Jesus and immersion? to exclude for drunkenness and other violations of the law of Christ when the trangressors would not reform? Was it not their custom, if a brother trespassed against another, that the offended brother should tell the offender his fault? Was it not their custom to assemble themselves together, to sing praises to God, to pray for one another, to exhort one another, to preach and to teach according to the best of their abilities? Was it not their custom to have a Moderator, or Bishop, to preside and keep order, when attending to any matter of discipline, and a Clerk to record every thing?

These are some of the most common usages and customs of the Elkhorn and South Kentucky Associations at the time of their union; have any of the North District churches departed from them? How, then, can you say, if any custom remains unchanged, you know not what it is?

You mention some customs that seldom call for attention from the Baptist churches; such as ordaining preachers and constituting churches. Name the church in this Association that has changed these customs; and name, too, the changes that have been made. The first knowledge that this Association has had of any such changes, has been derived from your own minutes!

But brethren, has the custom of the Baptists been uniform in ordaining ministers and constituting churches? We know that it has not been uniform. Your committee will report *next year* whether any such uniformity exists or not!

In reference to the Lord's Supper, you know, as well as we do, that there has not been uniformity; for it is known, not only to us, *but to you also*, that some of the oldest preachers in Kentucky do not break the bread in very small bits, but leave it, as some of ours do, in larger pieces. This, and our attendance on that ordinance rather more frequently, constitute the head and front of our offending in this matter!

As to the *words of baptism*—were they ever precisely the same among the preachers of the North District? Letters were sent to your meeting at Lulbegrud in April last, containing the baptismal words of different administrators; if you will show those letters, the world will see that the baptismal formulary has been diverse.

But what church has attempted to change either the baptismal words, or the mode of putting a candidate under water? You have named none; and not one has attempted it!

You say that one reason for deciding that the North District Association has departed from her Constitution is, that, in 1827, at Cane Spring, she neglected to attend to the complaints of Lulbegrud! But that church did not complain of any sister church by name. True, the name of a certain individual was read out, in a manner contrary to the usages of Baptists and the law of Christ; and the committee of arrangements were of opinion, as stated by one of them on the floor, that for this indecorous act, Lulbegrud deserved reproof!

Another reason stated is, that, in 1829, Goshen complained and she too received no attention! But Goshen complained of neither church nor individual. Besides, the majority of the committee of arrangements that year were of her own religious views, and they are still with you. Goshen's preacher, also, and her messengers, were all there, afraid or ashamed to name her complaints? And now you charge your own neglect on us!

Another reason is, that, in 1829, Cane Spring complained, and no one listened to her complaints! But she complained of no church. Her letter was full of misrepresentations of a certain individual, who was not even a member of the Association.

Another reason you give is, that, in 1829, Lulbegrud complained again, and her complaints still went unheard. We say again that Lulbegrud complained neither of any church nor individual! In a sweeping clause she says: "In consequence of changes taking place among the churches of North District in administering the Lord's Supper, we can not commune!" But she does not even name the change to which she objects! And yet the committee of arrangements, whose duty it was to bring business before the Association, never mentioned those things, although a member of the Lulbegrud church was on the committee, and a majority of them were then with you in your religious views!

For such reasons as these, you say that North District has departed from her Constitution, declaring at the same time, however, that you yourselves are the Association.

But, as the Goshen brethren say so much about Baptist customs, we ourselves will ask a few questions about those customs:

1. Is it Baptist custom to complain of sister churches before an Association, and yet name neither church nor offense?

2. Can a deliberate body attend to any complaint, unless the offense and the offender be named?

3. Is it Baptist custom to report any individual member to the Association, until he has been dealt with in private, or before his church?

4. Is it Baptist custom to report private persons, who are not members of the Association?

5. Is there any article in the Constitution of North District Association obliging her to attend to such complaints as those named above?

6. If there is no such article, could North District depart from her Constitution by neglecting them?

7. Would not North District have violated Baptist usage, as well as Gospel order, had she taken up any of those indefinite charges?

8. Seeing that the Constitution says expressly, That all matters shall be determined by the will of the majority, was it not a palpable violation of that Constitution for the Goshen minority to decide Associational questions?

9. Is it the custom of the Baptists for the minority of a church, or of an Association, to meet together and condemn the whole body to which they belong?

10. Is it the custom of the Baptists to neglect commemorating the Lord's death for two or three years together, as Lulbegrud has done, because *she thinks some changes have taken place in the sister churches?*

11. Is it the custom of the Baptists to call such persons together as may suit their own notions, and accuse, condemn, and exclude their brethren, without allowing those whom they accuse to say a word for themselves, as those Goshen brethren have done?

12. Is it the custom of Baptist churches to send two sets of messengers and two letters to the same Association the same year, as Lulbegrud did for four or five years?

13. Is it the custom of Baptist churches to have two Moderators in the same church, one in each end of the meeting-house, as Lulbegrud did for some years?

14. And will not these queries be of advantage to the Committee appointed by the Goshen meeting to prepare and report next year, *the uniform custom of the Baptists?*

The reference here made to Lulbegrud and Goshen, is not made in a retaliatory spirit, but to show that those two churches, or rather some members, through those churches, have caused much disorder, and that the Association has acted toward them with great forbearance.

We do not blame all the members of the nine churches that assembled at Goshen—Elder David Chenault's little fraction of Cane Spring we do not count as a church—but we blame the messengers themselves, who in a tyrannical manner drew off the churches without the consent of the same, from those with whom they stood united. Some, unwilling to submit to it, have since withdrawn from them.

Had the Goshen Council instructed their Committee to examine the New Testament, in order to find what was enjoined by Christ, and practiced by primitive churches and preachers, it would have shown that they intended to abide by the Terms of Union, which declare that the Word of God is our only rule of faith and practice. But to appoint a committee to examine some unauthoritative documents, in order to find a set of human customs and opinions, looks more like violating the Terms of Union.

But, finally, if you think that we have departed from the Constitution of North District Association, or embarrassed her supervisorship over the churches, or in any way changed her mode of administering her Constitution and Terms of Union, we ask you to call to your aid whom you please, and appoint your own time and place, anywhere within the bounds of the Association, and we will answer for ourselves; and the world will see whether North District has made such departures as you allege.

On Monday, the Association, having learned what had been done at the called meeting of the Franklin Association in June, passed, substantially, the following preamble and resolution, in reference to their action:

Whereas, there was a meeting held in Frankfort, on the ninth of July and the day following, 1830, of an extraordinary character (the minutes of which meeting claim for it the appellation of *The Franklin Asociation*), while the usual meeting of said Association is in September; and, *whereas*, this unconstitutional meeting manifested a belligerent spirit in withholding their Corresponding Letter to us, and in withdrawing the Corresponding Letter to Elkhorn which she directed to be sent last September, at her usual annual meeting, and in substituting one containing charges against certain individuals in the Elkhorn Association, which virtually overthrows all church power, and exalts Associational power at the expense of the churches; and, *whereas*, furthermore, the partiality and injustice of this strange meeting was glaringly manifested in her refusing to invite the members of the North District and Elkhorn Associations, and others, whom they thought unfavorable to her unconstitutional and illegal proceedings, and in her inviting to sit with her those who were thought favorable to her unauthorized course;

Resolved, therefore, That, under existing circumstances, the North District Association drop the correspondence of the Franklin Association for the present.

Before adjourning, Buckner H. Payne was directed to call on the former clerk, James French, and demand all the books and papers of the Association. They then adjourned, to meet for the last time as an Association, at Somerset meeting-house, on the fourth Saturday in July, 1831.

It was during this meeting at Spencer that John Taylor appeared as a vender of his book, called *Campbellism Exposed.* He had not come as a Corresponding messenger, for, of all men, he had the least sympathy with the great brotherhood that had assembled at Spencer's Creek. His business was to sell his pamphlet—not, it seems, from any desire to injure his brethren, but to raise the means to pay for its publication. Covered with the dust of a long ride, and carrying his saddle-bags, which were stuffed with copies of his little book, he approached John Smith, and said to him:

"Brother John, you have a bigger voice, and more assurance than any one I know here; so I would like to get you to announce from the stand that I have with me for sale the *Expose of Campbellism.*"

"Brother Taylor," said Smith, "you know that I told you, more than a week ago, at Brother Bullock's, that your pamphlet contained many erroneous statements, and, particularly, that you did William Morton great injustice. This, you know, I stated to you at the time. Now, I do think it is wrong for you to circulate such a document, and it would be wrong for me to advertise it for you. I care nothing for what you said about me—it gives me not the least concern;

but, certainly, you will not continue to misrepresent so good a man as William Morton."

"I don't intend to publish any more copies," said Taylor, who, of course, was not convinced of doing any one injustice.

"Well," said Smith, "if I advertise it at your request, I will tell the people what I think of it."

"That is what I expected you would do, anyhow," said Taylor, and he passed on through the crowd.

At a suitable moment, John Smith went upon the stand, where sat Elder Thomas Campbell, the Creaths, and others, and holding up a copy of the book in sight of the people, he said, in a voice that filled the grove where they sat:

"I hold in my hand a pamphlet, called *Campbellism Exposed*, written by Elder John Taylor, who is now present. He requests me to say to you that he has this book for sale, and wishes you to buy at least enough copies to pay for the printing.

"Now, friends, I have read every word of this book carefully, and of nearly every incident alluded to I have some personal knowledge. As I have said to Brother Taylor, so I now say to you: *it does injustice to facts throughout!* Particularly does it misrepresent the amiable William Morton, as I tried to show to the author himself a few days ago. What he has written concerning me, I care nothing about. You may read it and then think just what you please. But it is wrong to write, sell, or circulate a book so full of mistakes as this; for I do aver, that if all that is erroneous were cut out of it, there would not be enough left in any part of it to make a thumb-paper for a child."

"I thank you, Brother Smith, for your recommendation," said John Taylor; for he was present, and heard it.

"You are welcome to it, Brother Taylor," he replied.

CHAPTER XXXII.

THE ELKHORN ASSOCIATION usually met on the second Saturday in August, and the time was now near at hand. The leading Calvinists, like those of the North District, were resolved to bear with heresy and heretics no longer. The fate of such men as Jacob Creath, Jr., and Josephus Hewitt was, therefore, sealed; and even Jacob Creath, Sen., could not hope to live in peace with his old comrades any longer. He was still a member at Versailles, and if brotherly love could have shielded him from the devices of his enemies, he would have been safe in the bosom of that devoted church. But the strong arm of clerical power reached him even there. The Franklin Association declared that she would drop her correspondence with Elkhorn, if the Creaths, or the churches that sustained them, should be kept any longer in her connection; and, as we have seen, she had already preferred charges against them for their course at South Benson.

But it was more especially the distresses of the church at Clear Creek that stirred every orthodox heart with pity, and moved the Association to punish the destroyers of her peace. The conduct of the Creaths in organizing into a church, on the Bible alone, those who had refused to live under a human constitution, was ground enough, they thought, for dealing with them and the church to which they belonged.

Following the advice of John Taylor, Clear Creek had appointed a committee to treat with the Creaths for "the disorder of advising and setting up another church in her meeting-house, and for railing out against her Constitution." After an unsatisfactory interview, the committee publicly accused them before the church at Versailles. But that church postponed the trial, and called for a committee of helps from South Elkhorn, Providence, and Lexington. This course greatly offended the Clear Creek brethren; for, as they alleged, "two of those very churches were as far gone in the fatal delusions of Alexander Campbell as Versailles herself," and they resolved to lay the whole matter before the Association, on the ground that Versailles had not offered that satisfaction which was due to a sister church. In her letter to Elkhorn, Clear Creek thus, in effect, bewails her distracted condition:

We have lived, brethren, to see our Zion languish, and bemoan herself in sackcloth and ashes! "O that our heads were waters, and our eyes a fountain of tears, that we might weep day and night over the slain of the daughters of our people!" . . .

We attribute all our distress to the pernicious influence of the heretical sentiments of Alexander Campbell! But the principal authors of our trouble are our brethren, Jacob Creath, Sen., and Jacob Creath, Jr., whose conduct toward this church has been such that we are unwilling to recognize either them or the church to which they belonged, as entitled to our confidence or fellowship. . . .

Dear brethren, we are the same in sentiment as when we first had a seat among you. We have never changed; and we desire no change, except to be more like the dear Redeemer. As such, we call upon you to answer: Will you cause us to abandon you by continuing in your connection those who have attempted to destroy us?

It had been already announced by John Taylor, that Elkhorn, when convened at Silas, would certainly exclude the Creaths; and it seemed now to be the plan of the creed-men to cut off the church at Versailles in order to reach them.

In the meantime, the rights and powers of a Baptist Association came up continually for discussion. In the language of the anti-creed men, "The horns of the beast increased in power, and grew more and more wanton every day." While some maintained that no individual could rightfully be held to answer before an Association, unless for a breach of her rules, but was amenable to his church, and that no church could be rightfully cut off, save for a violation of the Terms of Union, on complaint made by a sister church; yet, others claimed that an Association had a right not only to govern herself, but to say who should stay in her communion. An old decision of Elkhorn, given, perhaps, in 1786, was quoted to sustain the singular position that, though she was but an Advisory Council, yet any church that should refuse to take her advice must be excluded!

Assured that an attempt would be made to cast out the church at Versailles, Josephus Hewitt, a few days before the meeting of the Association, withdrew from that church, and was received into fellowship at South Elkhorn. He hoped, by this step, to escape ecclesiastical censure himself, and, at the same time, to avert, or at least temper, the blow that was about to fall on Versailles. Jacob Creath, Jr., knowing that he was specially obnoxious to the clergy, followed his example, but took refuge among his brethren at Providence. The elder Creath was left alone at Versailles. Some fondly hoped that his gray hairs, and his forty years' service, would not only save him from oppression, but avert the wrath of his enemies from the church that he had so long nourished and loved.

The second Saturday in August came. Versailles, South Elkhorn, and Providence, persuaded that votes, and not arguments or entreaties, would avail anything in the Association, sent ten messengers each, instead of three, the number fixed by the rule of apportionment adopted in 1829. This, as they solemnly declared, they did in self-defense, claiming it to be their constitutional right to follow the advice of the Association or not, as they pleased. They remembered John Taylor's words, that "the Creaths may expect to face a charge at Silas! They may fancy that a few can hoodwink the many, as was done last year by means of their large representation; but Elkhorn has now guarded that point, so that the three churches which last year had twenty-four votes will this year have but ten."

In a grove near Silas meeting-house, the messengers of the twenty-three churches of Elkhorn assembled. Elder Gates, of Paris, delivered an appropriate address from John xiii. 35, *"By this shall all men know that you are my disciples, if you have love one for another.*" Thomas Bullock, the former Moderator, presided, and Benjamin S. Chambers, assisted by Jacob Creath, Jr., still acted as Clerk. The letters from the several churches were presented by their messengers, at a stand about a mile from the meeting-house, and, at the request of the Clerk, Jacob Creath, Jr., arose, and began to read them before the people. He had not been reading long, when Jeremiah Vardeman abruptly called him to order. Regardless of the interruption, Creath continued to read; but, again and again, he was assailed by cries of "Order!" for his relentless brother had resolved that no heretic should again lift up his head in the Elkhorn Association. Creath persisted in reading, and the aid of the Moderator was invoked to stop him; but neither Moderator nor Clerk saw fit to interfere. A tumult arose, which the voice of the venerable Lewis Corbin could hardly still. Order, however, was at length restored, and Jacob Creath resumed his reading. But the very sound of his voice seemed to awake again the spirit of confusion. Vardeman sprang to his feet, and, with his cane in his hand, lifted up his arm in much excitement, and exclaimed: "Brother Moderator, I must, and I will be heard!" At that word, Thomas Bronston, pushing his way through the crowd, hastily mounted the stage, and exclaimed: "*Now* you can read, Brother Creath; *I* am here!" The scene became more and more disgraceful; for the crowd grew noisy and demonstrative. At last, the Moderator, fearing a riot, requested Jacob Creath to desist, and let the Clerk read the letters; the floor was yielded, and the tumult ceased.

In due time the messengers repaired to the meeting-house, where the Association was organized by the election of William Suggett, Moderator, and Uriel B. Chambers, Clerk. But the spirit of strife, which had been quelled in the grove, was soon revived in the house. All the churches, save the three already named, had, in sending their messengers, conformed to the rule of apportionment. According to that rule, South Elkhorn should have sent but three, but, to the surprise of her sister churches, Josephus Hewitt had come forward, leading a delegation of ten brethren, and presenting a letter from that church, setting forth her reasons for not reducing the number of her messengers! Versailles, also, though entitled to but three, had sent Jacob Creath, Sen., and nine others. But that which most aroused the anger of the opposition was the appearance of Jacob Creath, Jr., as a messenger from the church at Providence, accompanied by nine others, nearly all of whom were known to be sternly opposed to creeds and clerical authority!

The question was soon raised whether these supernumerary messengers should be allowed to sit in the Association. The wrangling was sharp and protracted, and the assembly at last became more like an Ephesian mob, than a Baptist Association. John Smith, who had looked on the turbulent scenes of the day with painful emotions, arose, and begged his brethren from the non-conforming churches to withdraw their surplus messengers, and thereby avoid offense and misconstruction. The venerable Thomas Campbell, too, was present, but his patriarchal head was bowed in sorrow. Like a wise father, he, too, urged the messengers to withdraw. The advice of these prudent men was followed, and the sun of that stormy day went down in peace!

But on Monday the irrepressible strife arose again. On the complaint of Clear Creek, and of the Franklin Association, against Versailles, that "she held in her membership preachers that had taken part in constituting minorities of churches that had departed from the Faith and Constitution of the body," on motion of Jeremiah Vardeman, it was resolved:

1. That the church at Versailles be dropped from further correspondence with this Association.

2. That the church at Providence be dropped from further correspondence with this Association for non-conformity to the rules, and for receiving into her membership a preacher, Jacob Creath, Jr., who has in faith and practice departed from her Constitution, and who has taken part in constituting minorities who also have thus departed.

It was also voted that a committee be appointed to confer with the church at South Elkhorn, relative to certain grievances entertained against her for having departed from the Faith and Constitution of this Association, and for having disregarded her rule relative to an equal apportionment of

representatives in this body; and the committee were instructed to report at the next Association.

It is but just to say, in reference to these proceedings,
that no church had ever made known, either to Versailles
or Providence, any matter of complaint against them. Clear
Creek complained of Versailles, it is true; but she complained
to the Elkhorn Association only, and the accusations of that
church were admitted on no other testimony whatever. The
church at Providence had not been accused; for the charge
on which she was cut off was preferred by the very Association that judged, condemned, and excommunicated her!
The special ground on which that church was excluded, was
her reception of Jacob Creath, Jr., into her fellowship, and
the Association thus usurped the right to decide who should
be received or rejected as a member of an independent congregation!

The right to decide whether any individual has departed
in faith and practice from the faith, was, according to Baptist
doctrine, inherent in the church to which he belonged; yet
the Association assumed the right to declare that Jacob
Creath, Jr., had so departed, and proceeded to cast out the
church to which he belonged for presuming to receive him into
fellowship.

According to Baptist usage, it was the duty of the Committee of Arrangements simply to report the order in which
business, already properly introduced, should be taken up;
but that Committee, on their own responsibility, arraigned
for trial, by the Association, three independent churches—
an act which could have been lawfully done only by a sister
church.

But the course of the Association toward Providence, in
condemning her for non-conformity to the rule of apportionment, was harsh, even supposing that rule to have been
proper and binding on the churches; for, though Providence
had sent ten, instead of three messengers, yet the surplus was
withdrawn on Saturday, even before they had voted, or in
any other way influenced the action of the Association;
withdrawn, too, in order to conform to the rule of apportionment, at the request of brethren, and for the sake of peace.
It was certainly contrary to Baptist usage, also, to arraign a
church—the oldest one, too, in the connection—upon so

loose and ill-defined a statement as that "she was as far gone
in the fatal delusions of Alexander Campbell as Versailles"!

To all these proceedings, Jacob Creath, Sen., replied as
only he could have done. His defense was regarded, by those
who heard it, as the ablest speech of his life. They never
forgot his look and voice and manner as he stood that day in
the midst of his enemies, and plead with them, not to be
merciful or indulgent, but for their own sakes, and for the
honor of the Christian name, to proceed according to law
and precedent, saying, that if he or the Versailles church had
violated any law, human or divine, he would not refuse to
die.*

Thomas Campbell said that he had listened to the most
distinguished orators in Scotland and Ireland; but that
Jacob Creath's defense that day was the most masterly piece
of eloquence he had ever heard. The crowd had pressed
into the house until aisles and galleries were filled, and doors
and windows were thronged with people. Just as Creath
was about to conclude his address, there was heard a cry
that the gallery was falling; the screams of women, the rush
to the stairway, down which men fell in frantic confusion
—instinctive leaps for the doors and the windows, created
a scene that beggars description. But the alarm proved
groundless, and, in due time, order was restored. Had the
vote been at that moment submitted to the people who had
heard the defense of Elder Creath, there would have been
but one voice—and that voice would have acquitted him.
But, as one of their own party declared, "speaking, argument,
and evidence were unnecessary; for they had made up their
opinion before they came together."

There was another question, however, that now embarrassed them. John Smith had been sent as a corresponding
messenger from the North District Association: and, on
Saturday, at the proper hour, he had presented the letter or
that body, with a copy of the minutes of their recent meet
ing at Spencer, and also a copy of the Circular Letter. At
the same time, Reuben McDannold and others appeared as
corresponding messengers from the Council that had met at
Goshen, and which also claimed to be the North District

---

* Life of Jacob Creath, Sen., by his nephew.

Association. The question now arose, "Which body of Baptists shall be recognized by Elkhorn as the North District Association? Shall John Smith, or Reuben McDannold, be invited to sit with us?" When the discussion came on, it was apparent that Smith had already been prejudged; but he asked to be heard, and the Association lent him an impatient ear for a few moments. He said:

Brother Moderator, if any of the eighteen churches which I have the honor to represent in this meeting have departed, in any single instance, from our Constitution, as alleged, I beg these messengers from Goshen to point out the article which has been violated, and to name the church which has been guilty of such violation.

If the neglect, on the part of North District Association, in 1827, to notice the letter of Lulbegrud, which complained of departures from Baptist customs, was a violation of our Constitution, then these same brethren from Goshen are responsible for it; for they did not see proper to notice the complaint of that church.

If, in 1829, at Unity, when similar complaints were made, the Association again violated her Constitution by refusing to attend to those complaints, it was because these same brethren from Goshen opposed all investigation, while I and those with me urged it upon them as a matter of justice to the accused.

Brother Moderator, we can not consent to be bound by customs and usages that the Word of God does not authorize. If, then, these brethren from Goshen have withdrawn from us on that account, they, and not we, have disregarded the Terms of the General Union, for those Terms expressly declare that the Scriptures are the only rule of faith and practice among us!

But, brethren, the Constitution of North District, as well as that of Elkhorn, declares that all questions shall be determined by the will of the majority. Here, then, we tender to you a letter from eighteen churches, comprising an aggregate membership of nearly fourteen hundred brethren—more than two-thirds of the Association; while, on the other hand, these brethren from Goshen are here with some communication for you from a small withdrawing minority of our churches. Should you deny our Associational rights, and reject us, you would not only violate your own Constitution, but the plainest principles of justice and propriety.

But this straightforward argument had no effect upon an Association that, in the excitement of the hour, had laid aside the character of an advisory council, and assumed that of an authoritative hierarchy. They said, in their reply to Smith:

WHEREAS, It appears that two communications from North District have been sent to this Association, showing that a split has taken place in that body,

Resolved, therefore, That the ten churches which met in council at Goshen meeting-house, on the fourth Saturday in June, 1830, and in their minutes declare that the rest of the churches have departed from her Constitution in faith and practice, be recognized as the North District Association, and that our correspondence be continued with them as heretofore.

Finally, this remarkable session of the Elkhorn Association, which began with the excellent discourse of Elder Gates, on *Brotherly Love*, closed with the adoption of a Circular Letter which enlarged on the same theme—the entire Association joining with the Psalmist in the exclamation: "Behold how good and pleasant a thing it is for brethren to dwell together in unity!"

CHAPTER XXXIII.

THE victory gained by the Reformers at Red Lick, Madison County, in 1829, during the session of the Tate's Creek Association, was decisive; but the minority, now following the example of the Calvinists of Goshen, met at Viny Fork, in June, 1830, to consider, not how they might reclaim, but how they might exclude, their erring brethren.

They drew up a Protest against the teaching of Josiah Collins, Oliver C. Steele, Thomas S. Bronston, and others, which they published abroad among the churches. From that document we make the following extracts:

A number of our brethren in the ministry professing to teach the Ancient Gospel of our Lord Jesus Christ, are, more or less, holding forth the following unscriptural doctrines, viz.:

1. That there is no promise of salvation without baptism, and that it should be administered to all who say they believe that Jesus Christ is the Son of God, without examination on any other point;

2. That there is no direct operation of the Spirit on the mind prior to baptism;

3. That baptism procures the remission of sins and the gift of the Holy Spirit;

4. That the Scriptures are the only evidence of interest in Christ;

5. That obedience places it in God's power to elect to salvation;

6. That no *Creed* is necessary for the churches, but the Scriptures as they stand;

7. That all baptized persons have the right to administer that ordinance;

8. That there is no special call to the ministry;

9. That the law given by God to Moses is abolished;

10. That experimental religion is enthusiasm; and

11. That there is no mystery in the Scriptures!

Painful as it is, we feel it to be a duty which we owe to our Master, to our brethren, to the rising generation, and to ourselves, as professed followers of our *Lord Jesus Christ,* to inform you, that brethren T. S. Bronston, Josiah Collins, J. R. Pond, F. Shoot, O. C. Steele, and Samuel Willis, have, in their public exhibitions, held forth some of the above and other views which we think are inconsistent with the Gospel; for, by them, some of us have seen Associations thrown into commotion, churches divided, neighbor made to speak evil of neighbor, brother arrayed against brother, the father against the son, and the daughter against the mother. These are some of the sad effects of their Reformation! Now, as we are commanded to mark them which cause divisions and offenses contrary to the doctrines which we have learned, and avoid them, we enter our *Protest* against those brethren, and all who adhere to and advocate any of the above views contrary to our Constitution.

We intend to have no controversy, but to remain as we are, the *Tate's Creek Association of United Baptists;* and we now invite our brethren and sisters who feel willing to stand with us, to meet us at Providence meeting-house, in the county of Madison, on the Friday before the third Saturday in July next.

On that day about thirty-five delegates, from ten of the twenty-six churches of the Association, met, and were enrolled at New Providence, as supporters of the old Constitution; they then adjourned to meet again at Round Top, on the fourth Saturday in August, inviting all that approved the stand which they had taken against Campbellism to attend with them.

They met on the appointed day, and though but nine churches were represented, they called themselves the *Tate's Creek Association,* and resolved unanimously to drop their correspondence with every Association and church that tolerated the heresy of *Campbellism!*

Thus it was that while John Smith had been ostracised by

a few churches of North District for *innovation*, and the Creaths had been cut off from Elkhorn for *schism*, Josiah Collins and his brethren were excluded by Tate's Creek for *heresy!*

In the meantime, those brethren who had been published in the Protest as heretics, drew up a reply, which they put forth in a pamphlet of twelve pages, in substance as follows:

The charges that have been brought against us may be found in the Minutes of the Franklin Association, and in the *Baptist Chronicle* as well as in the bull of excommunication now issued against us.

1. *"That there is no salvation without baptism."* We answer: Except a man be born of water and the Spirit, he can not enter into the kingdom of God! This kingdom we understand to be the church militant, and not the church triumphant. We are of opinion that all who conscientiously love and serve the Lord, will be saved; and, we may add, we believe that all infants and idiots, and many Jews and Pagans, will be saved without baptism.

2. *"That baptism should be administered to all who say they believe that Jesus Christ is the Son of God, without examination on any other point."* We answer, that no person should be baptized on such a confession, unless he believes with the heart on the Lord Jesus. But to be more plain, if possible—for we desire to give you satisfaction—there must be a turning about from the love of sin to the love of holiness; we must repent of our sins and turn to God with full purpose of heart; the old man must be crucified; we must become dead to the world and alive to holiness; such is our faith.

3. *"That there is no direct operation of the Spirit on the mind prior to baptism."* We answer, that the religion of Jesus is spiritual, and not natural; and that our whole nature is in opposition to it. It is, therefore, through a spiritual communication that we are enabled to believe on our Lord and Savior Jesus Christ. This communication is directed to the mind whilst in a state of rebellion. The mind lays hold of the truth as it is in Jesus; the soul realizes a change in

its feelings, desires and anticipations; the bars of unbelief are broken; he is no longer a slave sold under sin; but, through faith and obedience, becomes an heir of God, and a joint-heir with our Lord Jesus Christ, and is made to rejoice in the prospect of a better world.

4. *"That baptism procures the remission of sins, and the gift of the Holy Ghost."* We answer, that baptism, abstractly considered, is worth nothing; but, when connected with faith and the blood of Jesus, which cleanseth from all sin, it is the act through which we become disciples.

5. *"That the Scriptures are the only evidence of interest in Christ."* We answer, that every disciple has the witness within himself, and has the Spirit of God dwelling in him; for our bodies are represented as temples for the Holy Spirit to dwell in. But the Scriptures are the proper rule by which we should measure ourselves.

6. *"That obedience places it in God's power to elect to salvation."* We answer, that we are elected through the sanctification of the Spirit and the belief of the truth.

7. *"That no creed is necessary for the church but the Scriptures as they stand."* All confessions of faith warrant us in this; for they declare that the Scriptures are to be the supreme standard by which all controversies in religion are to be determined. But why, then, it may be asked, are we in favor of the Constitution of the Tate's Creek Association, seeing it is merely human? We answer, there is a great difference between the church of God and an Association. The one is a number of disciples called out from the world, acknowledging one Lord, one faith, one baptism, and one Spirit which animates the one body or church, one Lord Jesus Christ, who is the head of the body, and the Scriptures of Divine Truth, as the only rule of faith and practice. Here every thing is complete from the beginning. Now, what is an Association but a being created by the churches, and consequently dependent upon them for its existence? We need not inform you that every body, whether it be political or religious, should have a constitution by which it should be governed, in order to the peace and harmony of the society. You therefore perceive that we are in favor of a constitution, whether it be in an Association or in a State.

8. *"That all baptized persons have the right to administer the ordinance of baptism."* We answer, that the charge is untrue.

9. *"That there is no special call to the ministry."* We answer, that there is a special call to the office of Bishop, Overseer, or Elder, and that their work, as well as the qualifications they should possess, is clearly laid down in the Scriptures.

10. *"That the law given by God to Moses is abolished."* Here we desire to be explicit: "Thou shalt love the Lord thy God with all thy heart, and with all thy soul, and with all thy mind; and thou shalt love thy neighbor as thyself." Now we conceive this to be the basis of all law; and that we are under it, not because it belonged to the Jews, but because it has been obligatory on all men, and is particularly enjoined on us under the reign of the Lord Jesus Christ. The dispensation under which we live, is a gracious one, and the only system that mankind is under for justification, is the system of grace, which is the effect of the atonement made by Jesus Christ. Man was to be justified meritoriously before his fall. Since his fall, he is to be justified gratuitously through the redemption that is in Christ Jesus by faith.

11. *"That experimental religion is enthusiasm."* We answer, that the religion of Jesus Christ teaches no such thing as enthusiasm; but many who profess his religion may be and are enthusiasts, no doubt. It depends much on his teaching what he experiences. If he is taught the pure principles of the Gospel, he will grow in grace and the knowledge of the truth, and will experience the indwelling of the Holy Spirit. If he is taught mysteries, and is made to believe that the Gospel has no influence on the mind, then his experience will be any thing but that which it should be. In fine, if he is Gospel taught, he will have a Gospel experience; if he is systematized, he will have a corresponding experience.

12. *"That there is no mystery in the Scriptures."* We answer, that the plan of salvation is no mystery; if so, who is authorized to unfold it, seeing that spiritual gifts have ceased? We acknowledge, however, that there are many sayings in both Testaments which we do not understand.

The *regular* session of the Tate's Creek Association for the year was held according to adjournment at Otter Creek meeting-house, Madison County, on the fourth Saturday in August. Eighteen churches, some of which were still strongly Calvinistic, were represented. After the usual introductory sermon by Joseph R. Pond, Moses Foley was elected Moderator, and J. Tribble and Thomas H. Christopher, Clerks. On Saturday, while they were balloting for speakers, according to custom, to address the people, some one charged that Jacob Creath, Sen., who was present, and whom many were anxious to hear, was ineligible to that honor. With a copy of the Minutes of the Elkhorn Association in his hand, he stood up and contended that it would be wrong to give such an honor to a man whom Elkhorn had excluded. Much debate ensued. John Smith maintained that Jacob Creath was worthy of all that Tate's Creek could bestow; and that a knowledge of facts would leave no doubt on the minds of the messengers that, according to both Baptist and Christian rule, he was constitutionally qualified to meet the wishes of the people on Lord's Day. He was about to relate some of the incidents which had taken place at Silas, when he was stopped by the Moderator, and ruled to be out of order.

"Then," said Smith, who was determined to let the people know all that Elkhorn had done at Silas, "if you will not let me speak here, I will go out yonder to that stump in the woods, and explain the whole matter to the people; I owe that much to Brother Creath, and to the truth."

The Moderator submitted the question to the messengers, and they voted that he should tell what had been done; and the people gathered in to hear him. When he had concluded his narrative, the ballot was taken, and both Jacob Creath and John Smith received the suffrages of the Association. Having thus received a full and accurate account of the proceedings of Elkhorn, they adopted the following preamble and resolutions:

Whereas, we understand that the Elkhorn Association, at her meeting at Silas, did, in the most violent and unprecedented manner, drop from her correspondence two of her churches, Versailles and Providence, without having either notified them or attempted to prove any allegations against them, and without calling on said churches or giving them an opportunity of answering for themselves; and, *whereas*, the said Elkhorn Association did recognize the refractory minority that broke off from North District Association in the most disorderly manner: now, dear brethren, seeing such a lawless stretch of Associational power,

Resolved, therefore, that we suspend our correspondence with said Association until we see whether the churches of said Association will sanction such proceedings on the part of their messengers who composed that body.

Smith, having been sent as a corresponding messenger to the Cumberland River Association, which met at Somerset, in Pulaski County, on the first Saturday in September, could not be present at the Bracken Association, which convened on the same day in the town of Washington, in Mason County.

Some of the churches of Bracken, anticipating the action of the Association, had, as independent bodies, already taken measures to rid themselves of the Reformers. It seems that in April preceding the meeting of that Association, a notice had been published throughout the country that a three-days' meeting would be held at Mayslick, on Friday before the fifth Lord's Day in May, and all brethren that were favorable to the restoration of the Ancient Gospel, and especially the public teachers among them, were earnestly solicited to attend. It was stated in the notice, also, that John Smith, Jacob Creath, Sen., Josiah Collins, William Morton, Jacob Creath, Jr., Josephus Hewitt, and other teachers named, would be present. Accordingly, on that day, a great number of people came together.

Alexander Campbell, who, with his father, Thomas Campbell, was with the brethren on that occasion, writing to the *Millennial Harbinger* (vol. 1, page 238), says:

We had the pleasure of meeting with many public, bold, and powerful advocates of the Reformation, and of uniting with them in prayers, praise, reading, exhortation, and in breaking the symbolic loaf. It was a very happy meeting, and, I trust, a very profitable one. All was harmony, Christian affection, and intense zeal for the purity, peace, and union of the disciples on earth. I could have wished that all the opponents of the Ancient Order of things had wit-

nessed this meeting, and heard and seen all that passed.
. . . The brethren, both public and private (and there was
a large assemblage of them present), parted as they had
met, in the strong bonds of Christian affection, with increased zeal and renewed energy in the great and good cause
of emancipating the brotherhood from the deadly influences
of human systems, and from the galling yoke of human authority in the kingdom of Immanuel.

This unauthorized breaking of the "symbolic loaf" offended many of the Baptists of the church at Mayslick, a
congregation numbering, at that time, about seven hundred
persons; and they resolved, as soon as practicable, to cast
out the Reformers from their fellowship.   They accordingly drew up and published the following curious protest
and resolution, which at once drove every man to his standard:

Our church being in a state of painful confusion result-
ing from attempts by Alexander Campbell and others to
produce a *reformation in society*, as they have been in the
habit of calling it—among other things, denying the direct
influence of the Spirit till after baptism—contending that
persons professing faith in Christ shall be baptized for the
purpose of actually receiving forgiveness of sins—denying,
and rather ridiculing, what we call Christian experience,
in part, at least; namely, a burdened heart on account of
sin, and a sensible manifestation of God's pardoning mercy
by faith in the blood of Christ—slandering the Baptist
society by saying they are in Babylon—against which sentiments, with many others referred to by them, we solemnly
protest.   Also, against the conduct of the Campbells, Creaths,
Smith, and others, who, in May, undertook to administer
the Supper in our meeting-house—a number of our brethren joining in that thing without the authority of the
church—some, likely, without thinking of the wounds and
distress they were bringing on their brethren.   Our brethren, a
number of them, also, have been encouraging preachers to
occupy our meeting-house that many of us believe to be Arians,
knowing they were trampling on our feelings, which we conceive to be contrary to good order.   We have made every effort

to place them and us on ground that we can live in some degree of peace, but in vain; and we are now compelled to adopt the following resolution:

That all of us whose names are hereunto subscribed protesting as above named against the Reformation (falsely so called), are willing and determined to rally round the original constitution and covenant of the church, which has never been disannulled—associating therewith the principles of the Union between the Regular and Separate Baptists which were adopted by the Elkhorn Association when this church was a member of that body, and according to which we have acted ever since, which is a fact as relates to Baptists generally, thereby occupying precisely the same ground we did before the confused and confusing system of things that has destroyed our peace, and the peace of many other churches among us. And that no person shall be considered a member of this church who will refuse to acknowledge the above by subscribing their names, or causing them to be subscribed, or who will encourage the above-named Reformers.

The church at Mayslick having thus been rent in twain, each party sent letters and messengers to the Association, and claimed to be the original church. The majority were at once received by the Association—not, however, on the ground that, according to Baptist usage, the majority should rule, or because the conduct or the creed of the minority, who were Reformers, was unscriptural, but as they declared, because the minority had embraced a system of things called *Reformation*, thereby departing from the principles of the United Baptists, and of that Association!

Bethel, also, a church in the same ecclesiastical connection, having divided, each party claimed to be the original church, and sent their messengers accordingly. But now, the minority, who declared that they stood on the old denominational platform, were received, while the majority, who professed to stand on Apostolic ground, were rejected!

The messengers from North District presented their letter also to the Bracken Association, and were strenuously withstood by the delegation from Goshen, who, on behalf of their brethren, claimed to be the only legitimate North District Association. Bracken did not, in this case, hesitate to decide in favor of the minority. She said:

A separation having taken place in the North District, produced, as we believe in the main, by the common evil that is destroying the Baptist society:

Resolved, therefore, That the ten churches which met at Goshen, and who manifestly stand opposed to the innovations of Mr. Campbell, and who are disposed to maintain original principles as believed and practiced by our society, be recognized as the North District Association, and that our correspondence be continued with them as heretofore.

Bracken, in her Circular Letter of that year, said:

We lament, dear brethren, that we have to say that a dark and gloomy cloud overspreads our horizon, unequaled since the establishment of the Baptist society in Kentucky. Associations and churches are dividing, and, of course, peace and harmony have departed. Our meeting has in some respects been unpleasant, several of our churches having separated, and each party presenting their claim to be the original church. . . . The manner in which some speak concerning the divine influence of the Spirit on the human heart; the making baptism the regenerating act, and the actual remission of sins to the believer in baptism; concerning experimental religion, the church being in Babylon, etc., is such that we confess, if it be the Gospel of Christ, and the way the Lord brings sinners to the knowledge of the truth, we have it yet to learn. This system being extensively propagated by the Bethany editor, and by many active and able advocates, tending to produce a revolution in our churches, called forth the efforts that our preachers and brethren have been compelled to use, to maintain, not mere matters of opinion indifferent in themselves, but the grand fundamental truths of the Gospel of Jesus Christ, and to resist the inroads making against us. And we want it to be distinctly understood that, so far as we know, none of the preachers or churches that are endeavoring to maintain original principles, are contending for any thing but what is common among the Baptists.

Such were the words, perhaps, of Walter Warder himself, the reputed author of the Circular, who, whatever may have been the grounds for once hoping that he would fully espouse the cause of the Reformation, was now zealously endeavoring to overthrow it. William Vaughn also withstood the progress of Reform, and at last succeeded in reminding Bracken that she was the daughter of Elkhorn, and in persuading her to stand dutiful and firm by the maternal side of that ancient and orthodox Association. It was generally believed that, had these two popular ministers accepted the *Ancient Gospel*, Bracken, like North District, would have gone almost bodily into the Reformation.

CHAPTER XXXIV.

On the third Saturday in September, 1830, the Boone's Creek Association met at *Indian Creek*, in Clark County. The six churches that, one year before, had voted to change or abolish the Constitution, viz.: Mt. Zion, Mt. Union, Nicholasville, Liberty, Friendship, and Lower Bethel, or North Middletown, still hoped that they might remain in communion with their brethren, and yet be free. But, when they all came together, it appeared that the spirit of Goshen would prevail. So sure were the indications of a proscriptive temper, that some, who had no heart for contention, and no hope of any reconciliation, returned home on Saturday in despair.

John Smith was again confronted by his opponents, and, although an accredited Messenger from North District, was rejected on the ground that he represented an heretical and disorderly faction of that body. Nor were the messengers from Tate's Creek more fortunate; that Association was adjudged to have departed from her Constitution, and her letter also was refused. The question was soon raised as to the course that should be pursued toward the six churches that had expressed dissatisfaction with the Constitution, and thus virtually denied the faith. A proposition to drop them from correspondence excited turbulent debate, in the course of which a certain preacher maintained that all those churches had been led astray by one man, whose bad zeal and false teaching had corrupted many others also. He set forth some of the ruinous doctrines "which," he said, "John Smith had been preaching to the people of North Middletown, and to other communities, until he had thrown the whole country into a blaze of excitement, and desolated many of the churches of the living God!"

On Monday, after William Morton and others had with drawn from the field in disgust and despair, Smith, who still lingered in the camp of the enemy, arose and respect fully asked for permission to speak. But he was vociferously ordered to take a seat. Grown familiar with these noisy but harmless demonstrations, he stood patiently before them and waited for silence. The Moderator, seeing that he was determined to speak, said to him:

"Brother Smith, I know you are too much of a Christian and gentleman to speak when brethren do not wish to hear you."

"But what sort of religion or courtesy is it," he replied "that falsely accuses a brother, and then rudely denies him the privilege of speech?"

"Put him down!" cried many voices at once.

The Moderator remonstrated: "Brother Smith, you see that the brethren do not wish to hear you."

"Will you not allow me," said he, "even to give a reason why I ought to be heard?"

"Certainly, you may do that, if you will only be brief."

"Well, then," said Smith, "instead of the doctrine which the brother on Saturday so unjustly imputed to us, we teach that Christ tasted death for every man; and that, after his resurrection from the death, he commanded the Good News to be proclaimed among all nations, and to every creature with the promise that those who would believe and be baptized should be saved. Now, if the people will not believe God's Word as thus declared, neither would they believe though he should speak to them directly by his Holy Spirit. This we believe and teach; and, if it is not the Good News of the Kingdom, I would be glad if that brother would tell me what the Gospel is."

"Will you not stop him?" exclaimed an old Calvinist, who had listened thus far in spite of himself. "He has told it nearly all right out."

"Brother Smith," said the Moderator, "will you not now take your seat?"

"Brethren," said Smith, "if you are determined not to hear me, I must sit down; but whether the religion of

Jesus Christ allows you to act in this way, let all these good people around me judge; I submit."

The proposition to drop the six anti-creed churches from the Association prevailed, and thus did the Calvinists of Boone's Creek *rid themselves of the Reformers.*

[Whatever may have been the temper or the indiscretions of a few, the greater part of the disciples among the churches of the Boone's Creek and of the North District Association, with John Smith at their head, honestly professed a wish to live in fellowship with their brethren, and prudently labored to avoid giving them any just ground of offense.] True, they demanded, as a condition of peace, that there should be freedom in all matters of opinion, and liberty in love respecting all things not expressly enjoined. While *faith and obedience* was maintained as the proper ground of union, they insisted that, beyond this, nothing should be required, one of another; that each should take the Scriptures alone for his guide; and, calling no man master, read and interpret for himself. Some popular opinions, it is true, were controverted, and certain long-established customs were disregarded by the Reformers; and it can not be denied that some were betrayed, at times, by their zeal or their resentment, into vain and unprofitable debate. But they seldom opposed a custom that did not make void the law of God, or controvert an opinion that had not been confounded with the faith, and made the ground or test of fellowship.

But illiberal minds sometimes espouse a liberal cause, and, in the name of freedom, strive to bring the free themselves into bondage. A few sectarian spirits, imagining that they were out of Babylon, when they had only climbed to their house-tops, very early obtruded themselves among the Disciples. While complaining of the yoke which they and their fathers had worn, they bent down their necks to other masters, and seemed unwilling to be free. Indifferent to the facts of the Gospel, they still wrangled for opinions; confounding example and principle—the letter and the spirit of the law—they went about railing at harmless old customs as unauthorized, and stickling for a puerile and lifeless ritual, under the name of the Ancient and Apostolic order of things.

The Baptists defended their ceremonies and order of worship on the ground of usage; but a few untaught ones among the Reformers, with but little spiritual discernment, imagined that they had found an outward rule or authoritative example for every accident of worship and point of order. The attitude of prayer—the hour of the day for eating the Lord's Supper—the chemical nature of the wine to be used—the propriety of a sermon, or even a benediction, after the Supper—the necessity of the loud *Amen* to all the public prayers—the number of deacons in a congregation— the holy kiss as a mode of Christian salutation—and many other such things, were discussed, not as questions of taste or expediency under the law of liberty, but as matters of grave import, or of positive legislation.

But, though the serious interest and decorum of a great religious controversy were occasionally disturbed by these disputations, yet broader minds and purer hearts consistently labored for union in liberty and love, on the basis of faith, as distinguished from opinion, and obedience, as distinguished from all legal and ritualistic observances. The plea for union on such grounds, maintained as it was by Smith and others with prudence and a fraternal spirit, could not, of itself, have dismembered the body of Christ, or produced schism in a single congregation. Exposed, however, as Reformers generally are, to peculiar temptations —to the fear of failure or the pride of success, to the enthusiasm of new ideas or the restless spirit of inquiry and debate—they must have been more than human had they been less indiscreet. The larger and better class of them strove to reform by argument and persuasive exhortation; they plead for union on unsectarian ground; they were tolerant when strong, and patient when weak. They conceded to others the right of private judgment and free speech, while resolutely claiming that right for themselves. This assertion of their liberty was, after all, the chief source of discord among the sectarian churches; for the jealous intolerance of the clergy regarded every dissenting view as heretical, condemned reform as innovation, and stigmatized freedom of thought and of action as licentiousness or downright apostasy.

When the disciples, therefore, proposed to maintain their connection with the Baptists, it was not on the condition that these should renounce their Calvinism, but that they themselves should be left free—zealous only for the truth, and subject only to the law of the King; but, when their Baptist brethren refused to remain in affiliation with them, it was on the ground that they would not observe the usages of the Church, or would not accept the doctrines of the creed.

"Why is it," said an impatient Calvinist one day to John Smith, "that you Reformers do not leave us? Go off quietly now, and let us alone."

"We love you to well for that," replied Smith. "My brother Jonathan once tried to swap horses with an Irishman, but put, perhaps, too great a price on his horse. The Irishman declined to trade, and, by way of apology, said: 'It would be a great pity, Mr. Smith, to part you and your horse, for you do seem to think so very much of him.' So we feel toward you, Baptist brethren; we love you too well to give you up; it would indeed be a pity to part us."

About that time John D. Steele, a man of exemplary piety and integrity, who, for many years, had been a zealous preacher of Calvinism in the valley of Green River, having read the debate between Campbell and McCalla, began, in consequence, to suspect the soundness of his own theological system. There was not at that time, however, in all the country where he lived, a friend that could show him, as he called it, *the way out of Babylon.* Hearing that there were a few Reformers in Lincoln County, he went to see them, in order to learn from them, if possible, the way of the Lord more perfectly. He returned home, and honestly declared to his neighbors that he had at last found the "old path," and that he was resolved to walk in it himself, and to make it known to the people.

He soon began to teach that human creeds, miscalled confessions of faith, were in the main but summaries of opinions, and that, consequently, they could not be a proper basis for the union of free and loyal Christians; that they were schismatic in their tendency, and ought to be abol-

ished. He was at once suspected of unsoundness, watched
and criticised, till grave heads shook sorrowfully, and restless tongues everywhere whispered against him; at last,
they judged him a heretic, and openly called him a *Campbellite!*

In the meantime, he had been appointed to preach the
Introductory Discourse at the Russell's Creek Asociation;
but his brethren on that occasion received him coldly. When
he reached the place of meeting he saw the messengers
gathered in little groups apart, conferring together. Soon
one of them arose, and announced to the people that the
messengers would forthwith assemble in the house, but
that the regular Introductory Address would be dispensed
with. But when the messengers had taken their seats, an
orthodox preacher, according to some previous arrangement,
came forward and addressed the people. Elder Steele bore
this treatment in silence; he took a seat unobtrusively in
the crowd, and heard the preacher to the close.

"Oh, Brother Steele!" said a good old sister present, grasping his hand, while tears of honest distress streamed down
her cheeks, "you are ruined; you have gone off with that
Campbell, and are ruined forever! I heard a preacher say
once, that he would rather go to hell from any other place
than the pulpit!"

The brethren at Union, in Adair County, to whom Steele
had long been preaching, patiently bore with him for awhile,
but, as he persisted in teaching that the Gospel should be
obeyed as well as believed—a doctrine which, one of them
declared, was not food for his soul—they, too, at last determined to dispense with his services. Accordingly, after
some preliminary proceedings, he was formally arraigned
on a written charge of having *changed his views respecting
the Law, Original Sin, the Atonement and the Call to the
Ministry.* When the indictment was read, he asked that
his doctrine might be investigated, promising, that if it
should be found to be erroneous, he would teach it no more.
But they replied that he was not charged with error in doctrine, and that, consequently, it was unnecessary to enter
upon any such investigation. "The simple question is," said
they, "have you *changed* your views or not?" Pleading

guilty to the charge, without reservation or excuse, he was at once dismissed, though by a small majority.

"Nancy," said John Smith, as he thoughtfully sat one evening at home, not long after these occurrences, "there is a good brother down yonder in the Green River country I hear they are going to kill; I am going down to help him."

He started at once, and, taking with him Josephus Hewitt, went on to Columbia, the county-seat of Adair; and, having been joined by Steele, they began boldly to preach everywhere the Ancient Gospel. The Baptists of Columbia, in the meantime, had sent for Elder John S. Wilson, a moderate Calvinist, but a relentless foe to the Reformation. He came promptly, and stood by his creed, resolutely denying every position of the Reformers. The people became intensely excited, and no house in the place could hold the multitude. A stand was erected for them in the woods, and, on Sunday, it devolved on Smith to meet the crisis. Rising above all controversy, and carrying his audience with him, he discoursed, for hours, of life and immortality through the Gospel. The conceits of orthodoxy and the jealousies of party were, for the time, forgotten; these carnal phases of religious zeal paled in the glory of the believer's hope which was now vividly set before them. Creeds and customs were as baubles that no longer amuse, and all differences of opinion were, for the moment, lost in a conscious unity of faith. When the speaker reached the height of his argument, the emotions of the people could find expression only in their tears. Eyes freely wept that never wept such tears before; and hearts, long obdurate and cold, melted in sympathy, penitence or joy. The impression made by that discourse was deep and lasting—the lapse of forty years has not effaced it from the memory and hearts of the people.

From Columbia, Smith went into Green County, having an appointment to preach at Mount Gilead. The day was bad, for a dismal, stormy sky lowered all the morning; yet the house was crowded, and the interest most intense.

"It is an ugly day," he said, on rising, "and I shall preach to you just as long as I please."

Having read Heb. viii., he explained the nature of the two covenants, presenting Judaism in contrast with Christianity—the Law as opposed to the Gospel. The people listened to his long discourse, not only without weariness, but with evident delight; and the power of his preaching was soon made manifest. At a private house in the neighborhood, where many had gathered in to hear him, he pressed the invitation of the Gospel, and affectionately urged every penitent believer to obey it. John Steele, with the wrestling ardor of Jacob, lifted up his voice in prayer, and the whole congregation, trembling with awe, bowed down with him in tearful devotion. The cross triumphed over prejudice, and the first fruits of the Ancient Gospel in all that region of country were now gathered in. Some of the most influential citizens of the community confessed the Christ, and were baptized for the remission of their sins.

From that place they continued their missionary tour to Mount Pleasant, of which church Steele was a member; thence to Edmonton, and through Barren County to the Dripping Springs. Here they met with Elder Ralph Petty, a staunch Calvinist, who, like John S. Wilson, honestly believed that those who preached the Gospel of Alexander Campbell, only "directed sinners to eternal pains!" The progress of these Reformers, thus far, had met with no other hinderance than argument or prejudice; but now they found themselves withstood by bolts and bars. The house at Dripping Springs was closed against them, and the keepers without were faithfully guarding the doors. Smith only smiled at this familiar but ill-devised expedient to stay the progress of truth; and the people, feeling an increased desire to hear a doctrine thus opposed, went, of their own accord, to the woods near by, and built a stand for the preachers, and gathered in crowds to hear them.

Turning southward, they preached through the counties bordering on the Tennessee line, and then Smith returned home by way of Greensburg and other towns in the Valley, leaving John Steele, now cheered and strengthened, to build on the foundation which had thus been laid.

"I believe," says Steele, "that John Smith's influence in the Green River Valley will continue to be felt through all time. He did a work there, which, in my judgment, no other man could have accomplished."

The subsequent history of John D. Steele illustrates well the proscriptive spirit that was everywhere aroused against those who were laboring to restore the ancient faith and order in the church.

He had been preaching monthly, as was the custom among the Baptists, to four influential churches of the Russell's Creek Association, sometimes taking the liberty of changing the day of meeting at any place, by previous notice, when the interests of the community seemed to require it. The preaching of Smith through that country had not only gained many friends to the cause, but had stirred up much bitterness of feeling against Steele. This opposition to him soon culminated in the Mount Pleasant congregation, of which he was a member. On one of their usual days of meeting, he had gone, agreeably to a previous appointment, to preach at another place; but, in his absence, a few members of that church came together, and, claiming authority to act by virtue of their presence on the regular day, proceeded to exclude him, for the alleged offense of "rejecting the principles of the general Union, *and other things*." This summary proceeding being noised abroad, a great multitude came together at the next meeting of the church, so that they crowded the house and the yard at Mount Pleasant.

When Steele arrived, the church was already in session, and another preacher, called for the purpose, was in the Moderator's chair. Steele asked for a full investigation of all matters of difference between them, with a view to reconciliation. He pleaded for it with tears, but he remonstrated and wept in vain. With a manly, but fraternal spirit, he then demanded to be informed respecting the *other things* charged in their bill of accusation, saying that, in time to come, when he should have passed away, good people, reading that language in the old church-book, might be led to suppose that he had been guilty of doing something wrong. This unforeseen demand greatly embarrassed them; and moved by fear of popular censure, or by an awakened sense of justice, they expunged the injurious words from their Record. Steele now arose, and holding up a copy of the New Testament, called on all that were willing to take that Book as their

rule of faith and practice, to come and unite with him in keeping its ordinances and commandments. Ten persons stepped
forth and stood with him on that foundation. At the next
meeting, others did likewise, and thus they continued to do
from day to day, until the greater part of the church went
with him into the Reformation.*

---

* "I have now—January, 1870—reached my seventy-seventh year," writes
Elder Steele, " and it has been sixty years since I made my first attempt at
speaking publicly for the Lord. In looking back over all the past, I can solemnly say that in all my labors in the Gospel, I have aimed at the glory of
God and the welfare of my fellow-men. In all this time, the Lord has been a
wall of fire round about me. and the glory in the midst. Yes, he has been to
me as the shadow of a great Rock in a weary land!"

CHAPTER XXXV.

DURING the winter and spring of 1831, John Smith, again relieved of all domestic care by the self-sacrificing zeal of his wife, went about among the rejected churches of the North District Association, confirming them in the faith, and setting every thing in order. He had but little trouble in persuading most of them to agree to a dissolution of the Association, when they should come together at Somerset in July; for, though originally and constitutionally an advisory body, it had, in its gradual assumption of power, become so proscriptive that it was but an impulse of liberty in the Disciples to declare themselves independent of it.

When the proper public sentiment, respecting the proposed revolution, had been formed, be began to feel an irrepressible desire to see his friends on the Little South Fork, and especially his old mother, who was living, at that time, with a son-in-law, in Overton County, Tennessee. He had often prayed that he might be spared to preach the Ancient Gospel in every place where he had once taught Calvinism. He longed, too, for an opportunity to vindicate himself, if he could, before those early friends who had heard so many rumors concerning his apostasy. The thought, that some of them might still be waiting the *Lord's time* in all the wretchedness of hope deferred, had caused him to pass many a sleepless night; and he had often said to his wife that, if he should die before he had preached the Gospel to them, he would die dissatisfied. And now, it seemed, the time had come to go, and tell them how they might be saved.

Accordingly, he set out in May, and reached the neighborhood of Monticello on Saturday evening, having made an appointment to preach in that village on the following day.

That night, in the hospitable cabin of one of his old ac-quaintances, many, that still loved him, gathered in to see him, and to hear him talk. They questioned him respect-ing his new faith, and, in their simple-hearted way, besought him, not without tears, to return to the good old paths from which he had wandered.

They had one test by which they judged whether a man was a Christian or not, and that test they now applied to him.

"Brother John," said one of them—an old man—"we would like to hear your experience again. It has been many long years since you told it; but we suppose you still remember it;" and they all sat together around him to hear it.

"I will give it to you," replied Smith, "but I shall expect each of you to do the same, for I want to know how the Lord has dealt with you all."

He related, with some minuteness, his experience, to which they listened with pleasure and surprise.

"Why," said one of them, "it is the very same that he used to give us years ago!"

"Certainly," said Smith. "I have never forgotten or de-nied my experience, for it was real, and just what I tell you. But I must now hear yours."

Each, in his turn, told his experience, varying some lit-tle in detail, but presenting substantially the same succes-sion of thoughts and feelings. Each had felt that he was the worst of sinners, and that God could not be just and pardon him. When they were all done he inquired:

"Do you really believe, brethren, that these discoveries were made to you by the Holy Spirit?"

"Yes, John!" said the same fatherly old Calvinist, whose meek face turned solemnly, but tenderly, upon him; "the good Spirit only could have made these things known to us."

"Do you believe, too," asked Smith, "that the Holy Spirit always speaks the truth?"

"Why, John! you *know* that the Spirit can't say any thing but what is true."

"But you say," continued Smith, "that the Spirit assured

you, that evening, as you sat disconsolate on the steps by
the door, that God could not pardon you, and be just;
and yet, on the next day, you got relief, and the same Spirit
then assured you that God had pardoned you, and was just!
If he really told you these things, did he not contradict
himself?"

At this the old man bowed his gray head in thought,
and his eyes, still moist with the remembrances of his own
conversion, rested musingly on the floor. Lifting up, at
length, his honest face, he said:

"Brethren, you may be sure that the good Spirit never
talks two ways."

"But, my brother," continued Smith, "the Spirit told
you that you were the greatest sinner in the world; now,
have you ever stolen any thing, or murdered any body?"

"Why, John!" he replied, "I never did such things in
my life!"

"But there are men, you know, that do commit these,
and even worse crimes. Were you a greater sinner than
they? Besides, the same Spirit told the brother sitting by
you that *he* was the greatest sinner in the world; and he
told the same thing to the *next* brother there; and he told
me, too, that *I* was the very worst of sinners. Now, how
could each one of us have been the worst of all?"

"Brethren," said the old man, solemnly, "rest assured the
Holy Spirit never contradicts himself!"

"Brother John," said another of them, whose harder
features betrayed the greater sternness of his prejudice,
"I have often said that if you should ever prove to be no
Christian, I would give up religion as a dream. But I see
now that you have never known what true religion is. You
seem to be utterly in the dark!"

Smith saw that it would be vain to attempt, by any further argument, to remove the scales from their eyes. They
had been blinded by their early religious education; they
were now all well advanced in years; and he could not
even disturb, much less remove, the prejudice of half a
century's growth.

He passed on down toward Stockton's Valley, sad with
the reflection that he would be met as an apostate by those
dearer friends whom he loved more than all others in the

world. He knew the depth of their prejudices, and he had
learned something of the nature of the rumors that had
gone before him; and he feared, not without reason, that
their confidence in him was lost, and that their ears would
be closed to his words. No disciples had yet preached the
Gospel, as he now understood it, in that sequestered region; the people had only heard of it, as a heresy that
denied the Holy Spirit and blasphemously declared that the
sins of men could be washed away with water! They had
heard, too, with sorrow and surprise, that their beloved
John Smith had renounced his old faith, ridiculed his experience and was gone, hopelessly gone, into that wretched
and ruinous delusion! They had wondered and wept at
his fall, and their hearts had long since given him up. He
knew all this; and as he journeyed along the familiar road
that led to the home of his youth, it pained him to think
of meeting those friends, still cherished, but now cold and
estranged.

He thought of Isaac Denton, his father in the Gospel,
venerable with age and godliness; and he dwelt on the
early kindness of that firm, but gentle-hearted pastor, till
he would have given the world to be assured that he still
loved him as a son. But, when he remembered his mother,
trembling with more than fourscore years, her religious
sentiments now past all change, and her prejudices too
sacred for a son to despise, he was moved with filial tenderness, and wept as he rode along his solitary way. His
mind, too, was much perplexed; for, with all his invention,
he felt that he could not frame a suitable apology or argument to meet her sorrowful reproaches. She was too infirm
to reason about doctrines, and he could not premeditate
any disingenuous plea even to win back his old place in that
mother's heart. Strong as he was, he dreaded the interview;
the thought of her distrust unnerved him, and he trembled
like a child. "I felt," he often said afterward, "that I
would rather meet, in fierce debate, a ten-acre field of men,
than that dear old mother, whose heart I had so deeply
distressed by a course that she could not be made to understand or excuse."

While indulging in these reflections, he suddenly met his
old pastor, Isaac Denton, in the road. He was then on his

way into Wayne County, where he had an appointment to preach. After much cordial greeting, they dismounted, and, hitching their horses on the roadside, sat down together on a log, and entered into conversation.

"I suppose, Brother Denton," said Smith, "that you have heard many unfavorable things about me—concerning my departures from the faith, and the errors into which I have run."

"I have, Brother John," said Denton, "and I am grieved —deeply grieved—to hear them."

"Brother Denton, you always professed to believe that I was candid and truthful, even when a boy."

"I have always believed that, John."

"I hope, then," said Smith, "that you will think I am candid now, and that I will tell you the whole truth about my departure from the faith."

"Yes," replied Denton; "Satan has never tempted me to doubt that you were a Christian from the day that I baptized you to the present moment. But you are gone—you are gone, John!"

"Where to, Brother Denton?" quickly asked Smith.

"From the faith of the Baptists," as quickly rejoined Denton.

"Well," said Smith, "I will tell you truthfully the whole route I have traveled: I have gone from the Philadelphia Confession of Faith to the Bible as my only guide in matters of religion."

"I have set down Alexander Campbell, John, as the most erroneous and corrupt man in the world," said Denton.

Smith, by no means diverted from his purpose by this denunciation, remarked: "I have heard, Brother Denton, that the doors of old Clear Fork meeting-house, where I told my experience many years ago, and where you received me into the church, have been closed against me!"

"Yes, they are," said he; "you will not be able to speak there."

"I am on my way to the Valley," said Smith, "and I expect to talk to the people; and now I ask you whether it will be agreeable to your feelings for me to preach in the house? I have often done so in times past, and I would like to do so in future, whenever I may come down to visit my friends."

"The church will not expect you to preach in their house, Brother John; and I think, myself, that you had better not do it."

"Brother Denton, you say that you have no doubt that I am a Christian; now, as you do not believe in falling from grace, I may have only gone into some error from which I may be brought back again."

"But I fear," replied he, "that you will do great injury to the cause before you are brought back."

"Will you not, then, turn, and go with me to the Valley?" asked Smith. "Let me preach in the house, and I will confess all my departures from the Baptist faith, and give my reasons for every change. When I am done, I will take it as the part of a father, if you will then get up and tell me wherein I have made any departure from the Word of God."

"No, no, Brother John; such a course would get us into controversy."

"Well, the controversy shall be friendly," said Smith; "and, my dear brother, it may convert me from the error of my way."

"You well know, John, that you can out-talk me."

"Were you standing on Gospel ground, Brother Denton, i have not the vanity to suppose such a thing; but, to tell you the truth, I do believe that I can out-talk any man, within five hundred miles of the place where we now sit, that will attempt to defend the ground you occupy."

"I must now go," said Denton; "but do not attempt to preach at Clear Fork meeting-house!"

And thus these old friends parted—each to his appointment—grieved that they could not part as brethren, after so many years of pleasant fellowship. Nor did they ever look upon each other's face again till, having laid aside the flesh, they met in that world where love, and not opinion, is the bond of union, and where deeds, not dogmas, are the tests of love!

The South Concord Association of Baptists, comprising many of the churches of Wayne, some of which were at that time enjoying the instructions of Isaac Denton, had, a few months previous to Smith's visit, published the following decree:

Whereas, Alexander Campbell and his followers have spread discord, by their influence, in different churches, therefore this Association resolves that our brethren of the churches that we represent are united to stand fast in the doctrines which they have received, and reject all those preachers that deny the agency of the Spirit from preaching in their houses, or their meeting-houses, so that our churches be not split and divided as some are.

Denton could not, therefore, have felt entirely at liberty to proffer even his own house to his erring brother had he felt a wish to do so. Laws, in those days, were often disguised as requests, and authoritative decrees frequently assumed the language of exhortation or advice.

On reaching his old neighborhood, Smith learned that the militia of the district had been mustered for exercise, that day, not far from Clear Fork, and he availed himself of the occasion to publish his appointments. After some conference with his friends, a preacher, by the name of Randolph, who belonged to what was then known as the "Christian Connection"—a body of believers, quite numerous in other parts of the State, that, many years before this, had discarded denominational creeds and names—went upon the muster-field, and, having obtained leave, turned to the battalion, and, hat in hand, proclaimed, in a loud voice, that "Elder John Smith would preach, that night, at the house of John Woods, and, on the next day, at the house of Alexander Hayes!" Smith intended to preach on Sunday, also, but he refrained from appointing at present a place of meeting, hoping that the people, after hearing him twice, would designate a suitable place themselves.

A large congregation gathered in that night at the house of Mr. Woods. The speaker presented, in clear and simple language, the chief points of the new doctrine, keeping the attention of his hearers fixed to the close. After the discourse, he informed them that he had that day seen Isaac Denton, who was opposed to his preaching in the meeting-house; that, consequently, he was forced to meet his friends in their own private houses. He was determined, however, that the people should hear him, if they were so disposed, for his doctrine had been much misrepresented. He owed it to his Master, whom he tried faithfully to serve, to his old friends and neighbors, whom he still loved, and to himself, to tell the people plainly what he believed and taught.

The Baptists present, and there were many, now took council together, and agreed that he should have the use of the meeting-house, if he desired it. "We want you to be heard, Brother Smith," said they, "and no other house in the neighborhood can hold the people that will come together;" and they insisted that he should preach at Clear Fork on Sunday. He accordingly made the appointment.

"And if I should defile the house, brethren," said he, with all apparent seriousness, "I will send for a priest to come with his holy water and make it clean again."

On Saturday, they again crowded into the house of one of his friends, and listened with increased delight, while he discoursed of *Heaven and Eternal Life;* and on Lord's Day, according to appointment, he discussed at Clear Fork the subject of the *Atonement*. These three discourses, the first ever delivered in that region of country by a preacher of the Ancient Gospel, were well received by the people; much prejudice was removed, a spirit of inquiry was awakened, and some were convinced. Although no one came out at that time in an open profession of the faith, yet his teaching proved to be as bread cast upon the waters.

There was present, at that time, a young student of medicine, from one of the northern counties of Tennessee, who had come over into the Valley on a visit to his friends, and was at the muster-field on Friday, when the announcement concerning John Smith was made. Curious to see and to hear the man of whom so many things were reported among the people, he went to the meeting that night. Pleased and encouraged, he sought his company the next day, and opened to him his heart. Though comparatively young, he had earnestly sought religion for eleven years, and had at last begun to despair. He had read the Scriptures as carefully as he could, anxious to know the truth and willing to obey it; but, like many others in that day, he had read them with the persuasion that, without supernatural aid, he could neither believe nor understand what the Holy Spirit revealed. He listened, therefore, with more than ordinary interest to Smith, who lost no opportunity of teaching the young stranger how to become a Christian. When they parted on Sunday evening, Smith, seeing his earnestness of purpose, his honesty and intelligence, pressed him to come to Montgomery, and study his profession with some of the physicians there, promising to give him his influence, and whatever religious instruction he might need. The young physician, however, returned to Tennessee, now fully persuaded that he had at last found the way of escape from his bondage. In three or four weeks from that time, he fled from his hard taskmasters, and was baptized into Christ, by Elder William D. Jourdan. Isaac T. Reneau, though he was educated for the profession of medicine, was too honest with himself, and too zealous for the truth, to look with indifference on the broad harvest-fields around him. The laborers were few; the toil, he knew, would be great; the trials many and severe, and the support, little or none; yet he went in, with a brave heart and strong faith, and for many long years since he has been gathering fruit unto eternal life.

On Monday, Smith went into Overton County, to the house of a married sister—Mrs. Matlock—with whom his mother was at that time living. The old matron saw him coming, and, with all the alacrity of childish joy, tottered out to meet him. She hung upon him in her doting fondness, and poured her tears into his bosom. All the years of his manhood rolled back in a moment as he felt the pressure of her palsied arms around him. He was a child, a tender-hearted boy again, and he wept his pious tears upon her head. He led her gently into the house, but when the greetings were over, her heart turned to its distress.

"They tell me, John, that you have left us! They say that you deny the good Spirit that once gave you peace, and that you tell poor sinners that water can wash away their sins! For a long time I would not believe them; but why didn't you wait till your poor old mother was dead and gone?"

"Mother," said he, "I confess that my mind has undergone some change in reference to the doctrines that I once held as true; but many of the things that you have heard about me are idle tales. I do not teach nor believe such things. I have never denied the Spirit, nor taught that water can wash away sins."

"But, if you had only lived and preached as you once did, a few years longer, John, it would not have hurt me; I could have died so much happier;" and she burst into a flood of complaining tears.

He tried, with all his art, to assuage her grief, but his words were powerless. He continued to sit by her side in silence, painfully conscious that he had not the address to wipe away her tears.

"Mother, on your account," said he, at length, "I would be glad if I were still a Baptist; but I could not, then, be true to my convictions of duty. It pains me, beyond expression, to wound the feelings of my mother; and I will now make you, as I regard it, a fair proposition: I will turn back and preach Calvinism as faithfully as I ever did, so long as you live, should I survive you, provided you will agree to answer for me, in the day of judgment, should I be found wrong in so doing."

"Ah, John," she replied, "I can't do that. I shall have to answer for myself in that day, and so must you, my poor boy!"

"Well," said he, "if I must answer for myself *then*, do you not think, mother, that I ought to believe and act for myself *now?*"

She mused for some time, and then, wiping her eyes, replied:

"I suppose you are right, Johnny; you ought to think for yourself. But you will have to account for it in the great day."

Thus she was reconciled; and, from that time, she did not cease to vindicate her boy to the day of her death. She could not, indeed, comprehend the nature or the ground of his apostasy; but she always said that she, at least, was not responsible for it—that John ought to be left free, for to his own Master he had to stand or fall.

Some of his old friends, however, could not be so easily conciliated, and they openly and abruptly cast him off. Meeting a prominent Calvinist of the South Concord Association, whom he had long known and loved, he greeted him cordially:

"Brother Floyd," said he, "I am glad to see you once more; how do you do?"

"Don't call me *brother* any more, Mr. Smith," said he, with repulsive solemnity.

"What have they turned *you* out of the church for?" replied Smith, with much surprise of manner. "What is it that you have done?"

"I have done nothing, sir!" said he.

"Well, but when I last saw you," persisted Smith, "you were in good standing with the brethren, and I called you brother; what in the world have you done that makes it wrong for me to call you brother now?"

While on this visit to his mother, he felt a desire to go and see his friends in Alabama again; and, leaving the seed which he had scattered around Clear Fork to spring up in its season, he mounted his horse, and, like a pilgrim, went to look once more upon the spot where the rod of his Father's love had chastened him. He could never forget his friends in the Hickory Flats; the memory of their kindness lay on his heart through life like a heavy, but precious, burden, which he felt that he could never repay, yet which he always loved to acknowledge by these grateful pilgrimages to their firesides.

On his way back home, he resolved to stop again at Monticello, and to lay siege to that place, if by any means he might deliver from bondage those dear old Calvinists, whose contradictory experiences, he hoped, had led them, by this time, to reflect on the ground of their confidence before God. Although weary from his long journey and incessant labors, he rallied his exhausted energies, and, for eight days and nights, he taught the people of Monticello in public, and from house to house. They received him kindly and listened to his doctrine with respectful attention; but no one received it, though some said they would examine whether it was from God or man.

He departed, at last, much worn down by his severe but fruitless toils. He left his old Calvinistic brethren as he found them; and they saw him go away with no less concern for his spiritual condition than when he came; for they were now more than ever persuaded that he knew but little or nothing about genuine, heartfelt, experimental religion.

As he rode along homeward that morning, dejected in spirit and worn down by labor and loss of sleep, he became so nearly exhausted before noon that he could hardly continue his journey. He almost sank from his horse in a blind and heavy stupor. While passing through the edge of a forest, he paused, intending to spread his saddle-blanket on the roadside and lie down for an hour's blessed sleep. "But suppose," thought he, "that while I am sleeping here, some Calvinist should pass by and find me thus?" and, shaking the slumber from his eyelids at the thought, he spurred forward, determined to keep awake till night. But even while fixed in this prudent purpose, he moved along for miles as unconscious as a statue; for nature had prevailed by stealth, and he had fallen asleep as he rode, upright in his saddle.

It should be mentioned that about this time, and, in fact, before this, John Smith's less honorable opponents, finding that they could not successfully meet him in argument, nor parry the shafts of his wit, which they dreaded more than his arguments, attempted to destroy his influence by detraction and slander. They shrunk from his presence, and, Shimei-like, from obscure hiding-places, cunningly threw their calumnies upon him as he passed along. Moved by these things only so far as they might affect the cause he loved, he watchfully guarded against every appearance of evil, carefully weighing his words and considering well his actions; beyond this, he gave himself but little concern that his defamers were secretly and persistently busy with his reputation.

CHAPTER XXXVI.

THE day for the gathering of the churches at Somerset arrived. A large majority of the Disciples, as we have said, were ready to dissolve the Association; but some were still fearful that the spirit of reform was becoming wild and revolutionary, and they paused to commend a more conservative policy. There was no express precept or example for an Association, they granted; neither was there any law to forbid it. "But may not such assemblies," they asked, "be proper, if, indeed, they are not necessary to the welfare of the Church?" All were determined, however, that, when they came together, nothing should be done through strife or vain-glory; that they would be one in action, though divided, it might be, in opinion.

On the 23d of July, 1831, the Association convened—save, indeed, seven churches and four parts of churches, which met at Howard's Upper Creek, on the same day—under the leadership of James French and David Chenault. Messengers from fourteen churches and four parts of churches, representing thirteen hundred and eighty-two Disciples, were formally enrolled under the old Constitution. Elder Thomas White was chosen Moderator, and Buckner H. Payne, Clerk. It was agreed that the *preaching brethren* present should decide among themselves who could most profitably address the people on Lord's Day; and, accordingly, John Smith, Peter Hon, and John N. Payne, a brother to the Clerk, occupied the stand, while Asa Maxey and Archibald Stewart addressed those who assembled in the house. A committee had duly prepared a table for the Commemorative Supper, and they all sat down, as one body, and broke the loaf together.

On Monday, the interesting question was asked: *Where shall the next Association be held?* Usually, many churches claimed, or begged the honor of entertaining the next Association; but now no such claim was set up, and no petition was preferred—not a congregation in all the bounds of North District proffered either house or grove!

"*Has the Association the right,*" was then asked, "*to impose itself upon any church, or to obtrude upon the hospitality of any community?*" and a decided negative vindicated the dignity of the Association and the independence of the churches.

Some one at this interesting crisis, perhaps in the goodness of his heart, sympathizing with the supposed embarrassment of the Association, proposed that it should hold its next meeting in the woods! He doubtless took it for granted that it must needs meet again somewhere; or, perhaps, he could not see that the glory of the old North District was about to pale before the rising of the Ancient and Apostolic Order of things. "Let us meet in the woods next year!" said he.

But the main question, which had been held in reserve, was now solemnly propounded: "*Is there any authority in the Word of God for this Association to meet at all?*" After some debate, in which nothing was said or done to give offense, they finally, and with much unanimity, resolved:

No church requesting the next Association to be appointed at any of their meeting-houses, and this body not having authority to force it upon any; and every church which appeared here by her letter and messengers unanimously agreeing that the Word of God is the only rule of faith and practice for Christians—on motion and second, *that the Constitution of the North District Association of Baptists be dissolved*—after consultation among the brethren, when the question was put, it was carried in the affirmative; and the said Association was thereby dissolved.

Upon after consultation, the brethren agreed to attend at Sharpsburg, at the request of her messengers in the name of the church, on the Friday before the third Saturday, and the days following, in August, 1832, and there communicate with one another, either by letter or otherwise, such information respecting the progress and affairs of each church as they may think of sufficient importance or interest to communicate.

North District Association thereupon, in the twenty-ninth year of its age, formally and quietly adjourned *sine die.*

The Disciples now ordered the publication of an address to the churches, from which we make the following extract:

DEAR FELLOW-CHRISTIANS:—We have concluded that it is best to notice the principal objections urged against us by some of our brethren, who have withdrawn their fellowship from us. And here we beg leave to remark that, let those brethren say what they will concerning us, let us never speak evil of them—never return railing for railing, or reproaches for reproaches. It is unbecoming our character as Christians so to do; for let them act toward us, or speak of us as they may, their improprieties should rather draw forth our Christian sympathies and prayers, and can never furnish us with a justification for violating that law of Christ which forbids our speaking evil of any man. To err is human; and we have no doubt that we have many errors to ask forgiveness for; and, whilst that is the case, we should always cultivate a forgiving, kind, and charitable temper, seeing that the Scriptures saith that "if ye forgive not men their trespasses, neither will your Father forgive your trespasses." We are fully aware that perfection belongs not to any man, or an entire exemption from error to any body of people; and we should ever be ready to accord to others that indulgence for their weakness and improprieties which we ask for ourselves. At the same time, we would remark that, to persist in error, if that error can be manifested from the Word of God, we utterly disclaim as forming any part of our character.

The first objection to which we shall call your attention, as presented by our brethren of the opposition, is, that we are charged with denying the "special operation of the Spirit in quickening the dead sinner."

In answer to this, we, in the first place, remark, that the expression *"special operation of the Spirit"* is nowhere to be found in the Bible. In teaching the Christian religion, in reference to man's receiving the Holy Spirit, we prefer using Bible terms to those invented by men, because the Apostles would not speak of those things in words taught by human wisdom, but in "words taught by the Holy Spirit."—I. Cor. ii.

13. We do not believe, neither have we ever taught, that men can be Christians without receiving the Holy Spirit; but the difference between us and our opposing brethren is this: We teach *that the Spirit is received through faith,* whilst we understand them to teach *that its first reception and operation is in unbelief.* We know of no promise of the Holy Spirit to any person, in the Bible, whilst in unbelief; but, on the contrary, the Apostle Paul expressly teaches, that "without faith, it is impossible to please God;" and the Savior says, John xiv. 17, that the Comforter, or Holy Spirit, which he would send, "the world can not receive." Our opposers say it can—Jesus says it can not. Our opposers say that the sinner must be regenerated by the Spirit before he believes; Paul says, Gal. iii. 14: "That we might receive the promise of the Spirit through faith," and not in unbelief. The Savior says, John vii. 38, 39: "He that believeth (not one that don't believe) on me as the Scripture hath said, out of his belly shall flow rivers of living water. But this spake he of the Spirit, which they that *believe* on him (not those who would not believe) *should* receive" (not had received before they believed). Again, Paul, Eph. i. 13: "In whom ye also trusted, after (not before) that ye heard the word of truth, the Gospel of your salvation; in whom also, *after that* ye believed (not before), ye were sealed with that Holy Spirit of promise," etc. Again, Gal. iv. 6: "Because ye *are sons* (not unbelievers), God hath sent forth the spirit of his Son into your hearts, crying, Abba, Father." And Peter, on the day of Pentecost, says, Acts ii. 38: "Repent, and be baptized, every one of you, in the name of Jesus Christ, for the remission of sins, and ye shall (not that ye had already received, but ye shall) receive the gift of the Holy Ghost." From the foregoing, it is evident that neither the miraculous nor common gifts of the Holy Spirit were *ever promised* to men in unbelief. Now, brethren, we know that if any man has not the Spirit of Christ, he is none of his; and we do teach men that they must believe and obey the Gospel, in order to the reception and enjoyment of the Holy Spirit.

The second objection is,"that we teach that the *mere* act of baptism, or immersion, *alone* can wash away sins; or, in other words, that mere baptism *alone* constitutes regeneration."

In answer to this, we say, we do not believe, neither do we

teach, that immersion *alone* can wash away sins, or that it is regeneration. But we do believe and teach that "he that believeth (not one that *don't* believe, or *can't* believe) and is immersed, shall be saved."—Mark xvi. 16. And we do teach that Peter (Acts ii. 38), did tell the believing Jews, or those who gladly received the word, to "repent and be immersed for the *remission* of sins;" and that Ananias, by the imme-diate *direction of the Lord*, did say unto Saul (not that his sins were washed away), but *"Arise, and be immersed*, and *wash away thy sins*, calling upon the name of the Lord;" that the eunuch, and the jailer with his household, *heard* the *word*, *believed* it, were *immersed* and did *rejoice* in the Lord, etc. And as the apostles did thus teach, so we believe and so we teach—and those things which God has joined together, *we will not* put asunder.

The third objection is, that we receive and administer bap-tism upon a "bare historical faith," or that we will baptize any person who merely *says* he believes that Jesus is the Christ.

As to the term "historical faith," it being an invention of men, of which the Bible knows nothing, we consequently have nothing to do with it; but we do teach that for a man to believe with all his heart, through the teaching or word of the apostles, according to John xvii. 20, and xx. 30, 31, and confess it with the mouth, that no man can forbid water: for proof of which we refer to Acts viii. 37. And *we know we are right* when we do as the primitive Christians did in the apostles' day, by the apostles' directions.

The fourth, and last objection which we shall notice for the present, is, that we deny "heart-felt religion or Christian experience."

This we do humbly conceive has arisen from a misapplica-tion of terms. We can not see how a man can have the experience of a *Christian* until he is one—all the workings of his mind before he becomes a Christian, we could only call faith and repentance, and not Christian experience—therefore, whatever an individual may feel or experience, either in mind or body, of either despondency, or hope and joy, before they become a Christian, we humbly conceive it would be a great prostitution of language to call *"Christian experience."* We, therefore, do not call it such, yet we believe that every Christian has felt these sensations more or less vivid; but we can not call or recognize (neither do they) any man or woman as a Christian until they have, by a confession with the mouth of their faith, and immersion, become one. They may have felt all the dark and desponding sensations commonly talked about, and all those happy and joyous feelings, and yet, unless they *obey* the Lord Jesus Christ, we can not call them Christians, or invite them to the Lord's Table; neither do, or will, any of our opposers. Whilst we admit, then, that those feelings and sensations are experienced by every person, more or less, before they are baptized, we can not, nevertheless, agree to call it a *"Christian experience,"* for the individual has not, as yet, put on Christ. We believe that it is by faith and obedience an individual has the promise of the Spirit, and that they do feel and rejoice in the promises of God; and we do set at naught all Babylonish terms and phrases not found in the Word of God, and all traditions, and all commandments, and doctrines of men, and we urge all to disregard every thing as matters of faith or practice not found in the Word of God. We, therefore, profess to be followers of our Lord Jesus Christ, and of no mortal man, and our enemies, who, by way of opprobrium, call us followers of Alexr. Campbell, do (while we are following in the footsteps of Christ) insult the King of Saints, by robbing God of his own glory and giving it to man.

CHAPTER XXXVII.

In taking leave of the North District Association, it is proper to relate that the few churches and parts of churches that had resolved to carry out the policy of the Goshen council. met, by their messengers, at Howard's Upper Creek, in Clark County, on the fourth Saturday in July, 1831. In order to guard against the entrance of all such mischief as that which had so lately tainted its orthodoxy and wasted its strength, this remnant of a once-powerful community, now one in temper and opinion, forever closed the door against heresy and innovation, by solemnly ordaining that henceforth no church should be received into their fellowship unless by unanimous consent.

But the principal business of these resolute Calvinists was the consideration and adoption of the report of the Committee on *Baptist Customs and Usages*. As before related, the few that met at Goshen, in 1830, having withdrawn from the majority of the associated churches for changing the old way of practicing the ordinances of Baptism and the Lord's Supper, and of administering the Constitution and the Terms of Union, appointed seven of their wise men to ascertain, during the year, *what the old ways of the Baptists were*, and to report the result of their research to the present meeting. Their report was read, carefully considered, and, after due revision, adopted.

Justice to those inflexible old men, who spared neither churches nor brethren, but renounced friendships, and sacrificed ecclesiastical influence, to preserve inviolate the baptismal and sacramental customs of their fathers, requires that the result of their grave and patient researches should be given to the reader.

After giving a history of the American Baptists from Roger Williams down to the general union in Virginia and Kentucky between the Regular and the Separate branch, they concluded •their lengthy report by setting forth the uniform practice of the churches, as follows:

We now proceed to state the way and manner of doing and performing those ordinances and religious rites before named, as practiced by the five classifications of Baptists embraced in this report.

*   *   *   *   *   *   *   *

Constituting Churches.—Two ordained ministers, at least, attend on them who are to be constituted a church. A constitution, covenant, or creed (whichever you please), being a compendium of Gospel principles and duties, is unanimously assented to and adopted by all included in the new constitution. The officiating ministers pray for them, and lovingly exhort, advise, and admonish them, give them the right hand of fellowship, and they to one another.

Subjects of Baptism.—All those who know, not only by education, theory, or credence of others, but by heart impressions, also, too deep and indelible ever to be effaced, that they are undone, ruined, and guilty before the Lord, and are without strength, or hope of deliverance from the wrath to come, save only by the grace of our Lord Jesus Christ.

Words of Baptism.—In the name of the Father, and of the Son, and of the Holy Ghost.

Mode of Baptism.—The administrator (an ordained preacher) and the person to be baptized standing in water of suitable depth, the minister, in an audible voice, pronounces the baptismal words; then lays the person to be baptized bacward into the water until the whole body is covered or overwhelmed with water; then raises the person to his or her feet.

Manner of Eating the Lord's Supper.—The administrator (an ordained preacher), standing at the table, after singing a hymn of praise, implores the blessing of the Lord, breaks the bread into pieces small enough to be readily taken into the mouth. The deacons receive the bread thus broken, and laid on plates, or some other like convenience, at the table, and present it to the communicants, that every one may take a piece. All being served with the bread, the administrator invokes a blessing, pours the wine into vessels of the cup kind, and the deacons bear it from the table to the communicants. A song of thanksgiving closes the solemnity.

That translation of the Scriptures called King James's is the version that the five names of Baptists treated of in this report receive, refer to, and confide in as authentic. The principles of government are exhibited in the proceedings of the council at Lulbegrud.

*   *   *   *   *   *   *

The committee think it due to the memory of the preachers who were constituted in North District Association, October, 1802, to state that no one of them, as far as known to the committee, had any agency in those associational derelictions and church departures noticed in the proceedings of the councils at Lulbegrud and Goshen; but that those innovations are derived elsewhere, and not from the original ministers and fathers of North District Association.

The Disciples of the North District having now formally repudiated all denominationalism by dissolving their Constitution and assuming the position of independent churches of Christ, John Smith went to be a witness of the final proceedings of the Elkhorn Association against those few Reformers who still lingered hopefully in her jurisdiction.

"How is it, Brother John," once asked Jacob Creath, "that you have singly captured so many Baptists in the North District, while we have been overpowered in the Elkhorn Association?"

"You have used honey only," replied Smith. "You have hornets, Brother Jacob, to deal with, and not flies; nothing but vinegar will do for them."

The church at South Elkhorn, where, it will be remembered, Josephus Hewitt had taken refuge from the wrath of his brethren, duly received the committee sent to confer with them in reference to the charges that had been exhibited against them at Silas. The question was asked by that church, "Who gave the information that we had departed from the faith and Constitution of Elkhorn?" and, though some of the committee present had introduced that charge in 1830, they responded, simply, that it was a matter of general rumor; that their business at the present time was not to debate questions or discuss points of difference; but to bring to them the Minutes containing the charges which had been brought against them at Silas, and to bear their answer to the Association, which was to convene at the Great Crossings in August, 1831.

The South Elkhorn Church, after proffering to the committee in the spirit of brethren, their affection and hospitality, during their stay in the neighborhood, proceeded, with Jacob Creath, Sen., as Moderator, to prepare a candid, but courteous response to the charges. In the conclusion of their answer, the church expressed the hope that the Association would reconsider her action at Silas.

"If they should find," said they, "that their proceedings on that occasion are, as we most firmly believe they are calculated to injure the happiness of God's people, we doubt not they will be rescinded; but, if they otherwise determine, we request that they consider us no longer of that body. From the Constitution we learn that the Association was formed for the mutual happiness, comfort, and welfare of the churches composing it; this object, we conceive, it now fails of securing.

"We do not wish to be understood, however, as renouncing fellowship with the brethren of the Association; far from it; we wish to love all who love our Lord Jesus Christ; but we do not wish to be involved in a continual struggle of unhappiness and distress."

Their messengers, now only three in number, bore their letter to the Association convened at the Crossings, and their names were duly enrolled. On Monday, the committee that had conferred with them, reported their proceedings, and, after mature consideration, the Association decided:

"Being satisfied that the church at South Elkhorn has departed from the doctrine and practice of this Association; and, further, that they countenance persons professing to be the ministers of Christ, who have proclaimed open war with our Constitution, and who have heretofore been excluded from our correspondence for heresy, we feel ourselves called upon, in the perpetuation of good order, to drop said church from our correspondence."

John Smith was present with the Tate's Creek Association, also, as a messenger from the Disciples that had dissolved their Association in July. He bore, of course, no letter; but he was cordially received as a *Disciple;* for the twelve churches, now assembled at Mount Nebo as the Tate's Creek Association, with Josiah Collins as their Moderator, were the same that had been censured by the unrelenting Calvinists at New Providence, in 1831. Smith occupied the stand on Lord's day, and with his usual power addressed the multitude, now, at last, in full sympathy with him, as one of the boldest, ablest, and most discreet of the Reformers.

On his return home, he was much gratified to find a letter from a prominent citizen of Monticello, who, though not a professor of religion, urged him to visit that place again, at his earliest convenience. He went down in October, and on presenting the Gospel to them, nine persons, among the best citizens of the place, professed faith, and were baptized for the remission of their sins. "Not," as Smith was wont to say, "that the water has any virtue to cleanse from sin, or that baptism or anything else that a sinner may do, can atone for the guilt of his soul; for pardon is only through the blood of Christ; but this is ordained to bring us to a knowledge and enjoyment of that pardon, which we receive only through the blood of the Lamb."

"But what shall we now do?" said those few Disciples, after they had been immersed; "no church here will receive us, and we have no one to teach us."

"Meet every Lord's day," replied Smith. "If others occupy the meeting-house, meet in your own houses and gather around your own firesides. If you can not exhort one another, pray together; or, if you can not do that, then read the Book and sing."

They followed his advice, and grew in grace and in knowledge; and soon, one of them began to speak in public, much to the comfort and edification of the little church.

CHAPTER XXXVIII.

THE reader will remember that the North District Association, in 1828, though composed largely of Reformers, had
with great unanimity, resolved to countenance no church
that would commune with *Arians.* Yet the Baptists of the
Mayslick church, two years afterward, complained that these
same Reformers had trampled on the feelings of their breth
ren by encouraging *Arians* to occupy their meeting-houses
The Bracken Association, also, about the same time, de
clared that the Reformers, whom they had just cast out,
"would not have been satisfied until they had brought into
the churches, and to the communion table, every thing that
professed faith in Jesus Christ, and had been baptized for
the remission of sins, regardless whether they were *Arians*
or any thing else."

Perhaps no two religious parties in the land, at that time,
were further removed from each other by mutual prejudices,
doctrinal differences, and diverse customs than the Baptists and these *Arians,* or, as they were invidiously called,
Newlights, or *Stoneites.* These differed from the Calvinists
in their views of the Trinity, and of the nature, ground,
and extent of the atonement. They had, besides, renounced
all human creeds, and, for a quarter of a century, had been
urging the union of all believers on the Scriptures as the
only standard of faith and duty. They had refused to be
called by any sectarian name, and had taken that of *Christian,*
in the belief that it was the name divinely conferred on the
disciples at Antioch. Though generally immersionists, they
fraternized with the unimmersed, and admitted them, without scruple, to their communion.

The Baptists, on the other hand, especially those of the

regular school, held, *as an essential element of the Christian faith*, and the very foundation of all communion with God, that in the divine and infinite Being there are three sub-sistencies—Father, Word, or Son, and Holy Spirit—of one substance, power, and eternity. Each of these has the whole divine Essence, yet the Essence is undivided. The Father is of none, neither begotten nor proceeding; the Son is eternally begotten of the Father, and the Holy Spirit proceeds from the Father and the Son. All are infinite, without beginning, and, therefore, but one God, who is not to be divided in nature and being, but is distinguished by several peculiar relative properties and personal attributes.

They held, also, that Christ underwent the punishment due to the sinner, and, by his perfect obedience, and the sacrifice of himself in the blood of his cross, made a proper, real, and full satisfaction to God's justice, and fully dis-charged the debt of those whom the Father had given to him, and for whom only he thus died; or, as they sometimes sang:

> " He for the sins of all th' elect,
>   Has a complete atonement made;
>   And justice never can expect
>   That those same debts should twice be paid."

They generally regarded a creed, or covenant, as essen-tial to the purity of the faith, and the unity of the Church. They wore their distinctive name, not only without distrust of its propriety, but with complacency, if not with pride. They were, as we have seen, almost without exception, strict, or close, communionists, and very zealous for the traditions and usages of their society.

Conceiving that no other view of the atonement could be scriptural than that which thus regarded it as a scheme of substitution and imputation, limited in application or design, they looked on the *Christians*, who rejected that view of it, as the worst of heretics, and but little better than infidels.

No doctrines had been more readily received or more tenaciously held by the Reformers while Baptists than the divine *Trinity* and the *vicarious atonement of Christ;* and they, too, had looked, with something like horror, on a people that denied, as they erroneously supposed the *Chris-*

tians did, the preciousness of the blood of Jesus, and taught that the blood of Paul, or Peter, or even of goats and pigeons, would have been just as efficacious. It was not strange, then, that, in 1828, the Reformers of the North District, ignorant of the real doctrine of the *Christians*, united with their Calvinistic brethren in a resolution to commune with such a people; nor was it strange that the Calvinists of Bracken, in 1830, regarded it as evidence of the hopeless apostasy of the Reformers that they could, at last, encourage these *Arians* to occupy their meeting-houses.

Though the Reformers had renounced creeds, voted out covenants, and dissolved Associations, yet many brought over with them, into their new estate, some of their old opinions, habits of thought, and even prejudices—the lees of orthodoxy and sectarianism—which were but slowly relinquished by some, and which clung to others as long as they lived.

"I rejoice in the freedom of the Gospel of Christ," said a distinguished Reformer, one day, to John Smith, while exulting in his imaginary deliverance from all his former errors and prejudices; "I rejoice in the liberty wherewith Christ has made me free. I feel that the last vestige of my old Calvinism has gone forever, and that its harsh spirit will never again cramp a single thought or impulse of my heart."

"My dear brother," said Smith, who well knew the power of Calvinism over a mind that had once been under its influence, and who had detected some traces of it still in the character or theology of his friend, "you have, it is true, given up your Calvinism as a system; you may have drained out the last drop from the cask, but the very hoops and staves smell of it still!"

But the more liberal *Disciples* were not long in discovering that the *Christians*, like themselves, had rebelled against the tyranny of opinion; that though they nursed with something like fondness their peculiar views respecting the doctrine of Reconciliation by Christ, yet they were neither Arians nor Latitudinarians. They saw, too, that those despised *Christians* had been laboring with good intent, and with a zeal that sometimes arose to enthusiasm,

to heal the wounds which schism had made in the body
of Christ; that, to this end, they had renounced all creeds
but the Bible, and all names but that of *Christian;* and
for this they had suffered reproach till they had become
a hissing and by-word to every sect around them. The
dream of a peaceful and universal brotherhood of believers had given them evangelical zeal; when they and the
rejected Reformers met, therefore, on the King's highway,
they talked freely together of the liberty which each, under Christ, had asserted at so much cost, and of their
common loyalty to him, whom each acknowledged as the
only Head of the Church. A common reproach daily weak-
ened their prejudices against each other, and quickened
the growth of sympathy between them, and they began at
last to feel that differences of opinion ought not to keep
apart those who were one in faith and purpose, and who
had, in fact, with equal firmness, renounced opinion as a
bond of union among the children of God.

Barton W. Stone, the earliest and ablest advocate of
the doctrines of the *Christians* in the West, was born in
Maryland, on the 24th day of September, 1772. His father dying while he was very young, his mother, with a
large family of children and servants, moved into the backwoods of Virginia. Here he went to school for four or five
years. In 1790, however, he entered an academy in Guil-
ford, North Carolina, determined, as he says, "to acquire
an education, or die in the attempt." His design at that
time was to qualify himself for the practice of law.

When he entered the academy, about thirty or more of
the students had embraced religion, under the labors of
James McGready; and, in about a year from that time,
after a long and painful *experience*, he, too, became a member of the Presbyterian Church, and turned his thoughts
to the ministry.

At the close of his academic course he commenced the
study of Divinity. Witsius on the *Trinity* was put into
his hands; but the metaphysical reasonings of that author perplexed his mind, and he laid the work aside as unprofitable and unintelligible. Having heard of Dr. Watt's
treatise on the *Glory of Christ*, he obtained the work, read it

with pleasure, and embraced its views. The presbyter on whom his examination devolved had himself embraced Watt's views of the Trinity, and his examination on this topic, to avoid discussion perhaps, was short, embracing no peculiarities of the system.

In April, 1796, he was licensed to preach, and, shortly afterward, he directed his course westward—first into Tennessee, and thence, about the close of the year 1796, to Bourbon County, Kentucky. Here he settled within the bounds of the congregations of Cane Ridge and Concord, where he labored with great zeal and success.

In the fall of 1798 he received a unanimous call from those congregations to become their settled pastor, and a day was set apart by the Presbytery of Transylvania for his ordination. Having previously notified the leading members of the Presbytery of his difficulties on the subjects of the Trinity, Election, Reprobation, and Predestination, *as taught in the Confession of Faith*, when he was asked, "Do you receive and adopt the Confession of Faith as containing the system of doctrine taught in the Bible?" he answered aloud, so that the whole congregation might hear, "I do, so far as I see it consistent with the Word of God." No objection being made, he was ordained.

Early in 1801, "the Great Revival" commenced in the southern part of Kentucky, under the labors of James McGready and other Presbyterian ministers. Determined to hear and judge for himself, he hastened to a great camp-meeting in Logan County, Kentucky, where, for the first time, he witnessed those strange exercises, of which we have elsewhere spoken.

Filled with the spirit of the revival, he returned to his congregations, related what he had seen and heard, and, with great earnestness and zeal, dwelt on the universality of the Gospel, and urged the sinner to believe now and be saved. The effects were immediate and powerful; the *"exercises"* made their appearance; a series of meetings followed; the work spread in all directions; multitudes united with the different churches; and, for a time, party creeds, names and feelings seemed to be lost in Christian love and union.

The "Great Cane Ridge Meeting" commenced in August

following. Many had come from Ohio and other remote parts, who, on their return, diffused the same spirit in their respective neighborhoods. Methodist and Baptist preachers united heartily in the work, and the salvation of sinners seemed to be the great object of all.

Stone and four other ministers, all members of the synod of Kentucky, now renounced the dogmas of Calvinism, and taught, wherever they went, that Christ died for all; that the divine testimony was sufficient to produce faith, and that the Spirit was received, not in order to faith, but through faith. At length, the friends of the Confession determined to arrest the progress of these anti-Calvinistic doctrines. One of them was taken under dealings by the Presbytery of Springfield, in Ohio, and the case finally came before the synod of Lexington, Ky., in September, 1803.

Discovering, from the tone of the Synod, that its decision would be adverse, the five ministers drew up a protest against the proceedings, and a declaration of their independence, and of their withdrawal from that body. They at once constituted themselves into what they called the *Springfield Presbytery.* They soon saw, however, that this name savored of a sectarian spirit; and they renounced it, and took the name *Christian.*

*In 1804, Stone's mind became embarrassed on the subject of the Atonement. He had believed and taught that Christ died as a substitute or surety in our stead, and to make satisfaction to law and justice for our sins, in order to justification. It seemed to him, on reviewing these principles, that either Universalism, or Calvinistic Election and Reprobation, necessarily followed. He indulged no doubt, however, that both of these systems were false. He determined, therefore, to divest himself as much as possible of all preconceived opinions, and to search the Scriptures daily for the truth. Driven from the doctrine of suretyship as unscriptural—wrong even in civil policy as well as in religion—he rejected that also which represented Jesus as dying in order to reconcile the Father to us. In the end, he came to regard atonement as meaning *at-one-ment*, or the restoration of the union between God and man. Sin, he saw, had separated God and man,

*Biography of Stone, by John Rogers.

who were formerly *at one*, when man was holy. Jesus was sent to save him from his sins, and to make him holy. This effected, God and man are at one again, without any change, however, in God, the whole change being in man; and this change is effected through faith in Jesus, who lived, died, and rose again. The whole efficacy of the blood of Christ passes on man to reconcile him to God—to lead him to repentance and to remission of sins—to justify and to sanctify him.

About this time the subject of baptism began to arrest the attention of the churches. Many became dissatisfied with their infant sprinkling, and wished to be immersed. But the question arose, who would baptize them? The Baptists would not do it unless they would become Baptists; and there were no Elders among the Christians that had ever been immersed. It was finally agreed that those who were authorized to preach, were authorized to baptize; accordingly, the preachers began to baptize one another, and then the people came and were baptized by them; and immersion soon became general among them.

Stone and some others now began to conclude also that baptism was ordained for the remission of sins, and ought to be administered in the name of Jesus to all believing penitents. But though he held and taught that view of baptism then, yet in time it strangely passed from his mind, and he was never fully led into the spirit of the doctrine, until it was revived by Alexander Campbell a few years afterward.

In 1809, aided by others, he began to preach far and near, and to found churches throughout Ohio, Kentucky, and Tennessee. In Ohio, at one time, he was providentially led to speak before an Association of Separate Baptists, already well disposed toward him and his brethren; and such was the influence of his character and the power of his discourse on that occasion, that the whole Association, including twelve Elders, resolved to throw away their creed and name, and, taking instead the Bible and the name Christian, to labor with him in the great work of Christian union.

Although he repudiated the orthodox views on the subject of the Trinity, Sonship, and Atonement, he never acknowledged the sentiments which were attributed to him by his opponents. In the latter part of his life, he often regretted that he had allowed himself to be driven, in self-defense, to speculate on these subjects as he had done. In the near prospect of death, he averred that he had never been a Unitarian, and had never regarded Christ as a created being.*

In the year 1826, while living in Georgetown, Scott County, Ky., he began to publish a periodical, called the *Christian Messenger*, which soon had a large patronage, and a great influence. The influence also of the *Christian Baptist* was already beginning to be felt, not only among the Baptist churches in Kentucky, but also among the Christians themselves. In a very few years, as we have seen, the Disciples, condemned and cast out by their brethren, as heretical or disorderly, had gathered themselves into churches, without any distinctive party name or man-made creed, as a bond of union. They were, in 1831, perhaps about eight thousand strong; the Christians were about equal in number.

"The only distinguishing doctrine between us,"† says Stone, in expressing his own view of the teaching of the Disciples at that time, "was that they preached baptism for the remission of sins to believing penitents. This doctrine had not generally obtained among us, though some few had received it, and practiced accordingly. They insisted, also, upon weekly communion, which we had neglected."

While the Christians had sought to effect the union of all Christ's people, by persuading them to accept the Scriptures as their only creed, and the name Christian as divinely called upon them, yet many were willing to adopt as more simple, scriptural, and practicable, the terms of union presented by Alexander Campbell.

"He developed to us,"‡ says one of the earliest and most devoted friends of Stone, "not only the true design of baptism, but also the true basis of Christian union."

The Bible as the only creed, and Christian as the only name, was the ground of union defined by Stone; while Campbell urged, that a belief with all the heart that Jesus is the Christ, the Son of God—which is emphatically the creed of every Christian church—and obedience to his authority in the ordinance of baptism, are the only Scriptural prerequi-

---

* James Shannon, in Collins' "History of Kentucky."

† Biography of B. W. Stone, p. 77.

‡ Elder John Rogers

sites to membership in any Christian congregation. He insisted, however, as necessary to the preservation of union, that opinions should be held in liberty and prudence, as private judgments, and that all public utterances respecting those abstruse questions which had divided Christians, should be strictly in the style and language of the Bible.

The great proposition, which asserted so broadly and unequivocally the essence of religious liberty, was set forth and maintained by both with equal zeal, if not ability. They both contended that no man or body of men have any divine warrant to set up their explanation of Scripture truths as tests of Christian character. The opposite position, that others have a right to interpret for us the Scriptures, the creed of each individual Disciple, and to impose their explanations upon us as essential to our salvation, was regarded as the very essence of religious bondage, and the source of religious persecution. This was practically the main issue between the two reforming brotherhoods, on the one side, and the denominational parties around them, on the other; and this was the vital principle, which in 1831 began to bring the Christians and the Disciples, in spite of their former prejudices, into sympathy and fraternal accord.

The position of Alexander Campbell, in reference to the union of Christians, was very early defined, in a practical way, by an incident which we here reproduce from the *Millenial Harbinger*, vol. 1, p. 147.

"Will you receive a Universalist?" some one is supposed to ask. No, not as a Universalist. If a man, professing Universalist opinions, should apply for admission, we will receive him, if he will consent to use and apply all the Bible phrases in their plain reference to the future state of men and angels. We will not hearken to those questions which gender strife, nor discuss them at all. If a person say such is his private opinion, let him have it as his private opinion; but lay no stress upon it; and, if it be a wrong private opinion, it will die a natural death much sooner than if you attempt to kill it.

In illustration of this most interesting point, I beg leave to introduce a narrative, which justifies the course here recommended, and presents it in a very eligible character, to the advocates of the Ancient Order of things:

In the year 1828, when the Gospel, as taught by the apostles, was proclaimed with so much power in the Western Reserve, Ohio, by our brothers Scott, Bently, Rigdon, and others, some of all sects obeyed it. Among these some Methodist and two Universalist preachers were immersed for the remission of their sins. One of these Universalist preachers appeared at the Mahoning Association, held in Warren, in the month of August, 1828. He was invited to deliver an oration at an early period of the session of the Association. He did so. Many of the brethren heard him with great pleasure; but some, remembering that he had, only a few weeks before, proclaimed Universalism, or some species of Restorationism, could not be altogether reconciled to invite him to a seat, and to treat him as a brother. Indeed, some worthy brothers were intent on having a motion made, calling on this Brother Raines for an unequivocal declaration of his opinions upon the restoration scheme, to which he was suspected, by some, as still partial. It was intended, by some members, to non-fellowship this brother if he avowed these principles. Some opposed this measure; but, finally, Brother Rains arose, and in a very clear and forcible manner, and with all deference, declared that when he obeyed the Gospel, he had, as he thought, virtually renounced sectarianism, and did not expect that the disciples of Christ were to judge him for his private opinions. It was true, he said, that many of his former opinions remained. These opinions he did not wish to inculcate; but, if he were asked to avow his private opinions concerning his former peculiarity, he must confess that he was substantially of the same opinion still.

This greatly alarmed some of the brothers, and they were prepared either to renounce him, or to withdraw from the Association if he were acknowledged. Some of us made a proposition that if these peculiar opinions were held as *private* opinions, and not taught by this brother, he might be, and constitutionally ought to be, retained; but, if he should teach or inculcate such private opinions, or seek to make disciples to them, he would then become a factionist, and, as such, could not be fellowshiped.

Whether he held those views as matters of faith, or as pure matters of opinion, was then propounded to him. He avowed them to be, in his judgment, matters of opinion, and not matters of faith; and, in reply to another question, averred that he would not teach them, believing them to be matters of opinion, and not the Gospel of Jesus Christ. Although a majority of the brethren were satisfied, still a number were not reconciled to this decision. It was repeatedly urged that it mattered not what his private opinions were on this subject, provided he regarded them only as matters of opinion, and held them as private property.

I urged this course from the conviction that, if these opinions were not agitated or discussed, the Ancient Gospel would cause them to wither away. This was my philosophy then, and, being much pleased with this brother, I had no doubt, from his very handsome address and acquirements, he would be a very useful laborer in the great field. I only heard of him a few times since; but the other day I received the following letter from him, which, I think, proves the wisdom of the course pursued, and goes far to recommend the principles contended for in this article.

*   *   *   *   *   *   *

Mr. Campbell continues:

Reason and experience unite their testimony in assuring us that, in the same proportion as individuals labor to be of one opinion, they disagree. The greater the emphasis laid upon opinions, the more rapidly they generate. The nearest approaches to a unity of opinion which I have ever witnessed, have appeared in those societies in which no effort was made to be of one opinion; in which they allowed the greatest liberty of opinion, and in which they talked more and boasted more of the glory and majesty of the great facts, the wonderful works of God's loving-kindness to the children of men, than of themselves, their views, and attainments.

I am greatly deceived in all my reasonings, and observation has misled me, if any society, pursuing the principle we have suggested, will ever be troubled with Unitarians, Trinitarians, Universalists, Arminians, Calvinists, etc.; and, under such a course of procedure as that recommended here, all will see that such systems and schismatical tenets could never originate. If I were to attempt to produce the greatest uniformity of opinion, I would set about it by paying no respect to opinions, laying no emphasis upon them, admiring and contemning no opinion as such. But, if I wished to produce the greatest discrepancies in opinion, I would call some damnably dangerous, others, of vital importance. I would always eulogize the sound, and censure the erroneous in opinion. We all know that strife is like the bursting forth of water—it always widens the channels; and many a broil in churches, neighborhoods, and families, would have been prevented if the first indication had been sympathetically attributed to the infirmity of human nature.

Barton W. Stone, in 1831 (*Christian Messenger*, **vol. v.,** p. 19), says, in substance:

Christians can not be blamed for their different opinions when they have honestly searched for the truth. My opinion is that immersion is only baptism; but shall I, therefore, make my opinion a term of Christian fellowship? If, in this case, I thus act, where shall I cease from making my opinions terms of fellowship? I confess I see no end. But one may say that immersion is so plainly the meaning of Christian baptism that he knows not how any honest man can be ignorant of it. This is the very language of all opinionists. . . . One may say my idea of baptism, as meaning immersion, is not an opinion, but a fact. So say the orthodox respecting many of their unscriptural opinions, and they are as firmly persuaded of them as you can be respecting immersion not being an opinion of baptism. Here, again, a disinterested umpire is needed. The case I shall leave *sub judice*, till a satisfactory determination of the matter be made.

"But," says one, "I can not have communion with an unimmersed person, because he is not a member of the Church of Christ, however holy and pious he may be." . . . Shall we say all are the enemies of Christ who are not immersed? We dare not. If they are not enemies, or if they are not against him, they are for him, and with him. Shall we reject those who are with Jesus from us? Shall we refuse communion with those with whom the Lord communes? Shall we reject those who follow not with us in opinion? Shall we make immersion the test of religion? Shall we center all religion in this one point?

Says Mr. Campbell, in reply (*Mill. Har.*, vol. ii., p. 103):

But opinions are always, in strict propriety of speech, doubtful matters, because speculative. If ever the word be applied to matters of testimony, to laws, institutions, or religious worship, we must be confounded in our faith and practice. If *opinion* apply equally to immersion and the doctrine of the Trinity, then it will apply equally to the Messiahship of Jesus, the resurrection of the dead, eternal life, and every item of the Christian faith and hope. . . . I know that *baptism* means immersion as certainly as I know that *manus* means a hand, and *penna*, a pen; or as certainly as I know that *sprinkling* is not pouring, and *pouring* is not dipping. . . .

We are represented as refusing communion with him with whom God communes, if we do not recognize as a fellow-citizen every one whom God regards as one of his people. Has God anywhere commanded us to sit down at the Lord's table with a person who refuses to be immersed because he was sprinkled? Or has he enjoined upon me to treat any person as a brother in the Lord, because he has recognized him as such, when he fails to keep the ordinances of the Lord? It is only in obedience to the Lord, not on the principle of expediency, but because the Lord has enjoined it, that we are to associate with any person as a brother in the Lord. Nor do I say that none are Christians but those who walk orderly: we only say that we are commanded to associate with those only who walk orderly. If we can dispense with the neglect or disobedience of one Christian, we may with another; and so on, till we have in the church all the vices of the world.

In August, 1831, Stone again writes (*Christian Messenger*, vol. v.):

The question is going the round of society, and is often proposed to us, Why are not you and the Reformed Baptists one people? or, Why are you not united? We have uniformly answered: In spirit we are united, and that no reason exists on our side to prevent the union in form. . . . We acknowledge a difference of opinion from them on some points. We do not object to their opinions, as terms of fellowship between us; but they seriously and honestly object to some of ours as reasons why they can not unite. These we shall name; and let all duly consider their weight:

1. That we have fellowship and communion with unimmersed persons. They contend—so we understand them—that, according to the New Institution, none but the immersed have their sins remitted, and, therefore, they can not commune with the unimmersed. On this point we can not agree with them; and the reason of our disagreement is, that this sentiment, in our view, will exclude millions of the fairest characters, for many centuries back, from heaven. . . . I know our brethren say: "*We do not declare that they are excluded from heaven, but only from the kingdom on earth. We leave them in the hand of God.*" But does not this sentiment lead to that conclusion? We believe and acknowledge that baptism is ordained by the King a means for the remission of sins to penitent believers, but we can not say that immersion is the *sine qua non,* without maintaining the awful consequences above, and without contradicting our own experience. We, therefore, teach the doctrine, "Believe, repent, and be immersed for the remission of sins," and we endeavor to convince our hearts of its truth, but we exercise patience and forbearance toward such pious persons as can not be convinced.

2. Another cause or reason why they and we are not united as one people is, that we have taken different names. They acknowledge the name Christian most appropriate; but because they think this name is disgraced by us who wear it, and that to it may be attached the idea of Unitarian or Trinitarian, they reject it, and have taken the older name Disciple. This they have done in order to be distinguished from us. Hence it is concluded that they wish to be a party distinguished from us, and have, therefore, assumed this name as a party name. This at once bars us from union in the same body; and we can not but believe it was assumed for this purpose by some. We should rejoice to believe the contrary. Until a satisfactory explanation be given on this subject, we must view ourselves equally excluded from union with the congregations of the Disciples, as from any other sectarian establishment. We object not to the scriptural name Disciple, but to the reasons why our brethren assumed it.

We are ready any moment to meet and unite with those brethren, or any others, who believe in and obey the Savior, according to the best understanding of his will, on the Bible, but not on opinions of its truth. We can not, with our present views, unite on the opinion that unimmersed persons can not receive the remission of sins, and, therefore, should be excluded from our fellowship and communion on earth. We can not conscientiously give up the name Christian, acknowledged by our brethren most appropriate, for any other, as Disciple, less appropriate, and received, or assumed, to avoid the disgrace of being suspected to be a Unitarian or Trinitarian. We can not thus temporize with divine truth.

Thus it seems, as Mr. Campbell observes, that it was not really because of any difference in their views of the design or meaning of baptism, that the Christians thought that they could not be one with the Disciples; for, in their views of this matter, they seemed generally to agree; but it was the *practice* of the former in receiving the unimmersed to their communion and fellowship that seemed to present a barrier to the union. Said Mr. Campbell, substantially:

But that God's rule or principle of rewarding men hereafter, is to be, as near as we can guess at it, the rule of our conduct to them in receiving them into his kingdom on earth, and in treating them as members of it, is inadmissible. The question is, Are we authorized to make the sincerity and honesty of a person's mind a rule of our conduct? It is God alone who is judge of this; and surely he would not require us to act by a rule which we can never apply to the case. Neither, perhaps, is it a fair position to assume that any man's sincerity in opinion or belief will have any weight in the final judgment; but whether it will or not, it can not be a rule of our proceeding in any case. We judge from actions; God judges the heart, and, therefore, we look for visible obedience, and, when we are assured that the Lord has commanded every man to confess him or to profess the faith, and be immersed into his name, we can never justify ourselves before God or man in presuming in our judgment of charity to set aside his commandment, and in accepting for it a human substitute. . . . We have no objection to the name Christian, if we only deserve it; nor predilection for the name Disciple, except for its antiquity and modesty; but, when it is plead for as of divine authority, and as the only or most fitting name which can be adopted, we must lift up our voice against the imposition, and contend for our liberty where the Lord has left us free. Would to God that all professors could be addressed as saints, faithful brethren, Disciples indeed, Christians.

In fine, while both labored for the union of Christians, Mr. Campbell thought that the only practicable way to accomplish it was to propound the Ancient Gospel and the Ancient Order of Things in the words and sentences found in the Apostolic writings; to abandon all traditions and usages not found in the Record, and to make no human terms of communion. Elder Stone urged, more emphatically, but not in opposition to this sentiment, the communion of Christians in the spirit of the Bible, rather than a formal union on that Book. He exhorted his brethren to seek for more holiness rather than trouble themselves and others with schemes and plans of union. "The love of God," said he, "shed abroad in our hearts by the Holy Ghost given unto us, will more effectually unite than all the wisdom of the world combined."

CHAPTER XXXIX.

JOHN T. JOHNSON, of whom Barton W. Stone said there was no better man, began, about the year 1829, while a member of the Baptist church at the Great Crossings, to examine, in the light of his Bible, what was vulgarly called Campbellism. He finally received it as the doctrine of the Scriptures, and contended for it with zeal in the private circle of his friends, till, at last, anxious that all should see and feel as he did, he began to preach it publicly as the faith once delivered to the saints. He saw, in the principles which he had embraced, the true basis for the union of Christians, and the only means for the conversion of the world; and he resolved to devote all his powers to the work of reforming the Church and saving the world. He prudently sought, first, to enlighten the congregation of which he was a member; but his efforts were scorned, and he went forth to build on the Bible alone. In February, 1831, he and only two others withdrew from the Baptist church at the Great Crossings, and formed themselves into a congregation of Disciples. Two or three more were added by baptism at their first meeting; and, from that time, having surrendered a lucrative practice of the law, he gave himself wholly to the work of preaching the Gospel.

"My emancipation from a sectarian institution," says he,[*] "resulted in an intimate acquaintance and firm friendship with that eminent man of God, Elder Barton W. Stone, deservedly the most eminent preacher in the Christian connection in the West." They lived together in, or near, Georgetown, and soon each plainly saw that there was no scriptural barrier to their union. They encouraged a

---

[*] Biography of J. T. Johnson, by John Rogers.

fraternal sentiment among the members of their congregations, and the brethren of both churches at last met and worshiped together. They all saw more and more clearly, every day, that they were indeed on the same foundation, in the same spirit, and with the same Gospel, and that there was no reason why they should not be of one family.

Among those who watched the development of this fraternal spirit among the Disciples and Christians about Georgetown, no one more deeply sympathized with it, or more cordially approved and encouraged it, than John Smith. There were but few, if any, of the persecuted *Arians* within the bounds of the North District Association; but his eye turned to the little handful of Disciples at the Great Crossings, and to the neighboring Christians of Georgetown—to Johnson and to Stone, as those who seemed to be called, in the providence of God, to lead in the work of uniting the two brotherhoods together. He could not, therefore, have staid away from them. In fact, they sent for him, and, in November, 1831, he went to the Great Crossings, and there labored in the Gospel for some days with Johnson and his brethren. Accessions were gained, and the number of Disciples at that place was increased to about forty.

"We rejoice," says Alexander Campbell, when speaking of that meeting, "to hear that the utmost harmony and Christian love prevailed, not only among the disciples composing that congregation, but between them and the disciples meeting under the *Christian name* in connection with Brother Stone, in Georgetown, notwithstanding the sparrings between us editors."

To further the cause of union, Johnson agreed to become a co-editor of the *Christian Messenger*, an arrangement which went into effect in January following. In the meantime, an informal and private conference was held in Georgetown some time before the close of the year, at which John Smith, John Rogers, and perhaps others, were present; the subject of a general union of the churches was discussed, its importance and practicability were admitted, and the time and manner of effecting it were considered. To this great work, John Smith was willing to give what time he could spare from his needy family, and, visiting the congregations of Christians and Reformers throughout the

State, labor to conciliate and unite them; and John Rogers was ready, if necessary, to do the same. They decided, however, to hold a four-days union meeting at Georgetown, embracing Christmas day, and afterward, a similar meeting at Lexington, on New Year's day, and to invite teachers and brethren from abroad to be present. On these occasions, many of both parties assembled and they worshiped and counseled together with one spirit and one accord.

At Lexington, especially, on New Year's day, pursuant to the notice very generally given, many Disciples and Christians came together to talk over, once more, and finally, the points of difference between them, to ascertain whether the proposed union were practicable, and, if so, to agree upon the terms on which it should be effected. It was not a meeting of Elders or Preachers only, but a popular assembly—*a mass meeting* of the brethren.

While many had laid aside their prejudices, and were ready to consummate the union, some of each party still cherished honest doubts respecting the doctrine of the others. Some Reformers still looked upon the Christians as Arians; and some Christians were adverse to the union, in the belief that the Reformers denied the influence of the Spirit, and attached undue importance to baptism. On the other hand, while the Christians still refused to give up their name, the others were willing to concede that it was no less scriptural and proper than Disciple. While all did not hold in the same sense that baptism was for the remission of sins, they all agreed that it was a divine ordinance, which could not safely be set aside or neglected. Finally, though they still differed on the question of free or restricted communion, each felt that it was his privilege to commune with the other, since they were all of one faith and one immersion.

On Saturday, the appointed day, a multitude of anxious brethren began, at an early hour, to crowd the old meeting-house of the Christians, on Hill Street, in Lexington. There were Stone, and Johnson, and Smith, and Rogers, and Elley, and Creath, and many others, all guarded in thought and purpose against any compromise of the truth, but all filled with the spirit of that grandest of prayers, "May they all be one, as thou, Father, art in me and I in thee; that the world may know that thou hast sent me."

Smith was informed that it had been arranged that one from each party should deliver an address, and plainly set forth, according to his own conception, the scriptural ground of union among the people of Christ. He was also told that he had been selected by the Disciples, and Stone by the Christians; and that it was the wish of the brethren that they should avoid the spirit and manner of controversy, and give their views of the plan of union freely, but without reference to party distinctions. When this had been announced, the two brethren went aside, and conferred in private. Neither knew certainly what the other would say in the critical hour which had now come upon the churches; nor did either, in that moment of solemn conference, ask the other to disclose his mind or heart, touching their differences, more fully than he had already done.

"What is your choice, my brother?" said Stone, at length. "Will you speak first, or last?"

"Brother Stone, I have no choice," said Smith. "I have already made up my mind about the matter; and what I have to say can be said as well at one time as at another."

"I wish you to talk first, then," said Stone, "and I will follow." And they returned to the house, as the hour for speaking had already come.

The occasion was to John Smith the most important and solemn that had occurred in the history of the Reformation. It was now to be seen whether all that had been said, and written, and done in behalf of the simple Gospel of Christ, and the union of Christians, was really the work of the Lord, or whether the prayers of Stone, and of Johnson, were but idle longings of pious, yet deluded hearts;—whether the toils and sacrifices of Smith were but the schismatic efforts of a bold enthusiast;—and whether the teachings of Campbell were only the speculations of a graceless and sensuous philosophy. The denominations around mocked, and declared that a church without a constitution could not stand, and that a union without a creed was but the chimera of a dreamy and infatuated heresy.

Smith arose with simple dignity, and stood, prayerful and self-possessed, before the mingling brotherhoods. He felt, as no one else could feel it, the weight of the responsibility that rested on him. A single unscriptural position taken—the least sectarian feeling betrayed—an intemperate word—a proud, unfraternal gance of the eye—might arouse suspicion and prejudice, and blast the hope of union in the very moment when it was budding with so many promises. Every eye turned upon him, and every ear leaned to catch the slightest tones of his voice. He said:

God has but one people on the earth. He has given to them but one Book, and therein exhorts and commands them to be one family. A union, such as we plead for—a union of God's people on that one Book—must, then, be practicable.

Every Christian desires to stand complete in the whole will of God. The prayer of the Savior, and the whole tenor of his teaching, clearly show that it is God's will that his children should be united. To the Christian, then, such a union must be desirable.

But an amalgamation of sects is not such a union as Christ prayed for, and God enjoins. To agree to be one upon any system of human invention would be contrary to his will, and could never be a blessing to the Church or the world; therefore the only union practicable or desirable must be based on the Word of God, as the only rule of faith and practice.

There are certain abstruse or speculative matters—such as the mode of the *Divine Existence*, and the *Ground and Nature of the Atonement*—that have, for centuries, been themes of discussion among Christians. These questions are as far from being settled now as they were in the beginning of the controversy. By a needless and intemperate discussion of them much feeling has been provoked, and divisions have been produced.

For several years past I have tried to speak on such subjects only in the language of inspiration; for it can offend no one to say about those things just what the Lord himself has said. In this scriptural style of speech all Christians should be agreed. It can not be wrong—it can not do harm. If I come to the passage, "My Father is greater than I," I will quote it, but will not stop to speculate upon the inferiority of the Son. If I read, "Being in the form of

God, he thought it not robbery to be equal with God," I will not stop to speculate upon the consubstantial nature of the Father and the Son. I will not linger to build a theory on such texts, and thus encourage a speculative and wrangling spirit among my brethren. I will present these subjects only in the words which the Lord has given to me. I know he will not be displeased if we say just what he has said. Whatever opinions about these and similar subjects I may have reached, in the course of my investigations, if I never distract the church of God with them, or seek to impose them on my brethren, they will never do the world any harm.

I have the more cheerfully resolved on this course, because the Gospel is a system of facts, commands, and promises, and no deduction or inference from them, however logical or true, forms any part of the Gospel of Jesus Christ No heaven is promised to those who hold them, and no hell is threatened to those who deny them. They do not constitute, singly or together, any item of the ancient and apostolic Gospel.

While there is but one faith, there may be ten thousand opinions; and hence, if Christians are ever to be one, they must be one in faith, and not in opinion. When certain subjects arise, even in conversation or social discussion, about which there is a contrariety of opinion and sensitiveness of feeling, speak of them in the words of the Scriptures, and no offense will be given, and no pride of doctrine will be encouraged. We may even come, in the end, by thus speaking the same things, to think the same things.

For several years past, I have stood pledged to meet the religious world, or any part of it, on the ancient Gospel and order of things, as presented in the words of the Book. This is the foundation on which Christians once stood, and on it they can, and ought to, stand again. From this I can not depart to meet any man, or set of men, in the wide world While, for the sake of peace and Christian union, I have long since waived the public maintenance of any speculation I may hold, *yet not one Gospel fact, commandment, or promise, will I surrender for the world!*

Let us, then, my brethren, be no longer Campbellites or Stoneites, New Lights or Old Lights, or any other kind of *lights,* but let us all come to the Bible, and to the Bible alone, as the only book in the world that can give us all the Light we need.

He sat down, and Stone arose, his heart glowing with love, and every pulse bounding with hope. "I will not attempt," said he, "to introduce any new topic, but will say a few things on the same subjects already presented by my beloved brother."

After speaking for some time in a strain of irresistible tenderness, he said "that the controversies of the Church sufficiently prove that Christians never can be one in their speculations upon those mysterious and sublime subjects, which, while they interest the Christian philosopher, can not edify the Church. After we had given up all creeds and taken the Bible, and the Bible alone, as our rule of faith and practice, we met with so much opposition, that by force of circumstances, I was led to deliver some speculative discourses upon those subjects. But I never preached a sermon of that kind that once feasted my heart; I always felt a barrenness of soul afterwards. I perfectly accord with Brother Smith that those speculations should never be taken into the pulpit; but that when compelled to speak of them at all, we should do so in the words of inspiration.

"I have not one objection to the ground laid down by him as the true scriptural basis of union among the people of God; and I am willing to give him, now and here, my hand."

He turned as he spoke, and offered to Smith a hand trembling with rapture and brotherly love, and it was grasped by a hand full of the honest pledges of fellowship, and the union was virtually accomplished!

It was now proposed that all who felt willing to unite on these principles, should express that willingness by giving one another the hand of fellowship; and elders and teachers hastened forward, and joined their hands and hearts in joyful accord. A song arose, and brethren and sisters, with many tearful greetings, ratified and confirmed the union. On Lord's day, they broke the loaf together, and in that sweet and solemn communion, again pledged to each other their brotherly love.

This union of the Christians and the Disciples was not a surrender of the one party to the other; it was an agreement of such as already recognized and loved each other as brethren, to work and to worship together. It was a union of those who held alike the necessity of implicit faith and of unreserved obedience; who accepted the facts, commands, and promises as set forth in the Bible; who conceded the right of private judgment to all; who taught that opinions were no part of the faith delivered to the saints; and who were now pledged that no speculative matters should ever be debated to the disturbance of the peace and harmony of the Church, but that when compelled to speak on controverted subjects, they would adopt the style and language of the Holy Spirit.

It was an equal and mutual pledge and resolution to meet on the Bible as on common ground, and to preach the Gospel rather than to propagate opinions. The brethren of Stone did not join Alexander Campbell as their leader, nor did the brethren of Campbell join Barton W. Stone as their leader; but each, having already taken Jesus the Christ as their only Leader, in love and liberty became one body; not Stoneites, or Campbellites; nor Christians, or Disciples, distinctively as such; but Christians, Disciples, saints, brethren, and children of the same Father, who is God over all, and in all.

His co-operation with Stone and Johnson in the work of bringing the two parties together, John Smith always regarded as the best act of his life. "But do you not fear," said a timid and dissatisfied brother to him that day, "that what you have now done will drive your Baptist brethren still further from you? You can not overcome their prejudices against the Arians; and it was certainly bad policy to raise this new barrier between them and the Reformation."

"I know not," said Smith in reply, "how that may be; but certain I am that the union of Christians, upon a scriptural basis, is right, and that it can never be bad policy to do what is right."

"Are there no differences of opinion between you and the Reformers?" inquired others about that time.

"We answer, we do not know," said the Christians, "nor

are we concerned to know; we have never asked them what their opinions were, nor have they asked us. If they have opinions different from ours, they are welcome to have them, provided they do not endeavor to impose them on us as articles of faith; and they say the same of us."

"But, have you no creed or confession as a common bond of union?"

"We answer, yes; we have a perfect one, delivered to us from heaven, and confirmed by Jesus and his apostles—the New Testament."

"How will you now dispose of such as profess faith in Jesus and are baptized? To which party will they be attached as members?"

"We answer, we have no party. It is understood among us that we feel an equal interest in every church of Christ, and we are determined to build up all such churches without any regard to their former names."

"But will the Christians and the Reformers thus unite in other sections of the country and in other States?"

"We answer, if they are sincere in their profession, and destitute of a party spirit, they will undoubtedly unite. But, should all elsewhere act inconsistently with their profession, we are determined to do what we are convinced is right in the sight of God."

It is worthy of mention that at the very time when these events were transpiring in Kentucky, the spirit of union was prevailing over sectarian prejudice in other States also. John Longley, a Christian, writing to Elder Stone, from Rush County, Indiana—the home of John P. Thompson—under date of the twenty-fourth of December, 1831, says:

"The Reforming Baptists and we are all one here. We hope that the dispute between you and Brother Campbell, about names and priority, will forever cease, and that you will go on, united, to reform the world."

Griffith Cathey, of Tennessee, on the fourth of January, 1832, writes, in substance:

The members of the Church of Christ, and the members known by the name of Disciples, or Reformed Baptists, regardless of all charges about Trinitarianism, Arianism, and Socinianism, and of the questions whether it is possible for any person to get to heaven without immersion, or whether immersion is for the remission of sins, have come forward, given the right hand of fellowship, and united upon the plain and simple Gospel.

It should be added, however, that in some parts of the country, especially in Ohio, the prejudices of many of the Christians could not be allayed, and some of them unkindly upbraided Stone and his brethren for their course. In fact, a few Disciples in those places, pushed reform to extremes, and, in abandoning one class of errors, ran with thoughtless zeal into others. Some publicly and zealously contended that sinners should not pray, nor Christians pray for them.* They would not even pray for the Divine assistance, when declaring the Word to the people. Thus, while one class of religionists in the country dared not preach the Word to sinners, in order that they might be left to the converting power of the *Spirit alone*, others would not now invoke the Spirit in their preaching, but trusted to the influence of the *Word alone*. Some, too, rejected from Christianity all that had not been baptized for the remission of their sins, and all that did not yet observe the weekly communion. Some Christians, concluding such to be the doctrine and feeling of all the Disciples, rushed to the opposite extreme, and opposed the Reformation as a spiritless, prayerless, and dangerous religion; and, instead of allaying prejudice, they strengthened it, both by their preaching and their writings.

In order to consummate the union, John Smith and John Rogers were requested, after due conference among the Elders and brethren, to visit all the churches of Kentucky; and the arrangement was announced in the *Messenger* of January, 1832, in the following words:

To increase and consolidate this union, and to convince all of our sincerity, we, the Elders and brethren, have separated two Elders, JOHN SMITH and JOHN ROGERS, the first known *formerly* by the name of Reformer, the latter by the name of Christian. These brethren are to ride together

---

* Biography of B. W. Stone, p. 78.

through all the churches, and to be equally supported by the united contributions of the churches of both descriptions; which contributions are to be deposited together, with Brother JOHN T. JOHNSON as treasurer and distributor.]

That *support* for the year 1832, which was one of unremitting toil, amounted to three hundred dollars to each; nor did these noble Evangelists ask for more. This sum was not, of course, regarded by the brethren concerned as a charge for their services; nor was it a stipulated salary, offered as an inducement to them to labor in the cause. The brethren in conference, knowing the dependent circumstances of their Evangelists, sent them forth with the assurance that while they were laboring for the Lord and the union of his people, their families would not be forgotten. The contributions raised were the freewill offerings of those whose prayers and sympathies followed these self-sacrificing preachers through all their toilsome journeyings and faithful ministrations among the scattered congregations of the State; and they went forth without binding themselves for any specified time or sum, but leaving it to those who selected them, to determine these matters in their fraternal councils.

Concerning the two congregations which were worshiping in Lexington at the time of the general union meeting, it is proper to add, that although they subsequently met and communed together, and even agreed on a day when they would consummate their union in form, yet before that day arrived, some discovered what they conceived to be an insuperable difficulty in the way of union. Many of the Christians held the opinion that none but Elders or Preachers could lawfully or properly administer the ordinances, while the Disciples denied the exclusive privilege of the clergy in this matter. As some difficulty in choosing a suitable Elder from the combined congregations was anticipated, some of the Christians suggested the expedient of inducing the Elder of some neighboring church to come and administer the ordinances for them; but the Disciples maintained that it was contrary to the ancient order of things to have one Eldership for two or more churches. Under the circumstances, therefore, many felt unprepared to go into the proposed union. After due reflection and conference, a meeting was held on the twenty-fifth of February, and the pledge of union was dissolved, and each party stood on its former ground.

Nor was a union between the two congregations finally and formally effected till in July, 1835, when Thomas M. Allen, who, for ten or twelve years, had been one of the most popular and efficient preachers among the Christians, and who was now preaching to them in Lexington with a view to their union with the Disciples, again proposed that measure to them. At his instance, they waived all prejudice and differences of opinion on the subject of order and clerical privilege—if, indeed, any such differences still remained—and not only consented to the union, but nobly proposed it to the Disciples.

CHAPTER XL.

IMMEDIATELY after the union meeting at Lexington, John Smith returned home, and found that the news of what had been done was already spread among the churches of Montgomery. In the very hour that he reached home, the elders of the church at Mount Sterling came to his house, and, with much concern, questioned him about the rumors that were everywhere afloat. He frankly detailed the whole matter to them, and vindicated his course.

The people of that region had neither read the writings of Stone nor heard his brethren preach; they, consequently, knew but little of their faith except from reports that misrepresented their views or defamed their Christian character. The elders were alarmed when they thought of the consequences that must follow from what they regarded as a great blunder on the part of their father in the Gospel. He saw that he had encountered prejudices too strong to be subdued in an hour's conversation. He judged also from the feelings of these brethren what must be the displeasure of others less liberalized by the spirit of the Ancient Gospel and less intelligent in the Scriptures. With a heavy heart he resolved to preach no more till he had reconciled the congregation at Mount Sterling to the measure, which, though they condemned it, was in harmony with every principle that they professed. He requested, therefore, that the church should be called together at an early day, to consider his action, and to determine, in the light of the Scriptures alone, whether he had done right or wrong. He asked, at the same time, that he should be heard with patience in his own defense. His hope was that he would be able to turn their thoughts to a more definite and practical view of Christian union, and to correct their misconception of the doctrine of Stone and his brethren.

The congregation assembled, and the interview, in the beginning, was painful enough; for, while they greatly loved him, they believed that, in the excess of his zeal, he had unwittingly betrayed the cause. They hung upon his words, however, with a tender, sorrowful interest, being willing to forgive, but still more anxious to justify. He spoke at much length, with great plainness and candor, answered their questions with patience, and then, not without some misgivings, left them to make up their verdict.

The question was submitted, "Has Brother Smith done right in affiliating with the New Light party?" Such had been the force of his reasoning, and such was the influence of his character, that, after due reflection, their prejudice gave way; they were persuaded, or convinced, and their confidence in him revived. They not only acquitted him of censure, but, for the most part, went cordially with him into the union.

He next went to Somerset, and thence to Sharpsburg and Owingsville—to the churches which he had planted amid persecution and distress; and it required all the weight of his influence, and all the power of the truth, to turn their censure into praise. Meeting Mrs. Ryan, who had so early and zealously labored with him in the Gospel, when friends were few and distrustful, she told him how it pained her to hear that he had united with the Arians; that she could pray, with all her heart, for union with such as really honored the Savior, but that she loved the truth too well to worship with a people that denied the Lord who bought them! In the freedom of sisterly remonstrance, she weepingly assured him that he had injured, if not ruined, the cause, and had wounded, beyond expression, the brethren that so much loved him. With many kind and patient words, he soothed her fears and justified his action, until, at last, she, too, began to see, in the union that she had opposed, the triumph of her own religious principles.

His travels as an Evangelist now began; and, with the same zeal that had inspired him in 1828, he went abroad, far and near, laboring unceasingly to reform, to unite, and to convert. His voice was heard along the valley of the Big Sandy in the east, and upon the banks of the Green River in the west. He proclaimed the unsearchable riches of Christ in the counties upon the Ohio, and constituted churches along the borders of Tennessee.

He soon discovered that while the disposition to affiliate with all true Christians, on the Bible alone, was very general among his brethren, yet their prejudice against B. W. Stone, growing out of their ignorance of his doctrine, was, in some other places also, a formidable barrier to union. Some, too, in their opposition to all measures of expediency in matters of religion, in their pious distrust of human wisdom, or their scrupulous devotion to the letter of the New Testament, demanded a special precept for the action of the elders and brethren about Georgetown in setting apart the two Evangelists, and pledging them a compensation for their services. Such men now refused their co-operation, and otherwise discouraged the execution of the plan adopted. "But we are fully able, and fully determined," said Stone, "to assist these Evangelists to support their dependent families, should all others forsake us."

For the benefit of those Reformers who honestly doubted the wisdom or propriety of the affiliation which he had helped to bring about, and which he was now laboring to extend and confirm throughout the State, Smith prepared and published an address, in which he endeavored to meet and remove their objections.

Concerning this address, John Rogers, his co-laborer, remarks: "The simplicity, the candor, the charity, the piety, the dignity and noble independence which this communication exhibits, are characteristic of the man who wrote it, and, what is better, of the religion which he professes. And I am much mistaken if it does not contain a fair and clear statement, as far as it goes, of the principles and practices of the Christian brethren in these regions, and not only here, but generally in the West. I do, therefore, confidently hope that it will be greatly useful in promoting the good work of union and co-operation among those who have acknowledged and submitted to the one Lord, one faith, and one baptism, the one God and Father of all, who is over all, and with all, and in all.

ADDRESS.

BELOVED BRETHREN: It becomes my duty to lay before our brethren and the public the principle from which I acted, when, with many Reformers, so-called, and many of those called Christians, we met together, broke the loaf, and united in all the acts of social worship. It will be recollected that all our remarks relative to the Christian brethren are confined to those with whom we have associated about Lexington, Georgetown, Paris, Millersburg, and Carlisle. When the Christians and the Reforming brethren united, as above named, we calculated at the time that the captious, the cold-hearted, sectarian professor, and the friends of religious systems formed by human device, would misrepresent and slander us. But we do not mind all this. It is no more than we expect from such characters; and we hope we shall always be able to bear reviling like Christians, and not revile again. We do not publish this address with the hope of satisfying or silencing our opposers; but hearing that some of our warm-hearted, pious, Reforming brethren, having heard many reports, and not being correctly informed on this subject, have become uneasy, fearing that the good cause of Reformation may be injured by the course which we have taken in relation to the Christian brethren, we therefore feel it to be a duty which we owe to our brethren, and to the cause which we profess, to lay before them and the public, candidly and plainly, the principle from which we have acted, relative to this matter—which is as follows:

When we fell in company with the Christian teachers, we conversed freely and friendly together. With some one or other of them we have conversed on all the supposed points of difference between them and the Reformers, and all the erroneous sentiments which I had heard laid to their charge, such as the following:

1. That they deny the Atonement. On this point I found the truth to be, in substance, about this: That they do not deny the Atonement, but they do deny the explanation which some give of it. At the same time they declare that pardon and salvation here are obtained through faith in the sacrifice and blood of Jesus Christ. They expect, and pray for, all spiritual blessings through the same medium,

and hope to overcome at the last, and obtain eternal salvation, by the blood of the Lamb, and by the Word of his testimony. This, substantially, if not verbatim, one of their principal teachers said to me; and this, I believe, they are all willing to say, so far as I have been conversant with them.

When I have conversed with them about the various speculations upon the character of Christ, or the *modus existendi* of the Divine Being, they have said that, by the misrepresentations and violent opposition of their enemies, they had been sometimes driven into speculations on that subject. They also say they are not only willing, but desirous, that all speculations on that subject may cease forever; and that all should speak of the Savior of sinners in the language of the inspired writers, and render unto him such honor as did the primitive Christians. So say I; and let Unitarianism, Trinitarianism, and all other human isms, return from whence they came, and no more divide the affections, prevent nor destroy the union, of Christians forever. Amen, and amen!

2. I have also conversed freely with the Christian teachers upon the subject of receiving the unimmersed into the church, and of communing with them at the Lord's table. They have said that they have had, and still have, in some degree, their difficulties on this subject. In their first outset they were all Pedobaptists. Having determined to take the word of God alone for their guide, some of them soon became convinced that immersion was the only Gospel baptism; and they submitted to it accordingly. They went on teaching others to do likewise; the result has been that all, with very few exceptions, belonging to their congregations in this section of country, have submitted to immersion. They have not, for several years past, received any as members of their body without immersion. And, with regard to the propriety of communing at the Lord's table with the unimmersed, they are determined to say no more about it, there being no apostolic precept nor example to enforce it. But whatever degree of forbearance they may think proper to exercise toward the unimmersed as best suited to the present state of things, they are determined, by a proper course of teaching, and practicing the apostolic Gospel, to bring all, as fast

as they can, to unite around the cross of Christ—submitting to the one Lord, one faith, one immersion—and thus form one body upon the one foundation, according to the apostolic order of things.

Here I must say, that when the Christian brethren have spread the Lord's table in my presence, they did not invite* the unimmersed to participate. When the Apostle said, "Let a man examine himself, and so let him eat," he did not say this to the unimmersed, or to those who were not in the kingdom, but to the church of God at Corinth, the members of which had heard, believed, and had been immersed. (Acts xviii. 8.) In a word, I believe that the Christian teachers with whom I have had intercourse teach as plainly, and as purely, what the primitive teachers taught, and require as precisely what they required, in order to the admission of members into the congregation of Christ, as any people with whom I am acquainted.

I have not written this for the sake of the Christian brethren, but for the sake of some of our Reforming brethren, who seem to be alarmed, fearing that I and some other Reforming teachers, have injured the cause in which we have been engaged, by sanctioning all the speculations and errors which have been laid to the charge of the people called Christians, whether justly or unjustly. That our Reforming brethren may be enabled to judge and determine upon the propriety or impropriety of our conduct, when we and the Christian brethren united in all the acts of social worship, we have thought it proper to lay before them what we understand to be the views and the practice of the Christian teachers, in the several important particulars named above.

If, in doing this, we have in any particular been mistaken, or have misrepresented them, we can assure them that we have not done it designedly; they will, therefore, have the goodness to correct the error, and pardon me. On the other hand, if the above-named views of the Christian brethren be correct, I would then ask any brother, what law of Christ is violated when we break the loaf together? Or when we meet with those on the King's highway, who have been immersed upon a profession of their faith in the Lord Jesus

---

* Nor debar them.—B. W. Stone and J. T. Johnson, ed. *Christian Messenger.*

Christ, and are walking in his commandments, by what rule found in the New Testament could we reject them, or refuse to break bread with them?

3. It may be asked, if the people called *Christians*, who have ceased to speculate upon the character of Christ, have given up their Unitarian opinions? And may it not as well be asked, have they who speculate upon the character of Christ before they became Reformers, given up their Trinitarian opinions? To both these questions I would answer, I do not know, neither do I care. We should always allow to others that which we claim for ourselves—*the right of private judgment*.

If either Christians or Reformers have erroneous opinions, they never can injure any person, provided we all have prudence enough to keep them to ourselves. Neither will they injure us, if we continue to believe the Gospel facts, and obey the law of the King. If all who profess to be teachers of the Christian religion would keep their opinions to themselves, teach the Gospel facts, and urge the people to obey them, the world would soon be delivered from the wretched, distracting, and destructive influences of mystical preaching.

4. Again, it is asked, when you break bread with those called Christians about Georgetown, etc., do you not sanction all the sectarian speculations of all those who are called by name throughout the United States? No. The Christian churches are not bound together by written, human laws, like many others; and even if they were, I should not believe that I had sanctioned any sectarian peculiarity which might be among them, because I find nothing either in Scripture or reason to make me believe so. If such an idea had been taught in the New Testament, surely the Reformers never would have acted as they have done, and are still doing. For example: after many of us became Reformers, we continued to break bread with many of those who continued to plead for all their old sectarian peculiarities and human traditions—even in our own congregation—without even so much as dreaming that we were sanctioning all or any of their unscriptural peculiarities, or those of the Associations with which we were in correspondence. You will say that all these had come into the kingdom by faith and immersion.

Granted: and so had those Christians with whom we broke bread, so far as we know.

Once more. It is well known that brother G. Gates, as yet, stands formally connected with the Elkhorn Association; and that all the Reformers cheerfully commune with him, as they ought to do, at the Lord's table, not thinking, for one moment, that in so doing they sanction all the peculiarities which belong to that body, and all the other Associations with which they stand formally connected. Similar cases might be multiplied, but we deem it unnecessary.

When our brethren shall have seen this, we hope they will be satisfied that we have not laid aside our former speculations, and taken up those of any other people. They can not think that we wish to amalgamate the immersed and the unimmersed in the congregation of Christ. We do not find such amalgamation in the ancient congregations of Christ. Therefore, whilst contending for the ancient order of things, we can not contend for this.

5. We are pleased with the name Christian, and do desire to see it divested of every sectarian idea, and every thing else but that which distinguished the primitive Christians from all other people, in faith and practice, as the humble followers of the meek and lowly Redeemer. And we do believe that the Christian brethren about Georgetown, etc., would be as much gratified to see this as we would be ourselves.

The friends of the Reformation may easily injure their own cause by giving to it a sectarian character; against which we should always be specially guarded. And in order to avoid this, and all other departures from the Apostolic order of things, we can not, we will not, knowingly sanction any tradition, speculation, or amalgamation, unknown to the primitive Christian congregations. On the other hand, we are determined, by the favor of God, to the utmost of our ability, to teach what the primitive disciples taught; and in admitting persons into the congregation of Christ, we will require what they required, and nothing more. We will urge the practice of all the Apostolic commands and examples given to the primitive Christians, and thus labor for the unity of the disciples of Christ upon this one foundation. And wherever we find others—whatever they may have been called by their enemies—laboring for the same object, aiming at the same thing, we are bound joyfully to receive them, treat them as Christians, and co-operate with them. And such we believe are the Christian brethren about Lexington, Georgetown, Paris, Millersburg, and Carlisle.

We have now laid before our brethren, candidly, and plainly, the principle upon which we have acted, relative to the union spoken of between the Christians and Reformers about Georgetown, etc., which, we think, is perfectly consistent with that from which we have acted for several years past. But if we have done any thing which the Gospel or the law of Christ will not justify, we would be glad to know it, as we do desire, above all things, to know the whole truth, and to practice it; and as we think that the best of us, either as individuals, or as congregations, are not fully reformed, but reforming.

We hope that the editors of reforming periodicals (Brethren Campbell, Scott, etc.), if they see this in the *Messenger*, will notice it in their journals, with such remarks of commendation or correction as they may think proper. We make this request because we think circumstances actually require it.

JOHN SMITH.

Concerning the doctrine of *baptism for the remission of sins*, it is proper to say, that while very generally received by the Christians at the time of the union, it had been perverted by imprudent teachers to the injury of the cause; so that some did not accept it, or held it in a sense different from that in which it was generally propounded. But views respecting the design of the ordinance were regarded as opinions that should not be allowed to prevent or disturb the union of those who were already of one faith and one baptism, and who acknowledged the Bible as their only standard of religious truth. While the spirit of investigation was encouraged, they were disposed to leave this matter to the private judgment of those who, believing in Christ with all their hearts, cheerfully and humbly bowed to his authority in the ordinance of immersion. John Rogers, the Evangelist, who held the prevalent view respecting the ordinance, uses the following language in March, 1832:

The doctrine of *baptism for the remission of sins*, has within a few years been brought before us, and much investigated. Some among us have embraced it cordially; others reject it. What then? Shall those who embrace it, condemn those who, though they believe in immersion, can not go the whole length with us in this matter? God forbid. Or shall those who do not receive it, condemn us who do receive it? I trust not. Charity forbids it. Our principles forbid it.

Stone, in his address to the churches of Christ, September, 1832, says:

Our opinions we wish no man to receive as truth, nor do we desire to impose them on any as tests of Christian fellowship. This is the principle on which we, as Christians, commenced our course many years ago; and I can not but view those as departed from this principle, who will not bear with their brethren because they believe in baptism for the remission of sins, and because they meet every Lord's Day to worship the Lord in praying, singing, exhorting, and breaking bread. O brethren! these are subjects concerning which many of us differ, but for this difference, we ought not to separate from communion and Christian fellowship. All believe that immersion is baptism—why should they who submit to the one baptism contend and separate because they do not exactly view every design of it alike?

CHAPTER XLI.

Early in March, Smith, still hopeful of planting the standard of the Ancient Gospel in those regions where he had once so successfully preached Calvinism, sent forward appointments for the ensuing month to the several places along his route to Stockton's Valley. He started for Crab Orchard about the first of April. When he reached Dix River, a crowd of people were assembled on the opposite bank, and, in crossing over, he was told that they had come out from town to meet him there, for several of them wished to be immersed. They had calculated the time of his coming, and now stood waiting at the edge of the water. He dismounted from his horse and baptized them, and then went on into town, a mile and a half distant, the throng following on, and gathering in at the appointed hour to hear him preach.

He passed on to Somerset, in Pulaski County, where there were but few brethren and many foes. Rising again to speak at the hour named a month before, he dwelt long and earnestly on the unfortunate schisms that divided the people of God, arguing that creeds engendered a party spirit among Christians, and imposed party names on those who, but for these things, might be one. Some were offended at his remarks, and left the house while he was speaking. "The wicked flee," he exclaimed, "when no man pursueth!" The rest now sat quiet till he was done.

While there, two brethren from Monticello came and informed him that the Methodists, in anticipation of his coming, had rallied in force under their Elder, taken possession of the court-house, then the only place for public worship in the village, and were threatening to destroy the last vestige of *Campbellism* in the place. They inquired of Smith what, under the circumstances, he was going to do.

"Brethren," said he, "I will be with you, God willing, at the promised time, and then we will determine."

While they were looking for him next evening, at Monticello, he rode into town. They were much cast down, but his presence revived them, though they were hopeless of gaining the attention of the people. That night, with his little band of brethren, he went into the crowded courthouse and heard the popular Elder preach to a people on whom, with many agonizing prayers, he had invoked the baptism of the Holy Ghost and of fire. When he was done, Smith arose and said that he had forwarded an appointment some four or five weeks since to speak, on the next day, in that house, not being apprised at the time that any other person designed to occupy it; he wished to say, however, that at eleven o'clock precisely, on the next morning, according to promise, he would meet such friends as might wish to hear him, at the old meeting-house, a little distance from town. It was a log-house of the early times, built by the Baptists, but long since abandoned and gone to decay; a few broken benches remained, and these, he thought, might be so arranged as to accommodate the women.

But in the morning, a citizen proposed that, as some desired to hear both speakers, Smith should preach in the court house in the afternoon. But to this proposal, the Elder would not agree, and Smith went out to meet his few friends in the old log-house. But the sympathy of many of the citizens was now turned in his favor, and they followed out in numbers to hear him. He made no allusion to the party in town, but presented the Gospel as the power of God to save all that would believe; and, at the close, three persons confessed their faith, and were immersed; some Separate Baptists, also, united with them.

The interest continued to increase, and the people, gradually deserting the town, gathered around him at the ruins. He gave notice, on Lord's Day, that at a certain hour in the afternoon, the Disciples would meet to be constituted into a church, at which time he would deliver a discourse appropriate to the occasion. Out came the Elder himself now, with many of his friends. Still the speaker studiously refrained from any allusion to him, or to his people. About a score of converts were regularly constituted into a church of Christ, and the people returned to town.

Smith reciprocated the seeming courtesy of the Methodists, and went to their meeting that night again. But another spirit had seized their preacher; some idle tongue had filled his heart with suspicion, and he publicly accused his prudent brother of speaking boastful things against him and the Methodists. Smith arose and replied in a proper spirit, and the audience was dismissed.

Next day, the unfortunate Elder had the mortification to see the crowds flocking by him at an early hour to the pulpit of Smith, and he turned, with a vexed spirit, into the courthouse again, and preached once more to the few that had not the heart to forsake him.

When the people returned that afternoon, they learned that he had adjourned his meeting, and was preparing to depart. Smith and his friends quietly took possession of the house, and he soon raised the newly-constituted church to forty members. Nor did they cease to grow in grace and numbers after he was gone. In a few weeks, ten more were added to them, and they continued thus to grow in numbers and influence—Elders Stone and Frisbie laboring for them in word and doctrine.

Speaking of John Smith's manner of preaching when at Monticello, one of those Elders remarks: "He presented the Gospel in its simplicity, adorned with nothing but the majesty of truth; he brought many matters, heretofore considered abstruse, and beyond the ken of ordinary minds, within the comprehension of the most common understanding."

Leaving Monticello, he hurried on to Stockton's Valley, for he had an appointment to preach at the residence of Elder Jonathan D. Young, then living in sight of the Clear Fork meeting-house.

On the day appointed, he appeared, and a large congregation of friends met him. From recent occurrences, they were much interested in the great matters which he had pressed upon their attention a year before; so now, after his discourse that day, he proposed what he called a *meeting of inquiry*, to be held at night, and he invited all to attend. The house was densely crowded, and the interview was profitable to all. "To me," says one who was present, "it was the most interesting meeting that I ever attended. It was a mental and spiritual feast. I confess that, when I heard John Smith that evening, it was the first time in my life that these nerves of mine were ever perfectly relaxed under the power of eloquence."

But it was on a subsequent visit that he began to reap in the Valley the harvest of his many labors and prayers. Some time in the summer of 1834 he was at Clear Fork again, on his way to Alabama. He spoke from a stand, in the oak grove near the meeting-house, and, on concluding a most persuasive address, he invited any that believed in Jesus as the Christ to arise, confess him, and be immersed. Dr. O. T. Ragland, an intelligent and influential gentleman of the neighborhood, accepted the invitation, and was immediately immersed in the waters of Clear Fork. He was the first person that was ever immersed in that country for the remission of sins. This practical exhibition of the Ancient Gospel deeply interested the people. They had been investigating it as a doctrine, and had discussed its peculiar features as a theory of religion, but they had never before seen it in practice, and its simplicity and novelty deeply impressed them.

Having announced that he would preach at Elliott's Cross Roads, near by, at the house of Colonel A. S. Bramlette, on a certain day, every thing was put in readiness for him. Notice was extensively circulated through the Valley; seats were placed in the rooms of the house, and in the long, airy porch, and through the ample, well-shaded yard without; and, when the hour for preaching arrived, more than one thousand persons crowded to the place. For three hours, Smith held the attention of that audience. He assailed creeds, sects, and parties, the tyranny of opinionism, and the vanity of all speculation in religion. He then presented the simple Gospel in contrast with these things, and closed his masterly discourse. Many hearts, touched by the power of his words, could find expression only in the stirring song that arose. Holding up his Bible in full view of the congregation, he exclaimed, in a voice louder than the swelling chorus, "Bow, you rebels! bow to your Lord and King!" and eight penitent souls heard the words as if a voice from heaven had spoken, and, coming forward, confessed, and were, soon afterward, immersed.

The cause was now established in the Valley. Other accessions were gained during the ensuing months, and in December—perhaps on the third Lord's Day—a church of Christ was organized near where the village of Albany now stands, with Jonathan D. Young, John Calvin Smith, Isaac T. Reneau, and others, as members—some of the old Christians uniting with them. Elder Young has long since rested from his labors—declaring, in his last moments, to Isaac Denton, that he had never regretted the course that he had pursued. J. C. Smith, now well advanced in years,[*] is still spared, though much afflicted, to be an elder of the church at Albany; and Isaac T. Reneau, their junior by many years, still preaches the Ancient Gospel among the people of the Valley and the adjacent country.

On one of his visits about that time, to Alabama, John Smith, while riding along, one hot summer morning, in Tennessee, stopped at an inn on the roadside, not far from Sparta, and called for his breakfast. The pleasant landlady received him politely, and ordered a servant to take good care of his horse, for he had traveled nearly twenty-five miles that morning. She immediately set about preparing breakfast for her guest, apologizing, at the same time, by saying that the younger members of the family had gone to a social gathering in the neighborhood, and she was left without help for the day. Smith soon found opportunity for conversation, and asked about the different religious denominations in the neighborhood.

"The Cumberland Presbyterians," said she, "have the largest congregations; but we have many Baptists and Methodists also."

Seeing that he was disposed to talk, she inquired from what part of the country he came, and on hearing that he was from Montgomery County, Kentucky, she put down her coffee-pot, and looking at him somewhat curiously, said:

"Travelers tell me that there is a strange sort of people up there in Kentucky called Campbellites."

---

[*] January, 1870.

"Yes, madam," replied he, "there are some in my own neighborhood."

"You have seen some of them then?" said she.

"Yes, madam, but they don't like that name."

"Well, how do they look?" said she. "Do tell me, sir."

"Those I have seen look pretty much like other people."

"I would really like to see one, so much," said she, musingly; "I'd give more to see one of those people than any show. I'm told that when any body wants to join them, they just put them under the water, and then let them go. One man told me that they would sometimes take people by force, and drag them down into the water; that they even chased after people, and ran them down; that they once took a fancy to a poor fellow, and ran him five miles before they caught him, and then, after putting him in, they just left him there to get home, or to heaven, the best way he could."

"That was a very long-winded fellow, ma'am," interrupted Smith, "to run five miles before the Campbellites caught him."

"I don't know what I wouldn't give to see one of them," said she, pouring out a cup of coffee, and handing it to her guest, who had taken his seat at the table with far more appetite than humor.

"How do you think a Campbellite would look?" inquired Smith, after breaking his fast a little.

"Well," said she, "I imagine they have a sort of wild, fierce, fanatical look about them."

"I think I can manage for you to see one," said Smith, as he received his second cup from her hands.

"I'd give any thing almost, if you would, sir," said the lady.

"Madam," said he, laying down the knife and fork which he had plied with more than usual assiduity, and raising his bland, good-natured face upon her, "look right at me, and you will see one! But don't be afraid," continued he, seeing her start, and then blush with confusion, "I am a *civil* Campbellite, and will not chase *you* into the water."

Having finished his meal, he withdrew from the table, and re-assuring her of his perfectly civil disposition, requested her to take a seat and listen to what he had to say about those singular people. He told her what they believed and preached, and corrected all the wicked stories that had been told against them.

"And now," said he, "we have some very smart men among us, and I wish that you could hear one of *them* preach, for I know you would love the religion which they teach and practice. But Antony Dibrell, the clerk at Sparta, whom perhaps you know, was at Monticello not long since, and made me promise to preach there on my return from Huntsville. Now, as you can not hear any of our great men, perhaps you will come and hear *me?*" She promised to do so without fail, and bidding her adieu, he went on to the Hickory Flats.

In due time, he was at Sparta. The Court of Appeals for that district of Tennessee was then in session, with Judge Catron and others on the bench. The appointment had with difficulty been published among the people. A Methodist camp-meeting had just closed in the neighborhood, and his friend, Mr. Dibrell, had gone out to have it announced; but they had refused to do it. Written notices had been put up, at different places, and Judge Catron, who had known Smith in Monticello, gave notice also, so that the people, after all, were expecting him. The business of the court was suspended, and all went to hear him. Dibrell had the old seminary building in readiness, and calling for the preacher at the village tavern, where he had put up that morning, he conducted him to the appointed place.

A large congregation of curious listeners awaited him. Judges and lawyers were before him, among whom sat also some Baptist and Presbyterian preachers. A nephew of Isaac Denton, a minister, was present, and came and sat fraternally with him in the pulpit. His kind hostess also was in the congregation. Smith looked over the crowded house for a moment, undecided how to improve his opportunity. "I regretted," says he, speaking of the occasion, "that I could have but one chance at them; for other appointments would hurry me away; so I determined to rake them with grape, and do as much execution as I could." He said:

There is but one Gospel, and woe to the man or the angel that preaches any other; let such a one, says Paul, be accursed. It behooves those who believe, as well as those who preach, to determine which is the Gospel of God's dear Son. Now, the Holy Spirit has put a mark upon that Gospel, by which every honest man may know it. If one comes to you, therefore, preaching any system of religion, look for that mark; if you find it not, reject him as a false messenger, who brings you another Gospel. And this is its sure and distinguishing sign: *He that believes it not shall be damned.*

One may preach Methodism as the Gospel; but has it the mark? Will all but Methodists be damned? They themselves will tell you, No. Methodism, then, is not the Gospel. Another may come preaching the doctrines of the Cumberland Presbyterians. Some of you may to-day remember when it was first announced among the people of this region. But has it the mark? Will all but Cumberland Presbyterians be damned?

My Baptist brethren, too, think they have the Gospel; and, verily, I long thought so myself, and yet I never once dreamed that my Methodist friends would be damned because they were not Baptists.

These *isms*, my friends, do not save those who believe them, nor do they damn those who reject them. They can not, then, be any part of the Gospel of Jesus Christ. Yet, while they are powerless to save, they set Christians at variance with one another, and mislead and bewilder those who wish to be saved.

But that religion which the devil and bad men call *Campbellism*, proclaims, first of all, that Christ died for our sins, according to the Scriptures, and was buried: and that he rose again from the dead the third day, according to the Scriptures. These glorious facts, attested by apostles, is the Gospel that Jesus commanded should be preached to every creature; —to which Gospel the precious promise is annexed, that he that believes it, and is immersed, shall be saved.

That Gospel we declare to you this day! Do you believe it? Then why tarry? Arise, and be immersed, and wash away your sins, calling on the name of the Lord. If you believe it not, and the risen Lord has spoken it, you must be damned!

His discourse made an impression on the people; but he could not remain to take advantage of it. Bidding his friends farewell, and commending his doctrine especially to his hostess, who had now both seen and heard a *Campbellite*, he set out that evening for Stockton's Valley.

He had hardly left the town when a stranger overtook him, and prayed him, with tears, to come back and talk some more to the people.

"For many years," said he, "I have been trying to learn from the preachers how to become a Christian; but never till this day had I a glimpse of light on the subject. Can you not return, and teach the people longer, for others, I know, are as blind as I have been?"

Though much concerned, Smith felt that he could not disappoint the people that would be waiting for him in the Valley. He, therefore, told the stranger where he could find brethren that would give him instruction. But the anxious man would not for awhile leave his side. He rode with him for ten miles of the way, and then, with a grateful heart, blessing the preacher that had brought him to the light, he left him to pursue his journey alone.

"Were you not very much embarrassed, John," said an old friend to him, in Stockton's Valley, "when you were preaching down at Sparta before all those great lawyers and judges?"

"Not in the least," said he; "for I have learned that judges and lawyers, so far as the Bible is concerned, are the most ignorant class of people in the world—*except Doctors of Divinity.*"

"But were you never embarrassed in your life, Brother John?" said John Calvin Smith to him.

"Well," replied he, "I have spoken before all the great preachers of Kentucky—Vardeman, and Creath, and others; and they were no more in my way than so many grasshoppers. But, I confess to you, Brother Calvin, the first time I ever preached before Aleck Campbell, I *did* falter a little."

CHAPTER XLII.

THE influence of the union was now seen in the success which everywhere attended the preaching of the Gospel. Immediately upon his return from Stockton's Valley, Smith resumed his labors among the churches in northern Kentucky, preaching at Georgetown, the Great Crossings, Versailles, Clear Creek, and South Elkhorn, and assisted at all these places by other preachers, both Christians and Reformers, now one in the work of uniting saints and converting sinners. Accessions were almost daily made to the churches.

During that summer and autumn, he was seldom at home, for his restless enthusiasm hurried him on from one three-days' meeting to another. Now he was laboring with the Creaths, at Clear Creek and Versailles; now with G. W. Elley, among the churches in Jessamine and Mercer, or mingling with F. R. Palmer, Thomas M. Allen, Thomas Smith, and others, in the happy scenes at Republican; now he was with Aylett Raines, or Walter Scott, or David S. Burnet, gathering vast crowds together at Minerva or Mayslick, and then, perhaps with brotherly pride, introducing some of the once despised Christian preachers to the reconciled brethren of Sharpsburg, Spencer, Mount Sterling, and Somerset—baptizing at every place, and, with the force of irresistible argument, breaking down prejudice and subduing opposition. Nor did he confine his labors during those months to the northern counties, but, crossing the Kentucky River, he went, alone, into Lincoln and Garrard—to the great strongholds of the opposition there—and preached, with increased boldness, the union of Christians in one faith and one immersion.

The meeting at Republican, near Lexington, about the first of June, was one of special interest. Many Christians and Disciples, no longer wearing these names distinctively, and caring no longer for differences of opinion, came together from all the surrounding counties, not so much to strengthen, as to enjoy their happy union. It was indeed a season of intense spiritual and social delight. Five hundred brethren and sisters, heretofore suspicious, or estranged, broke the loaf together; every eye was suffused with rapture, and every heart glowed with brotherly love. "I never saw a better meeting," says Thomas Smith, "at any time, in any country."

On the seventeenth of August, the first ANNUAL MEETING of the Disciples within the bounds of the old North District Association, was held at Sharpsburg, in Bath County, agreeably to a request of that church, made at Somerset, in 1831. All eyes were turned to this first great meeting of the brethren that had dissolved their Association as an unlawful assembly. It was confessedly an experiment, novel in its character and design, and complicated not only by questions of order and expediency, but by the timid inactivity or distrust of brethren that could not conceive how a meeting of the kind could be conducted without reviving the forms of the old Association, or adopting some other rules of procedure than those prescribed in the Inspired Constitution. Some, who had doubted the expediency of dissolving the North District Association, feared the result; while enemies hoped that *Campbellism*, now impious with engrafted Arianism, would practically refute itself in the wranglings of the mob at Sharpsburg.

John Newton Payne, the Elder of the church at that place, was a man of great piety and intelligence, and of fine administrative talnts. It was understood that the brethren from abroad were to be received as the guests of the congregation over which he so ably presided; but not as a foreign body distinct from that church. They had been invited to meet there, and to worship with them according to the spirit and tenor of the Book, as a congregation of disciples. No constitution, they judged, would be necessary to the good order and success of the meeting other than that which the Holy Spirit had already prescribed. The results we give in the words of those who were present. Elder Payne, after waiting to ascertain what effect had been produced on the public mind, says:

As far as I have been able to learn, the result has been most happy—our friends were pleased, our opposers silenced, and the neutrals, with the world, highly gratified. If there has been raised a single objection to our order or manner of conducting the meeting, by friend or foe, I have yet to learn it; and I do think it will go far in relieving the prejudices excited against us by dissolving what was called the North District Association, and in breaking down those preposses-sions that exist in favor of such unauthorized establishments.

John T. Johnson, F. R. Palmer, one of the ablest speakers in the Christian connection, Jacob Creath, Jr., and other preachers, were, also, present on that occasion.

Johnson writes:

I am constrained to say that I have never seen business conducted with more decency or in better order; nor have I ever seen any one who appeared to be more perfectly familiar with his duties than Brother John Newton Payne, the bishop of the congregation at Sharpsburg. We were captivated with the love which reigned among the brethren, and the zeal which was manifested for the conversion of sinners. Oh! that love and union may abound everywhere as at Sharps-burg! . . .

On Lord's day we partook, with several hundred, as near as we can guess, of the Lord's Supper. It was a most interesting scene. If sectarian leaders who busy themselves in misrepre-senting us—in charging us with impure motives, so far as a union of Christians has been effected—and who, according to their wishes, are perpetually crying out that the union can not last—had been present, they might have been convinced of the benefits growing out of one.

That visit to Sharpsburg, he afterward said, confirmed his convictions as to the glorious results about to be realized in the restoration of the Ancient Order of Things.

Many of those Disciples who had once belonged to the neighboring Boone's Creek Association, but who had been cast out, in 1830, for their unwillingness to approve any human terms of communion, now found strength and enjoy-ment in the general communion of their brethren in these simple annual meetings, which, from that time, were held from year to year, with the several churches of the District.

We may here add that the remnant of the Boone's Creek Association, animated with the same spirit that had, in 1830, proscribed those brethren for opinion's sake, came together again in Jessamine County, not long after the Sharpsburg meeting, under the leadership of a few elders still zealous for the ancient landmarks. Six or seven churches only were reported; four persons had been added to their number by immersion during the year, and thirty-one of their members had been dismissed or excluded!

This melancholy report was, however, in some degree, compensated for, by the appearance of Messengers from a newly-constituted church, that now asked to be received into their communion. True, the new church consisted only of about a dozen members, and the accession could add but little to their numerical strength; but the zeal of the little congregation was great, and what it lacked in numbers, it seems to have made up in orthodoxy, for, at the bottom of their letter praying for a correspondence with the Association, they boldly wrote these words: *"We discard A. Campbell and his doctrine!"*

On the adjournment of the annual meeting at Sharpsburg, John Smith resumed his travels as an evangelist—preaching in Nicholas and Fleming Counties with John Rogers, and in Clark County with William Morton. He writes to John T. Johnson:

I am constantly going, and am much encouraged. Prospects are flattering in every place where I have been. Since the commencement of the year I have had the pleasure of seeing many immersed by several teaching brethren. I have, with my own hands, immersed one hundred and thirty-five.

On one occasion, about that time, he was with Johnson at Georgetown, and at Dry Run. As they rode along together to the latter place, Johnson, who was a man of great dignity and much refinement of character, and was always frank but courteous toward his brethren, ventured to say to his companion and fellow-laborer that the cause which they were pleading was the most serious and solemn ever advocated by

man; and that, while there was every reason to rejoice and
be glad, in view of their success, yet he thought that the
preachers could not be too grave when bearing their message
to the people, and should never say anything from the pulpit
that could divert their serious and prayerful attention. Smith,
without attempting to justify his own occassional humor in
the pulpit, kindly received the gentle admonition, and resolved
to profit by it.

It had been arranged between them that, on Sunday, he
should discuss the subject of creeds. Accordingly, on that
day, he arose before the large congregation, and labored, with
much ability, and at some length, to show that man-made
creeds, instead of being bonds of union, engender strife and
schism. They have no unitive power, he contended, save
to make preachers *lock their horns together* in controversy.
In concluding, he remarked:

And now I would like to show you, by means of a little
incident, how every sensible and unbiased man regards a
human creed, when made the foundation of a church. With
your permission, I will illustrate the matter in hand by an
anecdote, if you will promise not even to smile, unless in the
gravest manner possible.

And he turned his pleasant face toward Johnson, who
sat before him nodding his ready promises with a thoughtless
confidence that said as plainly as words, "We are all sober-
minded Christians here, Brother Smith; so proceed with your
illustration." The speaker, in his deliberate manner, continued:

A Christian was once discussing the question of creeds with
a Calvinistic Baptist, who boldly maintained that his Confession of Faith was a better bond of union among Christians
than the Bible alone. So well satisfied was the anti-creed
brother, however, that both Scripture and common sense sustained him in the argument, that he proposed, in the end, to
submit the question to a Frenchman who had listened atten-
tively to the discussion, and who, from the negative character
of his own religion, could not have any prejudice in the
case. The matter was accordingly referred to him, and he
consented to judge between them. Making each disputant

take into his hand the creed that he had defended, he asked
of the man with the New Testament who it was that made
his creed.

"Jesus Christ," was the answer.

"And who, my friend," said he to the other, "made yours?"

"It was adopted in the city of Philadelphia, in the year
1742," replied the Baptist.

"Very well, then, gentlemen," continued the Frenchman;
"that is enough. If you follow your creed, Mr. Christian,
when you die, it will take you to Jesus Christ. Follow yours,
Mr. Baptist, and, when you die, you will go to *Philadelphie!*"

The amiable Johnson, taken by surprise, struggled very
hard to keep his promise and his gravity; but when he saw
his brother's droll look of admonition, bending down upon him
from the pulpit, he laughed outright!

On the second Lord's day in September, he was preaching
with Aylett Raines, Gurdon Gates, D. S. Burnet and others,
at Minerva, in Bracken County, when he again had occasion
to deplore the existence of sects among the people of God,
which evil he attributed to the influence of creeds and the
ambition of creed-makers. He illustrated, in his own peculiar
way, the sin of schism, and the reckless treason and impiety
of those who scatter and divide the flock of the Good Shepherd,
and, gathering them into different folds or pastures, put their
own spurious marks upon them, and call them by sectarian
names.

"Farmers," said he, continuing to illustrate his idea, "mark
their stock in different ways to distinguish them; one will
crop the right ear, another make a *swallow-fork*, or an *under-
bit* in the left ear, that each may know his own property from
his neighbors. Just so do the leaders of the different religious
parties put ear-marks on their flocks; they distinguish them
by various sectarian devices and names; they call some Presbyterian, some Methodist, or Baptist, so that all may know to
whom their converts belong. Now the Lord has put his own
mark upon his people; and the mark is this: *They follow me.—*
John x. 27.

"But these sectarian leaders," continued he, "have not
only broken the law of the King, in thus changing the mark
which he put upon his people, but they have enticed away from

God his own children, and bound them out to other masters. Now, it is against the law, in every civilized land, to treat a child in this manner, when his father is able and willing to provide for him; yet this is the very crime that has been committed by a sectarian priesthood; for the honest and pious people in those sects are God's own children, that have been taken by wile and stratagem from their Heavenly Father, and bound out to hard taskmasters, contrary to justice and law."

These remarks seemed to hurt the feelings of a Presbyterian lady, who was one of his hearers. That night, at the house of Jesse Holton, with whom he was staying, a good old sister informed him of the fact, and told him that she herself thought he was a little too severe, and ought to make an apology, which he readily promised to do.

On Monday, when he arose to speak again, he repeated what he had said, concerning the conduct of those who had pressed so many of the children of God into bondage to human systems. "But," said he, "I feel that I owe my sectarian friends an apology; for my kind of feelings on yesterday kept me from telling them, as plainly as perhaps I ought to have done, how very great their wickedness in this matter is. Now I say to all you poor, bound-out children of God, that hear me this day, I am willing to come back at any time to this place, institute a suit against your oppressors, impanel a jury of the twelve apostles, with the Lord and Redeemer as judge, and plead your righteous cause before him, till I convict your enslavers, and have them consigned to their own place; and this I will do, without fee or reward."

This apology seemed to be satisfactory to the lady, who was again present, and sat in full view of the speaker; for she received it with a smile that seemed to acknowledge as just the distinction which he had drawn between the culpable party-leaders themselves, and the good people whom they had led astray.

The great annual gathering of the Christians took place that year in October, at Clintonville, in Bourbon County, under the auspices of the church of Christ at that place, of which Thomas Smith was Elder. By virtue of his office in that congregation, he now presided over the general meeting, as on any ordinary occasion. It was duly announced that the object of their coming together was to worship God according to his Word, for the advancement of his cause and glory; that the church at Clintonville was not to be disturbed in its organization; and that the brethren and sisters from a distance were there as visitors, to assist one another in the work of the Lord. Here, among the many Christians assembled from different parts of the country, and in the presence of such men as Thomas Smith, F. R. Palmer, L. J. Fleming, and John A. Gano—all laboring to unite, in love, the true disciples of Christ—John Smith and John Rogers now rehearsed their travels, and cheered the friends of union and reform by their account of the remarkable success of the truth during the past few months. From their general report then given, it appears that several hundred persons in the few surrounding counties had, within that short time, been immersed into Christ, and that the two parties, in nearly every place which they had visited, had affiliated in work and worship as one people.

In his various tours through the State, Smith had discovered that besides the standard objections everywhere urged against the doctrine of the Reformers by the popular ministry, there was not unfrequently some special argument, or ingenious fallacy, peculiar to a neighborhood, which the people incessantly plied in their fireside controversies with the Disciples. These provincial, or local, objections, however futile in themselves when tried by reason or Scripture, acquired weight and importance from popular use, and sometimes greatly retarded the progress of the truth in certain neighborhoods.

Among the Shawnee Run Baptists of Mercer County, it was a favorite objection to the doctrine of the Reformers that it was, at most, but a noisy and useless clamor raised about things indifferent; that it did not profess to add any new element to the Gospel, but virtually conceded that the Baptists already had the essence of the matter.

"We have," said they to their reforming brethren, "as you all admit, the substance of the Gospel; why then disturb the peace of the Church by your unceasing clamor about the form?

John Smith, in company with Jacob Creath, Sen., and others, at last came among the people of Shawnee Run, for the first time since the division of that church on account of an effort to proscribe Josephus Hewitt. On Saturday, he spoke, as usual in warm weather, from a stand outdoors. Adapting his remarks to the audience, he [showed that the Gospel is not only a matter of substance, but of form also; so that if its form were changed, though the substance should remain, the Gospel itself would be destroyed. In concluding this discourse, he said:]

[It is the order in which the several parts of any thing are put together that determines its form. If every separate piece of that chair yonder were put into my hands, I would have the substance of the chair only; but it would now depend on the order in which I should re-arrange them whether the thing I make would be a chair again, a basket, or a bird-cage. In either case, I would still have the substance of the chair, but whether one or the other of these things would be made must depend on the order in which I arrange the parts.

Our sectarian friends may indeed have faith, and repentance, and immersion, and remission of sins, substantially, in their creed; but, if so, they have most awkwardly and unscripturally put these elements together. Hence, they present to the people, not the Gospel of Jesus Christ, but something called Calvinism, or Arminianism, which is no more like the Ancient Gospel than a bird cage or a basket is like that chair.]

That night he was taken very sick at the house of a gentleman in the neighborhood by the name of Woods, who at the time was not a professor of religion. He suffered much through the night, and at dawn Mr. Woods was summoned; he found him much prostrated, and in great pain. The kindest attentions were bestowed upon him, and after the lapse of several hours, he was much relieved. Still his weakness was extreme, and at times his pain was severe. When the hour for meeting approached, he requested that his horse should be brought out, for he would try and get over to Shawnee Run.

"Mr. Smith," said his friend, with some surprise, "you can not stand it. You can not make even a basket or a bird-cage to-day, much less preach the Gospel to the people. You must not venture out, sir."

"I will try it, anyhow," persisted Smith.

His host, seeing that he would not listen to admonition, at length helped him upon his horse, at a rather late hour, and rode by his side toward the meeting-house. Again and again, however, as he sickened, or paused to rest, on the road, his friend urged him to return to his bed, and give his body and mind one day's rest; but his heart was with Jacob Creath and the brethren, and he went resolutely on. When he reached the spot, they helped him to dismount, but he was unable to stand. The great congregation had assembled, and the morning exercises had begun; but many friends came and gathered anxiously around him as he lay exhausted on the ground. They made him, at last, a bed of their saddle blankets, over which some good sisters spread their riding skirts; and he lay down in much distress, upon this pallet, under a shade, not far from the speaker's stand.

A young woman, named Elizabeth Mizner, whom he had never seen before, but whose pleasant face was beautiful with compassion, came and brought him water, and such simple restoratives as she could find in the reticules of the older sisters; and she knelt by his side like a daughter, now and then moistening his hot lips, and gently fanning him to rest.

"Is she a Christian?" he asked of some one, after awhile, when she had left his side for a moment. Learning that she was not a member of the church, although much beloved for her virtues, he could not repress his emotion, but lay and wept, that so kind-hearted a creature should be without Christ in the world.

Jacob Creath was, in the meantime, addressing the people from the stand hard by; and his voice, toned with its wonted melody, rose and fell upon the sick man's ear, and helped to soothe him into quietude.

When the discourses of the morning were over, and the people had been dismissed for an hour's repast, Creath came to his brother, with no little concern for his condition. He expressed his regret that he was unable to preach; "for," said he, "the people are all anxiety to hear you, and they will be so much disappointed."

"Tell them," said Smith, rising partly up, "that, God willing, I will speak to them this afternoon."

When the hour came, he arose in his weakness, and making them gird his loins with a handkerchief, he was helped to the stand.

There, leaning on one of the brethren for support, while they occasionally refreshed him with water, he declared the Gospel to the people with singular power and effect. He returned to his pallet, and in his weariness now found a little sleep, while other brethren concluded the exercises of the day. After thus resting, he was refreshed, and then in the cool of the evening, returned to his place of lodging, distressed only at the thought, that so kind-hearted a creature should be living without Christ in the world!

CHAPTER XLIII.

JOHN SMITH's style of preaching was in striking contrast with that of the clergymen around him. He preached the Gospel in every discourse, usually contrasting it with Calvinism, the most popular religious system of that day, for he believed that its tendency was to render the Gospel powerless to convert and to unite. To sinners he preached Christ; to saints, union and reform. He never attempted to lecture. He had, in a great measure, lost, by neglect, the gift of evolving from a single phrase or clause of Holy Writ a theological system. He had ceased to scrap the Book for doctrine or duty, and to build upon some fragmentary text an imposing structure of thought or fancy. In exposition, he analyzed the entire context, and carefully sifted whole chapters, comparing spiritual things with spiritual. In a word, he interpreted and expounded the Bible by the canons of his own natural sense.

On a certain occasion, Smith went to hear a distinguished preacher, who addressed a large audience, in the town of Mount Sterling, from these few words, found in the Parable of the Sower, *"Then cometh the devil."* The speaker harped on his text somewhat after the following fashion:

The young man begins life with noble purposes and joyous hopes. The prayers of a pious mother go with him, and the counsels of a prudent father are, for a season, hid in his heart. He lays his plans in wisdom, and prosecutes them honorably until success gives him position in the world; but—*then cometh the devil!*

The politician, moved by a false ambition, abandons his peaceful fireside, renounces the endearments of home, and becomes the friend or servant of every man he meets. He bows and smiles himself, at last, into some office of trust, and—*then cometh the devil!*

The scholar, thirsting for distinction, relaxes his muscles, retires to his closet and trims his unwholesome lamp. He grows pale and thoughtful, and patiently wins the reputation of a man of learning; men approach and flatter him as an oracle in the land, and—*then, too, cometh the devil!*

The young tradesman, immured in his shop or counting-room, weaves golden dreams, and toils for years to realize them; and when at last he has gilded his humble name, and coffered his sordid idols—*then cometh the devil!*

Even the preacher receives a commission from the skies, and goes into the sanctuary of the Lord to break the bread of life to a hungering people. With the charms of ambitious oratory he steals away their hearts, and soon the multitudes begin to hang with idolatrous delight upon his lips, but—*then cometh the devil!*

The audience were enraptured, and the praises of the orator were murmured by the bustling crowd as they retired from the house. A good old sister of the church, whose pious heart had been stirred to its depths, accosted John Smith at the door, and claimed his meed of praise for her gifted preacher.

"Did you ever hear such a blessed, godly sermon, Brother Smith, in all your life?"

"Don't call it a *godly* sermon, sister," said he, "for there was no God in it, nor Christ; it was all *devil.*"

"But what do you think of it as a sermon?" she persisted, determined to make him confess his admiration. "Was it not fine?"

"It was the *devilishest* one I ever heard," said he.

In some places he found that the advocates of creeds were weakening the force of the anti-creed argument by exalting the Scriptures in the hearing of the people as the only ultimate rule of faith and practice, declaring that they were as strictly conformable to the directions of that Book as any people in the world; that those who were the most noisy in its defense as the only divine Rule, were not always the most faithful in observing it.

Riding along, one day, he fell in company with a Methodist preacher who was going on to fill some appointment. Their conversation soon turned upon the subject of creeds and other ecclesiastical devices. Smith's companion defended his Discipline on the ground of expediency, and claimed that his brethren were as faithful in keeping the commandments as the Reformers, though they did not make so much ado about it. This, Smith denied, and the discussion grew warm, though it continued kind.

A storm of rain coming up, the travelers hurried forward to a little village just ahead of them. They took shelter in a store, or small shop, where several farmers had gathered in out of the rain. The preachers were unknown to the company, but the shop keeper, seeing that they were cold and wet, set out a decanter of wine upon the counter, and pressed them to take a glass.

"You are the oldest, Brother Smith," said the Methodist, "help yourself first."

Smith went forward, and, filling the small wine-glass, drank it off.

"Why, Brother Smith!" said the Methodist, who had watched his opportunity, "you have been boasting for an hour past that you observe the Book more strictly than other people. I am surprised now to see that your practice does not accord with your profession, for you have just violated the plain injunction, that in all things, whether we eat or drink, we should give thanks!"

"I admit, my brother," said Smith, "the correctness of your teaching; but I think that among strangers, and on such an occasion as this, we may enjoy the good things of the Lord without making a display of our piety before men. I hope, though, that you will be as careful to observe all the commandments. Drink; you will find the wine good."

His companion, pouring out a glassful, set it down on the counter, and reverently closed his eyes; but Smith, seizing the glass unobserved, emptied it at a mouthful, and quietly replaced it on the counter. The Methodist took up the glass to drink; but, finding it empty, turned, amid the laughter of the crowd, and said:

"That was some of your mischief, Brother Smith, I know."

"Yes," said Smith, "and you have now let these good people see how a Methodist just half way obeys the Book. We are told to watch as well as to pray, my brother. You prayed well enough, but you neglected to watch, as the Scriptures command, and have lost both your wine and your argument by your disobedience."

He was once discussing the question of spiritual influence in conversion, with a worthy Baptist preacher, who lived in Lincoln County, near Stanford. His opponent had denied that the sinner could believe the Gospel on the simple testimony of the inspired witnesses, contending that in his natural, which meant his unconverted, state, he could not receive the testimony of such witnesses, for the Scriptures plainly declare that the natural, or unconverted, man receiveth not the things of the Spirit of God. But he claimed that the Spirit wielded a sword, with which he opened the sinner's heart; and he founded a specious argument on that metaphor of Paul. In reply to this argument, Smith said:

If the brother's position be correct, then it follows that no man will ever be converted while the world stands. No sinner can be converted by the Spirit alone, for Jesus declares that the world can not receive it; neither can he, according to the brother's theology, be converted by the words and testimony of the Spirit; for the unconverted, he says, can not receive these things of the Spirit. If, then, the poor sinner can receive neither the Spirit nor the words of the Spirit, by what sort of *hocus-pocus* is he to be converted at all?

My brother may argue, however, that though the sinner, in the hardness of his heart, may resist the Word and the Spirit alone, yet the Spirit wields a sword, which no man can resist. But, to place in the hands of the Spirit such a converting implement as that would be only a juggling device, to deceive the people.

True, there is a sword of the Spirit, but so called because the Spirit made it, and not because He wields it. It was made for the Christian warrior, who is commanded to take it in his own hand, and to go forth and fight against Satan and error. Now, that very sword is the Word of God itself—this blessed Book—which my brother says the unconverted man can neither understand nor believe!

The discussion having closed, the Baptist announced to the audience that, on the following Sunday, he would speak again on the subject of *Campbellism*, at another place in the neighborhood, which he named.

Smith informed him that he could not be with him on that day, but proposed that some brother, then in the audience, should go along with him and reply; but to this his opponent would not agree. "Then," said Smith, "I will select one of these good *sisters*, who will, I know, be more than able to defend the truth against all you may say."

A deist, who was present during this discussion, and who had long rejected the Gospel on the ground that while the preachers declared it to be good news, it was impossible to believe it without supernatural aid, now confessed that his infidelity had been only the disbelief of an error, and that he now saw that the Gospel was a rational thing, worthy of all acceptation.

At another time, while preaching through the same part of the State, he took occasion to discourse upon the sixth chapter of Ephesians, dwelling at some length on the sharpness and power of the Sword of the Spirit. No one having accepted the invitation of the Gospel, he was about to dismiss the assembly, when a Methodist preacher arose and asked the question:

"If your doctrine be true, Mr. Smith, why has the sword had so little power to-night?"

"Because," promptly replied Smith, "you teachers of human systems have so long hacked it against your traditions, and wrapped it about with your creeds and disciplines, and blunted it so against your anxious seats and mourning-benches, that sinners can feel neither edge nor point."

"I'd like to know the difference," said the discomfited preacher, "between your baptism and our mourning-bench."

"Difference?" said Smith, with much emphasis; "one is from Heaven—the other, from the saw-mill."

Speaking at another place, on the plainness and simplicity of the Gospel in contrast with the abstruse systems of men, a note was passed up to him from some one in the audience, containing this question: "If the Gospel is so very plain, as you say it is, why do you have to labor so hard to get the people to understand it?"

"I have often prepared ground in the wilderness for a turnip patch," replied Smith, "and though I had the kindliest soil, and the best of seed, and the sowing was easy, I never got top or root till I first took my ax, and hoe, and brier-knife, and went in, and whacked, and grubbed, and cleared away the ground.

"The Lord knows I do not esteem it hard work to preach the simple Gospel to those who are prepared to receive it; but it is labor indeed to root out prejudice, and cut down systems, and clean away the sectarian trash that cumbers the minds and hearts of the people."

Toward the close of the year 1832, the importance of retaining the two Evangelists in the field was informally discussed among the brethren about Georgetown. But even so late as October, the small remuneration proposed for all their toils and sacrifices had not been sent up by the churches. The brethren throughout the State were again urged by the treasurer to remit their contributions without delay; they were told not to fear that there would be an overplus, for, if there should be more given than the proposed allowance of three hundred dollars to each, it would be devoted to evangelical purposes during the coming year.

"We consider it highly important," said he, "to continue the same system of operations another year; whether we will do so or not, depends on the punctuality and liberality of the congregations."

All formal action, however, in reference to the re-appointment of the two Evangelists was deferred till April, 1833. In the meantime, they labored on in the cause, well assured that their brethren would do right, and—which was their chief temporal concern—that their families would not be forgotten.

Notwithstanding the result of the year's enterprise, some were still fearful that the union was in danger on account of the diversity of sentiment which still existed on the subject of baptism; not as it respected the act of baptism, for all were immersionists; nor the subjects of baptism, for none but penitent believers were immersed; nor, in fact, the design of the ordinance, for there were but few now that denied baptism to be for the remission of sins. But some thought that there were many in the kingdom that had received the remission of their sins, who had never been immersed; others indulged in all good hopes for such persons, but confessed that they had not sufficient scriptural evidence for an unwavering faith.

John Smith's sentiments on the subject of the communion were without the least shadow of change, the same as when he met Dr. Fishback in 1828. He had not knowingly sat down at the Lord's table with any unimmersed person, or when any such persons had been specially invited. There had been some few unimmersed members—generally old men— among the Christians of his acquaintance, but the last one of them, though quite aged, had been immersed not long after the union meeting at Lexington. But now, there was neither preacher nor any other member among all the churches, so far as he knew, that advocated the practice of receiving the unimmersed into the congregation, or of open communion with them.

CHAPTER XLIV.

SOMETIME in the month of April, 1833, the following notice appeared in the *Christian Messenger:*

It is requested by several brethren, in different churches, that there shall be a general meeting of the churches, by their Bishops and Deacons, for the purpose of co-operating with regard to sending out Evangelists to proclaim the Gospel, and to appoint four-days' meetings in every church, which may desire it, north of Salt River. The meeting is proposed to be held at Dry Run, near Georgetown, on the last day of April, 1833. The churches are earnestly requested to be punctual in their attendance.

Accordingly, on the thirtieth of April, the "Bishops, Elders, Deacons, and Messengers," from a number of churches of Northern Kentucky, met at Dry Run, and continued two days in worship and in consultation with respect to the best method of advancing the Truth. The question was raised, Whether the practice of keeping Evangelists in the vineyard of the Lord should be continued? In this they were all agreed; and John Smith and John Rogers consented to ride another year, and to go wherever they should judge it to be most profitable to the cause. Confident that the other churches north of the Kentucky River would co-operate with them, the brethren then assured these Evangelists that they and their families should be supported. John T. Johnson again consented to act as Treasurer; and the churches were requested to correspond, and to let him know, as early as possible, how much each was willing to give, and to remit to him in regular quarterly payments

It was also deemed proper to advise the churches throughout the State to meet, as early as they could, in their different sections, and appoint some of their most efficient teachers to ride as Evangelists; and each church was exhorted to give, according to its ability, as much as would keep them and their families from want.

They thought it proper, also, that on every Lord's Day there should be a general meeting of the brethren in the various congregations around, to continue for several days together, which appointments were to be made by the two Evangelists, and, in due time, published in the *Messenger*.

"Co-operation," said Johnson and Stone, in publishing to the churches the conclusion at which the brethren, in conference, had thus arrived, "co-operation is the life of any cause, and division its death. Let us frown on any attempt to divide us—banish speculation from among us, and let not opinions be ever introduced as tests of Christian fellowship. If ever this is done, there is an end to unity, peace, and love."

The opposition of the sects was now, if possible, greater than ever; and yet, the success of the disciples was unprecedented. The Baptists especially withstood its progress with a zeal which the shadow of the awful pestilence that was now approaching seemed not in the least to abate. "The *Campbellites*," said a prominent opposer, "have made the gulf between us impassable by throwing themselves into the arms of the Arians."

About the first Lord's Day in May, the two Evangelists, with Thomas Smith, William Morton, George W. Elley, and others, united in conducting a three-days' meeting at the Forks of Dix River, in Garrard County, a place but a few miles distant from Lancaster. A strong and influential body of Baptists, comprising about one hundred and sixty members, here met regularly, under the ministrations of Elder John S. Higgins. Their meeting-house was a rude, cheerless structure of stone, of no very pleasing appearance at best; but, when symptoms of heresy appeared among the members, and *Arian* or *Campbellite* teachers began to profane this sanctuary, bolts and staples and bars of iron were purchased, and every window and door was stoutly closed against them. A house thus rigged with stone and iron, and standing on the rocky roadside, could not fail to impress the passer-by with the sacrilegious conceit that it was a sort of prison for the lawless or the insane.

In March preceding the visit of our Evangelists, some four or five persons had seceded from the church at the *Forks*, and organized upon the Scriptures as their only covenant; and, on the same day, they were joined by ten or twelve others. They stood firm together on the Bible, asserting the right of private judgment as the inheritance of every free man in Christ.

John Smith reached the neighborhood on Friday evening. "We did not expect to see you, Brother Smith," said one of the friends, "for we heard, a few days ago, that you had been prosecuted in Mount Sterling, for stealing forty hogs, and had been put in jail."

He smiled at the story, and remarked that he thought it was a little unfair that his sectarian friends should insist on making him bear the sins of all the rascally Smiths in the country. But others, on the next day, assured him that his enemies were busy in spreading the scandal abroad, to his injury, and on Sunday, one of the elders begged him, for the sake of the cause, to notice the matter. Smith, at last, promised to put his defamers to silence.

Friends had erected a temporary stage for the speakers, and prepared seats for the congregation, not far from the stone meeting-house, for the Baptists had, as usual, locked their doors, and bolted the iron bars across the windows. When the hour came, he stood upon the stand among the elders, and before the multitude—all curious to hear what he would say.

"Friends and brethren," said he, "it has been asserted by some highly respectable, and, of course, very reliable, gentlemen, that I am now in the Mount Sterling jail for stealing forty shoats, and, consequently, that I am not expected to preach here to-day. Now, whatever may be true about the hogs, of one thing you may rest assured: I am not in jail to-day. Of this fact, even my sectarian friends will be convinced before I leave. The Lord knows, brethren, that in all my life, I have never looked on any place more like a jail than yonder lonesome house, with its cold, stony walls and iron bars. To my eye, that building is more like a place for criminals than a home for peaceful and happy Christians.

"But I am glad to find that my sectarian friends have become so morally nice as to condemn the stealing of a few hogs; we may now hope that they will quit worse crimes. Whatever may be thought of stealing, I solemnly affirm that, bad as it is, it is not so mean a thing, nor so injurious to society, as the wanton slander of an honest reputation!

"If a decent community ought to frown upon a thief that steals a few paltry hogs, perhaps to feed his hungry family, with what contempt should they spurn the wretch that defames, by falsehood, a preacher of the Gospel of Jesus Christ —a father, too, of innocent children, who can leave them no other legacy than a pure and reputable life! Truly,

> " 'He that steals my purse, steals trash;
> But he that filches from me my good name
> Robs me of that which not enriches him,
> And makes me poor indeed.' "

"Mr. Smith," said some one near him, as if conscience-stricken by his earnest words, "it was not you; it was another Smith."

"Do you, then, acquit me," replied Smith, "before I deny the charge?"

"But there is some mistake, sir," continued the man; "I heard that it was *Thomas* Smith."

Elder Thomas Smith was sitting on the stand, but unknown to the stranger who thus implicated him.

"Friends," continued the speaker, "here is a gentleman who informs me that the thief is one Thomas Smith, and not myself, as some of you have heard. And now, Brother Tom," said he, turning to the amiable and much-beloved Elder, who looked up at him with surprise, "I know it to be a city ordinance of Lexington, where you live, that no man shall suffer his hogs to run at large, or about the streets. If, then, you have those forty shoats, tell this gentleman where you have hid them."

"I know nothing about his hogs," said the elder, with some remonstrance in his tone.

"Sir," said Smith, addressing the stranger again, "Thomas

Smith, whom it seems you do not know, is now here on the stand with me; but he says that he knows nothing about those hogs. However, he will be here in the neighborhood for some days yet, and you can take him up whenever you please."

The accusers, who sat around, and whose names Smith had already learned, were dumb; and soon, one by one, they withdrew from the audience and disappeared.

At Mount Pleasant, near the little village of Keene, in Jessamine County, there was another large and zealous congregation of Baptists, to whom Edmund Waller had for many years been preaching. Some of his flock, however, had occasionally strayed into forbidden pastures, and had finally forsaken his fold altogether. About the middle of May, these dissenting members invited George W. Elley, of Nicholasville, to come and assist them in the organization of a church on the Word of God. Five names were duly enrolled at the first meeting; but in June, Elley, re-enforced by John Smith and William Moreton, again visited the little congregation, and its membership was increased to twenty-one earnest and intelligent disciples, most of whom were from the Mount Pleasant congregation.

On Saturday, George W. Elley, mounted on a stone step at the door, was about to address the people standing about on the wet ground—for a heavy rain had fallen—when a committee came and forbid his preaching on the premises.

"I suppose, gentlemen," he replied, "you have performed your duty; I must now perform mine. The house has been locked against us, and I shall proceed, therefore, to the worship of God, standing here on the step of this door."

The exercises of the day closed without further interruption; an appointment was made for a meeting next day, and a request was added that neither the house nor anything about it should be disturbed. The entire community, on various accounts, was deeply interested in this meeting, and, on the next day, a great many came together. Some persons had early taken possession of the flat rock near the door, and when asked to relinquish it for the use of the preacher, they refused, saying that the trustees had ordered that it should not be used as a pulpit again. They went to a horse-block close by, but they found a guard upon it also; the man that put it there had sent word that no Campbellite preacher must stand upon it.

Such opposition excited the indignation of a stranger that was present, and, although not a member of any church, he hurried off to his gig, and, pulling it into the yard, lashed its shafts to a walnut tree with the driving reins, scotched the wheels, stayed the bouncing springs with a rail, and then, turning to the preachers, politely said, "Now, gentlemen, you can preach from my gig."

John Smith, with all possible dignity, climbed into his novel pulpit, and, looking around upon the multitude, began to devise some means for seating the women. Two or three piles of flat rails were lying close at hand—for an old fence had been recently removed. Suggesting that these rails might be laid around on the grass for seats, some hurried to bring them away; but their opponents had anticipated them, and a guard was seated on the rails also.

For a moment the brethren were embarrassed; they expected to break the Loaf that day, and to hear two or three discourses besides. But the woods were full of horses, hitched to the trees, and, in a short time, they were stripped, and the green grass was covered with bankets and saddles. The women and the old men sat comfortably down upon them, and all were pleased, save those who, from the doorstone, the horse-block, and the rail piles, saw the failure of their petty scheme to break up the meeting.

Smith now stood up again. Adjusting his feet to the floor of the gig, and looking complacently around upon the scene, he said that when he left home, he had not expected to find at Mount Pleasant so elegant a pulpit; and he ventured to say that they had not dreamed of sitting so comfortably to hear him. He thanked his sectarian friends, through whose awkward contrivance he had found so pleasant a place from which to preach the Ancient Gospel to them. "In fact," said he, "I could not wish for a better, unless, indeed," he added, "they had a rope fastened by one end to that limb up there and the other tied about here"—putting his hand to his cravat. All feelings of resentment were allayed by his humor; and, without further allusion to the opposition, he began his discourse, and brought it to a most impressive close.

In the afternoon the cloth was spread upon the grass, the

bread and the wine were set forth, and the brethren and sisters, many of whom were from the Clear Creek church, gathered around, and partook of the solemn repast. A cheerful song concluded their worship, and Smith arose to dismiss them. Remembering that some of his brethren, in their extreme zeal for Ancient Order, had questioned the propriety of a benediction after the Supper, because there was neither precept nor precedent for it, he gravely adjourned the meeting, according to the new ritual, by saying: "*They* sang an hymn and went out; but *we* are out now."

Another three-days' meeting, at Mount Pleasant, was appointed for July; but, on account of the cholera, which was now raging through the land, it was postponed till August. In the meantime the brethren made, at a saw-mill near by, some rude seats, and, on the morning of the appointed day, they hauled them into the church-yard, and arranged them pleasantly under the shade of the trees. John Smith and George W. Elley were with them, according to promise. The worship on Saturday was uninterrupted, and the brethren went home in the afternoon, anticipating a happy meeting on Lord's day; but when they returned next morning they saw with surprise, and no little indignation, that their benches had been piled together during the night, and burnt to ashes; not one of them remained! Their feelings could hardly be restrained; but the influence of that religion, for which they were suffering insult and persecution, triumphed over their resentment. Smith, now asking leave of no man, stood upon the horseblock, which was charred and blackened by the conflagration, and spoke to the people:

"Bad as this is, my brethren, Christians have often fared much worse. *Your benches* only have been burnt; but *they* were bound to the stake and burnt to death for the sake of Jesus and his Word. Let us be patient toward our enemies, who can do us no more harm; and let us be thankful to our heavenly Father, that matters are no worse than they are."

He and Elley discoursed to the brethren and their friends, whom this outrage had multiplied, all seated, as before, in their gigs and on their blankets and saddles, or on the rocks, and door-steps, and even on the rails, which no one now ventured to refuse.

It must not be supposed that this silly and illiberal opposition was countenanced by all the Baptists at Mount Pleasant. There were Christian men and women among them, who, though they had no sympathy with the doctrine that had been the occasion of these disorders, condemned the spirit of violence which had possessed some of their brethren. In spite of continued opposition, however, the congregation rapidly increased in numbers, and soon the church at Keene, or *Liberty*, as the village was then called, became an influential society of brethren.

The interval between the June and the August meeting at Mount Pleasant, John Smith spent at home among the churches of Montgomery. Language can not describe the terror which seized the people, as the scourging cholera swept through the counties of Northern Kentucky. Persuaded that it was contagious, many fled from the infected towns and districts, and hid from the destroyer among the pines of the mountain solitudes. Whole households were scattered in sudden panic, and never all gathered to their firesides again. They fled, they cared not whither; their houses were open and tenantless; the morning meal was untasted on the board, and sometimes a corpse was left unsheeted in the silent chamber. Many who were away on duty or pleasure, when they saw the shadow of the coming pestilence, hastened home, and watched in awe till the plague had spent its fury, and the anxious days were over. In some parts of the country, farmers that lived on the public roads shut in their trembling families, and turned the belated traveler or terror-stricken refugee from their doors. Some were seen to stand like sentinels before their threshold, with gun in hand, and warn off the importunate that came for refuge or assistance. Farm-gates were locked, entrances were barricaded, and the beseeching helloa was unheeded.

After the meeting at Mount Pleasant in June, Smith went on to Frankfort for his daughter—then attending the school of Philip S. Fall—and at North Middletown, on his way home, he was seized with a fearful dysentery. For some days he struggled with the disease, which many supposed to be cholera; but he finally reached his house, though prostrated in body and mind.

It was not until the 26th of June that he was able to preach again; and then, and for some time afterward, he could only sit in a chair and talk, in his weakness, to the people. But his voice, though feeble, never fell more acceptably or more powerfully upon the ears of his congregations. He gathered them in his own and his neighbors' houses; he met them at Mount Sterling, and Spencer, and Somerset; but he seldom ventured, during the period of his convalescence, more than a few miles from home. Yet he talked, not weekly, but daily, to the people, who came from bedside watchings and burials to hear him. His only theme was the Gospel; and sinners, aroused by the fearful judgments of the Lord, listened to his invitations as the only voice, amid the wailing in the land, that was pleasant to their ears. Wherever he went, they were ready to hear and to obey. Accessions were daily received—and, sick as he was, he went into the water, sometimes twice a day, and immersed. Thus, in the five or six weeks that he was at home watching anxiously over his family, but disregarding himself, he immersed about three hundred persons with his own hands—all, save a score, within seven miles of his house! In fact, during the two months of July and August, within the bounds of a few counties in northern Kentucky, more than one thousand were added to the Church, under the labors of Smith and other faithful preachers, who toiled, through pestilence and sickness, for the salvation of souls.

It was during those months of terror that Mrs. Smith, alone one night, with her children, was aroused by some travelers that were fleeing from the cholera: they begged for shelter and rest till morning. The good woman took them in, and made them as comfortable as she could. In the morning, after they were gone, she began to fear that she had exceeded the requirements of hospitality, and had opened her own door to the plague, and exposed herself and her loved ones to the contagion. When her husband returned home, that day, she told him what she had done and how anxious she was to know whether she had done right or wrong.

"Nancy," said he, "you did exactly right, though we should all have to die for it. If we must die, let us die doing good."

CHAPTER XLV.

PREPARATIONS to keep the two Evangelists in the general missionary field for another year were early made; in fact, the congregations had so increased in liberality that hopes were now entertained that at least two more could be supported. Smith accepted the call of the churches, and consented to travel through the State as before, and to preach wherever the interests of the cause might require.

The year was ushered in, however, by a singular controversy between him and the Rev. Dewey Whitney, an accomplished Presbyterian clergyman of Mount Sterling. Believing that the people generally were ignorant of the doctrines of their creeds, Smith resolved to bring every dogma to the light, that they might be left without the apology of ignorance for their devotion to these denominational symbols. Accordingly, at several places, and with great plainness of speech, he had sifted the Confessions of Faith, and exposed every objectionable tenet that they contained.

"The people have not read their own creeds," said he, "and I do not believe they will indorse them when their errors are exposed."

Referring especially to the Westminster Confession, he declared it to be a doctrine of that creed that the officers of the church had power to remit sins; that it consigned non-elect infants to eternal perdition; that it slandered mankind at large, and even the Presbyterians themselves; and yet the orthodox preachers were bound to inculcate its unscriptural doctrines, or expose themselves to censure. Many were astonished at these declarations; some, for awhile, were incredulous; the Presbyterians were indignant; and the Rev. Mr. Whitney publicly charged him with willful misrepresentation.

Aggrieved by such a charge, he called on Mr. Whitney to make good his accusation or publicly to withdraw it. This led to a lengthy correspondence; but finally it was arranged, through the intervention of friends, that a public interview and a discussion of all the points at issue, should take place. A preliminary meeting was held on the 27th of November, 1833; but Mr. Whitney, though he had publicly accused Smith of falsehood, declined to make the specifications which were demanded. The accused determined, notwithstanding, to meet him. Moderators were selected, and clerks were appointed to take down the testimony and to report the discussion. The 22d of January, 1834, was fixed as the day of meeting; but, until the morning of that day, Smith was kept in ignorance of the special charges which he would have to meet.

. A little while before the debate came off, two Presbyterian preachers from some of the more eastern counties called, one evening, at his house, on their way to a meeting of the synod. He had been out, hard at work, all day, and had just come in with his dirty tow-linen apron on, and had thrown himself down on the floor, before the fire, with a chair for his pillow.

He heard the call of travelers at his stile, and went out himself to answer it. They begged permission to stay all night. It was quite dark: they had ridden far, through a wintry rain, and over miry roads, and they were weary, and hungry, and cold. He ordered their horses to be taken and well cared for, and then brought the travelers into the house. His wife, seeing that they were well-dressed persons, reminded her husband, in a whisper, of his unsightly apron, and asked him to go and pull it off—which he did; but he looked none the less rustic in the eyes of the genteel strangers. They had no suspicion who their rough-looking, but kind-hearted, host was, though the fame of "Raccoon John Smith" had long ago reached their ears. Perceiving that he was unknown to them, he signified to his wife a wish to remain so.

"Are you acquainted with the Rev. Mr. Whitney, sir?" asked one of them at length.

"Yes, sir," said Smith. "Ain't you both preachers?"

"Yes," said they, "we are now on our way to synod. How many persons have joined Mr. Whitney's church lately?"

"No one, as I know of."

"A great many, I suppose," continued the stranger, "have joined the new sort of Baptists, haven't they?"

"Yes, sir; I have seen hundreds of 'em baptized myself."

"They refuse to baptize little children, I believe?" they asked.

"Ah, sir; they won't do that," replied Smith.

"Why?"

"They say it ain't in their Book."

"Don't they know that the Bible commands fathers to dedicate their children to the Lord in baptism?"

"I reckon not," said Smith; "I never heard any of 'em read it that way. Please tell *me*, though, where the place is, in that Testament there, and *I'll* put it to some of 'em."

One of them took up the New Testament which was lying on the table, and carelessly turning over its leaves, said:

"I have not given you the very words, my friend, but that is what it means."

"If you would just read to me something in there about it, I would be much obleeged to you," persisted Smith.

"Well," said the first preacher, "do they believe that Peter immersed three thousand people in one day?"

"I've heard them talk about *that*, too," replied Smith; "they say that there was a hundred and twenty there beside Peter."

"You know, too," said the other preacher, "that infants were brought to Christ, don't you?"

"I've heard that read a hundred times," replied Smith; "but it says they came to git blessed, don't it?"

"My friend," said the first preacher, again, "all the hundred and twenty persons whom those Campbellites talk about, were not authorized to administer the ordinance of baptism; though I can't believe that all of them together could have immersed three thousand in one day."

"But," replied Smith, "one of their big men says, that about twelve of 'em were apostles that could do any thing almost; and seventy more had been preachin' about in pairs; which makes eighty-two preachers, the way they count. Now, one of you just please figure it up there for me—how many would each of them eighty-two preachers have to baptize, to git through with the whole of 'em, before dark?"

"Nearly forty," said one of the strangers; "but no one man can go into the water and immerse even forty persons in a day."

"Oh, you are mistaken about that, mister!" said Smith. "I seen a man baptize forty-one the other day; a Presbyterian held his watch, and it took just forty-five minutes. I seen that myself."

One of the preachers turned and looked at him curiously, and asked: "What man was that, sir?"

"Nancy," said Smith, "what was that man's name that done the baptizing up yonder on Slate?"

"It was Smith," said she, spoiling the jest, however, by an ill-suppressed laugh.

"So it was," said Smith; "it was a man of my own name."

"Are you not the very man yourself, sir?" demanded his guests.

"Yes, gentlemen," said Smith, laying aside all his assumed awkwardness, "I am the man."

"Well, well, Mr. Smith, what fools you have made of us!"

"No, gentlemen," said he, "*I* had no hand in that."

The matter was now pleasantly laughed off; though, before retiring, one of them again insisted that there were passages of Scripture that authorized the practice of infant baptism.

"There is not one such passage, gentlemen," said Smith, "in all the Book. However, I will grant you that there is one, and but one, can be made to serve your purposes."

"And what is that?" they eagerly asked.

"'Submit yourself to every ordinance of man,' I. Pet ii. 13," said Smith.

His guests, somewhat edified, left next morning. At Mount Sterling, they spoke in high terms of their host and his wife; but confessed that they had been no little deceived at first by Smith's rustic appearance and simplicity of manner.

On the morning of the 22d of January, a deeply interested audience assembled in the Presbyterian Church at Mount Sterling, when the Rev. Mr. Whitney, for the first time, made known to Smith his specific charges against him:

1. That Smith was in the habit of representing the Creed teachers as bound to preach their Creeds in opposition to the Word of God.

2. That said Smith has preached that the Methodists used to receive two-and-sixpence for sprinkling infants.

3. That said Smith has labored to make the impression that Creed teachers assume the same prerogatives as the apostles in the ministry of reconciliation to make and propose terms of salvation.

This last charge, however, was withdrawn, on the ground that all the testimony introduced related to a period subsequent to the date of the charge. But Smith informed his opponent that, when the present business was disposed of, he would reply to everything that he might see proper to allege against him or his doctrine. The other charges Mr. Whitney endeavored to prove by several witnesses, but their testimony was rebutted, and the allegations, in the judgment of the people, were not sustained. The investigation of these matters continued two days, and at length gave place to a more formal debate on the following propositions, which Smith boldly affirmed, and which Whitney as boldly denied:

The *Confession* and *Catechism* teach, substantially, 1. That the officers of the church have authority to forgive sins.

2. That non-elect infants, dying, go to perdition.

3. The Creed of the Presbyterians slanders them and mankind at large.

4. It does away with all grace on the part of God, in the justification of the sinner.

It had been stipulated that all references to Scripture should be made to the common English version. Smith was not willing to give his opponent any undue advantage over him by reason of his classical attainments, nor any opportunity to take refuge in the fastnesses of Greek and Hebrew literature; he was perfectly willing to confess, too, what, indeed, every body knew, that he was utterly ignorant of all the dead languages.

On the morning of the 24th he opened the discussion by

reading, in support of his first proposition, the following passages from the *Westminster Confession of Faith:*

XXX—i. The Lord Jesus, as King and Head of his Church, hath therein appointed a government in the hand of Church officers, distinct from the civil magistrate.

ii. To these officers, the keys of the kingdom of heaven are committed, by virtue whereof they have power, respectively, to retain and remit sins, to shut that kingdom against the impenitent both by the Word and censures; and to open it unto penitent sinners by the ministry of the Gospel, and by absolution from censures, as occasion shall require.

In explanation of this article of the Confession, Mr. Whitney said that it was found under the head of CHURCH CENSURES; that it meant, therefore, only, that the officers of the church had power to forgive members on proper acknowledgments, when they had sinned against each other, or against the government of the church; and, if due acknowledgments were not made, to retain their sins upon them.

Smith replied that the subjoined texts, on which the article in question is based, clearly refer to sins against God; that the language of the Confession must be interpreted in the light of those citations, and that the plain import of the words of the Creed itself sustained his charge. Besides, he argued, if Mr. Whitney's exposition of his own creed was correct, no private member could forgive his brother's trespasses, for that Creed restricts the power to forgive such sins to those who carry the keys.

In support of his second affirmation, Smith again read from the Confession:

III—iii. By the decree of God for the manifestation of his glory, some men and angels are predestinated unto everlasting life, and others foreordained to everlasting death.

iv. These angels and men thus predestinated and foreordained are particlarly and unchangeably designed; and their number is so certain and definite that it can not be either increased or diminished.

X—iii. Elect infants, dying in infancy, are regenerated and saved by Christ through the Spirit, who worketh when and where and how he pleaseth. So also are all other elect persons, who are incapable of being outwardly called by the ministry of the Word.

iv. Others, not elected, although they may be called by the ministry of the Word, and may have some common operations of the Spirit, yet they never truly come to Christ, and, therefore, can not be saved.

In addition to the reading of these articles, he argued that the non-elect at forty are non-elect at birth, and for such children, Christ, according to the Creed, did not die. "Now, do the non-elect never die in infancy? The deluge once swept a world away. Is it certain that all the children that then perished were elect? Earthquakes, famine, and pestilence respect neither age nor condition; do they always pass by the non-elect? Besides," said he, "is it any more cruel or unjust to send infants to hell than to let them live awhile, and multiply their sins, without the possibility of salvation, and then to deliver them over to preordained damnation? Kinder would it be in God, I do affirm, to let the poor babes perish in their infancy, and thereby save them at least from the wretchedness and sin of the present world."

To this, Mr. Whitney replied, in brief, in the language of the Confession—that the doctrine of this high mystery of predestination is to be handled with special prudence and care.

In support of his third declaration, Smith read from the *Larger Catechism:*

Q. 25. Whence consisteth the sinfulness of that estate whereinto man fell?

A. The sinfulness of that estate whereinto man fell consisteth in the guilt of Adam's first sin, the want of that righteousness wherein he was created, and the corruptions of his nature, whereby he is utterly indisposed, disabled, and made opposite unto all that is spiritually good, and wholly inclined to all evil, and that continually; which is commonly called original sin, and from which do proceed all actual transgressions.

It will better serve to illustrate Smith's peculiar manner of handling this passage, to relate a conversation held with a Presbyterian just before the debate, who. like his brethren generally, was charging him with misrepresentation of their views.

"I understand, Mr. Smith, that you say we do not believe our own *Confession*, and that it actually slanders us?"

"I did say so," replied Smith.

"Sir, we hold to every word of it as God's truth, believing it with all our hearts," said the Presbyterian.

"I think," said Smith, "I can prove that you do *not* believe it."

"Perhaps I may not credit your witnesses, sir."

"I need but one," said he, "and whether he is a credible one or not I will let you judge. *You* are that witness; now, will you depose with candor?"

"Certainly I will," said the man.

"Your creed says that you are wholly inclined to all evil. Now, in my neighborhood, we regard lying, theft, adultery, murder, and drunkenness as evil; were you, before your conversion, wholly inclined to these things? And we look upon honesty and truthfulness as good; were you always utterly indisposed, disabled, and made opposite to these things?

"Now," continued Smith, "some of your own brethren are my neighbors, and I might say, friends, although I can not indorse their creed. I have known them long and well—their sons and their daughters—and I can, in the most positive manner, vindicate them from this charge of utter and entire corruption. For, before their conversion, as well as since that time, they were not only disinclined to these evil things, but, from their very souls, they shrunk from the practice of them And do you, sir, now charge the love of such vices upon them, and confess, too, in open court, that you are just as guilty as they? If so, you are a worse man than I supposed, and ought, in justice, to be in prison, for your creed declares that, even since your conversion, this dreadful corruption remains in you!"

His fourth and last proposition—that the Confession of Faith makes grace on the part of God, in the pardon of the sinner, impossible—he maintained as a logical consequence of a commercial view of the atonement. If Christ actually discharged the sinner's debt and satisfied all demands against him, it may be *just* in God to pardon, but surely there can be no *grace* in his acquittal.

Besides, he argued, the Gospel, as a system of grace, is good news; but that which assures a man that he is a sinner by nature, and exposed to all the pains of hell forever—that there is no salvation for him unless arbitrarily elected without effort or conditions on his part, which election, too, it is always a point of merit to be doubtful of—such a revelation surely can not be good news, and it is not, therefore, the Gospel of the Lord Jesus Christ.

During the debate, Mr. Whitney, at one time, forgot the agreement that no appeal should be made to the Greek or Hebrew Scriptures. Closely pressed by one of his opponent's arguments, he introduced, by way of reply, a citation from the Greek. Smith's ear instantly caught the strange sounds, and he was about to rise to a point of order; but, looking over the large audience, he saw that not a man in the house, save his learned opponent himself, understood one word of the matter in hand. He suffered him, therefore, to proceed, without interruption to the close. He then arose, and, after replying to every thing relevant to the question, he said:

"It was my fortune, as you all know, my friends, to be raised on a frontier, where I had no opportunity to acquire a collegiate education. I am unable to say, therefore, whether the gentleman has spoken good Greek, or even Greek at all. But, lest some of you may suppose that there is argument in an unknown tongue, I will attempt to answer the gentleman's Greek also. When my father first settled in Kentucky, many Cherokee Indians used to come about on friendly hunting excursions. I was a lad then, but was always fond of hanging about their camp and observing their ways, and I learned, at last, a little of their language."

Suddenly turning to his reverend opponent and taking the attitude of an Indian brave in the act of letting fly an arrow at his foe, he exclaimed, with a strong Cherokee accent: "Segilluh unuhsohee unaka howee taw!"

With a stamp of his foot, he gave a startling emphasis to the last word; the bow-string twanged, the arrow sped, and his opponent started, as if a Cherokee warrior was upon him.

CHAPTER XLVI.

SMITH continued to labor that year as an Evangelist in the counties of Nicholas, Bourbon, Harrison, Scott, Woodford, and Fayette, till July, when he again made a tour southward, through the counties of Garrard, Lincoln, Pulaski, Wayne, and Cumberland, into Tennessee and Alabama, in order to instruct the Disciples, and to strengthen them against the formidable opposition that was everywhere arrayed against them.

"I can assure you," says he, in his report, "that the Christians in our own section of the country, see but a small corner of the field which *loudly* calls for laborers. In those parts through which I have recently traveled, there are thousands of people who have never heard the Gospel proclaimed in its primitive purity and simplicity. The sects are completely buried in the rubbish of their own traditions, and sinners do not know what they must do to be saved; and in many, very many, places there is no one to tell them. Hundreds are begging for some one to visit them, and teach them. I did not remain long enough at any one place to deliver more than one discourse, except in two cases; and of course had not an opportunity of gathering much fruit. Notwithstanding all the disadvantages, thirty-five made the good confession during my tour. If you wish to see a complete moral waste, take a journey through that part of the country; and I think your spirit will be stirred within you, to see the people wholly given to sectarianism. Still, the prospects for doing good are abundant and flattering. The great body of the people would hear and obey, if they had the opportunity."

The churches, generally, in northern and central Kentucky, were at last becoming alive to the importance of co-operative, evangelical enterprise. The result of the experiment, instituted in 1832, had demonstrated the wisdom of combined missionary effort to spread the Gospel. The success of John Smith and John Rogers now inspired the more zealous brethren with the hope that, if these first Evangelists of the church could be longer sustained, and properly re-enforced, the last vestige of sectarianism would, in a few years, disappear from the State.

An interesting four-days' meeting was held in August, in the town of Shelbyville, by Elders Morton, Rogers, Allen, Gates, Hall, Thomas Smith, and others. These brethren, with the church at that place, in a special conference on the last day of the meeting, took the whole subject of evangelizing under prayerful consideration. They discussed the importance of employing additional means for setting in order the things that were wanting in the churches, and for preaching the Gospel to the world—agreeing unanimously that, in order to convert the world, "something should be done which the churches were not yet doing." They endeavored to ascertain the scriptural plan and method of procedure, and finally concluded that, "As the church is the light of the world, the pillar and support of the truth, and as the word of the Lord sounded out from the primitive churches, and as the church at Antioch sent Paul and Barnabas, and as other churches sent Timothy and others, and helped them on the way, so it is the duty of the churches now to send and support Evangelists in the great and necessary work of the preaching of the Word."

But there were others who still refused their aid to sustain Evangelists, on the ground that no such functionaries were needed—it being the mission of the Church itself to convert the world. Some maintained that the power to convert was in the inspired Word alone, and that the Bible, and not the preacher, was the true missionary to the world; others, again, admitted the necessity of public religious teachers of some sort, but could find no authority for any other than the bishop or elder of a congregation.

At the close of the year 1834, many became solicitous to learn whether John Smith and John Rogers would continue their labors as Evangelists for another year.

"We are happy to have it in our power to answer in the affirmative," writes Johnson. "No two men would be *more* acceptable; and none, we are well assured, could render more essential service to the cause in which we are engaged. They have labored with an untiring zeal, devotion, and prudence, becoming their high calling as Evangelists of the King of saints. Several thousand have been benefited by their work of faith, labor of love, and patience of hope in the Lord Jesus Christ. They seem to have constantly before their mind the great sacrifice which the Son of God made to redeem sinners. Thus influenced in the cause of our King, they are determined, for the present, to continue in the field and contend for laurels that will never fade away."

John Rogers, however, in the April following, was compelled to abandon the general missionary work. An afflicted wife and dependent children demanded his constant presence at home. The loss of his valuable services at this crisis was greatly felt. Still he labored with success among the churches in his neighborhood, endeavoring more especially to restore the Ancient Order in every congregation. In the letter which this good and useful man wrote to Johnson, after reviewing the past, and gratefully acknowledging the kindness of all the brethren, he adds, with impressive emphasis and candor:

There is one thing in this retrospect that greatly mars my peace, which I think it my duty to state: That, while we made converts by hundreds, *we did not more strongly urge conformity to the apostolic order of worship established in the first churches.* I am now thoroughly convinced that, where this order is not established, but little is gained in the cause of Christian reformation. Converts we may make by scores, but, if this order be not set on foot among them, they will either go to the world again, or degenerate into sectarians.

. . . And it is certain that our want of conformity to the whole will of God upon which we so much insist, has done, and is doing, us more harm than all our opponents; nay, than all other causes together. We have directed our attention to proselyting more than to training the proselytes.

. . . I must be permitted to say again what I have often said in effect in my public addresses; that, unless this Reformation be greatly reformed, we may not hope to succeed.

There must be less conformity to this world, and more conformity to the will of God.

In the spring or summer of that year—1835—John Smith became involved in a controversial correspondence with the Rev. Edward Stephenson, an able minister of the Methodist Episcopal Church. This gentleman had been appointed, in the autumn of 1834, to the Mount Sterling station—some of his friends declaring at the time that it was for the special purpose of arresting the progress of *Campbellism* in that region of country. Not long after his arrival, he announced to the public his intention to deliver a series of lectures upon the main, distinctive items of doctrine as found in the writings of Alexander Campbell. He added afterward that, when his series of lectures was concluded, he would, if called on, meet *the well-known and acknowledged leader of the Reformers* in that section of the State, on the propositions assumed.

He was in due time requested by John Smith and Buckner H. Payne to name the man alluded to by him as a *leader,* and to state definitely, in writing, the propositions, which, as opposed to Mr. Campbell's views, he would endeavor to sustain. After some delay he replied that John Smith was the individual whom public opinion had long since identified as the prominent leader, in that region at least, of the religious community with which he stood connected. Just at that juncture, however, Alexander Campbell himself, returning from Nashville, reached the town of Mount Sterling on his way to Virginia; and Mr. Stephenson immediately addressed him a note, in which, after referring to his correspondence with Smith, he proposed:

"If it be your desire to assume the place of Mr. Smith in this case, your wish shall be gratified provided Mr. Smith will give me·an explicit avowal of his disposition to decline the place."

"You have as much mistaken my character," said Mr. Campbell, in reply to him, "as you have the Christian system, if you imagine that I feel myself in duty bound to turn aside from my appointments to debate on Methodism or Presbyterianism, with any person who takes it into his head to distinguish himself with the title of the Defender of the

Faith of his party. The note you have had presented to me, *after the bearer had clearly ascertained* that I was leaving town this morning to meet my appointments in Mason County, informs me that you have challenged Brother John Smith, of this county, on some propositions excogitated in a series of lectures, of the literary and moral character of which I have learned nothing, delivered, or to be delivered, by you in this place, touching the Christian religion. I have no doubt but that gentleman is every way qualified to defend the Christian religion from your assaults; and am not without some faint hope that, if he should not be able to convince *you*, he may be the instrument of saving some of your brethren from the delusions of a sectarian religion."

Smith, after waiting till near the middle of June for Mr. Stephenson to conclude his lectures on Campbellism, which he had begun in January, now pressed upon him the contemplated discussion; but after a voluminous correspondence, which dragged on till September, he found it impossible to agree with his opponent on any propositions that properly set forth the distinctive doctrine of Mr. Campbell and his brethren.

In the meantime, having sold his farm in Montgomery, Smith bought land near Owingsville, in Bath County, to which he moved in the month of August. He still continued to preach, however, to the congregations in Montgomery, laboring especially to set every thing in order, and to advance them in the knowledge and observance of all things that had been commanded. He had found it very difficult to induce the country churches, whose members were scattered over a widely-extended district, and who had been accustomed to meet but once a month, and then mainly to hear a sermon, to come together regularly, every Lord's Day, for social worship and mutual instruction. Few were willing, as yet, to take upon themselves the office of bishop, although zealous enough in the private defense of the truth. It was not till the year 1836 that the brethren, even at Spencer and Somerset, agreed to meet every Lord's Day to observe the ordinances as they were delivered.

The resignation of John Rogers as an Evangelist, and the probability that John Smith also would be constrained to retire from the field, together with the known wants of the churches, and the general condition of the cause, as reported by these faithful Evangelists, weighed on the heart of Johnson and others, until, finally, they resolved on a plan of operations, which they believed would, if generally adopted, meet the demands of the cause with respect both to the church and the world.

During an annual meeting at Mount Carmel, in Bourbon County, which commenced Friday before first Lord's Day in September, 1835, the preachers and other brethren met at the house of the excellent Noah Spears, for the purpose of taking into consideration the subject of evangelizing. After an interchange of views on the subject, the following propositions were unanimously agreed to:

1st. That there should be men employed to set the churches in order, and to preach the Gospel to those without the king dom—men of intelligence and moral worth—efficient men who could give themselves wholly to the work of an Evangelist.

2d. It was agreed that the most successful method of operating was for each Evangelist to take a small district of country for the field of his operation, say one or two counties, and cultivate it well.

3d. That the most certain and satisfactory way of ob taining the means of support was by subscription.

It was then agreed that there should be a meeting appointed at Georgetown, commencing Friday before the first Lord's Day in November following, to which a messenger should be sent by every congregation favorable to the project.

Accordingly, on the 31st day of October, 1835, messengers from several congregations in each of the counties of Fayette, Woodford, Jessamine, and Scott, met with the congregation of Christ at Georgetown.

From the contributions reported, and the cheering prospects ahead, it was deemed advisable to make provision for, and to solicit the appointment of, four highly gifted Evangelists.

It was thereupon resolved, that John Smith, Jacob Creath, Jr., B. F. Hall, and J. P. Lancaster were suitable persons to be engaged in so noble an enterprise, and the congregations of which they were members were recommended and solicited to appoint them to the work in the field of labor for which they were considered so well qualified.

The most entire confidence and unabated affection was expressed for the two former Evangelists—Smith and Rogers—and it was even a matter of astonishment that so much had been accomplished by them on so large a theater. But it was considered that the former system was very inefficient, and had fallen short of achieving the most desirable results, owing to the vast extent of the field of labor, and the lack of a regular plan of operations within a prescribed boundary.

There being, as was thought, prominent defects, it was determined that the field of their labors should be limited, *primarily*, to the four counties formerly named. By these means, it was designed to make a fair experiment of the success and transforming power of the Gospel when announced, sustained, illustrated, and exemplified by such able and efficient Evangelists and teachers. It was designed to cultivate this field of labor to the highest point of perfection of which it was susceptible with the means employed, that, independent of the invaluable local blessings to be enjoyed therefrom, the world might be profited to the greatest possible extent by the model of Christianity thus presented. It was hoped that the liberty, zeal, and efficiency of the congregations thus co-operating would create a laudable Christian emulation all over the country.

The sacrifices heretofore made by the Evangelists and public teachers were deeply and sensibly felt and expressed; and it was resolved to awake to a sense of duty—to bear a part of the sacrifices, and to share some of the honors and joys of the victory.

It was resolved, therefore, that not less than $500 could, with *any* regard to the circumstances around them, be tendered to each of those brethren. Less than this was conconsidered as falling too far short of the remuneration proper to be made for such great sacrifices.

The congregations contributing were requested to appoint each a Treasurer, to take charge of the funds contributed, whose duty it should be to transmit the same to G. W. Elley, the General Treasurer, at Lexington, to be paid over to the Evangelists quarterly.

John Smith was urged to accept the call; and, feeling deeply the importance of the proposed work of restoring the ancient order in the congregations, he agreed to undertake it, in connection with the others, provided the church at Mount Sterling, of which he was still a member, and other congregations, would release him. He was informed that his compensation would be not less than five hundred dollars; but, as he had incurred some indebtedness by his removal to Owingsville, a certain wealthy brother privately pledged to him, on his own responsibility, one hundred dollars more.

John T. Johnson was requested by the committee that had the matter in hand to visit Mount Sterling, and obtain the consent of that church to the proposed arrangement. But the brethren, believing that his services were needed within his old bounds, declined to give him up, and he, accordingly, refused to leave them.

Thus obedient to the wishes of his brethren in Montgomery, he devoted himself, for the year 1836, to the welfare of the churches in that county, in Bath, and in Clark, without the promise of any specified salary—trusting, as he had formerly done, to the liberality of his brethren for a support. The year closed—he had neglected his own affairs, and toiled faithfully for the good of others; Johnson, having afterward visited some of those churches, describes them as being animated with new life and zeal; and yet their faithful teacher received, after all, but little that year for his services.

He now quietly retired to his farm, at the beginning of the new year, donned his tow-linen apron again, put in with his own hands a heavy and profitable crop, delved and plowed and hewed as he had done in earlier days, until his strong nerves were shattered, and an incurable palsy began to shake his arms. "When I work hard," writes he, in 1839, "my nerves are so much affected that I can hardly write my name. I have no doubt that I shall be completely palsied, in a few years, if life should last."

CHAPTER XLVII.

JOHN SMITH, though not a politician in any sense of the term, was as decided in his political as in his religious opinions, and as frank and candid in expressing them. Every one, in fact, knew on which side of any important question to place him. While distinguished for prudence, he was incapable of any timid or truckling concealment. His deliberate judgments belonged to the public, if they chose to ask for them; and he declared them in a manner so frank and kind that he left no reasonable ground for misunderstanding or offense.

In 1837, a very exciting political contest occurred in the Congressional District where he lived, between the Hon. Richard French and Richard H. Menifee, then in the twenty-eighth year of his age. This distinguished young orator and statesman was born in Owingsville, in the year 1809. Left an orphan at four years of age, he struggled with poverty and averse circumstances till the age of sixteen, when he was taken to Mount Sterling by Edward Stockton, with whose assistance he was enabled to acquire an education. Admitted to the practice of the law at the age of twenty-one, he was at once appointed Commonwealth's Attorney for that District, and, in his twenty-seventh year, was returned as a member from Montgomery to the House of Representatives of Kentucky. In 1837, he was made the standard-bearer for the Whig party in the Congressional campaign for that year, in opposition to Judge French, a distinguished Democrat. Never did a greater career of usefulness and splendor dawn upon the vision of any young man. To the most brilliant gifts of oratory, he added the loftiest virtues of manly and heroic character. The history of his boyhood—his early struggles for knowledge, his spotless honor, and extraordinary talents—early won the heart of John Smith, who loved him with almost parental fondness. The political strife of that year was intensely earnest. As the day for the election drew nigh, almost every other interest was forgotten. Quiet neighbors waxed warm with disputations; partisan hurrahs were mingled with their harvest songs, and political wranglings profaned, on Sunday, the very precincts of the sanctuary. The brilliant Menifee, with his boyish face and delicate form, moved like a meteor from one highland barbecue to another, and the mountains sent up their shouts of enthusiasm when he appeared. The voice of the people, at length, prevailed, and the popular honors rested on the brow of the young statesman.

Smith could not have been an indifferent spectator of that remarkable contest. Sympathy for his gifted young friend was natural and proper, and would alone have interested him in the result. But he, too, was a Whig; and, though his brethren were divided in sentiment, it was impossible for him to disfranchise himself on that account, and to hide his honest sympathies or convictions from the world; he quietly, but promptly, cast his suffrage for Mr. Menifee. The consequences might have been foreseen—they probably were anticipated, but certainly they were not regarded. Some took offense, and declared that they would hear him preach no more. Disaffection soon sprang up; misunderstandings ensued; other occurrences, misconceived or misinterpreted, fomented strife, till finally the peace of the church was destroyed.

Smith was necessarily involved in these dissensions, and he found himself, at last, in direct conflict with some of his brethren. But in this, as in every other controversy—and they were not a few—into which he was forced by duty to himself or to the cause, he was vindicated by his brethren.

We may here mention the fact that, in the October following the election of Mr. Menifee, a son, the last of fifteen children, was born to Elder Smith, and he at once received the name of the illustrious young Congressman.

In the spring of 1840, Smith received a pressing invitation to visit the city of Covington, and, if possible, to resuscitate the cause in that important place. James G. Arnold, who, it may be remembered, first met Smith in the Bracken Association at Wilson's Run in 1828, had been a teacher of considerable reputation at Washington, and then at Maysville, in Mason County. Such men as John Newton Payne, Buckner H. Payne, the Holtons, and others, whom he had instructed, bore testimony to his ability as a sound, practical educator of young men. From Maysville, Arnold, with but limited means, went to Covington, then comparatively a village, and soon afterward began to collect together the few scattered Disciples of that place, amounting, perhaps, to about forty-five souls. With the aid of James Challen they were organized into a church; but the cholera of 1833 destroyed or dispersed the little congregation, and the cause seemed hopelessly to perish away. But in March, 1840, Arnold resolved to make an effort to revive it. He fitted up his own tobacco warehouse, near the first Market-space, for the accommodation of an audience, appointed a day for meeting, and then sent for John Smith to come and address the people. He accordingly went down, and, finding deism in great strength, spoke much in defense of the simple Gospel, affirming that infidelity is often but the rejection of sectarian systems of religion which are as unreasonable as they are unscriptural. The deists themselves came to hear him, and showed him every remark of respect. The meeting lasted for nearly a week, and closed with fifteen or twenty accessions.

Arnold at once determined to build a house of worship for the Disciples. He had been successful in business, after his removal to Covington; and now, without asking a subscription from any person, he selected a lot on Third Street, employed laborers, superintended the work, and paid for it all *in silver half dollars* from his own pocket. The house was nearly completed in 1843, when John T. Johnson, the Evangelist, with John Newton Payne, appeared and consecrated it by a warm and successful protracted meeting.

In the following May, the first of those great gatherings of the churches called *State meetings*, took place in Harrodsburg, Mercer County, at that time the seat of Bacon College; and Smith, though much pressed by business at home, set out for that place.

Some of the brethren were again contending that the name Christian had been imposed by divine authority— that it was the new name of which the prophet speaks, and that the followers of Christ should always be called by it. Others still believed that it was either given by enemies, or assumed by the early disciples themselves; and, while they did not object to wearing it, they thought that the name Disciples, or Saints, or Holy Brethren, was just as proper, and that, in fact, these names might be used indiscriminately. Some, in their zeal for the name Christian, had gone so far as to confer it, formally and publicly, with some ceremony, on young converts after their baptism. The controversy on this subject had ceased to be profitable, and, in the opinion of many good brethren, it was doing harm, and ought to be dropped.

When Smith reached Georgetown, on his way to Harrodsburg, he found that Johnson himself had prepared an essay on the subject of the Name, which he was about to send to the papers for publication, and he now read it to Smith.

"If Brother Campbell loves you one-half as much as I think he does," said Smith, on hearing it, "he will certainly not do you the injury to print it."

"Brother Scott, I know, will print it," said Johnson.

"Yes," said Smith; "Walter, too, is half crazy about this matter of the name, and he will print it; but you ought not to send it to him. Brother Campbell has dropped the controversy himself, and I think you *all* ought to quit. Rest assured, you never will, by all your writing, induce any one who understands the Book, to adopt one of these names to the exclusion of the others; for we know that, after the name *Christian* was given at Antioch, the sacred writers, speaking of the brethren, still call them disciples; and no matter who gave the other name, they were willing to wear it and to suffer under it."

At Harrodsburg, he found Walter Scott, and he soon expressed a desire to have an interview with him and Johnson. They met accordingly at a private house, and, while sitting in the parlor, with a number of brethren and sisters around them, Johnson inquired:

"Brother Smith, is the matter about which you wish to talk to us of a private nature, or can you communicate it before these brethren?"

"Nothing that I wish to say," replied Smith, "needs be said in private."

"Proceed then," said Johnson; and all present gave their attention.

"I never did pretend, brethren, to rank myself with great men, but my age and experience I hope will give me the privilege of expressing my opinion for the advantage of brethren younger than myself. This controversy about our name is likely to get up a party feeling among the brethren, and, therefore, it ought to be dropped. Brother Campbell has quit writing about it, and I think you should all do the same."

"Why, Brother Smith," said Scott, with some enthusiasm "I have an article on hand, which I will publish next month, proving conclusively that God never acknowledges his people, or their works, until they receive their right name."

"If you prove *that*," replied Smith, "you will kill a thing I love as dearly as I do my own life."

"What is that, Brother John?"

"The name *Christian*," replied Smith.

"How will we do that?"

"You learned men have been teaching us that it was some ten or eleven years from Pentecost till the meeting at Antioch. Now, will you indeed prove that God never owned the disciples of Jesus, nor the ten years' preaching of the apostles, nor the thousands of converts they had made, till the time of that meeting? This, surely, you will not attempt to do. But, if God can not acknowledge his children until they have the right name, as you say— and if, however, he *did* acknowledge the apostles and their works before the Antioch meeting—then the name *Disciple*, by which they had previously been called, is the right one, and that of *Christian* is gone forever!"

"But, Brother John," replied Scott, "only one-half of the Christian body was formed within that period. The Church was then composed of Jewish Christians; but, when the other half was added from the Gentile world, the whole received its right name."

"Now, just think of it, brethren!" Smith rejoined. "The Church of Christ, during all that time, with its thousands of members, and the apostles at their head, was not a body, but a one-legged, one-breasted, one-armed, one-eyed nameless thing, waiting for its fellow-half to get a name!"

"Really, that won't do, Brother John," said Scott.

"No, Walter; and if you had not been *hypoed* in some way, you would have seen that it would not do."

"But, Brother Smith," asked Scott, "don't you and your wife give your children names?"

"Walter," replied Smith, "you and other great men have been writing much about the patronymic, or family, name. Now, Nancy and I were so ignorant that we thought our children were all *born* Smiths—that they were entitled to this patronymic name by virtue of their birth. True, we give them proper names, in order to distinguish them from one another; but we never had any other idea than that they were all *Smiths* when born. Did you ever quarrel about whether your children should receive, by inheritance, your own family name?"

Scott was silent; the general laugh that followed relieved him from any reply, and Smith let fly another shaft.

"Walter," continued he, "you recently wrote a piece inviting the brethren to send you their written views as to the time when it was proper to confer the name *Christian*. Now, I do wish that some school-girl had been at your elbow when you thus wrote, and told you that it was when one was baptized into Christ, and thus put him on—being born into the Kingdom and the Name, when born of water and the Spirit; and that you had no more right or authority to confer it by a subsequent ceremony than you had to celebrate the Romish mass.

"Suppose," Smith still persisted, without mercy, "that I had been called on to celebrate the rites of matrimony between you and your wife, and that I had duly married you, and pronounced you man and wife; that, in a few days afterward, I had returned, and, calling your friends together, summoned you to the parlor, and informed our sister that I had come to confer upon her her new name —that it was now proper that she should take upon herself your name; would she not, with much surprise, have informed me that she had already acquired that name by virtue of the law that had made her your wife, and that she would continue to wear it, too, as long as she. lived, without the aid of any of my pow-wowing?"

It may be added that the articles with which the Church was, at that time, threaened, never made heir appearance; but when Scott returned home, he penned and published the following description of John Smith:

Quality of voice—guttural, dry, and husky; articulation— measured, slow, perfect; enunciation—full; emphasis—natural and striking; pause—irregular; tone—drawing; action —nervous, indicating, *Down with the enemy!* language— always sifting out the sense; logic—sure, sharp, killing; rhetoric—borrowed from all sources: in nature, from the sun down to the spark of a firefly; in society, from the king to the beggar; in art, from the sublimest to the meanest of human fabrications; and, in religion, everything; eloquence —sparkling, shrewd, and bordering sometimes on the indescribable. But let a man take care how he resigns himself to Smith's wit. It is used as some dangerous animals use their feelers—simply to ascertain where the prey lies: when that is done, the wit is ended, and then woe betide the man that smiled; *he must die the death.*

CHAPTER XLVIII.

ELDER SMITH, while carrying on his farm near Owings-ville, was by no means inactive, either as a teacher or an evangelist. He continued to visit the churches at Somerset, Spencer, Sharpsburg, North Middletown, Bethlehem, which he had organized in 1833, and other places in that portion of the State. He was often away, too, on distant preaching tours, now laboring again with Rogers in Nicholas and Fleming, now with the indefatigable Johnson, who was everywhere, and now operating alone, as the frequent calls of the brethren, or his own zealous impulses, determined him. Occasionally he would appear unexpectedly in some distant place, where, though personally unknown, his fame had already preceded him.

During one of his tours, perhaps in the summer of 1840, he appeared at Madison, in Indiana, late one afternoon. Being a stranger, he called on one of the elders of the congregation, and introduced himself.

The few brethren that could be seen, were at once noti-fied, and the chapel was lighted up. The weather was warm and the evenings short; and upon such a notice, not more than twenty-five or thirty came together. He began his discourse by saying:

"I am rather a singular sort of man, my brethren; at least, I am generally so regarded. One thing in which I differ from most other preachers is, that on occasions like this, when very few come out, I preach my very best sermons; whereas others keep theirs back for big meetings, associa-tions, and the like. This, I think, is not right; (I always preach as well as I can.) And now if you will give me your attention, I think I can promise you something worth hearing.

I hope that none of you will go to sleep; for, if you do, the number left awake will be very small indeed."

He read a portion of Eph. iii. "And he fulfilled his promise," says Elder F. W. Emmons, who was present. "Never did I listen to a discourse that interested me more. I remember the doctrine, and the impression its presentation then made upon my mind is vivid still." *

Smith's exordiums were often enlivened with some little pleasantry, that seldom failed to win the attention of the listless to his more serious discourse. It was the unstudied play of nature, however, rather than any art of the orator. His mind seemed like a giant in repose, till, by a little quaint humor, he had brought his audience within his reach and then, whether he reasoned or exhorted, the speaker had his will.

Other preachers of the day may have surpassed him in fervid or imaginative oratory, but none equaled him in that wonderful impressiveness which leaves a doctrine in the mind and heart forever.

"Thirty-five years ago," says one, "I heard him preach in a cabin near Monticello. I was then a boy, but I could not keep from listening; and to-day I distinctly remember that sermon—the text, the doctrine, and the arrangement. No recent discourse is so vivid in my mind."

"He was preaching once at Walnut Flats, near Stanford," says another, "when I was a youth, and living in that village. Hearing that there would be a gathering at the *Flats* on Sunday, I went out with some other young persons for amusement. The day was very warm, and the house and woods around were full of people. After loitering awhile, I went in from idle curiosity, but could get no further than just within the door. Observing the preacher, whom I did not know, for I had never seen John Smith, I concluded, from his appearance, that it would not be worth the while to stand and listen to him. He had rode some distance that morning, and, on account of the heat, had pulled off his coat, and carried it on his arm. He had entered the house and the pulpit in that guise; his shirt collar was unbuttoned and lay open around his neck; and thus he sat waiting for the hour to arrive. In a few minutes he arose,

* 1865.

buttoned and carefully adjusted his collar, put on his coat, and at once assumed the air of a grave, earnest, and thoughtful man.' He began by saying: 'Doubtless many of you will be much disappointed to-day, as I understand that Elder Thomas Smith was expected to speak. I am not that learned and excellent man of Lexington, but simply John Smith, or, if you will understand me any better, *Raccoon John Smith, of Montgomery*.' I felt at once drawn to the man; I was fixed to the spot where I stood; and in spite of myself, I listened to him for two hours and a half."

"The first time that I ever heard John Smith preach,' says Aylett Raines, "was at Mayslick, I think, in 1830—forty years ago. His text was I. Cor. x. It was a powerful discourse. His introduction was characteristic of the man. 'I expect,' said he; 'to deliver a sermon to-day that will please everybody—though if any shall be displeased, I suppose it will be my own brethren: for if I should say anything which, according to the usual laws of interpretation, the sects might not believe, let them take the same liberty with my words that they do with those of Christ and his apostles—let them say that Brother John don't mean what he says, and then they may make my words mean just what they like, and, of course, can't be displeased.' "

While preaching regularly for the church at Bethlehem, in Clark County, a Universalist began to disturb the people. So many, in fact, seemed to be carried away with his doctrine that he talked at last of constituting a church there. Smith, having declared, on one occasion, that, by the mode of reasoning which the Universalists employed he could prove that all men would be damned, was pressed to make good his assertion.

"You will never undertake to do that," said a Universalist.

He accordingly announced that, on his next visit to Bethlehem, he would preach on *Universal Damnation*. When the time came, an immense crowd assembled; for the singular promise had been published far and near among the people. On rising, he remarked:

"I am going to deliver a discourse to-day, brethren, which the Lord knows, and you know, I do not believe one word of; but, to expose the absurdity of a doctrine which you have been hearing, I will show that, applying the Universalist's mode of interpretation, all men, without exception, will be damned. And what if I should succeed in proving that the devil will get the last one of you? I fear it is nothing more than you all richly deserve, anyhow."

He then laid down a copy of Pingree's "Defense of Universalism" on the desk, and, beside it, his own manuscript —the first and only discourse that he ever wrote—and he proceeded to demonstrate at every point that, according to the logic of the author, the Scriptures consign all men to perdition.

"And now," said he, in conclusion, "if you will give me your attention thirty minutes longer, I will prove to you that neither Mr. Pingree nor myself have told you the truth."

This discourse saved the church from Universalism. That doctrine was, in the estimation of the people, successfully confuted, and the preacher that had disturbed their orthodoxy retired, and left the field to Smith.

"Doctor," said he to a brother, not long afterward, "I preached a very singular discourse the other day. Not a man that heard it believed one word I said; I did not believe it myself; nor is it believed in heaven, earth, or hell; for there was not a particle of truth in it. But, what is stranger still, I never preached a sermon in my life that did more good!"

In the beginning of the year 1843, John T. Johnson visited Owingsville and Sharpsburg, and, assisted by Smith, held very successful meetings at those places; and the two congregations, feeling their responsibility as bodies organized for the support and propagation of the Gospel, combined their means, and agreed to sustain John Smith as their Evangelist. In the meantime, the brethren at Georgetown, Dry Run, Leesburg, and Old Union appreciating the importance of a mission to St. Louis, made their arrangements, and solicited Smith and Johnson to visit that place; and, accordingly, on the twenty-third of April, they appeared there unexpectedly among the brethren. They labored eight days, with but little apparent success. Smith took an excursion into Illinois before returning home, while Johnson remained two weeks longer on the field. About thirty-five accessions were gained before he finally departed.

In the fall of that year, the debate between Alexander Campbell and the Rev. N. L. Rice took place, in Lexington. It was conducted in the presence of Dr. Fishback, President Shannon, John Smith, and Aylett Raines, on the part of the Reformation, and four others on the part of Presbyterianism —the Hon. Henry Clay being president of the board. The discussion began on the 15th of November.

On that day, John Smith, who had left home some time before, was summoned back by a message like that which came to him one morning at dawn, when he was away from home, among his father's friends, in Alabama.

On the day before, while some men were engaged in slaughtering his hogs, his youngest son, then in the seventh year of his age, the darling of the household—his little Menifee—came in from school, and, with childish curiosity, hurried to the spot where the work was going on. Some one having called for a hoe, Richard ran to get it. It was lying across a hogshead filled with boiling water, over which a blanket had been spread. He climbed up quickly, and, the blanket giving way, he fell headlong into the scalding water. He was taken out immediately, but too late. He lived but eight hours, through sufferings too heart-rending for description, and then expired.

The unfortunate father set out at once on horseback for his home, sustained along his wretched journey of forty or fifty miles by the hope that his darling would recover, or that at least he would see again the little sufferer before he died.

"I remember well," his daughter * writes, "how my father looked that day, when he reached home, weary and worn almost to exhaustion, but with hope beaming in his eye. When told that his boy, the pride of his old age, was no more, he dropped down in the doorway apparently lifeless. The fatigue of his hurried journey and the shock of Richard's death were too much for him; he was unable to get to his room till we applied such restoratives as his case required."

In October, 1849, Smith, now in the sixty-sixth year of

---

* Mrs. Emma S. Ringo, of Missouri.

his age, incapable at times of any sort of manual labor by reason of his increasing palsy, his older surviving children all married or scattered abroad, and the cherished boy that had been at once the pride and the hope of his declining years taken away, disposed of his farm, and, with the concurrence of his wife, removed to Mount Sterling, with their two youngest daughters, Emma and Mary, to spend there the rest of his days in peace. He bought a pleasant home just within the limits of the town, and, dividing one-half of his time between the church in that place and his beloved Somerset, he devoted the remainder to such labors of love as the wants of the brethren abroad seemed to require.

He had enjoyed this happy repose from worldly care but a short time when a preacher, almost entirely unknown in that community, appeared, and, greatly pleasing a number of the brethren, was called to preach to the congregation one Sunday in each month. But soon the peace of the church was destroyed by his indiscretions. The distant congregation of which he was a member having arraigned him on account of some reported improprieties, and, subsequently, having excluded him for alleged indiscretions at Mount Sterling, dissensions arose that threatened to ruin the cause in several places.

Smith withdrew his services, as a preacher, from the congregation at Mount Sterling, and, not long afterward, he was constrained, by a sense of duty to himself and to the cause, to remove his membership also. Other prominent brethren withdrew at the same time, and the church was left to stand or to fall with the new preacher whom they seemed determined, if possible, to vindicate.

A cruel assault was now made upon Elder Smith. Some charged him with jealous efforts to ruin a persecuted man; others, misled by misrepresentations, or inflamed by sophistries, pursued him with ungrateful animosity.

The brotherhood generally looked on these proceedings with surprise. Finally, however, their judgment found utterance through committees properly called together—one at Mayslick, from certain churches in Mason and Fleming and Bracken; and another at Somerset, from certain churches in Bourbon and Clark and Bath. These tribunals patiently investigated the facts in the case, and their decisions, though made in reference to different points of the controversy, sufficiently vindicated those who had fallen under the hasty censures of the church, and confirmed the sentence of wrong-doing against him who had led so many good brethren and sisters into error.

Finally, after eighteen months of estrangement, John T. Johnson and William Morton visited Mount Sterling and brought about peace and reconciliation.

At the very time that the brethren were thus so happily reconciled at Mount Sterling, he who had been the occasion of their grievous dissensions, having wandered southward into Stockton's Valley; where every grove and cabin chronicled some good deed of John Smith, publicly renounced the Reformation and became a Baptist, telling his Calvinistic brethren at the time that his heart had been with them for a year!

In the meantime, a month or two before the visit of Johnson and Morton to Mount Sterling, the venerable Smith, robbed of the beautiful hope that he would live out his patriarchal days among a people whom he loved as his children, now turned away from the scene of his earliest and noblest struggles, and with a heavy distress upon his heart, went to live in Georgetown, near the beloved Johnson, where the spirit of Stone still breathed its peaceful influence on the people and the church. Having sold his pleasant cottage and grounds in Mount Sterling, he purchased property in Georgetown, and removed to that place with his family in October, 1851.

It was not the least of the afflictions of this faithful man of God, that, in removing from his old field of labor, he would have to withdraw his services from the church at Somerset. He had preached there regularly on the third Lord's Day in each month since the year 1829; and, indeed, previously to that time, from 1817, he had taught them and their fathers at old Grassy Lick. To leave them now was like the abandonment of his own children. They, too, felt their orphanage when he departed; for two years had hardly passed when troubles arose, and they sent to beg him to return.

The church at Mount Sterling, also missing, in time, his wise counsels, finally, for the sake of the cause, urged him to preach to them again; and the venerable father, forgetting the recent past, in the love of earlier years, held a successful meeting there in 1854, and afterward preached to them occasionally as before. The spirit of peace returned, and, from that time, the church grew in numbers and in influence.

CHAPTER XLIX.

Soon after his removal to Georgetown, Smith was chosen Elder of the church, and by word and example, in public and in private, he continued to edify the brethren, to maintain the ancient customs in the church, and to commend the cause that he so much loved, to the world around him. The years passed pleasantly by; and while the field of his labors was more and more contracted by reason of his infirmities, his zeal burned on, and his usefulness was as great as ever. Whether warning young disciples against the fascinations of the dance and other popular amusements, or discouraging all departures from the Ancient Order in the public assemblies, he was the same prudent but resolute opposer of every thing that he believed to be unfavorable to a pure, spiritual life and worship among the children of God.

He sometimes forgot or disregarded his bodily infirmities. Though palsied to such a degree that he had to be fed ilke a child, he would frequently ask the family to pack his portmanteau for a journey, and, taking a servant-boy as his only companion, he would make short tours among his old friends, or their children, who always greeted his coming with delight. In 1857, he presided at Ghent as a Moderator in the discussion between Benjamin Franklin and the Rev. T. J. Fisher, and in September, 1858, he sat among the brethren of Missouri in their State Meeting at Columbia. It was on that occasion that he was pressed by Elder Daniel Bates and others to prepare an autobiography for the press before he should be called hence to receive the reward of his labors.

"I have never aspired to any notoriety, my brethren," said he, in reply. "My only object, through all my public life, has been to do all the good I could, without the least craving after what the world calls fame."

They continued, however, to urge it upon him as a duty, and he promised at last to take the matter under consideration. At their suggestion, other brethren afterwards wrote to him, and affectionately pressed the subject upon his attention.

In 1860, he was again in Missouri, and was present at a debate in Brunswick, between Elder Moses E. Lard and the Rev. Mr. Caples. An incident is related as having occurred on that occasion, which shows that nearly eighty winters had not chilled the ever-flowing vein of humor that had freshened and sparkled through the years of his vigorous manhood.

It was, perhaps, just after the close of some morning discussion, that he remarked to the brethren, who were standing around the rostrum, that he had concluded to start home next day. Mr. Caples, who was near by at the time, gathering up his books and papers, and who was himself a reputed wit, reached over and touched the venerable man, saying:

"Mr. Smith, don't leave until this debate is over, for I want to take a 'coon hunt with you."

"That would just suit me," replied Smith, putting his palsied hand on Caples's shoulder, "for when I go a 'coon hunting, I always like to have a good *dog* along."

Mr. Caples stepped back, bowed politely, and, taking off his hat, handed it to him, saying:

"You can take my hat, sir."

The old man, recognizing the well-known military principle, that "to the victor belong the spoils," took the hat and started off the field with it, amid the laughter of the company; but, after passing almost out of the crowd, he turned and brought it back.

"Take your hat, Mr. Caples; it's of no use to me, and your head will need all the protection it can get before this debate is over."

"I thought, Brother Smith," said Aylett Raines to him one evening, seeing him rather indifferent to a shower of rain that was falling upon him, "I thought that you immersionists did not like sprinkling."

"Ah! Aylett," said he, "that was one of the times you were mistaken. With me, it depends altogether on the administrator. When it comes from Heaven, I like it very well, but, from the fingers of a priest, *I despise it.*"

When the rebellion broke out, John Smith occupied no ambiguous position toward it. He was politically for the preservation of the Union, and religiously loyal to the Government. Discussing the question of secession, in 1861, with a prominent politician of Kentucky, he met the arguments of his opponent with so much candor and power, that the latter, dropping the question of State rights, demanded:

"You certainly will not deny that it is to the *interest* of Kentucky to go with the South?"

"I never look for *interest*," said he, "where no *principle* is invested."

On his way to his residence one evening, while a party of troops held the town, and a guard was placed at every street, a soldier in gray halted him, and demanded his pass.

"What is it that you want?" said Smith, not exactly comprehending the situation at the moment.

"Have you got a *pass?*" asked the guard.

"Yes, sir," said Smith.

"Out with it, then," said the soldier.

Smith stepped toward him, and, raising his shriveled fist, shook it at the stalwart soldier, saying:

"This is *my* pass, sir!"

"Get along, old man," said the soldier, laughing, as he shouldered his musket, and marched away on his beat.

CHAPTER L.

On the 4th of November, 1861, Nancy Smith, one of the best of wives and mothers, died, in Georgetown, and was laid to rest by the grave of her son, James Harvey, in the beautiful cemetery at Lexington.

The incidents in the life of this good woman are domestic; they belong to her family—to her children, and her children's children. Necessity early circumscribed the sphere of her activities, where, through all her life, she displayed the most eminent of womanly virtues. To a sound judgment, untiring energy, and great force of character, she added an earnest but noiseless piety. She had a heart that was kind and patient, almost to a fault; a manner, at all times, and in every place, the most artless and unobtrusive She was guileless of speech, plain, and without ostentation. She affected no modern tastes or prejudices, but lived and died an exemplary matron of the olden times. She was frugal and provident, and, in all her domestic arrangements, scrupulously neat, orderly, and Quaker-like. She lived for her husband and her children; to them, under God, she consecrated her life; and in that devotion consisted her happiness and her usefulness. But for her noble self-sacrifice, perhaps the labors of her husband would have been lost to the church; it was through her heroic, but unrecorded struggles with poverty and care, that he was at last known in the gates, when he sat among the elders of the land.

She was the mother of eleven children—only five of whom survived her. Eliza Blaze, her first-born, died in 1819; William Pinckney, in 1824; Joshua Carroll, in 1827; Richard Menifee, in 1843; John Duke, in 1846; Eliza Ann Freeman, in 1856; and James Harvey, in 1859.

The story of her life would be beautiful if told; but it is sacred. Other than human pen has kept record of her deeds of love, her sacrifices, and her toils; and in that day when the books shall be opened, and the small and the great of earth shall stand together, no fairer page will be unrolled and read than that which bears the humble name of NANCY SMITH.

After the death of his wife, Elder Smith went to live with his daughter, Mrs. MARIA M. LEE, of Owingsville—spending much of his time, however, with his younger daughter, Mrs. EMMA S. RINGO, of Mexico, Audrain County, Missouri. Some months, also, he now passed at the Daughters' College, near Harrodsburg, Kentucky, where he detailed to the writer many of the reminiscences of his long and eventful life. But, whether in Kentucky or Missouri, he spent the remainder of his days still pleading for the Ancient Gospel, and for the liberty of the children of God.

In the fall of 1865, while preparing to spend the winter in Missouri, he received a copy of the new Constitution of that distracted commonwealth. After reading the oath required to be taken as a condition precedent to the exercise of the functions of a minister of the Gospel, his son-in-law, Mr. Lee, inquired:

"Father, can you take that oath?"

"No, I can not," said he, with much emphasis.

"Then you must not go to Missouri: you will get into difficulty; and you are too old to be troubled."

"No," said he; "I am just at the right age, for my days are few, and I can not be troubled long."

Others tried to dissuade him from going, but in vain; he felt that it was his duty to go to his children, and he went, fixed in the determination to do what was right in the sight of God, and leave the consequences to him.

It had of late been his habit to speak of his preaching as only *talking*, and, when he reached Mexico, he announced that he would *talk* to the people on the next Lord's Day. Some took advantage of his language, and, wholly ignorant of his character, said he would evade the law. Having heard of it, he entered the pulpit, on Lord's Day, and be-gan his discourse by remarking:

"Last winter, when I was with you, I sat down and *talked;* to-day I will stand up and *preach.*"

He continued thus preaching, every Lord's Day, until the following April, at which time the spring term of the circuit court was held in Mexico. Having made the acquaintance of the judge, and found him to be a pleasant and very intelligent gentleman, he said to him, one day:

"Judge, you have doubtless heard that I have been preaching here without taking the oath required by the constitution of the State."

"I have heard of it, Mr. Smith, and I think it a little strange, for I understand that you have always been a Union man, and a truly loyal one."

"I have always been such," said Smith; "and, so far as the politics of the oath are concerned, I can take it with as clear a conscience as any man in Missouri; but it involves other principles, that conflict with my conscience. I know it may be said that I am not to judge of the constitutionality of a law; but I am compelled to decide in this matter— not as setting a law aside, or declaring it null and void, but as a question of private conscience. I regard the new constitution as the first bold attempt that infidelity has ever made in this country to dethrone Jehovah. Were I to take this oath, I would no longer preach by the authority of Jesus Christ, but by that of an unbelieving legislature. It would be rebellion against my rightful Sovereign, and, to save my life, I could not do it."

The April term of the court having closed, Smith received information that the grand jury had indicted him, and he was advised to give the usual bond and security for his appearance. Some even urged him to anticipate the time set for his departure to Kentucky, and to go at once, and escape the annoyance of arrest.

"No, friends," said he; "I can not go aboard a train of cars and endure the ride, with a consciousness that I was fleeing as if I had been guilty of wrong. I will do right, and fear nothing."

On the morning of the tenth of May—the day set for his departure—he bade his children adieu, and started to the depot. While crossing the street, the sheriff, who had put off the arrest till the last moment, accosted him.

"Mr. Smith," said he, "you will have to stop. I have a *capias* against you;" and he proceeded to read it.

"Mr. Sheriff, what have I done?"

"We all know that you are a Union man, but you have preached without taking the oath."

"I have done so," said Smith, "and I shall preach on without taking it. I say this, not in the spirit of resistance of law, but, with the example of the first Christians before me, I submit to law, and take the penalty; *I will not take the oath.* You will have no trouble in conducting me to jail; but tell my friends to build them an arbor near my window, for I will still try to preach to them. You can keep me, Mr. Sheriff, in a chicken-coop as well as in a jail; I never flee from civilized man."

"Mr. Smith," said the officer, "I have a penal bond drawn up, and any one will go on it as your security. If the law permitted, I would do it myself."

"Mr. Sheriff, you can not go on my bond. I am well assured, too, that there is not a man or woman in Mexico that would refuse; but no one shall do it. I will just request my son-in-law to have my baggage taken to his house, and then I will be at your service."

His son-in-law, Mr. Ringo, in the meantime, had learned what was going on, and, coming up at the moment, received directions concerning the baggage. The sheriff handed him the bond.

"Father," said he, "I want you to sign this; I will attend to every thing else. Take the cars, as you purposed, and go on to Kentucky; every thing will be right."

"Do so," urged the sheriff; "it is all that is necessary."

"Mr. Ringo," said the old man, "I would do as much for you as for any man in the world, for you have always been kind to me; but I can not gratify you now."

Just then he was taken aside, and informed that one hundred men at least had resolved to deliver him, at the risk of life, if he should be thrown into prison. Blood would doubtless be shed in the attempt, and possibly some of his own friends might fall. He reflected a moment, and faltered;

his resolution gave way, and, with a hand shaking with the infirmities of more than eighty years, he put his reluctant mark to the bond, and, with a sort of dissatisfied conscience, stepped into the cars, and came on safe to Kentucky.

The bond was given for his appearance on the 15th of October, 1866—the very day on which he would complete his eighty-second year; but the trial was postponed till April following. In the meantime, the oath was set aside by decision of the Supreme Court, and Elder Smith was, on motion of the District-Attorney, Mr. Boulware, discharged at the April term of the Circuit Court.

The winter of 1866-7, Elder Smith spent in Kentucky; but in March following, he made arrangements to return to Missouri. He seemed to have a premonition at the time that he would never see his friends in Kentucky again; yet the anticipation that he would soon be with Christ, whom he had faithfully served for more than sixty years, filled him with serene cheerfulness, and he loved to talk of his decease. He called for the last time to see the friend who was then engaged in preparing his memoirs at Ashland, near Lexington, Ky. He spoke of his probable death in Missouri—of the disposition to be made of his remains—of his funeral, and, with eyes suffused with tenderness, he alluded to older friends, then living, that had stood by him for fifty years, whom, perhaps, he would never see again in the flesh.

He sat at the fireside at Ashland among those who were to him as children; and his mind, kindling with the hope of the Christian, arose to the contemplation of that sublimest of all historic scenes, the Transfiguration. For an hour, he sat and described the amount, the trembling disciples, the heavenly visitants, and the glory that invested him at whose feet lawgiver and prophet laid down their honors.

"His raiment," said he, "was exceeding white as snow. I once saw the fields and forests robed by a sleety storm in marvelous splendor; the morning sun arose without a cloud, and shone upon a world of ice—the snow itself was dim. There is a brilliancy whiter than snow, and it clothed the Son of God upon the holy mount."

Inspired with his theme, he seemed to hear the very words which the glorified spoke concerning the decease which

Jesus should accomplish at Jerusalem. He carried his little audience, with the charms of dramatic art, to Gethsemane and to the cross. Cords and spikes and hammers lay around, and amid the angry surges of the multitude, Jesus sighs out the tender prayer, "Forgive them, Father!"

"I love to think," said he, "that my life should spring from his death; my healing, from his wounds; my glory, from his shame. If God forsake him not, I can not be accepted. If thorns press not his temples, I can never wear a crown of glory. Now, in the grave he lies; he must conquer death, or I must sleep forever. If there ever was a time when all the harps of heaven were still, and not one note of angel music sounded through the skies, 't was when that lifeless, mangled form was lying in the rich man's tomb' But the voice of God pierces the gloom and silence of the grave; angels attend upon his second birth; with a glorious escort, he passes upward in his chariot of clouds, and enters in through the everlasting gates. Those doors were closed when Adam fell; they now receive the conqueror of sin and death. And, glorious thought! they are still unbarred; and I, and you, and all that follow him in life, shall one day enter through the gates into the everlasting city of our God."

He passed on next day to Georgetown, and thence to Frankfort. Here he rested for the night in the hospitable mansion of John L. Moore. This—March 14th—was the last night that he ever spent in Kentucky. He was wholly unattended on his journey, and, knowing the anxiety of his friends, he wrote to them from this point that all was well with him thus far. He remembered, too, that there was in the city a negro boy that had once waited on him; he now sent for him, and gave him money, some counsel, a blessing, and a last farewell. Next morning, he bade adieu to his friends in Frankfort, and set out for Missouri.

Through the summer and fall of that year, he preached far and near, as opportunity offered for doing good, visiting the counties of Audrain, Callaway, Boone, Warren, Pike, and Monroe. The following letter from Elder D. T. Wright, editor of the *Pioneer*, presents an interesting picture of the brave old man, forgetful of age and bodily decrepitude in his zeal for the cause:

JOHN AUGUSTUS WILLIAMS:

Dear Brother—Our venerable and beloved brother, John Smith, has been with us nearly two weeks, preaching the Gospel of Christ with the zeal and ability that would have done him credit twenty or thirty years ago. He arrived here to attend the Consultation on the 3d inst., and left on Monday the 14th. At first, I mistook his physical strength, and did not give him the opportuntiy to speak as often in the forepart of the meeting as I should have done. His strength, for one of his age, is indeed remarkable, and the presence of mind and the ability he manifests are truly astonishing. He was listened to by large audiences with the deepest interest. On one occasion, he mounted on a bench while the invitation hymn was being sung, and exhorted the people to come to Jesus, with the pathos and strength of a young man. Some twenty odd were added to the Church while he was with us. One of our best citizens, who was upward of seventy years of age, came forward at the close of one of John Smith's discourses; he arose in the pride and dignity of manhood, though bowed with years, and, for the first time in his life, confessed Christ. Brother Smith took his confession, and the next morning I immersed him. Brother Smith's health is good, and he·is one of the most cheerful and happy men I have ever seen. He speaks of the future with a familiarity that is most affecting indeed; such strong and ennobling faith I have never seen manifested by any man before. The Lord be praised for this illustrious hero of the faith in the nineteenth century.

D. T. WRIGHT.

The last error that John Smith came in conflict with was *Spiritualism*. In the fall of 1867, a woman from some of the New England States delivered a series of lectures on that subject in Mexico. At the instance of his son-in-law, the venerable Smith was present. The lecturer, having heard much of her distinguished auditor, approached him at the close of one of her addresses, and demanded his opinion of the matter.

"I hold myself ready, madam," he promptly replied, "to

prove, at any time, to the entire satisfaction of an intelligent audience, that the whole thing is from the devil."

When this·remark was noised abroad, a number of citizens solicited him to appoint a time to address them on the subject, and assured him that he should have a full house and a patient hearing. He accordingly announced to his congregation, on Sunday, that if it would be agreeabe, he would deliver a discourse on *Spiritualism* on the next Lord's Day, and would hold himself bound to prove from the Bible that it was all of and- from the devil.

The day, which was some time in January, arrived, and, in the opinion of many that heard him, he fuly redeemed his promise. They declared that such an array of scriptural testimony they had never heard presented on any subject.

After closing his argument, he took a seat, as was his custom, in front of the pulpit, facing the congregation. Just as the song was concluded, a lady, who was a Spiritualist, and who was occupying a seat immediately to the left of the stand, arose, and with closed eyes, as in a trance, began to reply to the argument which she had just heard, saying that it was wicked thus to malign the spirits that had been sent hither to warn those in the form. The brethren were dumb with amazement; they knew not what to say or to do, and the whole audience became restless with embarrassment. "If Father Smith," whispered a brother to another at his side, "can not deliver us from this dilemma, the Lord only knows what will become of us."

The old man just then slowly put his hand into his pocket, drew forth his tobacco-box, took a chew, and then deliberately returned the box to its accustomed place. Turning to the woman, with a motion of his palsied hand, and, in his peculiar tone of voice that betrayed a little impatience, but not the least trace of ill-humor or embarrassment, he said:

"Oh! we don't want to be interrupted now with such stuff as that."

"Excuse me," said the medium, who was now sitting with her head thrown back, her bonnet fallen off, and her eyes still closed; "excuse me," she said, "I am not responsible for what I say; I have no control over myself."

"Well," said he, "you are in a bad fix if you have no control over yourself, and you had better go home."

She immediately arose to her feet, and stepped forward; extending her hand to him, which, however, he refused to take, she said:

"Well, I will go. Farewell, my brother; I hope to meet you in another world."

"It depends, madam, on which world you are going to," said he, "whether I wish to meet *you* or not."

At this, she seemed to get angry, and started abruptly down the aisle. Just as she passed out at the door, he closed the scene by saying:

"I raised the devil, and have now cast him out!"

CHAPTER LI.

DURING the winter of 1867-8, the health of Elder Smith was unusually good. In the month of January, he went on the cars to Wellsville, and thence in a sleigh to Middletown, a distance of twelve miles, to attend a debate between Elder Ford and a Methodist preacher; and, though he exposed himself to more fatigue and rough weather than usual, he was afterward more active and cheerful than he had been for some time.

The 9th of February, 1868, was one of the coldest days of that winter. It was Sunday, and, notwithstanding the weather, the venerable man remarked, at breakfast, that he would go to Sunday-school that morning, and preach, as usual, at the regular hour. Remonstrance was in vain, and refusing a carriage, he started early, and walked over the icy path to the meeting-house.

Those who heard his discourse that day will never forget the power and zeal with which he spoke; it was the last, and one of the best discourses that he ever delivered. The day grew colder every hour. When he returned home in the early afternoon, his bloodless, shivering frame alarmed his daughter, and she hastened, with much concern, to administer a stimulant.

"I do not remember," he remarked to her, "that I have ever been so cold in all my life."

A cup of hot coffee was prepared; and after his usual meal, he retired to his room, and fell asleep. He awoke somewhat refreshed, and would have gone out again to meeting that night, but all joined their entreaties, and persuaded him to stay at home. He retired early, but the morning found him suffering intensely from inflammation. Dr. Ringo, who lived in the house, was promptly summoned, but he continued to grow worse, in spite of the tenderest nursing and the most assiduous medical attention. Other physicians were called in, at length, but only partial relief was found; his disease seemd to baffle all human skill. Between his paroxysms, during the first week of his illness, he lay in a stupor from which he could hardly be aroused.

On Tuesday, the 18th, his mind became more active, and his voice more natural. This gave his anxious friends some hope; and, in fact, for several days, he seemed, at least, to grow no worse. When not suffering, nor too heavy with stupor, his remarks were strikingly characteristic; even his genial humor would sometimes well up unconsciously, though from a heart already touched by death.

He talked cheerfully of his approaching dissolution, and seemed even to rejoice that his race was nearly run. They would sometimes express to him a hope that he would soon be well; but he begged them not to give him such assurance; for it would make him unhappy to think that, after suffering so much, he would have to endure it all again, when he came at last to die.

"Still," he would say, "while I ought not to wish to live, I would like to look a few more times upon the sun."

He desired such of his brethren as should mention him in their prayers, to petition that he might be reconciled to his Father's will, whatever it might be. His conversation was not characterized by that enthusiasm or ectasy which is sometimes manifested by dying saints; he was calm, thoughtful, and self-possessed.

"My prospects," he said to Elder Wm. J. Mason, "are entirely satisfactory. I have no fears, whatever, about the future. I am nearly home."

"What a great failure after all," he remarked, "would my long and checkered life have been, but for this glorious hope of a hereafter!"

On Tuesday, the 25th, he sent for all the members of the family who were near him, and made such a disposition of his temporal affairs as he thought best, and then remarked:

"I am as calm and as much composed as I ever was in

my life; and I leave the earth with but one single regret: my sons-in-law are not Christians! What would this whole world avail *me* now, if I had not tried to live a Christian."

Turning to Mr. Ringo, and grasping his hand, he exclaimed: "My son! my son!"—But his feelings overcame him, and he could speak no more.

It should be mentioned that Mrs. MARY VANCE STEELE, his youngest daughter, who was then residing in or near Mexico, was, also, in a very feeble state of health at this time, and that JONATHAN, his oldest son, was lying at St. Louis in the last stage of consumption.

Elder Smith now expressed a wish to see his brother, John Augustus Williams, of Kentucky; and he requested his daughter to write to him to come and be with him in his last hours—to assist in conveying his remains to Kentucky, and to deliver his funeral discourse at Lexington.*

To Elder J. T. Brooks, who had called, he said: "Don't you wish, Brother Brooks, that *you* were as near your journey's end as *I* am?"

On Friday, the 28th, he remarked to Mr. Guthrie, a Baptist minister, who approched his bedside: "I am suffering greatly, but not too much, I suppose. I am nearly well, and will soon be home."

On that day, indeed, he grew much worse, and his friends assembled in the room, for they knew that the hour of his deliverance had come. He called them each by name to his bedside, and, as they approached, he pressed their hands affectionately; but his emotions were unutterable, and he was silent. In a little while, he asked to be raised up and supported in his bed. He then called his daughter to him, and, putting his arms tenderly around her neck, said: "Daughter, I want some music to cheer me through this dark Valley."

Brethren were immediately sent for, and their trembling

---

* The news of Elder Smith's extreme illness, and of his dying request, did not reach the author at Harrodsburg, Ky., till it was too late. A telegraphic dispatch about the same time informed him that his venerable friend was dead; but Mr. Ringo was already on his way to Kentucky with his remains. After due conference, however, with the friends of the deceased, he delivered the memorial discourse at Somerset, in Montgomery, on the third Lord's day in May following.

voices cheered the dying saint with that favorite old song that breathes of hope and Heaven:

> "Since I can read my title clear,
> To mansions in the skies."

After this he rested more quietly; and then, calmly and sweetly breathing out his life, he fell asleep in Christ at half-past eight o'clock, P. M.

On Monday, March 2d, uncertain rumors reached the brethren at Lexington, Kentucky, that John Smith was dead, and that his remains would reach that place from Missouri on the following day. On Tuesday morning, however, dispatches were received announcing that his remains would arrive by the eleven-o'clock train on Wednesday. Every arrangement was made to pay to his memory a last tribute of affection. The thought that he was now gone, who had been so long a wise father in Israel, filled every heart with sorrow. J. W. McGarvey writes:

A committee of brethren, with hearse and carriages, met the remains at the depot, and bore them to the church. A large audience was assembled, including a number of preaching brethren. It had been agreed that some of these should follow each other in short addresses. Brother Graham was called upon to open the exercises with reading and prayer. Brother Elley, who had been longer acquainted with the deceased, and had labored more with him in early years, than any present, then made a brief and appropriate address. He was followed by several others in the expression of such sentiments as the occasion suggested. There was no fulsome eulogy; for how could such be spoken over the remains of John Smith? but the brethren spoke of incidents in his life which reflected the greatness of his soul, and joyfully bade adieu to the old visitor as one who had fought long enough and well enough to be allowed an eternal rest.

It was expected by the members of his family that Brother John Aug. Williams, who is his biographer, would be present on the occasion to deliver a formal oration; but the shortness of the notice, not admitting of such preparation as the subject demands, rendered this impracticable.

After the brief but touching services at the church, the

remains were borne to the cemetery, followed by a long procession of brethren and sisters.

Elder Smith left few written records of any part of his eventful life. He loved the approbation of his brethren, but he was wholly indifferent to what the world calls fame. No man of equal merit was ever more modest; not that he was characterized by any weak and timid self-distrust, for he properly estimated his peculiar gifts; but his was a modesty that accomplished great things in a boastless manner, without parade, and for no reward. Few men ever achieved so many single-handed victories; and yet he never put a trumpet to his lips to sound abroad his triumphs.

He was honest, in the noblest sense of the term —honest before God, toward his fellow-men, and with himself. His candor was perfect; he would not disguise himself by the thinnest gauze of affectation or deceit; he was ever guileless and transparent. With all his humor, he never toyed with truth, nor pointed a jest at her expense. Exact in his language, scrupulously punctual to his appointments, cautious and precise in his statements, and faithful to every promise, he was ever the manly impersonation of honor and truth.

He was singularly conscientious; not like Saul the persecutor, who, with his eyes closed against the light, dreamed that he was doing God's service, but he was conscientious in the higher sense of seeking the light, and walking firmly in it. He was, of course, without the slightest tinge of bigotry. His former religious opinions had been early inwrought into his very being; and yet he was the first to see his errors; and, when the light came, he followed its guidance, at the sacrifice of friends, and of every worldly interest and honor.

To support such conscientiousness, and to give it power and majesty before the people, he had the most undaunted moral courage. When the cause he loved was in jeopardy, or any truth that he held was assailed, he regarded neither danger nor suffering in its defense. Whether he attacked error, or vindicated truth, he never counted his enemies; it mattered not to him whether they were ten or ten thousand strong; he went within their lines, dallied with their sentries, and sat, composed or defiant, at their very camp-fires. He often fought error on her own ground, and was, therefore, sometimes aggressive in his warfare; but, whether he assailed or defended, his moral courage was sublime.

With all his manly and heroic virtues, he was as gentle and simple-hearted as a child. Benevolence tempered down the harsher elements of his nature, and mellowed his character with a pleasing, sunny softness. Naturally of a quick and impulsive temper, he had learned patience from much affliction. Age, which usually dries up the fountains of youthful love, gave freshness and volume to his affections. No one ever grew old more gracefully. Time whitened his locks and furrowed his brow, but the frosts of more than eighty winters never chilled his affection; decay itself put neither stain nor wrinkle on his heart. There was a youthful freshness, a bloom and warmth, about his love, that made the dear old man companionable in extreme old age. In truth, only his fleshly tabernacle seemed to fade with years; the spirit that dwelt within resisted the influences of outward decay.

Even little children loved him, and sought his presence as they sought the sunshine. He loved them too—not with the doting fondness of a feeble old man—but for their guilelessness and faith.

A public man thus truthful and intrepid, would necessarily have provoked opposition, notwithstanding his amiability. Even John Smith had his enemies. Who, then, may hope to live without them? Still, he rarely made an enemy on his own account. Those who opposed him, hated the cause that he advocated, and struck, through him, at what they would destroy. Toward such foes, however, he felt no malice or revenge. But against the impostor and the hypocrite, his indignation was ever passionately aroused, and he pursued them with the most unsparing lash. He was especially watchful against those insidious foes that sometimes creep unawares into the Chruch to corrupt its members or disturb its peace; none could play the part of a pretender or schismatic in his presence, and be safe; for then, indeed, the lion of his nature was terribly aroused.

While such was his temper toward those who must be

called his enemies, his tender, faithful and unselfish devotion to his brethren was a beautiful and prominent trait of his character. His heart never let go a friend. If that friend prospered, he rejoiced, and if reverses overtook him, he flew to his relief. If a brother, in his weakness, stumbled, or even fell—no matter how low—*if only honest*, John Smith still clung like a brother to him.

While he was one of the most independent and self-reliant of men, he was, at the same time, one of the most grateful. Those yet live who won the heart of this good man by some little favors done him more than fifty years ago; and, yet, in all that flight of years, those deeds of kindness never were forgotten—gratitude glowed like a vestal fire in his heart till death.

Unlearned in books, his mind drew all its nourishment from the Book of books; and in his love and knowledge of the Scriptures lay the foundation of all his greatness— the secret of his influence and his power.

He rests from his labors by the side of his wife, among many of the beautiful and the gifted of Kentucky. Close by him sleeps JOHNSON, the Evangelist; and the statue of CLAY looks down from its lofty pedestal upon his humbler grave. A simple but tasteful shaft of marble marks his resting-place; and the pilgrim brother that may seek the hallowed spot, will read the few but expressive words which filial piety has inscribed: [See following page.]

IN MEMORY OF

JOHN SMITH,

AN ELDER OF THE CHURCH OF CHRIST.

BORN

OCTOBER 15TH, 1784;

DIED

FEBRUARY 28TH, 1868.

True, genial, and pious, the good loved, and all respected him. Strong
through affliction, and wise by the study of the Word—he gave up
the Creed of his fathers for the sake of that Word. By its power,
he turned many from error; in its light, he walked, and
in its consolations, he triumphantly died.

———————

In all his sacrifices and service, his companion shared. She gave her life
to God, and her death was precious in his sight.

NANCY SMITH

WAS BORN

NOVEMBER 15TH, 1792;

DIED

NOVEMBER 4TH, 1861.